The Parlement of Paris After the Fronde, 1653–1673

The Parlement of Paris After the Fronde
1653–1673

ALBERT N. HAMSCHER

UNIVERSITY OF PITTSBURGH PRESS

Copyright © 1976, University of Pittsburgh Press

All rights reserved

Feffer and Simons, Inc., London

Manufactured in the United States of America

LIBRARY OF CONGRESS CATALOGING IN PUBLICATION DATA

Hamscher, Albert N
  The Parlement of Paris after the Fronde,
1653–1673.

  Bibliography: p. 247
  Includes index.
  1. France. Parlement (Paris)—History.
2. France—Politics and government—1643–1715.
I. Title.
JN2428.H28   347'.44'035   76-6661
ISBN 0-8229-3325-X

To my Mother and Father

Contents

Tables

Acknowledgments

In preparing this study, I benefited immensely from the advice of many historians. My greatest debt is to J. Russell Major, who directed my graduate study and continually exposed me to superb teaching and high scholarly standards. Others who read the entire manuscript in various stages of preparation and kindly offered constructive criticism include George Cuttino, John Hurt, A. Lloyd Moote, David Sabean, Paul Sonnino, and J. H. Shennan. One of these gentlemen gently reminded me that if I accepted the counsel of all, I would "wreck the book." An exaggeration, perhaps, but his comment serves to underscore that all decisions about content and organization remained mine, and in consequence I alone am responsible for any errors in the text. I also wish to thank my colleagues at Kansas State University, who read portions of the manuscript and made valuable suggestions for its improvement; Charles Fieker in particular was very helpful on matters of style and organization. In Paris and London, the staffs of nine libraries and archives enthusiastically suggested research materials and, in some cases, graciously applied their paleographic skills to difficult documents. I am especially indebted to Michel Antoine for acquainting me with conciliar records and for impressing on me that a good study of the Parlement of Paris required familiarity with a wide variety of sources. Finally, I dedicate this book to my dear parents, who sacrificed so much to ensure that their son received the education that the Great Depression had denied them.

Financial assistance from the Ford Foundation, Emory University, and Kansas State University made possible the research and writing of this volume.

Introduction

D espite the great quantity of historical literature devoted to the reign of Louis XIV, the fate of traditional institutions after the civil wars known as the Fronde remains obscure.[1] This neglect stems primarily from the widely held assumption that the monarchy so consolidated its power after the Fronde that its former opponents suffered considerable loss of authority and influence. To be sure, few would deny either that the crown emerged from the abortive rebellion with its domestic strength enhanced or that in subsequent decades the king and his ministers undertook many ambitious reforms. But because this resurgence of royal authority has rarely been seen from the vantage point of traditional institutions, any generalization about the changes imposed on them is questionable. Indeed, so long as the monarchy's relations with established authorities remain unclear, our understanding of the broader issue of the nature and consequences of "royal absolutism" in the post-Fronde era will be incomplete and distorted.

The state of historical research on one such institution, the Parlement of Paris, illustrates the gaps in our knowledge about the domestic history of France in the second half of the seventeenth century. Parlement, one of the oldest and most powerful courts of law in the *ancien régime*, was a focal point of opposition to the crown in the early stages of the Fronde. For decades preceding this conflict, its members had continually challenged many royal policies and had forcefully defended their wealth, authority, and prestige from the eroding influence of administrative centralization. During the Fronde itself, many of the judges had boldly asserted for their court a legitimate constitutional role to approve and supervise royal actions and to participate with the king in the solution of national problems. Despite the importance of Parlement in the origins and course of the Fronde, however, no book or scholarly article has treated in any detail the history of the court after the conclusion of hostilities in 1653, and conventional interpretations about its decline in subsequent years lack firm roots in archival sources. This neglect is regrettable, because the successful assertion of royal authority after the Fronde depended in large measure on the obedience of this frequently recalcitrant institution.

This book assesses how and to what extent the crown controlled the Parlement of Paris in the two decades after the Fronde. Such a study is warranted, because in the history of early modern France only the reign of Louis XIV after the Fronde remains *terra incognita* as regards the activities of this court. But more important, an examination of the relations between the crown and Parlement reveals in microcosm the methods, achievements, and limitations of royal absolutism in this period. The study begins in 1653, when Cardinal Mazarin returned to Paris from exile, and terminates in 1673, when Louis XIV reduced to a mere formality Parlement's right to protest, or remonstrate, royal decrees. This time period, though restricted, offers several advantages. First, it enables us to compare the policies of Mazarin, who retained his post of first minister after the Fronde, with those of Louis XIV, who assumed personal rule upon the cardinal's death in March 1661. Second, the history of institutions at its best requires an investigation of more than political and constitutional conflicts. The social composition of Parlement, its judicial authority, and the economic interests of the judges also bear directly on the problem of royal control, and a limited time period allows the full exploration of these often neglected subjects. Finally, the decades immediately following the Fronde were the most crucial to the formation of the relations between the monarchy and Parlement for the remainder of Louis XIV's reign.

The details of Parlement's organization and authority as well as the activities and interests of the judges will emerge throughout this study, but a brief survey of the court's evolution through the Fronde provides a context for later developments. Primarily a judicial institution, Parlement was the superior court of law in an area covering nearly two-thirds of the kingdom. Each year the *parlementaires* judged hundreds of civil and criminal cases in first instance and on appeal. They also regulated and supervised the conduct of the lesser tribunals in their area of jurisdiction. As the most prestigious court of law in France, Parlement exercised a necessary and useful function for the monarchy.

The internal organization of Parlement in the seventeenth century was complex. There were five *chambres des enquêtes* and two *chambres des requêtes*, the former collecting information on litigation and the latter hearing requests for justice. In addition to these seven chambers, there were three superior chambers of the court. The most prominent was the *grand' chambre*, the administrative hub of Parlement which distributed cases to the other chambers and had final say on all judicial decisions. There was also a chamber that judged criminal litigation (*chambre de la tournelle*) and another that decided cases involving Protestants (*chambre de l'édit*). An interim *chambre des vacations* sat while Parlement was in recess in the autumn of each year.

Approximately two hundred magistrates staffed Parlement. Junior judges, both lay and clerical, sat in the chambers of *enquêtes*, held many of the seats in the *requêtes* on commission, and proceeded to the *grand' chambre* on the basis of seniority. Each chamber of *enquêtes* and *requêtes* had two presidents to supervise its judicial activities. The *grand' chambre* was composed of approximately thirty senior judges who were headed by eight *présidents à mortier* and a first president. The chambers of *tournelle*, *édit*, and *vacations* were composed of judges from the *enquêtes* and *grand' chambre* on a rotating basis. The first president, the chief official of the court, was assisted by the *gens du roi* (collectively known as the *parquet*), including a *procureur général* and two *avocats généraux*. Like the first president, these officials gave advice on litigation, delivered royal messages and decrees to the magistrates, and in theory represented the king's interests in the court. In addition to this regular membership, honorary councillors, dukes and peers, and *maîtres des requêtes* had the right to enter and sit in Parlement. Four *maîtres des requêtes* at any given time and all the dukes and peers also enjoyed full voting privileges. Finally, a host of advocates, clerks, guards, notaries, and solicitors aided the magistrates in their judicial business.

Besides its considerable judicial activities, Parlement had acquired over the centuries a number of administrative duties and privileges that rendered the court a formidable political force in the kingdom. By the sixteenth century, the judges had established the right to register and supervise the enforcement of many types of royal decrees. The French kings often turned this prerogative to their own advantage because judicial review at Parlement endowed their acts with a quality of public consent. But such a symbiotic relationship occasionally disintegrated when Parlement opposed a particular decree, refused registration, and voiced its objections through the right of remonstrance. On some occasions, the kings were able to command obedience only by sitting in a *lit de justice* at Parlement itself. The *parlementaires* could also pressure the crown and disrupt the implementation of its programs by holding plenary sessions to discuss public affairs, by modifying decrees before proceeding to registration, and by actually issuing their own judicial and administrative decrees contrary to the royal will. Moreover, Parlement's substantial police duties in the capital city, its supervisory powers over lesser courts, and its claimed role of defender of the Gallican church further enlarged the judges' sphere of political influence. Indeed, Parlement's conduct could have national importance because other Parisian and provincial officials frequently looked to it for support and leadership in their own struggles to preserve their privileges and prerogatives; and quite naturally, still other discontented groups—be they peasant, urban, or noble—commonly welcomed disturbances at Parlement as one way to justify their own protests or rebellions. Clearly, then, Parlement's superior legal status and its varied administrative duties meant that the judges could never have been content with strictly judicial functions. Because of its perennial contact with public affairs through litigation and registration, Parlement had developed early in its history a keen desire to participate with the king and his advisers in the resolution of major issues. In addition, the magistrates had gradually accumulated the administrative machinery necessary to oppose those royal policies that offended them. The lack of a precise definition for Parlement's legitimate role in the vaguely defined realm of "affairs of state" provided a constant source of friction between the crown and its leading court of law.

By the opening decades of the seventeenth century, Parlement had also developed into a social corporation. Like most royal officials in *ancien régime* France, the *parlementaires* purchased their posts (*vénalité des offices*), owned them as negotiable property, and enjoyed the right to sell or bequeath them to candidates of their choice by paying an annual tax (*droit annuel*) to the royal treasury.[2] These procedures of officeholding profoundly influenced the social composition and collective mentality of Parlement. In the first place, ownership of an office and control of its transmission provided a judge with both security in office and freedom from royal appointment. The *parlementaires* thus could afford to act with remarkable independence in their relations with the monarchy. Equally important, the magistrates' right to choose their successors permitted them to recruit Parlement's membership along both family and social group lines. This in turn fostered social cohesion and pretensions among the judges that easily reenforced their political claims. *Parlementaire* families built dynasties in the court and intermarried; the judges developed a sensitivity to the social background of candidates for office and in time considered themselves to be the highest and most influential members of what contemporaries called the "nobility of the robe." The way that the magistrates acquired and transmitted their posts, therefore, had both social and political consequences that dovetailed with Parlement's traditional prestige and authority.

For a number of reasons, then, the Parlement of Paris that confronted the French kings of the seventeenth century possessed considerable judicial and administrative powers, cherished a tradition of political involvement, and exhibited strong sentiments of social elitism. Unquestionably, the magistrates could serve the monarchy well, and since the court's origins in the thirteenth century, successive kings had extended their influence in the realm with the aid of their leading judges. By the middle decades of the seventeenth century, however, the interests of the crown and Parlement had begun to diverge, and the judges obstructed rather than supported the growth of royal authority.

When France officially entered the Thirty Years' War in 1635, relations between the crown and Parlement deteriorated rapidly as the governments of Cardinals Richelieu and Mazarin relied on a host of financial expedients to support their foreign involvement. In order to compensate for the insufficiency of revenue from ordinary sources, these ministers and their advisers established new taxes and extended older levies, attempted to reduce judicial salaries and interest payments on government bonds (*rentes*), created and sold additional offices, and occasionally resorted to forced loans. They also sought out the services of financiers and tax farmers, who, with royal acquiescence, subverted regulations against fraud in financial administration and made huge profits at the expense of taxpayers. Moreover, in order both to enforce their financial policies and to increase administrative efficiency, Richelieu and Mazarin introduced other innovations aimed at circumventing the cumbersome, venal bureaucracy that protested and obstructed the monarchy's drift toward expediency. Intendants, nonvenal officials directly responsible to the king, entered the *généralité* level of the financial administration and usurped the functions of the established local officials, the *trésoriers de France* and the *élus*. They also interfered with the duties of the financial courts—the chambres des comptes and the cours des aides—and their inevitable involvement in judicial matters threatened both the authority of lesser judicial tribunals and the appellate jurisdiction of the superior courts, including the Parlement of Paris. While the intendants grew in number and authority, the king's councils extended their own administrative activities. The crown increasingly relied on conciliar decrees to authorize its policies in order to avoid registration procedures at Parlement and the other sovereign courts.[3] The councils also freely nullified the judicial and administrative decrees of Parlement and evoked from it litigation that concerned royal programs. In moments of desperation, the government even established extraordinary judicial commissions, exiled its most vocal opponents, and attempted to force royal officials into submission by threatening to revoke the *droit annuel*. The two cardinals justified all such actions by asserting that whenever the needs of state (as perceived by the king and his highest advisers) conflicted with the traditional privileges of established bodies, the latter must yield to the former.

Although all these royal measures appeared intermittently, they clearly represented a trend toward administrative centralization that one historian has recently referred to as a "governmental revolution."⁴ Obviously, many groups in France objected to the monarchy's campaign to break free from the traditional restraints on its power. Peasants, already plagued by bad harvests and an abundance of financial burdens, resented the new levies, and the first half of the seventeenth century was rife with agrarian discontent. Townsmen too were angered not only by the proliferation of taxes, but by the steady erosion of their semiautonomous position in the state. The great nobles (*les grands*), resentful of a loss of influence in the highest circles of power and always anxious to enhance their material welfare, frequently aroused their clients to rebellion and exploited the grievances of others to advance their own cause.

Like all these groups, the crown's own venal officials, including those in Parlement, opposed the governmental revolution. Many of the financial expedients that Richelieu and Mazarin introduced undermined the *parlementaires'* economic vested interests, and threats to revoke the *droit annuel* jeopardized the market value of their posts as well as their security in office and control over Parlement's recruitment. Moreover, the crown's reliance on its councils and the intendants to accomplish its goals raised serious jurisdictional issues. Parlement interpreted the government's attempts to combat venal officials by transferring their duties to other royal agents as a direct challenge to its own functions, prestige, and claim to a participatory role in affairs of state. On a more general level, the *parlementaires* deplored the monarchy's arbitrary methods and the violation of normal legal procedure. The Parlement of Paris, that premier defender of law and tradition in France, found intolerable both the recent changes in the existing order imposed from above and the increasing disrespect which the king and his closest advisers showed for constituted authorities. By mid-century, the two-pronged financial and administrative attack on royal officials had created such an atmosphere of resistance that they temporarily suspended their perennial fratricidal struggles and united in opposition to the crown. In 1648, a growing constitutional crisis and sporadic rebellions in France exploded in the civil wars known as the Fronde, an early and significant aspect of which was the revolt of the judges.

In June and July 1648, representatives of the Parisian sovereign courts assembled in the Chambre Saint-Louis at the Palais de Justice to end the governmental revolution. Whether the actions of these men were rooted in self-interest or altruism, and whether they were reactionary or revolutionary, are questions that will doubtless always be the subject of some controversy. Perhaps the best way to understand the *parlementaires'* position is to recognize that a variety of motives underscored their protest. This can be illustrated by reference to the many decrees that the crown either issued or sanctioned in May, July, and October 1648 in response to the collective opposition of the sovereign courts.

Unquestionably, this legislation reveals that the *parlementaires* had their own vested interests at heart and that they were concerned primarily with rectifying past abuses. They and the other judges pressured the government to guarantee the payment of judicial salaries and interest on *rentes*, to continue the *droit annuel*, to recall the intendants from all but a few frontier provinces, and to promise that the king's councils would act within the confines of sixteenth-century ordinances. Other provisions, however, such as those which reduced the *taille*, suspended the collection of extraordinary taxation, and assured the better supervision of financiers and tax farmers, showed that the magistrates intended their actions to benefit others than themselves. Furthermore, the *parlementaires* proved to be reformers as well as critics. To be sure, they were not a revolutionary group. Parlement derived its very existence, status, and powers from the king, and the judges never challenged the continuation of the monarchy or advocated fundamental social and economic change in France. But within the monarchial framework they promoted several constitutional concepts which, if successfully imposed on the crown, would have not only increased the authority of their court, but changed the daily operation of the royal administration. Underscoring all their demands and implicit in royal concessions were the principles that royal finances fell under the jurisdiction of judicial officials, that the judicial review inherent in the registration procedures amounted to veto, and that in general Parlement stood above the king's councils and was capable of initiating legislation and checking executive authority. In 1648, therefore, the traditional conservatism and self-interest of the judges combined with an impulse to promote state reform and to relieve some of the burdens on the rest of the populace.

The subsequent evolution of the Fronde beyond this peaceful "parlementary" phase into the violent civil war known as the "Fronde of the Princes" and the gradual dismantling of the judges' reforms are well known and require little elaboration here. Let it suffice to note that a variety of forces undermined the judicial revolt of 1648. The expansion of hostilities into a destructive duel between Mazarinists and the supporters of the great nobles placed the judges in a difficult position. Reformers, not revolutionaries, the *parlementaires* deplored the violence and excesses exhibited by both sides. Their response to constitutional crisis was strictly legalistic, and the government's promise at the Peace of Rueil in April 1649 to preserve the legislation of 1648 had removed all but a few extremists from an active role in the conflict. But Parlement thereafter rapidly lost control of events, and its efforts to mediate a settlement and to preserve its earlier gains collapsed in the force of arms. Ultimately, the success of the judges' program depended on both the favorable disposition of the crown toward reform and the willingness of other groups to confine their demands to what the sovereign courts had already achieved. But the pressures of foreign and civil war made the termination of financial expedients and administrative centralization unacceptable to Mazarin and his advisers, and the great nobles never appreciated the ingrained legalism of the judges.

These problems were symptomatic of a more general disintegration of the united front of 1648. As the Fronde unfolded, *parlementaires* increasingly quarreled among themselves about their objectives, Parlement itself soon lost contact with and control over the other sovereign courts and lesser tribunals, and the many other groups involved in the conflict each pursued their own grievances. In short, the *frondeurs* were united only by negatives: their hatred for Mazarin and their antipathy to recent crown practices. The rebellion lacked the cement of common goals and alternatives to fuse the government's enemies together. This situation was conducive to anarchy rather than to cooperation, and the factionalism among his opponents and several fortuitous military victories enabled Mazarin to survive the onslaught. By 1652, order was restored in Paris and the royal administration already had begun to violate the concessions granted the judges in 1648. The cardinal's return to the capital city in the following year and the fall of the last *frondeur* city, Bordeaux, symbolized the collapse of the Fronde, and with it the revolt of the judges.

But the conclusion of hostilities failed to ensure a clear path for the unchallenged assertion of royal authority. Any attempt to trace the crown's relations with traditional institutions in the following decades must recognize that the defeat of the Fronde did not give the monarchy a *carte blanche* to embark on a program of radical innovation or to run roughshod over its recent foes. Mazarin's triumph was extremely tenuous, having resulted as much from the division among his critics as from his own force of arms or popularity. For the moment, the government certainly benefited from war-weariness in France and the disarray of the *frondeurs*. But the widespread hostility to the governmental revolution did not die in the civil wars, and the cardinal and his advisers had no guarantee that they would not provoke renewed domestic strife if they continued their previous policies. Indeed, one reason why historians have traditionally viewed the Fronde as such a tragic episode in French history is precisely because no one emerged from the conflict with a clear victory. The fundamental issues in contention between the crown and its opponents remained unresolved.

As regards the Parlement of Paris specifically, the Fronde was but a violent interlude in a long period of constitutional conflict that extended beyond 1653. Despite the erosion of its reforms and the humiliation of defeat, the court survived the civil wars with its membership, authority, and pretensions remarkably intact. Certainly, the judges were even less likely than before to propose revolutionary solutions to their grievances. But they still possessed the power and commanded the respect to obstruct the execution of unpopular royal policies, and the crown had little assurance that the court would not revive its call for reform or by its recalcitrance raise the spectre of a new Fronde. Thus, the famous *lit de justice* of October 22, 1652, at which a teen-aged Louis XIV boldly forbade the judges to interfere in "affairs of state," particularly royal finances, did not necessarily inaugurate an era of *parlementaire* submission. The magistrates had ignored similar prohibitions in the past, and no one in 1652 could predict how long their present quiescence would last. Even after the general pacification of the realm and Mazarin's return to power, therefore, the direction of Parlement's future activity was of utmost concern to the government. The major problem that confronted the cardinal and later Louis XIV was how to control this recalcitrant court of law. The principal problem for the historian is to determine what methods they chose and how well they succeeded.

Because it is essential to consider Parlement not only as a judicial court, but also as a social corporation with substantial political influence, the format of this study is primarily topical. The first two chapters analyze Parlement's membership in the period 1653–1673 to determine whether the crown attempted to control the court by recapturing the appointment of judges or by dissolving the social and family ties that often reenforced and directed the members' political expressions. For this reason, all royal legislation that had a potential impact on the councillors' right to choose their successors, the social relations among them, and the monetary value of their posts receives detailed consideration.

In the decades preceding the Fronde, the monarchy frequently alienated the magistrates by pursuing policies that threatened their prosperity. The third chapter evaluates the intent and effect of royal policies that influenced the sources of *parlementaire* wealth during the post-Fronde decades, asking whether the administrations of Mazarin or Louis XIV tried to avoid potentially volatile conflicts with Parlement by satisfying the financial vested interests of the judges, or whether they attempted to submit the magistrates to the royal will through a variety of economic sanctions.

The following two chapters concentrate on Parlement's political influence, its opposition to royal policies, and its participation in affairs of state. The discussion focuses on the issues that generated conflict between the crown and Parlement, the methods that each employed to secure the primacy of its views, and the degree of success that they enjoyed.

Judicial administration was Parlement's primary responsibility. During the first decade of his personal rule, the king issued several important ordinances that reorganized judicial procedures at every level. Because the future definition of Parlement's judicial authority and methods were at stake, the final chapter analyzes the legislation that comprised Louis XIV's famous "reformation of justice" and assesses its impact on the judicial functions of the magistrates.

There were thus a variety of ways that the crown could have controlled Parlement, all of which reflected the complex interaction between the procedures of officeholding, the court's judicial and administrative traditions and authority, and the judges' financial and political aspirations. The discovery of which alternatives, if any, the cardinal-minister and young king decided to pursue and successfully employed will both define their relations with a powerful and prestigious sovereign court and provide additional perspectives on the broader question of the rise of absolutism in the mid-seventeenth century, a period of redefinition of corporate prerogatives and royal authority.

The Parlement of Paris After the Fronde, 1653–1673

CHAPTER ONE

The Office of Councillor at Parlement in the Reign of Louis XIV

The procedures by which judges at the Parlement of Paris acquired and passed on their offices had important implications for their political activities, social attitudes, and financial interests. Because the *parlementaires* purchased their posts on the public market and owned them as negotiable property, they were free from royal appointment and therefore enjoyed remarkable independence in asserting their political claims. Except for the first president and the *gens du roi* of the court, who held their offices on royal commission, the judges also had the right to choose their successors. This control of recruitment in turn had important consequences for the social composition of Parlement and the collective mentality of its members. Not only did the judges build family dynasties in the court, they frequently rejected candidates for office whom they considered socially unworthy. These practices, in addition to the evasion of royal regulations designed to prevent family relationships in the court, enhanced social cohesion among the judges and nourished sentiments of social elitism that easily reenforced their political pretensions. Moreover, because an office in Parlement represented a considerable capital investment, the magistrates naturally had a vested interest in preserving the procedures of officeholding and a high market value for their posts. In several significant ways, therefore, the methods of office tenure and exchange in Parlement affected the attitudes and actions of the *parlementaires* and exercised considerable influence on their relations with the monarchy. For this reason, the policies of Cardinal Mazarin and Louis XIV toward officeholding bear directly on the problem of royal control of Parlement after the Fronde.

OFFICES AS NEGOTIABLE PROPERTY

The exhaustive studies on the *vénalité des offices,* or the trade in public functions, by Roland Mousnier and Martin Göhring explain both the 3 mechanics of the system and its implications for French institutions and society.[1] The sale of offices in France dates to the early Capetians, but it was during the reign of Francis I that *vénalité* became institutionalized. Francis and his successors created large numbers of venal offices for sale on the public market, an expedient that provided a lucrative respite for hard-pressed royal coffers. The *parties casuelles* was organized as a branch of the royal treasury in 1522 to receive the funds prospective officials paid to the crown for their posts. Slowly, even the offices of established institutions, including the Parlement of Paris, became venal. The size of the French bureaucracy grew as Francis and his successors tried to raise additional funds.

In some cases, the crown permitted officials to transmit their offices to whomever they pleased: a lineal heir, a distant relative, or the highest bidder. However, a compulsory clause in the standard resignations, called the forty-day reservation, specified that if a *résignant* (the official who desired to dispose of his post) should die within that period after the transaction, the office would revert to the crown without indemnity to either party. Because the transfer of an office was frequently a deathbed act, this clause stood throughout the sixteenth century as a serious threat to commercial security in the purchase of a post. Equally important, it jeopardized the transmission of offices within individual families.[2] Throughout most of the sixteenth century, however, there were alternatives available to many officials to avoid the forty-day reservation. Often an official could obtain, with the payment of a fee, letters of *survivance* which allowed him to pass his office at any time either to his lineal heir or to a prospective buyer (process called *resignatio in favorem*). By the 1580s, the crown also occasionally sold outright grants of heredity for some offices.

During the reign of Henry IV, the hereditary tendencies already present in the transmission of offices became firmly established. The famous declaration of December 1604 stipulated that if an officeholder paid an annual tax of one-sixtieth the value of his office (based on the price at which the crown sold the post or on later revaluations by the Conseil d'Etat), he was assured the freedom to bequeath his office at any time to whomever he pleased. The buyer who had paid his *marc d'or* (tax paid to the crown upon the assumption of a post) seldom failed to secure his royal letters of provision in due course.[3] Thus, as the system of *vénalité* combined with *resignatio in favorem* in 1604, the control of institutional recruitment passed from the crown to the public market and the officials themselves.

The system of *vénalité* and the annual tax, called the *droit annuel* or simply the *paulette* after the financier who proposed it, held significant consequences for the relations between the monarchy and its judicial and financial officials. The immediate results benefited the crown. Kings welcomed the extra revenue that office sales and the *paulette* provided, and by granting officials the privilege of choosing their successors, the monarchy disrupted the powerful nobility's control of many officeholders through patronage.[4] The crown also won the gratitude of officials who appreciated both the tacit recognition of the hereditary tendencies in officeholding and the rise in the capital value of their posts owing to their control of office transmission.[5] Furthermore, the *paulette* was subject to renewal every nine years, and by periodically threatening to abolish it the monarchy could hope to prevent the coalescence of officials with rebellious malcontents such as *les grands*, who frequently incited all segments of the population to protest unpopular royal policies. There are many examples in the first half of the seventeenth century of officials, including those in Parlement, subordinating their urge to join other discontented groups against the "governmental revolution" in favor of their still more pressing self-interest to preserve control of their offices. To the most eminent historian of venality and the *paulette*, the monarchy's capacity to neutralize its judicial opponents in this fashion signified an important stage in the growth of royal absolutism in the seventeenth century.[6]

Despite these advantages to the monarchy, the fact that many royal officials did indeed seriously challenge the "governmental revolution" during the Fronde reveals that any absolutist tendencies generated by the *paulette* were extremely fragile and undependable. If one looks back over the political and financial turmoil that accompanied the Wars of Religion, the advantages of the *paulette* seem obvious. But a forward glance into the seventeenth century reveals equally significant liabilities for royal authority. For if the *paulette* originally helped the crown to secure the independence of its officials from the great nobles, it was only a matter of time before these officials began to assert their independence from the crown itself. As a result, much of the administrative history of seventeenth-century France focuses on the monarchy's efforts to regain control of its own venal officials.[7] Successive royal administrations had to grapple with the basic problem that it was the officials, not the king, who recruited the membership of traditional royal institutions. Free from direct royal appointment to venal posts, the judges in Parlement could afford to oppose royal policies that offended them. At the same time, they became committed to defending the procedures that bestowed security in office and increased the capital value of their charges. If threats to abolish the *paulette* might temporarily bring recalcitrant officials into line, they did not offer a fundamental solution to the freedom of action officials gained by the control of their offices. In fact, if royal tampering with the *paulette* coincided with other grievances on the part of the judges, as was the case in 1648, it could intensify their resistance to the point of civil strife.[8]

In addition to these political implications, the combination of venality with the *paulette* had social consequences that could adversely affect royal authority. French institutions became the preserve of the wealthy, for it was only they who could afford to purchase an office. This was especially the case after 1604 when the commercial security in an office conferred by the *paulette* increased the market value of most venal offices. At the same time, owing to the freedom in office transmission offered by the *paulette*, officials increasingly chose their successors along both family and social group lines. As social cohesion matured within judicial and financial institutions, officeholders became more attentive to excluding prospective members who did not fit the social composition of the corporate group. French institutions were no longer simply administrative units with certain judicial, financial, or political functions; they were also social corporations with an intense awareness of social status and privilege. This in turn gave administrative and political pretensions a social base. The crown's highest venal officials easily employed sentiments of social elitism to substantiate their claim for an active role in those public affairs the king and his councils increasingly saw as their own exclusive responsibility.

The Parlement of Paris was very much involved in this process. During the fifteenth and sixteenth centuries, prospective councillors secured their offices by one of three procedures: royal appointment, election by the magistrates (often on the basis of merit), or *resignatio in favorem*.[9] Although family dynasties in Parlement appeared as early as the reign of Charles VIII, they were relatively few in number and still in a nascent stage of development.[10] His successor, Louis XII, had tried to limit Parlement's use of election and *resignatio in favorem* to prevent the court from becoming a "closed body narrowly recruited from a certain number of Parisian officer families."[11] As the trend toward *vénalité* developed in the sixteenth century, however, Parlement became more the preserve of certain social groups and wealthy families than an institution whose members were selected on the basis of merit.[12] By the end of the century, Parlement was staffed almost entirely with members whose social origins lay in established *parlementaire* and lesser robe families and the upper segments of the wealthy bourgeoisie.[13]

The institution of the *paulette* tax in 1604 profoundly influenced the social mentality of the magistrates in the Parlement of Paris. Many families established dynasties in the court, and the concept of *noblesse de robe*, whatever its legal ambiguities, developed to the point that the judges considered themselves the equals of any other nobles in France. Mousnier believes that as a result of the *droit annuel*, the *parlementaires*, who already enjoyed a high degree of social status owing to their elevated judicial function, "separated themselves from the rest of the officials." The *présidents à mortier* and their sons considered themselves members of the *haute noblesse*, while ordinary councillors joined the *petite noblesse*. "It seems," concludes Mousnier, "that all the magistrates of Parlement rose socially as a body and left the third estate."[14] In the course of the seventeenth century, the *parlementaires* frequently used their conception of themselves as a privileged social elite to buttress their asserted administrative and political prerogatives in the struggle against royal centralization.

The governments of Cardinal Mazarin and Louis XIV had two alternatives regarding the venality of offices and the *paulette* after the Fronde. The one best suited for controlling Parlement was to attack the system directly, ending the sale of offices and abolishing the *droit annuel*. At one stroke this would recapture the control of institutional recruitment for the crown and weaken the resistance of the court to royal policies by removing the security in office that the magistrates enjoyed. Such drastic reform could also dissolve the social basis of political pretensions by breaking the family and social group monopoly of offices in the court. On the other hand, the crown could leave the procedures intact. The judges could continue to control the recruitment of their membership and to portray Parlement as a prestigious social corporation. If the royal administration chose the latter course of action, it would have to devise other methods to subdue this powerful and traditionally troublesome court of law.

PARLEMENT AND THE PAULETTE AFTER THE FRONDE

The *droit annuel* expired every nine years, thus providing the government with a periodic opportunity to revoke it if and when circumstances permitted. The first expiration date after the Fronde fell in 1657. The analysis of the government's decision in that crucial year, however, will be better understood in the context of the important edict on the *droit annuel* of October 6, 1638, which described the conditions under which the tax operated during the first few years of Louis XIV's reign.

The 1638 edict had its origins in the turbulent relations between the crown and Parlement during the last years of Richelieu's administration. The financial pressures of the Thirty Years' War had compelled Louis XIII and his first minister to introduce a host of extraordinary financial measures to meet rising costs.[15] The royal administration imposed new taxes, created additional venal offices, and further utilized the provincial intendants to circumvent the resistance of provincial branches of the royal administration to the crown's programs of expediency. It came as no surprise when Richelieu turned to the Parlement of Paris as a source of needed revenue. At a *lit de justice* held on December 20, 1635, Louis XIII registered several extraordinary tax edicts and office creations, among which were more than twenty new councillorships and presidential posts at Parlement. Interpreting these additions as a threat to their prestige and the capital value of their posts, the judges refused to accept the new appointees and instead issued a barrage of remonstrances to protest the king's policy. Louis's first response to this obstruction was to exile some of the more recalcitrant *parlementaires*. But pressure from Parlement was so strong that in March 1636 the crown suppressed several of the new court offices as a concession to the magistrates.[16]

The turmoil of these years provided the immediate background for the 1638 edict on the *droit annuel*, the terms of which revealed the positive and negative aspects of the procedure for royal authority.[17] By making it known in Parlement that the renewal of the *paulette* depended upon the judges' acceptance of his most recent policies, Richelieu certainly convinced the court to consent to the financial decrees and most of the new officials. The edict also increased the official value of offices and the *droit annuel* fees by 25 percent, thus guaranteeing an increment in royal revenue.[18] Nevertheless, that the judges also benefited from the edict's provisions underscores the essence of compromise between the cardinal and the *parlementaires*. The edict flatly recognized that the venality of offices and the *droit annuel* were integral parts of French institutional life, thus confirming the status of offices as private property at the disposal of a judge. The *droit annuel* was extended for another nine years, and the *parlementaires* successfully negotiated their exemption from a clause stipulating that officials pay an additional tax in the form of a loan (*prêt*). The detailed clauses describing how widows, heirs, and those who had received *resignatio in favorem* were to validate their claims in no way interfered with a magistrate's privilege to dispose of his office as he pleased so long as he punctually paid the *paulette*. The judges therefore retained a basis of independence from the crown, guaranteed for another nine years by Richelieu's timely extension of the *paulette*. Even the increase in the official value of venal offices did not threaten the judges because the market value of their posts had risen far more than 25 percent since 1604; for example, the increase of 1638 raised the official value of the office of lay councillor to 24,000 *livres*, but Mousnier indicates a going market price for this office in 1635 of 120,000 *livres*.[19]

From Richelieu's death in 1642 until the outbreak of the Fronde in 1648, Cardinal Mazarin continued to pursue his predecessor's and patron's policies of expediency. As his relations with Parlement steadily worsened, he too apparently hoped that threats to abolish the *droit annuel* would silence his critics in the court. By an edict of May 1648, Mazarin actually suspended the continuation of the *droit annuel*, but his move so angered Parlement and other officials that he quickly restored it on June 30. The *paulette* was continued for another nine years; there was no official revaluation of office values (despite the fact that their market value continued to rise), and Parlement was again exempted from the forced loan.[20] But as the most recent historian of Parlement's role in the Fronde has noted, even this fleeting attempt to revoke the *droit annuel* had already done its damage by provoking the judges of the Parisian sovereign courts to convene their famous meeting at the Chambre Saint-Louis, the act that ushered in the parlementary Fronde.[21] Manipulation of the *paulette*, which had occasionally worked for Richelieu, had backfired for Mazarin.

Parlement was still the recalcitrant institution it had been before and during the Fronde when the *paulette* again came up for renewal in 1657. The specific issues involved in the conflict between the crown and Parlement will be examined in subsequent chapters. The issue presently at hand is to determine whether Mazarin saw the *droit annuel* as a means to control Parlement. In order to understand the cardinal's sentiments on this subject, it is important to recognize that it was a consistent feature of his policies toward Parlement to choose immediate rather than long-range solutions to problems that arose. Mazarin seemed literally to formulate his policies on a day-to-day basis. Much of this vacillation stemmed from the influence enjoyed within governmental circles by Nicolas Fouquet, who jointly exercised the posts of *surintendant des finances* in the ministry and *procureur général* of Parlement. Fouquet shared Mazarin's proclivity for placing problems only in their immediate context. This wily minister was far more concerned with securing desperately needed finances through intrigue than facing Parlement squarely over issues of conflicting interest. Several of Mazarin's other trusted advisers, notably Secretary of State for War Michel Le Tellier, *Surintendant* Abel Servien, Jean-Baptiste Colbert, and Chancellor Pierre Séguier, deplored the cardinal's reluctance to deal firmly with the court. Despite their influence, Mazarin time and again followed Fouquet's advice and pursued a policy of compromise and pacification.

In July 1656, Fouquet was in the process of negotiating the registration of several lucrative financial edicts at Parlement.[22] Faced with "diverse difficulties" in the court, he advised Mazarin that the solution, "in a word . . . is that one could secure this considerable affair only by according the *droit annuel* [to the judges]."[23] The cardinal eventually adopted this advice and granted the *paulette* for an additional nine years by an edict of January 15, 1657. The conditions were those of 1648; there was no revaluation of office values and no loan to pay in addition to the *droit annuel*.[24] But this solution was hardly an example of the crown using the renewal of the *paulette* to force the judges to accept distasteful policies. Fouquet's financial edicts continued to meet stiff resistance in the court despite the renewal of the *paulette*, and only after he modified them significantly did the judges proceed to registration.[25] It is possible that Mazarin and Fouquet regretted having granted the *paulette* so easily, but no doubt memories of events in 1648 convinced them to let the matter rest.

Compromise had been the essence of Cardinal Mazarin's relations with Parlement. When young Louis XIV announced upon the cardinal's death early in 1661 that he would assume personal management of his government, however, Parlement quickly realized that bargaining with him would prove more difficult than it had been with his preceptor. It seemed that Louis issued reforms from his reorganized councils daily. As early as July 1661 he ordered the Conseil d'En haut to publish a decree that attacked a major fulcrum of the court's political authority: from that time all decrees of the king's councils were to have precedence over those of the law court. In the same year, the king arrested the last of "Les Mazarins" whose policy it was to compromise with the court. Nicolas Fouquet came to trial for corruption before the *Chambre de Justice*, which Louis had established in 1661 to punish those responsible for the financial abuses that marked his minority.[26] As the expiration date for the *droit annuel* drew close in late 1665, the *parlementaires* began to wonder whether Louis would renew it. What were they to expect from this zealous king and his powerful minister, Jean-Baptiste Colbert?

Well before the cardinal's death, Colbert had expressed dissatisfaction with the way Mazarin and Fouquet managed the affairs of the kingdom. Despite his personal attachment to Mazarin, Colbert time and again emphasized that basic reforms were necessary if the royal administration was to function smoothly. Upon his own initiative, Colbert wrote a lengthy memorandum to the cardinal in October 1659. Although his particular motive in writing was to complain about Fouquet's financial administration, Colbert swiftly proceeded to what he considered to be the broader issues involved. He emphatically argued that the personal attitudes of Mazarin and Fouquet were in part responsible for the problems they encountered in managing affairs of state. He condemned their tendency to define problems only in an immediate context, to believe "that it is not useful to think into the future, but only the present"; defining problems from a perspective of expediency yielded only "confusion." Furthermore, he stressed that the difficulties in financial administration could be fully appreciated only if they were viewed as part of the larger problem of particularism in the French state. The sentiments of provincialism, the power of the nobility in the countryside, and the independence of the venal officials all contributed to minimize the intended effects of royal policy. As to the officials, Colbert noted that the security of the *droit annuel* not only protected royal officials who, like the magistrates of Parlement, consistently resisted the king's will, but it also provided no incentive for them to exercise efficiently their professional duties. Colbert offered the cardinal a simple solution, at least in theory: curtail the sale of public offices, reduce the number of existing officials, revoke the *droit annuel*, and reform the regulations that supposedly defined the officials' duties.[27]

After the cardinal's death and Fouquet's arrest, Colbert gradually became Louis's most trusted adviser, and as such he remained interested in the problem of *vénalité* and the *paulette*. When in 1665 the *droit annuel* came up for renewal, Colbert wrote three memoranda in which he synthesized his views on the connection between the *droit annuel* and the conduct of royal officials.

In a "Memoir on the Administration of Justice," Colbert complained about how poorly justice was administered throughout France: the judgment of both civil and criminal litigation at all levels of the judiciary was lengthy, inefficient, and expensive.[28] He encouraged the king to send deputies from his councils to Paris and the provinces to report on the abuses they discovered in the judiciary. On the basis of these reports, councillors of state would formulate a new set of procedural codes to be applied uniformly throughout the kingdom.[29] But Colbert told the king that he already knew the cause of the abuses the deputies would eventually document. He recognized that abuses in judicial administration, as in the area of financial management, largely resulted from the excessive number of venal officials who enjoyed freedom of action because of the *droit annuel*. Echoing his sentiments of 1659, Colbert encouraged Louis to end the sale of offices and to abolish the *droit annuel* over a period of four years. He realized that this action might "ruin an infinite number of families, particularly the officials of the courts called Sovereign," but the alternative was continued disorder in royal administration. Colbert further suggested that the king reduce and stabilize the value of existing offices and enforce age requirements for entrance into the judiciary.[30] He believed that these reforms would result in more experienced judges who would charge litigants less if their own investment in offices were reduced.

In another memorandum entitled "Advice on the *Annuel*," Colbert further elaborated the reasons why the *droit annuel* should be abolished. "The establishment and long use of this right has greatly increased the consideration and credit of the judicial officials in the kingdom," thus reenforcing their desire to extend their political pretensions. If the king abolished it, Colbert assured Louis "that all the consideration and credit of the *gens de robe* would be entirely reversed at a single blow." Louis could

then recapture control of institutional recruitment and "render those provided [with an office] wiser and more moderate in important occasions."
Colbert further explained that the sale of offices siphoned a great deal of
the kingdom's wealth into underproductive sectors of the economy. Instead of investing in trade and industry, the wealthy bourgeoisie, hungry
for position and status, willingly paid exorbitant prices for offices. If
venality were curtailed, "merchants [who now scrambled to purchase offi-
ces] would be more highly considered in the kingdom, which would in
turn yield great [financial] advantages [to the crown]." Finally, Colbert
reiterated that the reformation of justice required fewer and more docile
judicial officials.[31]

Colbert firmly believed, therefore, that the sale of offices and the *droit
annuel* stood as obstacles to the complete assertion of the monarch's will.
Their revocation would improve the administration of justice in the kingdom, increase the flow of funds into productive sectors of the economy,
and allow the king to render royal institutions docile through his control of
the recruitment process. However, in his third memoir to Louis dated
October 1665, just two months before a final decision on the *paulette*,
Colbert dramatically reversed his views regarding the Parlement of Paris.
The best way to control Parlement, he asserted, was "to act with time and
patience [and] without precipitation." If the law court was treated rudely
and its authority reduced "at a single blow," the magistrates would easily
reassert their pretended authority during a future weak reign or minority.
The path to control of Parlement, he explained, was the gradual erosion of
the court's political authority. Colbert advised the king "to treat these
matters only in their ordinary conduct, and not to resort to extraordinary
means."[32]

Although Colbert did not elaborate these views in detail, he clearly
advised Louis to continue the *droit annuel* for Parlement. What he seemed
to advocate was that the king conduct his offensive against the court on the
judicial and political level and curtail the mechanisms Parlement used to
exert political influence: the court's plenary sessions, its right to remonstrate, and its practice of issuing decrees contrary to those of the
king's councils. Surprisingly, Colbert viewed control of Parlement's
membership as a short-range expedient. Certainly he was not ignorant of
tactics intended to reduce Parlement's status as a social corporation. His
desire to stabilize office prices and to enforce age requirements for entrance into the court would have had, if enforced, an impact on the composition of the court. On the other hand, by relinquishing direct royal supervision of the recruitment process, Colbert in effect advocated continued
control by the magistrates over the transmission of their offices. In 1665,
therefore, Colbert and Louis XIV had arrived at a crossroads in the tactics

to be employed in silencing Parlement. In assessing the "three faces" of the court—social, political, and judicial—Colbert and Louis decided not to concentrate their efforts on the first.

Unfortunately, the sources are silent as to why Colbert shifted his tactics in this third memorandum, and any assessment must be tentative. One possible explanation is that he viewed the renewable *droit annuel* as a way periodically to threaten the judges into submission. But such an absolutist interpretation neglects Colbert's forceful condemnation of the procedure in his earlier memoranda. Furthermore, for the remainder of his reign Louis granted the *paulette* as a matter of course without extensive bargaining. In December 1709, he even dispensed with the fee altogether, thus officially sanctioning an official's control of his post.[33] Perhaps the most plausible explanation of Colbert's change in attitude lies in the risk he faced in enacting his suggestions for reform. The crown lacked the funds to repurchase most venal offices, and there was no guarantee that the abolition of the *paulette* would not provoke the unified resistance of the kingdom's many officials, resistance that might mushroom into civil strife as in 1648. The death of Philip IV of Spain in September 1665 further complicated the feasibility of reform. The prospect of war increased the influence of Colbert's chief rival, Michel Le Tellier, in the council. Colbert might have feared the erosion of his own influence with the king if he urged full reform of the judiciary at a time when military priorities within the council were ascendant.[34]

Whatever Colbert's motives ultimately were, the edict on the *paulette* that Parlement registered at a *lit de justice* on December 22, 1665, reflected his most recent advice.[35] The *paulette* was again extended on the conditions of 1638, except that there was no revaluation of office values and no forced loan for superior judges. The only major alteration of previous edicts was that the *paulette* would come up for renewal every three years instead of the usual nine, thus giving the king more frequently the opportunity of revoking the tax, an opportunity which, as noted, the crown never sought to exploit.[36] A contemporary did indicate that Louis later threatened to revoke the *droit annuel* in a declaration of February 1669, but that he only exercised his threat for certain groups of lesser officials.[37] The Parlement of Paris, however, enjoyed the privilege of the *droit annuel* throughout Louis XIV's reign until the edict of 1709 abolished the fee altogether.[38]

Thus, neither Mazarin nor Louis XIV and Colbert changed the magistrates' control of office transmission. Because offices in Parlement remained venal and transmissible under the conditions of the *paulette*, the interference of the crown in Parlement's recruitment was by definition extremely limited. The judges retained security in office because their posts remained negotiable property, and Parlement was free to continue to develop patterns of membership along social group and family lines.

The history of the office of councillor of Parlement, however, is far from complete. The edict of December 1665, besides continuing the *droit annuel*, contained several other clauses that reduced the official value of offices and stabilized tbe prices that prospective buyers could pay for an office in the high judiciary. The edict also established minimum age requirements for entrance into the court. Another edict registered at the same *lit de justice* stipulated that the relatives of financiers and tax farmers could freely hold posts in all branches of the judiciary, including the Parlement of Paris. Louis and Colbert issued still another edict in 1669 prohibiting candidates from entering a court where they had relatives as members. None of these edicts would have totally placed recruitment for Parlement in the hands of the king, but their enforcement could have seriously impaired social structure and family membership trends in the court. A full analysis of officeholding in Parlement in the post-Fronde era requires that each of these subsidiary expressions of royal policy be examined in turn.

PARLEMENT AND THE STABILIZATION OF OFFICE PRICES

Two historians who have recently written about the Parlement of Rennes during the reign of Louis XIV agree that the clauses of the December 1665 edict that reduced the official value of offices and stabilized the legal prices to be paid for posts in the high judiciary damaged the financial position of the Breton magistrates. They assert that the reduction of office values seriously jeopardized the judges' capital investment in their posts and threatened to reduce their court's prestige and political influence.[39] Though perhaps valid for the Breton judges, these conclusions are not applicable to the Parlement of Paris for several reasons. First, because of certain social tensions within the Parlement of Paris, the reduction and stabilization of office values actually benefited the court's development along specific social lines, a phenomenon that increased the judges' self-esteem and social pretensions during the reign of Louis XIV. Second, the majority of magistrates did not suffer the serious financial loss that supposedly accompanied the edict. Finally, drawing too direct a correlation between the value of an office and an institution's esteem or political authority can be misleading. Not only did offices in the high judiciary remain attractive for reasons other than their financial worth, but the reduction in office prices in no way threatened the duties and powers that a judge relied upon to sustain his political activities.

The market value of offices at the Parlement of Paris had steadily increased in the first half of the seventeenth century. Mousnier estimates that the price of the office of councillor was 11,000 *livres* in 1597. The market value rose to 21,000 in 1600, 36,000 in 1606, 60,000 in 1616, and 120,000 *livres* in 1638.[40] The high prices of the thirties continued through the Fronde and into the 1660s.[41] In 1665, on the eve of the edict that stabilized prices, the government had *trésoriers de France* estimate the market value of offices throughout France. The figures in table 1 demonstrate how rapidly the prices for offices at Parlement had risen since the 1638 evaluation.[42] Even granting possible inaccuracy on the part of the *trésoriers*, it is apparent that the market value of offices had soared up to 500 percent more than the amount which the government officially recognized and upon which it pegged salary payments and the *droit annuel*. The situation was the same for the offices of the other Parisian and provincial sovereign courts.[43]

The reasons for this dramatic rise are complex. Occasional and periodic fluctuations in the general index of all prices might have been in part responsible. Mousnier grants this possibility, but he notes that most prices never rose as rapidly as those for offices. He chooses to emphasize the *paulette* as a key factor because it provided security in the possession and transmission of offices that had not been present in the sixteenth century.[44] Another notable causal factor was the periodic increase in salaries that magistrates purchased from the crown with a lump sum. These raises were little more than forced loans because several decades in office were required for a magistrate to regain his investment. But, because salary

TABLE 1
VALUES OF OFFICES AT PARLEMENT, 1638 AND 1665

Office	Official Value in 1638 (in *livres*)	Estimated Value in 1665 (in *livres*)	Droit Annuel Paid on 1638 Value (in *livres*)
Président à mortier	66,666	500,000	1,111
Avocat général	40,000	150,000	666
President of *requêtes*	40,000	180,000	666
President of *enquêtes*	36,000	150,000	600
Maître des requêtes	28,000	280,000	466
Lay councillor	24,000	120,000	400
Clerical councillor	20,000	110,000	333
Commission to *requêtes*	4,000	20,000	66

increments were hereditary (following the office, not the individual), they did contribute to raising the market value of a post. Perhaps another explanation, which Meyer has offered from his study of the Parlement of Rennes, is that the political prestige of the sovereign courts, including the Parlement of Paris, made judicial offices more attractive to prospective buyers.[45]

Each of these explanations has validity, but only partially so. The introduction of the *paulette*, for example, would have naturally increased the value of an office immediately after 1604, but it does not explain the dramatic rise in subsequent years. Similarly, although salary increases were frequently enacted, they were never of a magnitude to create a significant and sustained rise in prices. As regards Parlement's political pretensions, these had certainly been asserted long before the seventeenth century.

The most plausible explanation of the phenomenon, and the most durable over a long period of time, is that competition for offices by extremely wealthy prospective buyers caused the value of offices to rise. At Paris, the competition was provided by the children of wealthy bourgeoisie, tax farmers, financiers, and recently ennobled *secrétaires du roi*. In his *Annales politiques*, the Abbé Saint-Pierre reflected on the Fronde era and expressed what he considered to be a well-known fact: "Just as in Rouen the merchant families secured offices at the Parlement of Normandy . . . so at Paris the financier families daily seized the posts in the Parlement of Paris."[46] Why these groups desired offices in Parlement is clear enough. The political prestige provides a partial explanation. More important, Parlement had the reputation of an elite social corporation with a tradition of dignity and nobility. To possess an office at Parlement offered the wealthy commoner or noble of recent extraction an excellent opportunity to introduce his family into a prestigious judicial institution with a high degree of social status.[47]

The magistrates, however, did not sympathize with the desire of tax farmers and financiers to place their relatives in the court. Social considerations partially account for their hostility. Once a member of Parlement, a judge quickly forgot that he might have had a bourgeois background, whether by birth or marriage. He became sensitive to the social background of prospective members, and he particularly resented the opulence of successful financiers. Their "bourgeois blood" was seen as a threat to Parlement's prestige, and their competition for posts so inflated office prices that it seemed that only these undesirable elements could enter the court. At the beginning of the Fronde, a councillor named Laisné expressed the opinion of his fellow magistrates when he complained that "the price of a post is so expensive that it seems that only tax farmers are able to enter the court."[48]

Sentiments of social elitism might seem contradictory given that the judges did not refrain from amassing riches themselves or marrying the daughters of financiers for their wealth. But the contradiction is less puzzling if the social tensions within Parlement are seen in context with the political and administrative policies of the crown before the Fronde. The magistrates firmly believed that tax farmers and financiers were the passive servants of royal administrations whose "governmental revolution" eroded Parlement's wealth, function, and prestige. By aiding the notorious intendants, and by extracting profits from funds earmarked to pay judicial salaries and interest on government bonds, the tax farmers and financiers ensured the judges' enmity toward them.[49] That the judges took these social and political grievances seriously is evident because they could have made sizable profits by selling their offices at inflated prices. Most of them minimized their financial vested interests, however, in favor of their social and political claims. At the beginning of the Fronde, the court issued the famous decree of October 23, 1648, which excluded tax farmers, financiers, and their children from office in Parlement.[50]

As office prices remained high in the 1650s, the magistrates renewed their attack on tax farmers and financiers, whose relatives continued to enter the court despite the 1648 decree. In February 1658, a councillor at the Parlement of Metz named Garnier presented his letters of admission to the Parlement of Paris, but the judges postponed his reception because they suspected that his father had been "interested in the tax farms."[51] Ignoring a royal prohibition to discuss the case, President Molé asked his colleagues to enforce the 1648 decree and to reject Garnier's candidacy.[52] In December, the magistrates decided to consider seriously Molé's proposition. Deputies from the *enquêtes* and the *requêtes* requested that all chambers be assembled to discuss the issue, and, confronted with this unified protest, First President Lamoignon was obliged to comply.[53] Parlement was very agitated over this issue. One of Chancellor Séguier's informants wrote that the judges considered rejecting all relatives of tax farmers and financiers from the court; he feared that eventually Parlement might apply these restrictions to all levels of the judiciary.[54]

In January 1659, Parlement discussed Molé's request. Fortunately, a speech delivered by one of the *avocats généraux*, Denis Talon, and a rare written opinion of a councillor named Miron have survived.[55] They testify to Parlement's resentment of the tax farmers on both social and political grounds. Both concluded in favor of Molé's request. Talon's stirring speech condemned the vile activities of the tax farmers in the provinces as a threat to Parlement's judicial authority. "[They act] with destruction in the villages . . . as if they were in a conquered nation," he said. "They are enemies who consider the legitimate authority we [the *parlementaires*] exercise as an obstacle." Furthermore, he charged that the tax farmers and financiers paid "millions" for an office in the court, thus excluding more socially acceptable candidates. They also married their daughters to prestigious *parlementaires*. "If the disorder continues, all the grand and illustrious families of France will be despoiled." Talon concluded that Parlement "has the duty to carry out an exact examination of the conduct of those who aspire to charges in the judiciary . . . [and to require them to be] incorruptible and exempt from reproach and suspicion, and not men of luxury and corruption. . . . Those who sit under the *Fleurs de Lys* have the responsibility to reflect on their condition . . . and not to dishonor their posterity with the mixture of impure blood."

Miron advanced political reasons for his dislike of the tax farmers and financiers. Not only did they profit handsomely from the kingdom's financial difficulties, he asserted, but they undermined Parlement's authority by passively implementing royal policies of expediency. The stability of the French monarchy "is attributed to the fact that the parlements moderate absolute authority and render royal administration more acceptable to the people. . . . It is the duty of this court to be the arbiter of the intentions and interests of the king and the people, . . . to moderate the rays of the sun [while the tax farmers], to the contrary, resemble these flashing rays."

On the basis of such opinions, Parlement decided to reject Garnier's candidacy.[56] The court issued decrees that called for the enforcement of the October 1648 decisions and extended the prohibition to *all* relatives of the tax farmers. Any magistrates who had married the daughters of tax farmers in the past, or did so in the future, were denied mobility to higher positions in the court. The decrees also stipulated that the chambers of the *édit, tournelle, enquêtes,* and *requêtes* would collectively investigate and vote on the family backgrounds of future candidates for office.[57] Other Parisian sovereign courts quickly followed Parlement's lead and issued similar decrees.[58]

How valid was the judges' claim that the relatives of tax farmers and financiers invaded the court? An examination of the backgrounds and the marriages of the councillors received at the court during the second half of Mazarin's administration indicates that their fears were more imaginary than real. The genealogies of the ninety-six councillors received at Parlement between 1653 and 1661 reveal that only 12.5 percent of the new councillors had fathers who could be classified as bourgeois, financier, or *secrétaire du roi,* and only 18.7 percent of their grandfathers had such origins.[59] As regards the marriage alliances these councillors contracted, only 18.7 percent wed the daughters of individuals who were bourgeois, financiers, or *secrétaires du roi*. This sample, of course, does not include those members who already sat in the court before 1653. Furthermore, it is limited to the councillor and his father and grandfather. No doubt the inclusion of all family members and their alliances would increase the frequency of the judges' contact with the tax farmers and financiers. On the other hand, the figures presented here include all genealogical references to *secrétaires du roi*, bourgeois, and financial posts that financiers frequently held. This tends to inflate both the percentage of the relatives of tax farmers and financiers in the court and the councillors' alliances with them by marriage, because not all *secrétaires du roi*, bourgeois, or royal financial officials were tax farmers and financiers. With this proviso, these figures do provide a reliable estimate of the extent of a "bourgeois" or "tax farmer invasion" into Parlement, and it indicates that such an influx might well have inflated office prices, but it was not of the magnitude that some literary sources and the *parlementaires* themselves would have us believe.

Perhaps the best explanation of why the judges exaggerated the threat posed by tax farmers and financiers to the social composition of the court in the 1650s resides in Parlement's conflicts with the crown on other issues in the same period. At both times the issue of Parlement's social composition flared up, in 1648 and 1658–1659, the judges also were challenging Mazarin's financial and administrative policies. Sixteen forty-eight, of course, was the eve of the Fronde; 1658 and 1659 were years marked by renewed judicial opposition to jurisdictional encroachments by the royal councils and to the plans of Mazarin and Fouquet to reduce interest payments on government bonds that many magistrates held. The *parlementaires* naturally found the social issue a convenient method of pressing political grievances against the royal administration by attacking the visible symbols of royal financial expedients, the tax farmers and the financiers. It is possible that Mazarin recognized that Parlement attempted to add a social dimension to its complaints, and he did not wish to intensify further Parlement's anger on other affairs, especially at a time when he delicately pursued negotiations for a peace treaty with Spain. On the other hand, perhaps the cardinal was unconcerned with this internal matter of the court and hoped that if the magistrates had their way he could render them more docile. In any case, the royal administration did little to interfere with the court's decrees of 1659 against the tax farmers and the rejection of Garnier's candidacy.

Despite these predominantly political motives behind Parlement's activity in the 1650s, the judges' claim that tax farmers and financiers threatened Parlement's social composition was not without foundation in the following decade when the influx of the relatives of these detested individuals into the court did increase perceptibly. This influx provides the immediate background for the edict that stabilized the prices for offices in the sovereign courts, and it holds the key for assessing the social consequences of this stabilization in the Parlement of Paris.

Parlement might well have been intent on enforcing its decrees of 1659. For example, in May of that year the judges postponed the reception of a Monsieur Hervart at the court because they believed that his father, an *intendant des finances,* had been involved in tax farming. After a year of deliberation, Parlement finally rejected the younger Hervart's candidacy.[60] Nevertheless, an examination of the backgrounds and marriages of the councillors received at the court during the years 1661–1673 demonstrates that Parlement did not long enforce its regulations. Of the 112 new councillors admitted into the court, 25.9 percent had fathers who could be classified as bourgeois, financiers, or *secrétaires de roi* (compared to 12.5 percent in the period 1653–1660) and 27.6 percent of their grandfathers had similar backgrounds (compared to 18.7 percent during the years 1653–1660). Furthermore, 23.5 percent of the marriages contracted by the new members fell into the same group (compared to 18.7 percent in the 1653–1660 period).

It was in the midst of this influx that the king issued the edict of December 22, 1665, which, in addition to extending the *paulette,* reduced the official value of offices in the high judiciary and fixed the prices that prospective buyers could pay for them. The stated intent of this stabilization was to open the judiciary to competent candidates who could not afford offices at current price levels. The edict no doubt also reflected Colbert's belief that high office prices led judges to demand higher fees from litigants as well as his conviction that lower office prices would channel more of the nation's wealth into productive sectors of the economy. Table 2 compares the market values of offices in 1665 before the edict with the prices legally established for future purchases.[61]

The immediate effect of the edict was to reduce the capital value of offices anywhere from 30 percent (for a president) to 15 percent (for a councillor). Ormesson relates in his journal that when news of the changes leaked as early as March, and when the edict was registered in December, "all the officers were confused and upset."[62] Just six days after the judges registered the edict at a *lit de justice,* deputies from the chambers of *enquêtes* and *requêtes* asked First President Lamoignon to call a plenary session of the court to discuss its provisions. Lamoignon replied that he had consulted with the king and Chancellor Séguier about holding such a session, but that Louis had informed him that he intended the court to obey the edict without further discussion.[63] A few weeks later several judges again

TABLE 2
PRICES OF OFFICES AT PARLEMENT: THE REFORM OF DECEMBER 1665

Office	Official Value in 1638 (in *livres*)	Estimated Value in 1665 (in *livres*)	Official Price in December 1665 (in *livres*)
Président à mortier	66,666	500,000	350,000
Avocat général	40,000	150,000	150,000
President of *requêtes*	40,000	180,000	90,000
President of *enquêtes*	36,000	150,000	100,000
Maître des requêtes	28,000	280,000	150,000
Lay councillor	24,000	120,000	100,000
Clerical councillor	20,000	110,000	90,000
Commission to *requêtes*	4,000	20,000	15,000

pleaded with Lamoignon to intercede with the king on their behalf. Under royal orders, however, the first president simply repeated his previous speech. The clerk of Parlement's registers noted the frustration of the magistrates by adding to the official transcript that, upon hearing Lamoignon's identical words, "the entire court ended the session without saying a word, and with no deliberation [on the edicts]."[64]

In his memoirs, Louis XIV spoke of the resistance of Parlement to this edict and his determination to stand firmly behind his decision:

So as to let it be known that I did not regard [the *parlementaires*] highly, I ordered [Lamoignon] to assemble Parlement and tell the councillors that I no longer wanted them to discuss edicts verified in my presence, and to see if any among them dared to disobey me. Because, in fact, I desired to use this event as a shining example of the entire submission of this court and of my just severity to punish them. . . . [Yet, when Parlement ended its session] I received perfect witness of the total reestablishment of royal authority.[65]

Sympathetic biographers of Lamoignon emphasize that he perceived Louis's desire for a confrontation, warned the court, and advised the passivity that its clerk poignantly recorded.[66]

At this point two crucial questions arise. First, what was the impact of the stabilization of offices prices on the composition of the court? This question can be answered only in light of the increased influx of relatives of tax farmers and other "bourgeoisie" into Parlement in the early 1660s. Second, do the protests of the *parlementaires* against the edict indicate that a reduction in the capital value of their offices threatened their financial ruin?

The reduction and stabilization of office values ultimately had its intended effect. The prices paid for offices in Parlement, which had remained high until 1665, began to stabilize at the legal levels by no later than 1682.[67] But that more than a decade elapsed before prices finally stabilized indicates that the *parlementaires* temporarily evaded the terms of the edict and did not suffer financial loss. For example, those magistrates who rushed to sell their posts because of the edict often found loopholes to recoup their losses. They could charge a prospective buyer an additional "under the table fee," called a *pot de vin*. Ormesson writes that he sold his charge of *maître des requêtes* for 150,000 *livres*, a net loss; he made up the difference by demanding an additional 84,000 *livres pot de vin* from the purchaser. He then boasted "that instead of losing on my charge, I made [50,000 *livres*] profit."[68] A contemporary biography of Colbert, moreover, took note of the widespread evasion of the edict and asserted that "it did not at first have its effect and the officials eluded the will of the king by *pots de vin*, which were given secretly and which augmented considerably the prices established by the fixation."[69] Thus, while one cannot exclude the possibility that some councillors who sold their offices lost money, the evidence that exists on this matter suggests that others fared quite well.

The judges also escaped serious financial loss because of the very values to which the edict pegged office prices. Although the *présidents à mortier* suffered the most because of the large difference between the market value of their office and its new official price (150,000 *livres*), the losses of the councillors were considerably less.[70] Also, it is quite probable that most of the councillors had purchased their offices when they were worth even less than the new regulations stipulated. Only those who purchased an office during recent price booms would suffer; but even in this case, the *pot de vin* expedient was open to them. The edict's effect upon the various presidents of the court was not as severe as the figures would show, since these offices were almost entirely hereditary and had been purchased in generations past at prices below even those established by the edict.

As to the question of the edict's impact on the membership of Parlement, the long-range consequences of price stabilization were to strengthen social cohesion within the court. This fact makes the edict a landmark in the development of social patterns and mentality within Parlement. Because office values were reduced, established *parlementaires* were encouraged to hold on to their offices and to transmit their charges, when they did sell, to other Parisian and provincial official (or robe) families. For example, whereas ninety-five councillors left their posts in the last eight years of Mazarin's ministry, only seventy-eight did so in the eight years following the 1665 edict. Moreover, a wealthy tax farmer or rich bourgeois lost the one edge he had possessed in bargaining for offices—money. With prices lower, the magistrates could sell their offices to other robe families who could once again compete financially for offices. This important implication of the edict was not immediately perceptible, no doubt because the use of *pots de vin* kept prices temporarily inflated. Of the seventy-eight new councillors received at the court between 1666 and 1673, 16 percent had fathers and 18 percent had grandfathers who fell into the category of bourgeois, financier, tax farmer, or *secrétaire du roi*. Their entrance had tapered off, but had not been curtailed. After an important edict outlawed *pots de vin*, however, prices did stabilize by 1682 and Parlement became even less tainted with those elements.[71] Bluche found that by 1715, "from the commission of the first president to the simple office of councillor, the issue of birth was the basis [of a candidate's] reception, suspension, or delay. . . . The number of offices available to the bourgeoisie was minimal. . . . The court was rarely open to new men."[72] Meyer has discovered a similar development in the Parlement of Rennes. Until 1665 wealthy bourgeoisie frequently entered the court, but the trend reversed after the issuance of the 1665 edict: office prices declined, the wealthy bourgeoisie was excluded from the court, and the *parlementaires* increasingly rejected candidates whose origins were not in official (or robe) families.[73]

The royal administration did recognize that by lowering the prices of offices, the relatives of tax farmers and wealthy bourgeoisie would inevitably be excluded from Parlement. At the *lit de justice* of December 1665, Louis presented another edict to the court in which he pardoned the tax farmers for past crimes (for which he had recently prosecuted many in the *Chambre de Justice*) and ordered that "the said tax farmers and their children will be admitted without discrimination in all charges of the military [*épée*], judicial, and financial administrations."[74] As noted above, such people did continue to enter the court, but this was owing more to the *pots de vin* than to the king's edict. First President Lamoignon himself made this clear. On December 15, 1667, Lamoignon reported to the court that the king had summoned him to learn why the judges continued to disobey his December edict by refusing to admit the relatives of tax farmers into the court. Lamoignon admitted to the king that Parlement still considered its own decrees of 1659 against the tax farmers valid. He attacked the tax farmers, "to whom all dignities were available because of their excessive wealth and because they were supported by alliances with many powerful families." He asked Louis "to remember the excesses that these types of people had brought to all things and the confusion they had added to the affairs of the state." This issue "was essential to the dignity and purity of his Parlement." Then he proceeded to the question of why tax farmers and financiers still entered the court. He did not cite Louis's edict of 1665, but instead referred to the *pots de vin*:

Even Your Majesty desires that the price of charges be fixed and not rise to the excesses of the past. [Yet] it will be impossible to conserve this rule as long as the tax farmers have entry into Parlement, because they always seem to discover a thousand ways to evade the regulations. [Because of their wealth] they have replaced many old families [in the court].[75]

Despite Lamoignon's fears and Louis's refusal to bargain on this issue, the number of councillors related to tax farmers and wealthy bourgeoisie did decline in time, a phenomenon resulting from the curtailment of *pots de vin*. As prices stabilized, Louis's edict allowing the relatives of tax farmers in the court became a dead letter. His edict could not force a *parlementaire* to sell his office to someone he considered to be undesirable. The continuation of the venality of offices and the *droit annuel* ensured the magistrate this prerogative. From its inception, moreover, this royal afterthought to allow wealthy financiers entrance into the court was doomed: it had already been condemned by the policy that authorized the stabilization of prices. Colbert had made it quite clear in his memoranda of 1665 that one of the reasons he wanted the prices of offices stabilized was to ensure that the wealthy bourgeoisie invested more of their funds in productive sectors of the economy and not in offices. Louis's permission for them to enter the court was but a point of honor, and if enforced, it would have led to the destruction of Colbert's policy.

One additional aspect of the stabilization of office prices warrants assessment: its impact on the prestige and political influence of Parlement. Perhaps Colbert hoped that the reduction of an office's value would yield a reduction in its status and political leverage. In his contemporary history of Louis's reign, Paul Pellisson maintained that Colbert hoped the edict would symbolize "regulations that would, in general, seem to humiliate the robe."[76] Such a cause and effect relationship, however, never materialized. On the one hand, there were many reasons why contemporaries desired an office in Parlement; the political pretensions of the institution and the monetary value of its posts were only two. The imposing traditions of the court, its judicial preeminence, and the social status attached to it were far more durable and appealing than fluctuating prices or political fortunes. Office prices had continued to rise, for example, even after a royal decree of July 1661 made all decrees of the king's councils superior to those of the court.[77] On the other hand, that Parlement easily reasserted its political claims upon Louis XIV's death in 1715 should underscore the low correlation between political activity and office prices.[78]

The edict of December 1665 was therefore not as disastrous for the *parlementaires*' interests as we might imagine. The magistrates had clearly been upset with the crown's tampering with office prices, and the royal administration might well have hoped for a general offensive on the prestige of the court. But in the long run Parlement's status as a social corporation benefited from the edict. With the *droit annuel* continued and the magistrates released from the temptation to sell their offices to those who could bid extraordinary sums, Parlement was able not only to control its recruitment, but to direct this recruitment along social, and not simply financial, lines. Moreover, the stabilization of office prices neither spelled financial ruin for the judges nor prohibited them from continuing to elaborate Parlement's asserted prerogatives in the political and administrative life of the state.

PROCEDURES TO CONSOLIDATE FAMILY CONTINUITY AND SOCIAL COHESION

One of the most popular methods the magistrates used to recruit along family lines was the age dispensation, which the judges solicited from the king, often for a fee. The procedure allowed the magistrates to transmit their offices to relatives who had not yet reached twenty-five, the legal age required for entrance. The age dispensation was often used in conjunction with a procedure called *concurrence*, which permitted two relatives to hold an office jointly. Only one of them received remuneration for his service, but the holding of posts *en concurrence* allowed the younger judge to assume the office automatically when the elder died because legally they both owned the post.

On March 31, 1662, the king sent letters patent to Parlement prohibiting age dispensations and reminding the judges that candidates for the judiciary must be twenty-five years old. Although the letters were primarily a response to Colbert's desire to exclude young and frequently inexperienced individuals from assuming high judicial posts, the enforcement of age requirements could have also seriously disrupted the transmission of offices within *parlementaire* families. Sensing this implication of these letters, Parlement postponed registration.[79] When Louis sent identical legislation to the court on February 3, 1663, the court registered it, but for all practical purposes rendered it ineffective by adding the modification "that nevertheless, age and service dispensations would continue to be granted on important occasions and for considerations of merit." In order to make their intentions clear to the king, the judges added that "the king will be humbly supplicated to give proper consideration for his officials of Parlement and grant their children age dispensations so they may enter the court."[80]

Acting on the advice of Colbert, Louis once again decided to end age dispensations. In the famous edict of December 22, 1665, he stipulated that in order to hold office in Parlement, a *président à mortier* had to be forty years old, an *avocat* or *procureur général*, thirty years old, and a councillor, twenty-seven years old.[81] The first indication that the magistrates evaded his edict was that Louis was obliged to draw up two additional supporting decrees on August 13, 1669, and February 27, 1672.[82] Moreover, a list of age dispensations compiled from manuscript sources indicates that during the period 1653–1673 the crown granted them to the sons and nephews of eighteen magistrates in Parlement.[83] Of the forty councillors received at Parlement from 1669 to 1673, 15 percent received age dispensations. In 1674 alone, thirteen judges received age dispensations for their relatives.[84] Bluche has analyzed the ages of councillors when they were received at Parlement between 1659 and 1715, and his figures demonstrate that their average age upon entrance was below the legal minimum. This trend continued into the eighteenth century, as shown in table 3.[85]

The clear evasion of the regulations distressed Achille III de Harlay, the *procureur général* of the court after 1667. Apparently, he frequently complained that officials at all levels of the judiciary easily obtained age dispensations from the king, for in a letter dated June 29, 1678, Le Tellier, who had become chancellor in the previous year, wrote in detail to the *procureur général* about the profusion of these grants. His explanation provides the key to the royal administration's inability to execute its will:

The reason why these sorts of graces [dispensations] have been accorded these past years is well known to you [Harlay]. You will judge well that I have not been at liberty to refuse to seal [letters of dispensation]... for all those who have been presented with age dispensations when it appears that those provided have paid adequately for them. There is reason to hope that with peace, the king will find himself beyond the necessity to use these extraordinary means to augment his finances, and that we will only very rarely see age dispensations for the officials of the judiciary.[86]

Such an opportunity never arose. Faced with the problem of financing his foreign wars, Louis resurrected the extraordinary policies of his predecessors and sacrificed his ideal of curtailing all age dispensations. Convinced that the regulations could not be enforced, Colbert finally legalized age dispensations for a fee of 1,500 *livres* in November 1673.[87] Government policy in this matter never evolved from intent to enforcement.

The formation of family dynasties within Parlement and the marriage alliances *parlementaires* forged with one another were also important factors

TABLE 3
AVERAGE AGE OF COUNCILLORS RECEIVED AT PARLEMENT, 1659–1715

Years of Reception	Average Age of Lay Councillors	Average Age of Clerical Councillors
1659–1703	25.8	32.3
1704–1715	22.8	30.8

in the development of social cohesion in the court. Colbert had several reasons for wishing to dissolve these personal and social bonds. On the general level, he wanted to correct the many abuses prevalent in the administration of justice. One of the abuses that the councillors of state whom Colbert requested to draw up reports on malpractice in the judiciary cited most often was the high frequency of familial ties and intermarriage among members at all levels of the judiciary. Universally these patterns had produced partial judges and rampant corruption.[88] Colbert also realized that family ties within a given court were conducive to the development of sentiments of social elitism and solidarity, which could always become dangerous when combined with political pretensions.[89] He sought to solve these problems in an "Edict of General Regulations for the Judicial Officers of the Kingdom," which Parlement registered on August 13, 1669.[90] In addition to provisions previously noted—the prohibition of age dispensations and reiteration of the prices to be paid for offices in the high judiciary—the edict also stipulated that candidates for an office could not be received in a court where they had relatives of the first, second, and third degree (father, son, brother, uncle, or cousin). It further prohibited councillors from marrying the daughters of other councillors in the same court and abolished the practice of holding offices *en concurrence*. First President Lamoignon personally requested the king to suspend these articles, but to no avail; Louis was determined to execute all the provisions of the edict.[91]

Closer analysis of the implementation of the edict, however, reveals that, as with the age dispensations, there was a difference between what the royal administration desired and what it actually achieved. The procedure of *concurrence*, for example, appears to have been curtailed somewhat; yet on May 14, 1671, Alexandre Petau received permission to hold his office *en concurrence* with his son for ten years.[92] The prohibitions against judges marrying the daughters of other magistrates certainly remained a dead letter. Of the marriages contracted by the forty councillors who entered the court after the edict (from 1669 to 1673), four (Amelot, Boucher, Caumartin, and Monthullé) married the daughters of other councillors, four others (Bazin de Bezons, Maignart, Berthier, and Vialart) married the daughters of *maîtres des requêtes*, one (Chauvelin) married the daughter of an advocate at the court, and another (Morant) married the daughter of a *greffier en chef* (chief clerk) of Parlement.[93] Because the government lacked the legal authority to annul marriages, and because the councillors owned their offices, there was little the crown could do but accept these marriages as *faits accomplis*. Moreover, as with age dispensations, the financial needs of war obliged the king by the 1670s to sell dispensations for family relationships (*parenté*) within the court.[94]

The continuation of the *droit annuel,* age dispensations, intermarriage among the magistrates, and the procedure of *concurrence* made inevitable the entrance of young councillors into the court who were related to the other magistrates by blood or marriage. Bluche has demonstrated this fact in the Parlement of the eighteenth century. The Gilbert des Voisins family, for example, was related to seventy other *parlementaire* families; even such a relatively minor figure as Hurault de Bernay was related to seventeen families.[95] This situation held true for the period from 1653 to 1673. The records of the Conseil d'Etat and the Privy Council can be used profitably to demonstrate the familial ties among the magistrates. Whenever the *parlementaires* became involved in personal litigation, some of their cases eventually came before Parlement. If the magistrate had an excessive number of relatives in the court, the opposing party could file for an evocation, a procedure whereby the councils sent the litigation to another parlement if the claimant could prove his charge. The evocations, filed with the Privy Council or the Conseil d'Etat, are particularly instructive because they cite the magistrate and his alliances in the court. In March 1670, for example, a Dame d'Huart had a case before Parlement against a *greffier en chef,* Jean du Tillet. She asked that the case be sent to another jurisdiction because Tillet was related to five *maîtres des requêtes,* one *président à mortier,* one president of the *enquêtes* and thirteen councillors.[96] In November 1664, a president at the Parlement of Metz, Philippe de Loynes, requested that his case before the court involving a councillor, Jacques Pinon, be evoked because Pinon had thirteen relatives at the Parlement of Paris.[97] Similarly, in February 1665 the Marquis de Boischerpin asked for an evocation since the defendant in his civil suit, Dame Michele de la Barde, had thirteen relatives at Parlement through her deceased husband who had been a councillor at the court.[98] In February 1665, Claude de Rochechouart was granted an evocation of his case to the Parlement of Bordeaux because his opposing party, the honorary councillor Jacques Mesgrigny, had multiple alliances in the Parlement of Paris.[99] Literally hundreds of such depositions exist in conciliar records, all leading to the same conclusion: despite the prohibitive edict, the *parlementaires* were extensively related to each other through birth and marriage.

Other genealogical sources corroborate this conclusion. Such notable families as the Harlays were closely allied with the Lamoignons, Bellièvres, and Boucherats;[100] the Fieubets to the Nicolaïs, Longueils, Gilberts, Caumartins, and the Feydeaus;[101] the Lamoignons to the Harlays, Novions, and Aguesseaus.[102] Even families that exhibited less dynastic impulse were closely allied to other families in the court: the Gilliers had connections with the Berengers, Betauts, Le Ferons, La Forests, Maignarts, and Vachers.[103] The genealogist of the Petau family provides a detailed list of Paul-Alexandre's relatives in the court:[104]

Etienne d'Aligre, *président à mortier*, cousin (4th degree)
Claude Anjourard, councillor, cousin (4th degree)
Blaise-Claude Meliand, councillor, cousin (3rd degree)
Guillaume-Urbain de Lamoignon, *maître des requêtes*, cousin (3rd degree)
Jacques de Gourges, *maître des requêtes*, cousin (3rd and 4th degree)
Anne Le Clerc d'Aulnay, councillor, cousin (5th degree)
Jacques-François de Gourges, councillor, cousin (5th degree)
Dominique-Jacques de Gourges, councillor, cousin (5th degree)
Paul de Fieubet, *maître des requêtes*, cousin (4th degree)
Louis-Gaspard de Fieubet, councillor, cousin (4th and 5th degree)
Pierre Gilbert des Voisins, president of *enquêtes*, cousin (4th degree)
Pierre Gilbert des Voisins, *maître des requêtes*, cousin (4th and 5th degree)

Royal legislation, therefore, had little effect upon those methods the *parlementaires* used to build family dynasties and to develop mutual solidarity through the ties between them. Age dispensations, the holding of offices jointly by father and son, and intermarriage persisted through the post-Fronde period. The survival of these practices, in addition to the continuation of the sale of offices, the *droit annuel*, and the social considerations implied in office transmission as a result of the price-fixing edicts, meant that the *parlementaires* retained the freedom not only to select their successors, but to channel recruitment along family and social group lines.

THE CROWN AND THE TRANSMISSION OF OFFICES

Because offices remained on the public market and subject to the *droit annuel*, there was little the royal administration could do to interfere in the transmission of offices and "pack the court" with its own candidates. It is, of course, difficult to establish this point definitively. The historian has no reliable method to discover the motives behind each and every office exchange, and royal intrigue is not easily documented. However, some existing financial records containing 116 entries of office transmissions at Parlement for the years 1653–1673 reenforce the impression that the magistrates, and not the royal administration, controlled the transmission of their posts.[105] Although only 21 of the 116 transfers (or 18 percent) were between a magistrate and a lineal relative (such as a son or a brother), the records clearly show that the *résignant* who had paid his *droit annuel* determined who would replace him at the court. There are several entries, for example, of offices sold by widows whose husbands had died *en charge* before contracts of transmission had been drawn up. The widows enjoyed this privilege because the deceased magistrates had paid their *droit annuel*.[106] Only one of the 116 entries notes that the office had been forfeited to the king because the *résignant* owed a substantial debt to the royal treasury.[107]

Moreover, even when offices did become available to the crown, financial and personal considerations often frustrated the royal will. Ormesson provides one such example. When in September 1666 the lieutenant civil of Paris, Dreux d'Aubray, suddenly died, Louis hoped that a loyal *parlementaire*, President Le Pelletier, would assume the vacant post. Le Pelletier declined, however, because the charge was far too expensive (upwards of 600,000 *livres*).[108] Here is a situation involving an office that was not even subject to the *droit annuel*, but one the king could not fill with his chosen candidate! The royal administration also often failed to coordinate its efforts effectively enough to control those offices that escheated to the king or his representatives in the court. In December 1665, for example, Lamoignon received the office of the deceased councillor Verneuil because of a debt the latter owed him. But when Lamoignon sold the office, he upset Colbert and Le Tellier because he had not passed on the charge to a candidate whom they preferred.[109] As late as June 1683, Louis had the opportunity to fill the offices of two deceased councillors which were disputed by a host of supposed heirs. When shown a list of the available candidates, however, the king simply favored the two among them who had the soundest legal basis for their claims.[110]

Finally, the concessions the royal administration made to Parlement at the end of the Fronde further reduced the possibility of replacing hostile magistrates with more reliable candidates. By the terms of the declaration of October 22, 1652, the government granted amnesty to almost all of the *parlementaires* for their participation in the civil wars.[111] Only a few of the most recalcitrant judges like Fleury-Machault and President Viole were persuaded to sell their offices and leave the kingdom. Many others whom the king exiled were allowed to return to Parlement in subsequent years because of the persistent remonstrances of the court. The exiles had not forfeited their offices.[112] A rare manuscript list of all the presidents and councillors of the court dated September 7, 1654, testifies to the presence of many old *frondeurs* who had weathered the storm: Daurat, Amelot, Deslandes-Payen, Broussel, Portail, Presidents Molé and Nesmond, and so on.[113] Perhaps one of the reasons Parlement continued to oppose many policies of the royal administration after 1653 was the presence in the court of all but a few of the old *frondeurs*.

After the Fronde, therefore, the magistrates remained firmly in control of the recruitment process of their court. Although the king and his successive ministers expressed an interest in recapturing the appointment of councillors, the continuation of the sale of offices and the *droit annuel* made it highly unlikely that they could ever achieve their goal. Even policies that might have restricted Parlement's development along family and social group lines missed their mark. Whether by working at cross-purposes, as was the case of the edicts that stabilized office prices, or through the need to pursue extraordinary financial policies, as in the case of age dispensations and prohibitions against parental ties and intermarriage within the court, the government found it difficult to enforce its edicts. The magistrates easily evaded them. How the composition of Parlement's membership reflected specific social patterns and contributed to the magistrate's view of his role in state and society is the theme of the following chapter.

CHAPTER TWO

The Social Composition of Parlement and the Concept of Noblesse de Robe

T he system of *vénalité des offices* and the hereditary tendencies inherent in the *paulette* procedure encouraged sentiments of social elitism at Parlement. The magistrates, however, were never content to rest their claimed status as a privileged group in French society upon the concrete results of *vénalité* alone. At the heart of their social pretensions was the conviction that they were members of the nobility. The magistrate's fundamental belief in his nobility in turn provided the touchstone for the more complex group conception of nobility of the robe. It will be the task of this chapter to define and relate the two—nobility and robe—as they applied to the *parlementaire*, and then to establish their factual basis both in the composition of the court and in the magistrate's conception of his role in state and society during the post-Fronde years. Such an investigation reveals sources of strength in Parlement that survived the resurgence of royal authority during the reign of Louis XIV.

THE PARLEMENTAIRES AS NOBLES OF THE ROBE

The personal nobility of members of the Parlement of Paris had been recognized, if not by legal pronouncement, then at least by custom in the sixteenth century.[1] It was not until the appearance of the works of the great jurists of the seventeenth century, however, that the nobility of the *parlementaires* received more precise definition. The leading jurists— notably Bacquet, Loyseau, and La Rocque (who first published in 1580, 1610, and 1678 respectively)—divided the nobility of France into two groups.[2] The first was the *noblesse de race*, which included those nobles who enjoyed perfect, or hereditary nobility. Although this group often included old military families, the jurists did not explicitly state that such origins were the sole criterion for entrance into the *noblesse de race*. They were far more concerned with the transmission of nobility through generations, that is, whether the nobility was personal (enjoyed by a single individual but not his children) or hereditary. As might well be expected, the age of a family was thus quite important. Those families whose genealogies seemed to be timeless often had the good fortune to be classified as perfect, hereditary *noblesse de race*. The jurists were more exact in defining the second category of the nobility, referred to as *noblesse par bénéfice du Prince* (Bacquet), *noblesse provient des dignitez* (Loyseau), or *noblesse politique et civile* (La Rocque). This group included those individuals and families who either had their nobility granted as a gift from the king or who were ennobled through the exercise of an office that carried with it the rights and privileges of the nobility. The nobility of the second category was usually only personal, not hereditary, and the acquisition of nobility could be dated in time to the original assumption of the office.[3]

The *parlementaires* were almost universally placed into the category of those who were ennobled by their office. Bacquet, for example, places the magistrates with other officials who enjoyed nobility by virtue of their charges: *maîtres des requêtes*, councillors at the Chambre des Comptes and Cour des Aides, and the *trésoriers de France*.[4] As members of this group, the magistrates did not enjoy perfect, hereditary *noblesse de race*, but only personal nobility. Bacquet noted, however, that a *parlementaire* could confer hereditary nobility on his heirs if his father and grandfather had also held office in the court. This three-generation principle, called *patre et avo consulibus*, derived from Roman law and was well represented in the jurisprudence of the seventeenth century.[5] It was quite possible, therefore, for a councillor at Parlement to enter the *noblesse de race* as defined by Bacquet.

The great jurist of the early seventeenth century, Charles Loyseau, was far more complete and detailed than Bacquet in defining the hierarchies within the nobility. According to Loyseau, there were several functions that carried perfect, hereditary nobility immediately upon assumption of the charge by the incumbent: the great offices of the crown (chancellor, *grand écuyer*, *grand amiral*, etc.), the governors of the provinces, members of the royal household, and councillors of the Privy Council. It is notable that Loyseau assigns the *présidents à mortier* of Parlement the rank of privy councillor and thus the status of *noblesse de race*.[6] Simple councillors remained under the aegis of "lesser offices" and thereby enjoyed only personal nobility. Like Bacquet, however, Loyseau insisted that the councillors could acquire *noblesse de race* through the principle of *patre et avo consulibus*.[7]

Despite his reluctance to grant perfect nobility to the councillors of Parlement and his general distaste for venality of offices, Loyseau did attest to the dignity of the magistrates and their undeniable right to the status of nobles. He maintained that virtue, which was the essence of nobility, emanated from both military and judicial functions. "This nobility enjoyed by the officials of the Parlement of Paris is not founded solely on the fact they are the heirs of the Roman Senate or the Council of State of France, but also because they are the judges of the King, and exercise with him his sovereign justice."[8] The magistrates of Parlement were members of the "vraie noblesse"; although their nobility was personal and not transmissible to their heirs (except by the three-generation rule), the *parlementaires* were never included with those nobles who had usurped their titles or acquired nobility by prescription ("living nobly"). Such individuals, referred to by contemporaries as *nobles hommes*, were held in disdain by Loyseau.[9] If by the early seventeenth century authoritative jurists had testified to the nobility of the magistrates at Parlement, opinions had changed little at the end of the century. In 1678 we find La Rocque repeating the same principles Loyseau had postulated half a century before.[10]

That the magistrates enjoyed the same rights and privileges as other members of the second estate reenforced their claim to noble status. They were exempt from such taxes as the *taille*, *gabelle*, and *aides*. They were not burdened by the *corvée*, nor did they have to submit to the quartering of royal troops in their households. They also exercised certain honorific rights at state processions.[11] As members of a sovereign court, the magistrates enjoyed special privileges not common to the nobility in general. For example, they had the right of *committimus*, which empowered them to carry personal litigations directly to the king's council and they were exempt from many feudal dues, such as the *lods et ventes* which the rest of the nobility continued to pay.[12] Finally, as members of the Parlement of Paris they enjoyed additional exemptions, the most notable being from the *franc-fief* and the *ban* and *arrière-ban*.[13]

Throughout the seventeenth century, the nobility of the magistrates received further support by a combination of royal decree and judicial recognition. For example, La Rocque cites a decree of the Privy Council given in April 1669 declaring that Simon Chevalier, councillor at Parlement, was "noble et écuyer" (enjoying perfect nobility in the terminology of the jurists) under the principle of *patre et avo consulibus*.[14] But only during the troubled minority of Louis XIV, when Mazarin and Anne of Austria desperately bargained for political support, did the *parlementaires* receive the charter of perfect nobility. By the terms of an edict of July 1644, the councillors, presidents, *gens du roi*, and *greffiers en chef* of Parlement were to enjoy perfect nobility and have equal status with the *noblesse de race*.[15] The same provisions were renewed in an edict of November 23, 1657, when Cardinal Mazarin once again tried to solicit the support of Parlement for his policies.[16]

During the period of his personal rule Louis XIV confused the legal definition of a *parlementaire*'s nobility by issuing a series of contradictory decrees. A general edict of 1669 nullified those of 1644 and 1657 and restored the old rule of personal nobility and the provisions of *patre et avo consulibus*. This was rescinded, however, in another edict of 1690, only to be reestablished again in 1715.[17] The confusion caused by these royal pronouncements perplexed contemporary legists. In 1667 and 1669, for example, two lawyers at the Parlement of Paris, Desmaisons and Jovet, published compendiums of notable decrees and *règlements* of the court. Desmaisons, writing in 1667 while the 1644 and 1657 edicts were still in force, maintained that the magistrates of Parlement enjoyed only personal nobility and could only enter the *noblesse de race* through the three-generation principle.[18] On the other hand, Jovet, who should have emphasized Louis's recent restoration of the ancient principles, instead maintained that the magistrates enjoyed the perfect nobility of the *noblesse de race*.[19] Each of these informed *avocats* therefore cited the very principles that were *not* in force at the time they assembled their digests! As regards Louis's reasons for changing his opinions on this subject, we can only assume that it was a matter of expediency. In 1669 Louis was in the midst of attacking Parlement on other issues of social importance: age requirements, nepotism, intermarriage among families in the court, and so on. In 1690, the king included the grant of perfect nobility in an edict creating two presidential posts and four councillorships in the chambers of *enquêtes*. Doubtless he hoped that the grant of perfect nobility would make registration of the edict more palatable to the magistrates.[20]

Despite the ambiguities that crop up from time to time in the definition of a seventeenth-century *parlementaire*'s nobility, two points are clear. First, at no time did Louis XIV retrace his steps to the extent of denying the essential nobility of the magistrates. The principles of personal nobility and *patre et avo consulibus*, which were so dear to Bacquet and Loyseau, remained unquestioned. Second, by the end of Louis's reign, the noble status of the *parlementaires* was universally recognized by royal decree, judicial confirmation, and the dictums of the jurists.[21]

It is worth noting at this point that most histories of Parlement refer to the magistrates as "nobles of the robe" in order to distinguish them from the other commonly used category for the aristocracy of the second estate, the "nobles of the sword." Contemporaries were fond of these terms and used them extensively. Their intention was clearly to differentiate among nobles with similar privileges on the basis of social status and source of nobility. Members of the *noblesse d'épée* claimed their nobility through the exercise of a military charge (however this function might have diminished over time), which was often synonymous with the possession of a very old genealogy. The *noblesse de robe* comprised those individuals and families (including the *parlementaires*) who enjoyed the rights and privileges of nobility by virtue of their offices in the high judiciary, but who did not enjoy social prestige equal to that of the sword group owing to their more recent ascension in the social hierarchy. The two categories roughly paralleled the distinction made by the jurists between *noblesse de race* and the more recent *anoblis* who were deemed noble by virtue either of their office or a specific grant of nobility by the king. We must recognize, however, that the robe and sword dichotomy was one rooted more in popular conception than in legal fact or jurisprudence. The jurists were always quick to point out that military positions produced *anoblis* while certain offices carried perfect *noblesse de race*, including the *présidents à mortier* of Parlement and even simple councillors if they met the requirement of *patre et avo consulibus*. Despite the definitions of the jurists and governmental legislation, however, the robe-sword distinctions doggedly preserved themselves in the mentality of the *ancien régime*.

In recent decades historians have been less willing to accept the robe-sword dichotomy as an accurate description of social reality, especially for the eighteenth century. In his history of Parlement during the reign of Louis XV, François Bluche argues for a thorough revision of the meanings of the two terms. He maintains that the term *robe* should not imply the status of a separate class or caste within the nobility. Instead, members of the robe should be viewed as individual nobles who simply chose a profession (*état* or *métier*) within the aristocracy. In support of his thesis, Bluche emphasizes the high frequency of both functional and social interaction between the robe and the sword in the eighteenth century. Both groups commonly held posts in the royal administration usually considered the exclusive province of either one or the other, and a high rate of intermarriage between them further blurred social distinctions. In addition, both robe and sword shared similar privileges and conceived of their nobility as a birthright. Most of them saw the acquisition of landed wealth as befitting their station. Few historians of the *ancien régime* will deny that in terms of daily life-style, the wealthy and powerful nobles of both robe and sword had more in common with each other than with their poorer and less professionally endowed counterparts in the provinces. What Bluche argues, therefore, is a thesis he expresses by the title of his last chapter, "The Equality of All the Nobility." He portrays the eighteenth century as a time when the categories of robe and sword became outmoded; the two groups merged, put aside the distinctions of the past, and began to think more in terms of their common interests as aristocrats.[22] Franklin Ford, of course, had earlier expressed similar views in his *Robe and Sword* to reenforce his theory that the eighteenth century witnessed a coalescence of robe and sword, a social transformation that proved to be of utmost political importance as members of the robe began to defend the rights and privileges of all the nobility in their sovereign courts.

Without question, Bluche and Ford have exposed a major shift in aristocratic opinion during the eighteenth century. But the historian of the seventeenth century must resist the temptation to apply their arguments out of context. During the reign of Louis XIV, the *parlementaires* still identified with the concept of *noblesse de robe* and promoted the sense of exclusiveness it implied. The magistrates in Parlement conceived of themselves as members of the "nobility of the robe," and not just the "nobility," despite the fact that authoritative jurists and royal decrees never officially recognized such a category. A simple example will illustrate this point. Bluche estimates that between 1715 and 1771 approximately 81.5 to 89 percent of the new councillors received at Parlement were already nobles and did not need their offices to gain such status.[23] Although it is difficult to be precise about the previous status of the councillors received at the court between 1653 and 1673, it is clear that in this period also many councillors were noble before their reception, if for no other reason than that many were direct descendants of other councillors (*patre et avo consulibus*) or of *secrétaires du roi*, an office that conferred hereditary nobility. But when the magistrates spoke of their nobility, they almost always did so in terms of the group concept of robe and not in terms of their previous status as nobles or the definitions provided by royal decrees and the jurists.

The *parlementaires* must thus be met on their own grounds. It is insufficient to define the nobility of the judges solely through the dictums of the government and the jurists. These authorities believed that the judges were ennobled by their charges and eligible for the *noblesse de race* through the three-generation principle. But the magistrates were not satisfied with this alone. Above all, they sought to base their elite status on the group principle of robe. Furthermore, Bluche's insistence that the robe be viewed as a simple matter of professional choice can also be misleading for the seventeenth century in several respects. First, it tends to underemphasize the importance the judges themselves assigned to their participation in the robe. To be a judge at Parlement was more than just employment: it was a way of life which fostered a group mentality and corporate solidarity that separated the *parlementaires* from the rest of society and reenforced their claim for a prominent role in affairs of state. Second, the coalescence of robe and sword associated with the eighteenth century was still in a nascent stage of development in the seventeenth century. During the reign of Louis XIV, the judges continued to share similar backgrounds in the magisterial and official segments of society and to marry predominantly in this group. This led the judges to think of the robe not simply as a professional group, but also as a social group, an identification that strengthened the bonds between them and intensified their sentiments of exclusiveness. At the same time, gentlemen of old family continued to resent the social ascension of the *parlementaires* and to erect barriers against merging with them. Far from destroying *parlementaire* pretensions, however, this hostility compelled the judges to glorify the robe all the more as a defensive reaction.[24]

The concept of *noblesse de robe*, therefore, stemmed from a combination of the *parlementaires'* status as nobles, their occupation as the king's highest judges, and their social origins and ties with one another. How all these elements interacted and influenced the magistrates' perception of their role in state and society during the reign of Louis XIV will emerge from an analysis of the court's composition and an examination of how the judges expressed the concept of robe.

PARLEMENT AS A SOCIAL CORPORATION

The solid adherence of the magistrates of the Parlement of Paris to the concept of robe was fully described in some of the notable literature of Louis XIV's reign and in the speeches and writings of the *parlementaires* themselves. But an examination of the professional and social composition of Parlement in the decades after the Fronde indicates that the concept of robe also had a structural base in the court's membership. A study of the genealogies of the magistrates who entered the court between 1653 and 1673 provides an adequate demonstration of this point. These twenty years illustrate general membership patterns in the immediate post-Fronde period and allow a comparison of structural changes that occurred during the administration of Mazarin and the early years of Louis XIV's personal rule. The analysis presented below is based on three-generation patrilineal genealogies of the 208 councillors who entered Parlement between 1653 and 1673: 96 of them began service between 1653 and 1660, the last eight years of Mazarin's administration, and 112 were received between 1661 and 1673, the first thirteen years of Louis's personal rule.[25] Because approximately 200 magistrates sat in the court at any given time, the figure of 208 represents a theoretical, if not actual, turnover of membership. Moreover, this group of 208 councillors offers an additional advantage for statistical analysis because it represents a total of 175 families: 146 contributed one councillor, 25 provided two, and only 4 families sent three new councillors to Parlement.[26]

The professional backgrounds of the fathers and grandfathers of the councillors are listed in table 4 and divided in two ways: first, according to the time of a councillor's reception, and second, into six categories that reveal social patterns in Parlement's recruitment.[27] The division according to the decade in which a councillor entered Parlement indicates any changes in the composition of the court that occurred after the direction of royal affairs passed from Mazarin to Louis XIV in 1661. The distribution of the councillors' ancestors into categories shows the comparative representation of various groups in Parlement. The two categories of judicial posts, for example, isolate those councillors whose fathers and grandfathers were magistrates and thus associated with the robe. The distinction between judicial offices of high and lesser prestige reveals any change in the frequency of lesser magisterial families entering the court.[28] The next three categories (nonjudicial officials, *secrétaire du roi* and bourgeois, and sword) enable us to determine the number of councillors whose immediate origins were in groups other than the robe. The separation of officials from nonofficials in these three categories serves a dual purpose: first, to establish the rate at which families from the wealthy bourgeoisie and nobility of the sword gained access to Parlement, and second, to emphasize that nonjudicial officials, though not formally associated with the robe, had more in common with the magistrates than did individuals who did not even hold office in the royal administration.[29] Table 5 lists the six categories and gives the percentage of the fathers and grandfathers of the councillors received by Parlement between 1653 and 1673 who fell into each category.

TABLE 4

PROFESSIONAL BACKGROUNDS OF THE FATHERS AND GRANDFATHERS OF COUNCILLORS RECEIVED AT PARLEMENT, 1653–1673

Position	Fathers of Councillors Received		Grandfathers of Councillors Received	
	1653–1660	1661–1673	1653–1660	1661–1673
1. High Judiciary				
Chancellor of France	1	0	1	0
Secretary of state	1	3	1	3
Councillor of state	3	5	0	2
Maître des requêtes	12	11	4	4
Président à mortier at the Parlement of Paris	5	1	3	3

(*continued*)

TABLE 4 (continued)

Position	Fathers of Councillors Received		Grandfathers of Councillors Received	
	1653–1660	1661–1673	1653–1660	1661–1673
Gens du roi at the Parlement of Paris	2	2	0	1
Councillor at the Parlement of Paris	31	17	18	14
Greffier en chef at the Parlement of Paris	0	0	1	0
President of a sovereign court in Paris (except Parlement)	6	7	1	1
Gens du roi of a sovereign court in Paris (except Parlement)	0	2	0	1
Councillor at a sovereign court in Paris (except Parlement)	11	13	14	12
President of a provincial sovereign court	1	1	1	1
Lieutenant particulier of the Châtelet (Paris)	0	0	1	0
Prévôt des marchands (Paris)	0	1	0	1
Ambassador	1	0	0	0
Bailli of the Palais (Paris)	0	0	1	1
2. Lesser Judiciary				
Councillor of a provincial sovereign court	2	3	0	2
Lieutenant général of a bailliage, seneschal, or presidial court	1	0	2	0
Secretary or *greffier* in the king's councils	1	1	0	0
Trésorier de France	0	5	3	2
Mayor of a town	0	1	1	1
Échevin of a town	0	1	1	2
Maître des eaux et forêts	0	1	0	1
Greffier in the *chambre de l'édit* (Parlement of Paris)	0	0	1	0
Advocate or *procureur* in the Parlement of Paris	1	0	8	4
Advocate (elsewhere)	0	0	2	2

TABLE 4 (continued)

Position	Fathers of Councillors Received		Grandfathers of Councillors Received	
	1653–1660	1661–1673	1653–1660	1661–1673
Bailli of justice in a cathedral chapter	0	0	0	1
Notary	0	1	0	1
Commissaire of *saisies-réelles* at the Parlement of Paris	0	0	0	1
3. Nonjudicial Officials				
Surintendant des finances	1	0	0	0
Contrôleur général des finances	0	2	1	0
Intendant des finances	0	1	0	0
Trésorier de l'Epargne	1	0	0	0
Maître de l'Hôtel du Roi	0	1	0	1
Contrôleur ordinaire de la Maison du Roi	0	1	0	0
Contrôleur de l'Argenterie du Roi	0	1	0	0
Contrôleur général des gabelles	0	0	1	0
First man of the *Compagnie des Ordonnances*	1	0	0	0
Intendant or secretary of a noble house	1	2	1	1
Secrétaire or *trésorier des guerres*	0	0	1	3
Secrétaire de la chambre du roi	0	0	0	1
Orfèvre du roi	0	0	0	1
Receiver of demesne, *taille,* or *taillon*	0	0	1	3
Receiver and payer of salaries at the Parlement of Paris	0	0	0	1
4. *Secrétaire du Roi* and Bourgeois	9	20	11	20
5. Sword	2	3	2	3
6. Unidentified	2	5	14	17
Total	96	112	96	112

The most obvious conclusion these figures offer is that an overwhelming majority of the councillors had fathers and grandfathers who were associated with the robe through their strictly magisterial functions (74.6 percent of the fathers and 60.1 percent of the grandfathers), and clearly most of them were members of the high judiciary. If all officials are included, the figure increases to 80.4 percent for the fathers and 67.8 percent for the grandfathers. Even after the turbulent civil wars, therefore, the court was staffed with new councillors who had solid magisterial and official backgrounds, while those councillors who represented nonofficial families remained a distinct minority. Family background in the sword was a mere 2.4 percent, thus calling into question a seventeenth-century application of Bluche's thesis of professional interaction between robe and sword. That few councillors had immediate family origins in the wealthy bourgeoisie also exposes the contemporary belief in a "bourgeois invasion" of the court as a myth, or at best, an exaggeration. Furthermore, as noted earlier, the perceptible increase in the number of councillors with this background who entered the court in the 1660s was eventually curtailed by the edicts that stabilized the prices for offices in the high judiciary.

If these figures are further divided according to the decade in which the councillors were received by Parlement, structural changes through time become perceptible. Table 6 shows the results of this division. Analysis along two time periods does indicate some change in patterns between the backgrounds of those councillors received during the Mazarin years and those who entered the court during Louis's personal rule. It is apparent, for example, that the councillors whose fathers and grandfathers were in

TABLE 5

PROFESSIONAL BACKGROUNDS OF THE FATHERS AND GRANDFATHERS OF COUNCILLORS ENTERING PARLEMENT, 1653–1673: TOTALS BY CATEGORY

Category	Fathers		Grandfathers	
	No.	%	No.	%
1. High Judiciary	137	65.9	90	43.3
2. Lesser Judiciary	18	8.7	35	16.8
3. Nonjudicial Officials	12	5.8	16	7.7
4. *Secrétaire du Roi* and Bourgeois	29	13.9	31	14.9
5. Sword	5	2.4	5	2.4
6. Unidentified	7	3.3	31	14.9
Total	208	100.0	208	100.0

TABLE 6

PROFESSIONAL BACKGROUNDS OF THE FATHERS AND GRANDFATHERS OF COUNCILLORS
ENTERING PARLEMENT, 1653–1660 AND 1661–1673: TOTALS BY CATEGORY

Category	Fathers of Councillors Received				Grandfathers of Councillors Received			
	1653–1660		1661–1673		1653–1660		1661–1673	
	No.	%	No.	%	No.	%	No.	%
1. High Judiciary	74	77.1	63	56.3	46	47.9	44	39.2
2. Lesser Judiciary	5	5.3	13	11.6	18	18.8	17	15.2
3. Nonjudicial Officials	4	4.2	8	7.1	5	5.3	11	9.8
4. *Secrétaire du Roi* and Bourgeois	9	9.4	20	17.9	11	11.5	20	17.9
5. Sword	2	2.0	3	2.7	2	2.0	3	2.7
6. Unidentified	2	2.0	5	4.4	14	14.5	17	15.2
Total	96	100.0	112	100.0	96	100.0	112	100.0

the high judiciary decreased somewhat, thus revealing that there was mobility into the court in the reign of Louis XIV. The number of councillors whose fathers and grandfathers fell into the lesser judiciary and nonjudicial official groups increased in time: from 9.5 percent (fathers) and 24.1 percent (grandfathers) in the first period to 18.7 percent (fathers) and 25 percent (grandfathers) in the years from 1661 to 1673. This increase of lesser families (both robe and other officials) into the court no doubt reflected the initial effects of the edicts that stabilized office prices. As prices slowly began to decline, many families whose financial resources were obviously limited could once again compete for offices. This is all the more obvious if the backgrounds of those councillors received after the 1665 edict are examined. Of the seventy-eight councillors who entered Parlement in those years, 24.3 percent of the fathers (over 18.7 percent for the years 1661–1673) and 27.6 percent of the grandfathers (over 25 percent for the years 1661–1673) fell into the lesser judiciary and nonjudicial official groups. The lesser judiciary alone made gains of 14.5 percent of the fathers (compared with 11.6 percent for the period 1661–1673) and 18.8 percent of the grandfathers (compared with 15.2 percent for the period 1661–1673). In the same post-1665 period, those councillors with immediate bourgeois backgrounds continued to enter the court, but their number remained relatively stable: 14 percent for the fathers and 16 percent for the grandfathers.

The increased frequency with which bourgeois, nonjudicial official, and lesser robe families entered the court naturally had its impact on the number of councillors whose immediate family backgrounds were in the high judiciary, and within that category, at the Parlement of Paris itself. While 77.1 percent of the fathers and 47.9 percent of the grandfathers of the councillors received at the court in the 1653–1660 period were in the high judiciary, the number drops to 56.3 percent of the fathers and 39.2 percent of the grandfathers in the latter period. The same pattern emerges from an analysis of those councillors whose fathers and grandfathers had been Parisian *parlementaires*. Between 1653 and 1660, 39 percent of the fathers and 23 percent of the grandfathers of the new councillors had held office in Parlement. During the years 1661–1673, this representation declined to 18 percent for the fathers and 16 percent for the grandfathers. It appears, therefore, that some of the dynastic structures in Parlement changed as more bourgeois, lesser judicial, and nonjudicial official families entered the court in the 1660s.

The cause of such change, however, should be assigned to the individual buying and selling patterns of the judges and not to the policies of the royal administration. The themes discussed in the first chapter should make this point clear. The magistrates had kept control of their offices through the continuation of the *droit annuel,* and those regulations that might have weakened family dynasties within the court (curtailing age dispensations and holding offices *en concurrence*, prohibition against entering a court where relatives sat, etc.) were unsuccessful. Moreover, another potential explanation for the phenomenon, that *parlementaires* rushed to sell their offices as a result of the price-fixing edict, is equally untenable because only seventy-eight judges sold their offices in the eight years after the edict compared with ninety-five in the last eight years of Mazarin's administration. It seems that the decline in the dynastic element was but a short-range perturbation in the selling habits of the magistrates: the stabilization of office prices caused a rearrangement of patterns in the court as regards the family backgrounds of the new councillors. But the situation apparently stabilized during the rest of Louis's reign because Bluche has established the existence of many powerful family dynasties in the court at Louis's death in 1715.[30]

Two additional analyses will further illustrate the mobility of new families into the court during the reign of Louis XIV. The first, the rate of functional mobility through generations, shows the percentage of those councillors for whom a position at Parlement represented an improvement, a regression, or no significant change from the positions held by their fathers and grandfathers. Of the 208 councillors who entered the court between 1653 and 1673, sufficient data exists for 203 to permit an analysis of functional mobility through three generations. Of these 203 new councillors, fully 60 percent of them had progressed upwards in the scale of professional status when compared with their fathers and grand-fathers. For example, Jérôme Murard's father, François, was a *trésorier de France* at Lyon, and his grandfather, Jean-Baptiste, had been an *échevin* in the same city.[31] Another case in point is Nicolas II Le Pelletier, whose father, Nicolas I, was a *maître des comptes* in Paris, as was his grandfather, Martin.[32] The father of Jean-François Petit was a *procureur* at the Châtelet, and his grandfather was a "riche hostellier."[33]

For a substantial 39 percent of the councillors, a position at Parlement was not as prestigious as the posts that their fathers and grandfathers had held. But one must remember that it was often difficult for a young man beginning a career to attain the preeminent posts held by his ancestors. Thus, although Charles Amelot's grandfather, Jacques II, had been a councillor at the Parlement of Paris, his father, Jacques III, was the first president of the Cour des Aides in Paris.[34] Similarly, Antoine d'Aubray's grandfather, Claude, had been a *trésorier de France* at Soissons, but his father, Dreux, was both *lieutenant particulier* at the Châtelet and a *maître des requêtes*.[35]

Finally, 10 percent of the councillors held posts similar to those of their fathers and grandfathers. Most often, this stable group included council-lors whose fathers and grandfathers had remained in Parlement for life. Both the father and the grandfather of Nicolas IV Le Camus had been councillors in the Parlement of Paris.[36] Nicolas Bauquemare's father, Charles, was a president in one of the chambers of *requêtes*, and his grand-father, Jean, had been a councillor in the court before he became a *maître des requêtes*.[37]

Another indication of mobility into the court is the frequency with which councillors came to Parlement from other, lesser posts in the judiciary. Such mobility was as high as 17.7 percent in the period from 1653 to 1660. The figure would rise to 25 percent if religious offices were included; they are omitted because they are difficult to correlate in terms of status with judicial offices, and because a cleric rarely relinquished his religious post when he assumed a judicial one. The following are the offices held prior to their reception by councillors who entered Parlement from 1653 to 1660:

Councillor at the Parlement of Metz	6
Councillor at the Parlement of Rouen	6
Abbot	5
Bishop	1
Councillor at a bailliage	1
Councillor at the Châtelet (Paris)	1
Councillor at the Grand Conseil	1

Lieutenant particulier of a town	1
Page of the king	1
Prior	1

Just as the number of councillors with family backgrounds in categories other than the high judiciary increased in the 1660s, the number of councillors who had occupied other, less prestigious posts before entering Parlement also rose in the 1661–1673 period:

Councillor at the Châtelet (Paris)	14
Councillor at the Parlement of Metz	12
Abbot	5
Professor of theology	2
Advocate at the Châtelet (Paris)	1
Auditor, Chambre des Comptes (Paris)	1
Avocat général at the Parlement of Metz	1
Bishop	1
Commissaire des gabelles	1
Councillor at the Conseil de Bresse	1
Councillor at the Parlement of Dijon	1
Lieutenant général of a bailliage	1
Provincial post (undetermined)	1
Trésorier de France	1

Thirty-one percent of the new councillors in this period had exercised a previous judicial, and in a few cases financial, position. If clerics were added, the figure would rise to 38 percent. Again, the edicts that stabilized the prices of offices may have interceded on behalf of families who were better able to enter the court with office prices lowered. This is particularly striking with regard to the large number of councillors from provincial parlements and the Châtelet of Paris who were able to enter the most prestigious of sovereign courts.

Two general conclusions emerge from the above analyses. First, the councillors who entered Parlement during the twenty-year period extending from 1653 to 1673 had a substantial background in the robe and official groups. Over three-quarters of their fathers and two-thirds of their grandfathers had held offices in the royal administration; at least half fell into the most prestigious category of the high judiciary. At least one-fifth of the councillors had a father or grandfather who had sat in the Parlement of Paris itself. Second, the internal rearrangements within the six categories—with more councillors of bourgeois, nonjudicial official, and lesser robe backgrounds entering after 1661 (the sword group remaining stable)—indicate that there was mobility into the court during the reign of Louis XIV. This mobility, however, was largely restricted to individuals with magisterial and official backgrounds, a situation that became more pronounced after 1665 when the edict that stabilized office prices began to take its toll on the number of bourgeois who entered the court.

In terms of the family backgrounds of its membership, therefore, the Parlement of Paris had a structural basis to support a sentiment of allegiance to the group concept of robe. As a matter of speculation, it is likely that the limited influx of lesser families actually fostered the robe sentiment during the reign of Louis XIV and postponed coalescence of the *parlementaires'* identity with the rest of the nobility, a phenomenon that Ford and Bluche describe as a significant development in the eighteenth century. The newer families were highly attracted to the robe concept because it was an improvement over their previous status, and newly discovered pretensions were thus able to flourish. If the court had continued to be dominated by numerous family dynasties and individuals solely from the very high judiciary, the process of identification with other nobles might well have proceeded more rapidly than it actually did because these older, more prestigious families felt confident enough to broaden their perspective. Certainly, those councillors with family backgrounds in the high judiciary remained predominant in both decades. But their numbers had decreased through time in favor of lesser families for whom the concept of robe was exhilarating and well worth defending. It is quite possible that these lesser families added just enough leavening to keep the concept of robe and the prerogatives the judges claimed under its auspices alive during the reign of Louis XIV.

An interesting departure that helps to explain further why the concept of robe remained a vital force in the Parlement of Louis XIV is an analysis of functional mobility out of the court; that is, the frequency at which *parlementaires* left the court to assume higher posts in the royal administration. The rate of such mobility was far greater during the Mazarin years, 1653–1660, than for the first thirteen years of Louis's personal rule. Of the 96 councillors who entered the court in the first period, 38 (or 40 percent) later assumed higher posts, usually *maîtres des requêtes* (26 of the 38, or 68 percent).[38] But during the second period, 1661–1673, only 33 (29 percent) of the 112 councillors who entered the court eventually left to assume a greater position, again, usually that of *maître des requêtes* (22 of the 33, or 66 percent). This trend is understandable in the light of the above patterns of the councillors' backgrounds. On the one hand, the edicts that stabilized office prices made councillors reluctant to sell their offices, hoping that prices would rise in the future; this accounts for the fact that fewer offices changed hands in the post-1665 period than in previous years. On the other hand, owing to the mobility of lesser families into the court, fewer judges had the financial resources to afford the substantial sum of money required to purchase a higher office. The result of this decline in functional mobility out of Parlement was that councillors increasingly made their parlementary post a career. In the long run, this more pronounced continuity of membership enhanced both the solidarity among the magistrates and the advancement of the privileges and prerogatives that the *parlementaire* claimed for himself and his institution. These patterns of functional mobility also negate any thesis that would portray Louis XIV as a benevolent despot who rewarded silence in his Parlement by holding the plum of advancement before the magistrates. Louis had little control over who entered the most attractive of post-Parlement positions, the *maîtres des requêtes*. These offices, like those of Parlement, were venal and personally transmissible under the auspices of the *droit annuel*. The *maîtres*, like the *parlementaires*, decided to whom they would sell their charges. Louis XIV neither "packed the court" with his personal appointees nor determined who would enter those other venal posts that officials owned as personal and negotiable property.

The marriage patterns of the councillors who entered Parlement between 1653 and 1673 reveal that the magistrates usually restricted their alliances to other magisterial and official families, thus enhancing Parlement's status as a social corporation. The sample of marriages includes 80 of the 96 councillors received at the court between 1653 and 1660 and 85 of the 112 councillors who entered Parlement in the second period, 1661–1673. The sample is smaller than that for family background because not all the lay councillors married, and few of the clerical councillors contracted alliances. Table 7 gives the distribution of the 165 marriages according to the positions (if any) that the father of the wife held in his lifetime. Following the procedures established to study patterns of family background, totals by category are presented in table 8.

TABLE 7
MARRIAGES OF COUNCILLORS ENTERING PARLEMENT, 1653–1673

Profession of Wife's Father	Councillors Received 1653–1660	Councillors Received 1661–1673
1. High Judiciary		
Chancellor of France	1	1
Councillor of state	4	2
Maître des requêtes	12	7
Président à mortier at the Parlement of Paris	2	0

TABLE 7 (continued)

Profession of Wife's Father	Councillors Received 1653–1660	Councillors Received 1661–1673
Gens du roi at the Parlement of Paris	2	1
Councillor at the Parlement of Paris	9	10
Greffier en chef at the Parlement of Paris	0	2
President of a sovereign court in Paris (except Parlement)	3	6
Councillor at a sovereign court in Paris (except Parlement)	11	10
Gens du roi of a provincial sovereign court	3	1
Lieutenant particulier of the Châtelet (Paris)	1	1
Ambassador	1	1
Greffier en chef of the Parlement and Estates of Brittany	0	1
2. Lesser Judiciary		
Councillor of a provincial sovereign court	3	3
Greffier in the king's councils	0	1
Trésorier de France	2	0
Prévôt of a town	1	0
Lieutenant général of a town	0	1
Advocate or *procureur* at the Parlement of Paris	1	2
Procureur at the Châtelet (Paris)	1	0
Notary	1	0
3. Nonjudicial Officials		
Intendant des finances	1	1
Trésorier de l'Epargne	1	0
Contrôleur de l'Argenterie du Roi	0	1
Contrôleur général des gabelles	0	1

(continued)

TABLE 7 (continued)

Profession of Wife's Father	Councillors Received 1653–1660	Councillors Received 1661–1673
Secrétaire de la chambre du roi	0	1
Surintendant des finances for the brother of the king	0	1
Payer of *rentes* at the Hôtel de Ville (Paris)	0	2
4. *Secrétaire du Roi* and Bourgeois	11	16
5. Sword	2	5
6. Unidentified	7	7
Total	80	85

The conclusions derived from these figures closely parallel those that emerged from the study of family background. Nearly two-thirds of the councillors received between 1653 and 1660 married the daughters of officials in the high judiciary, and over one-half of the councillors followed suit in the subsequent period. If lesser judicial and nonjudicial officials are

TABLE 8
MARRIAGES OF COUNCILLORS ENTERING PARLEMENT 1653–1673: TOTALS BY CATEGORY

Profession of Wife's Father by Category	Councillors Received 1653–1660		Councillors Received 1661–1673		Councillors Received 1653–1673	
	No.	%	No.	%	No.	%
1. High Judiciary	49	61.3	43	50.6	92	55.8
2. Lesser Judiciary	9	11.3	7	8.2	16	9.7
3. Nonjudicial Officials	2	2.5	7	8.2	9	5.5
4. *Secrétaire du Roi* and Bourgeois	11	13.7	16	18.9	27	16.3
5. Sword	2	2.5	5	5.9	7	4.2
6. Unidentified	7	8.7	7	8.2	14	8.5
Total	80	100.0	85	100.0	165	100.0

added, the figures increase to 75.1 percent and 67 percent respectively. Over the entire twenty-year period, 71 percent of the marriages contracted by the councillors were with women whose fathers were in the royal administration. Furthermore, the new *parlementaires* often married the daughters of other magistrates in the court despite governmental prohibition: 15 percent in the 1653–1660 period and 16 percent in the period extending from 1661 to 1673. Only 2.5 percent of the councillors in the first period and 5.9 percent in the second period married women whose fathers fell into the "sword" category.[39] Here again, the interaction between robe and sword that Bluche and Ford emphasize for the eighteenth century was barely present in the seventeenth century. Surprisingly, marriages with the wealthy bourgeoisie were relatively few, falling between 13.7 percent and 18.9 percent for both periods combined. Councillors thus did not refrain from marrying the daughters of the wealthy bourgeoisie, although they may have objected to entrance of these families into the court. But this contact was less frequent than contemporaries would have us believe. The genealogies reveal that the fathers and grandfathers of the councillors contracted more marriages with the wealthy bourgeoisie than did the councillors themselves.

The methods employed above to trace functional mobility through three generations can be profitably applied to determine the social mobility of the councillors as revealed by these marriages. Of the 165 councillors whose marriages have been verified, there is information on the marriages of the fathers and grandfathers of 145. The patterns that emerge closely parallel those previously observed in functional mobility: two-thirds of the councillors married better than their fathers and grandfathers. Despite fluctuations in Parlement's political authority, the court remained an attractive place to be for purposes of contracting a favorable marriage. Drawing too close a correlation between the institution's political authority and its social appeal breaks down under rigorous investigation. By purchasing an office in Parlement, an individual, especially of lesser robe origin, was assured of an upward path for himself and his family. In fact, the vast majority of councillors married only after assuming their posts in Parlement. Examples of the 66 percent of the councillors who married more prestigiously than their fathers and grandfathers include the case of Adam-Pierre Barthémy, who wed a daughter of another councillor in Parlement. His father and grandfather, who had held posts in the Chambre des Comptes of Paris, both had married the daughters of bourgeois.[40] Louis Bechameil's grandfather, a bourgeois of Rouen, had married the daughter of an *élu*, and his father, a *secrétaire du roi*, had married the daughter of a *contrôleur des bâtiments du Roi*. Louis contracted his marriage with the daughter of a president in the Parisian Chambre des

Comptes.[41] Another example is Jean-Baptiste Machault, who contracted an alliance with the daughter of a councillor in the Parlement of Paris. His father, a *maître des requêtes*, had married the daughter of a *trésorier de France*, while his grandfather, a *maître des comptes* in Paris, had married the daughter of a *secrétaire du roi*.[42]

Only 21 percent of the councillors married less prestigiously than their fathers and grandfathers. Often, but not always, this occurred when a councillor selected the daughter of a bourgeois or a *secrétaire du roi*, doubtless because of the lucrative financial possibilities opened to him. Thus, while Claude de Hère's grandfather, a councillor at Parlement, had contracted an alliance with a daughter of another councillor in the same court, and his father, a councillor of state, had married the daughter of an *écuyer* in Champagne, Claude wed the daughter of a *secrétaire du roi*.[43] Guillaume Boucherat's grandfather, an auditor in the Chambre des Comptes, had allied with the daughter of an *écuyer*, and his father, also an official in the Chambre des Comptes, had married the daughter of another official in the same court. Guillaume, however, only succeeded in marrying the daughter of a simple *procureur* at the Châtelet and widow of a wealthy *trésorier de France*.[44]

Finally, the marriages of 13 percent of the councillors were stable in terms of social mobility, that is, they were almost identical to those of their fathers and grandfathers. Robert Bigot and his father, a *président à mortier* at the Parlement of Rouen, both wed daughters of councillors in that same parlement.[45] Likewise, both Nicolas IV Le Camus and his father, also a councillor at the Parlement of Paris, married the daughters of other councillors in the court.[46]

A word of caution must be appended to all the foregoing analyses. The genealogies used in this study deal with the fathers and grandfathers of the councillors to the exclusion of other family members—brothers, sisters, uncles, cousins, and so on. It is quite possible that the figures cited to delineate patterns in the composition of the court's membership would change somewhat if entire families had been included; for example, more contact between the *parlementaires* and nonofficial, sword, and bourgeois families might well have been detected. It is hoped that the more narrow approach of this study will not result in a tunnel vision that excludes the possibility of more extensive outgrowth by *parlementaire* families into other groups in society. But even if the results are qualified to allow for more contact between *parlementaire* families and other nonofficial or nonrobe groups, the fact remains that an overwhelming majority of the magistrates in the Parlement of Paris itself had extensive family backgrounds in the judicial and official segments of society, and that they contracted marriages almost exclusively within this group. The magistrates were well suited by family background, marriage, and their current position in the court (especially if they emanated from lesser official families) to carry the banner of the robe throughout the reign of Louis XIV.

Still other aspects of the judges' backgrounds reenforced the group sentiment of robe. As noted in the previous chapter, the *parlementaires* were extensively related to one another, and they evaded royal regulations that prohibited them from entering the court if their relatives sat there or from marrying the daughters of their colleagues. In addition to these personal ties, many *parlementaires* were also heirs to a long tradition of participation in the robe. Most notable were the families of the *présidents à mortier* who had exercised those posts for many generations: the Novions, Longueils, Nesmonds, Bellièvres, Lamoignons, and so on. Even less prestigious families, however, could boast a long history of participation in the judiciary. The genealogist of the Gourreau de La Poussière family was able to write at the end of the seventeenth century that "this family has produced a *maître des requêtes*, an *avocat général* at the Parlement of Brittany, a president of *enquêtes* at [the Parlement of] Paris, a *maître des comptes*, two councillors at the Cour des Aides of Paris, a *procureur* of the king at a *prévôté*, three councillors at a presidial court, one professor of law, a provincial *prévôt*, four *échevins* and two councillors in the town of Angers."[47] Another case in point is the Sevin family: in the first half of the seventeenth century alone, it had contributed magistrates to the Parlement, Requêtes de l'Hôtel, Grand Conseil, and many provincial courts.[48] The genealogies reveal that such extensive participation in a wide variety of judicial institutions was almost universal among *parlementaire* families.

In terms of their family backgrounds and social contacts through marriage, therefore, the magistrates at the Parlement of Paris had a solid base in the composition of their court on which to build their self-conception as members of the robe. We must now examine how the judges themselves expressed the concept of robe and what position in state and society they claimed under its auspices.

ROBE PRETENSIONS

When contemporaries spoke of the robe, they often referred to all officials and institutions in the royal administration, especially its judicial branch. But the *parlementaires* frequently employed a more narrow definition: the robe was synonymous with the Parlement of Paris. There was little doubt in the minds of the judges that their institution was the supreme sovereign court, and certainly superior to the lesser judicial bodies of the realm. The Parlement of Paris was the elite of all the courts, *la première compagnie du royaume*.[49] An established *parlementaire* family and most certainly those families who had recently struggled to reach the top of the judicial administration demanded privileges for themselves and the prestigious court to which they belonged. The *parlementaire* saw himself as separate from the rest of society and the rest of the nobility by virtue of his charge. He viewed the court of law as an eminent intermediary between the king and his subjects. Such ideas remained alive after the Fronde and continued to be expressed during the reign of Louis XIV despite his attempt to curtail the court's nonjudicial activities.

An incident that reveals the magistrates' sensitivity to questions of status occurred in 1658 when the *présidents à mortier* of the court and the bishops of France quarreled over which group had precedence at official gatherings. At the end of July, several correspondents informed Cardinal Mazarin that Parlement was upset because several bishops had left a Te Deum at Notre-Dame before the presidents.[50] Although Chancellor Séguier had informed the acting first president, François-Théodore de Nesmond, that this had been done in error, "Parlement used this occasion to emphasize that there was not enough firmness applied to sustain the dignity of the court."[51] The judges then ordered the bishops to return to their dioceses in one month or forfeit their personal ecclesiastical income.[52] The bishops disobeyed the decree, held meetings of deputies at Fontainebleau, and remonstrated to the king that Parlement had unjustly usurped their ecclesiastical prerogatives.[53] Mazarin did the best he could to cool tempers and mediate the conflict. He promised the bishops of Fréjus and Coutances that he would give serious attention to their protests, while at the same time he assured the magistrates that he would ultimately decide in their favor.[54]

The issue was finally resolved by compromise: Parlement withdrew its decrees against the bishops in return for the right of precedence. Even those of Mazarin's advisers who were usually hostile to the pretensions of Parlement, such as Servien and Séguier, opted for the judges in this encounter. As Mazarin explained to the Bishop of Fréjus, the presidents had the best case because "the Parlement of Paris meets continually . . . and is a body independent of all others. I have my doubts," he continued, "that the same can be said of two or three bishops who happen to be at court by accident."[55] On their part, the judges believed that a victory in this matter firmly established their precedence over all the bishops (and thus most members of the first estate), and they emphasized in the court's registers that they had conserved "the first corporation of the realm in the status and prerogatives that were established by the king and his predecessors, and that it has enjoyed for several centuries."[56]

Although the seemingly endless wrangling over questions of precedence strikes the modern reader as petty and as just one more indication of the vanity of the contestants, the underlying importance of these conflicts was not lost to contemporaries. What might have begun as a simple issue of ceremonial formality often developed into a conflict where the basic issues of social status and political authority were at stake. There is no better example of this than the conflict that raged from 1662 to 1664 between the *présidents à mortier* of Parlement and the *ducs et pairs* of France.

The quarrel had its inauspicious origins in the ambiguity of who should offer advice first to the king at a *lit de justice*, the presidents or the peers. The real issue, of course, had nothing to do with the advice each offered the king because the procedure was purely ceremonial by the seventeenth century. The important point was who occupied a higher status in state and society—the presidents or the peers. Father Avrigny, who published his *Mémoires pour servir à l'histoire universelle* in 1733, believed this issue important enough to be included in the annals of world history. He seized the essence of the conflict when he referred to it as "this famous dispute that interested the first persons of the Sword and the Robe."[57]

In January 1662, Louis XIV had held a *lit de justice* at Parlement and had asked the peers to submit their advice before the presidents. The magistrates protested this procedure with such vehemence that the king allowed each side to draw up memoirs to support their respective positions.[58] In their first memoir, the peers provided only a short, sketchy defense of their prerogatives. Citing only a few historical precedents, they argued that their group, and not the presidents, "since their origin have formed the first sovereign court of your kingdom."[59] The presidents countered that it was they, not the peers, who stood closer to the monarch because the kings of France had created Parlement in the thirteenth century to balance the influence of the peers. Relying also upon historical precedents, the presidents claimed that they had given their advice first at twenty-eight of thirty-three *lits de justice* held between 1597 and 1662.[60] But the *parlementaires* did not stop here. They made one claim that, if accepted by either the king or the peers, would have theoretically enhanced their social status and political authority:

Parlement is certainly not a member of the Estates General, nor is it part of the three bodies that compose them, because it is separated from the rest of the subjects of the king, which form their corporations themselves: Parlement . . . is immediately attached to the crown, without which it forms no body or community.[61]

In effect, the magistrates had injected the issue of their superiority over the Estates General to underscore their belief that Parlement was the single most important corporation in the state. The conflict with the peers had left the realm of ceremonial formality.

In their second memoir, the peers were quick to exploit this pretension of Parlement. They reasoned that if Parlement claimed to be above the estates, and if the king himself summoned the estates, then Parlement had indeed claimed to be above the king.[62] The *parlementaires* did not capitalize on the faulty logic of the peers in their second memoir. Doubtless realizing that their assertion would upset the king, they let the issue of supremacy over the estates drop. Instead, they reverted to an argument based solely on historical precedents.[63] Because of the passion exhibited by each side, Louis informed the presidents and the peers that he wished to hear no more on the issue. First President Lamoignon pressed the king to reconsider his decision, but he held firm.[64]

Louis was mistaken if he thought that the affair would pass, because the magistrates again protested when he asked the advice of the peers before the presidents at a *lit de justice* held in January 1664.[65] This time, the king decided to settle the issue definitively, and on January 7 the *gens du roi* informed the judges that they were to draw up another memoir to justify their pretensions.[66] The memoir Parlement submitted was shorter than those of 1662, but it was very well organized and to the point. The opinions expressed provide an excellent indication of the social status and political authority that all the *parlementaires*, not merely the presidents, claimed for themselves.[67]

Following the lines of argument established in 1662, the magistrates reiterated that Parlement had originally been established to offset the influence of the peers in later medieval France. Although the peers had a just claim to a deliberative voice in the court, it was the *présidents à mortier* who presided over sessions in the absence of the first president and who had the right "to hold a rank and function superior to the peers at all times."[68] The magistrates did not hesitate to extend this reasoning to an attack on hereditary dignities in general, conveniently forgetting the hereditary tendencies in their own court caused by venality of offices and the *paulette*. "Thus, there is a [major] difference between hereditary dignities, which exist by themselves, pass along in families, and represent only what they are by appearances, like the dukes and peers—about which one can say with some validity that the king only participates when he gives them [titles]—and the charges of [royal] officials who receive their authority, their function, their support, and all their subsistence from the king's authority."[69] In essence, the presidents attempted to attach themselves directly to the monarch, placing themselves above the peers; if the king decided in favor of the latter, his authority would suffer because Parlement was but a reflection of his will.

As had been the case in 1662, the judges did not neglect to equate the superior status of the *présidents à mortier* with the prestige and authority of the larger corporate body. The memoir asserted that if the peers "make a separate body, they are in no way able to take precedence over Parlement, which is the first of all corporate bodies in the state, never superseded by anyone, and which is superior even to the Estates General . . . [because] it [Parlement] is not party to the three bodies that compose them. . . . On the contrary, Parlement is attached immediately to the crown."[70] The *parlementaires* not only claimed an individually higher status than the peers because they were the king's highest magistrates, but maintained that Parlement was the preeminent body in the state. Only the king stood above them.

After the submission of this memoir to the king, several councillors of state discussed its merits in the presence of Louis. According to Ormesson, who was present at the session, Colbert spoke highly of the *présidents à mortier* and "gave the impression that he seemed willing to conclude in their favor." But Colbert's final advice was that the king should decide in favor of the peers because Parlement had been so recalcitrant during the civil wars.[71] All those present agreed with Colbert, and on April 26, 1664, the Conseil d'Etat issued a decree awarding precedence to the peers.[72]

Despite Parlement's defeat on this issue of precedence, some essential points about the resolution of this controversy warrant additional comment. Colbert did not reject the claims of the *parlementaires* on historical grounds, nor did he question the theoretical framework they had constructed to support the superior status of their body; this was not done until the following year when Louis began referring to the sovereign courts as "superior courts."[73] Instead, Colbert proposed a policy of political expediency: Parlement had misbehaved during the Fronde (he conveniently avoided the fact that many peers had done the same), and a decision in favor of the peers would be a sign of punishment. Colbert's advice and Louis's decision should therefore be placed in the context of the other actions the royal administration took against Parlement at the same time—the abolition of age dispensations, the prohibition against a councillor entering the court if he had relatives there, and so on. Moreover, just as royal policy was often unsuccessful in these areas, so it was in the question of precedence. Quite literally, the magistrates felt that they had lost a battle, but not the war. The *parlementaires* continued to challenge the peers on questions of precedence after 1664. One of the most celebrated conflicts centered on the issue of whether the first president should remove his hat to the peers at *lits de justice* as he did to the king and the assembled Parlement. Although this *affaire du bonnet* developed fully only in the eighteenth century, an extant manuscript memoir indicates that the struggle had begun as early as 1670, after the 1664 decision, and well after the king had begun to curtail Parlement's interference in "affairs of state."[74]

However the political status of Parlement may have declined in the eyes of the monarch and his advisers, the *parlementaires* continued to exalt their social prestige and political role.

A fascinating document that testifies to the continued social and political pretensions of Parlement throughout Louis's reign is a book published in 1701 by a *parlementaire*, François Bertaut de Fréauville, under the combative title, *Les Prérogatives de la robe*.[75] Bertaut, as a councillor for life in Parlement, had excellent credentials to serve as a commentator on contemporary opinions in the court.[76] Equating the term *robe* with the Parlement of Paris, he postulated that the social status of the *parlementaire* and the political authority of the institution were inseparable and mutually reenforcing. After discussing the origins of the court and the sedentary quality given to it by Philippe Le Bel, he disagreed with those authors who had maintained that Parlement's permanent residence in Paris had slowly eroded its right to "participate in the solution of affairs of state. . . . It is certain that the successors of Philippe Le Bel and Louis Hutin not only have taken counsel of Parlement in all important affairs of state, but have been pleased to judge individual cases there."[77]

Throughout the text, Bertaut emphasized the dignity of the court, not only in judicial administration, but also in "les plus grandes affaires de l'Etat."[78] He stressed that many members of the sword aristocracy sat at Parlement in positions subordinate to the magistrates and that the French kings had always viewed Parlement as a source for personnel in "les plus grands emplois."[79] Even the costume of the *parlementaire* commanded respect because it dated to the Roman Empire.[80] Bertaut went as far as to assert again that Parlement was superior to all other corporate bodies in the state, including the Estates General, a popular *parlementaire* argument during the conflict with the peers in 1662 and 1664. According to him, the estates and the Assemblies of Notables (which always had peers and sword nobles as members) were inferior to Parlement in several respects. First, the estates and notables only met when the king summoned them, while Parlement met without interruption. Second, in the estates, three bodies gave opinions; in the notables, each individual offered advice; but in Parlement there was only one voice, that of the king. Third, the estates represented the people; the notables, the aristocracy alone; but Parlement represented the king. Parlement was therefore a "sovereign" body, while the others were purely consultative.[81]

Bertaut related the high status of Parlement as a judicial institution with considerable political influence to his claim that the magistrates occupied a preeminent place in society. More particularly he placed the "high robe" (synonymous with Parlement) squarely above the "high sword" in terms of social prestige. He was fond of the thesis that all categories of French nobility, including robe and sword, originated from the judicial and municipal officials of ancient Rome. In the past, he asserted, the peers of France "were nothing but judges and councillors; ... it is still more true that the dignities of peer and count had passed from judicial officials to those who carry the sword."[82] Bertaut thus went beyond pure historical precedent and met the sword nobility on its own ground: if they claimed to be old, the magistrates were older.

In France, there are two sorts of nobility, that of the robe and that of the sword: one can say with assurance that the nobility of the robe is established on more ancient and solid foundations than the sword because it [the robe] is derived from Roman laws.... [In Rome], no one spoke of military families, but of patricians, not of *patre et avo militibus*, but of *patre et avo consulibus*. [83]

Moreover, because of their judicial activities, the *parlementaires* "are above simple gentlemen." After all, if Parlement registered letters of *anoblissement* and daily judged the cases of nobles in the court, then "having become the judges of nobles, [they are] raised above them, or at least they are their equal."[84] Bertaut also accepted the definition of a *parlementaire*'s nobility as established by the jurists, which clearly stated that a magistrate could become a *noble de race* if he met the standards of the *patre et avo consulibus* principle.[85]

Finally, Bertaut discussed the system of venality of offices, which he noted had always been used by the nobility of the sword to separate themselves from, and raise themselves above, the nobility of the robe. He challenged the sword on this point from two directions. First, he emphasized that nobles of the sword were just as guilty of venality as those of the robe: many military, courtier, and provincial government offices were bought and sold. Second, and more important, he insisted that the venality of offices was acceptable in France because the hereditary tendencies it encouraged were beneficial to the administration of the realm. "When they [offices] remain in families (there are many which have been in some families for an entire century), they are transferred to men who assume them solely for the dignity that is attached, and not for the revenue they produce," he claimed. Family control of offices is necessary "to acquire the experience and time that are needed to pass to greater employment [in the state]."[86] Undoubtedly many of Bertaut's contemporaries remained skeptical about this attempt to de-emphasize the motive of personal gain among the judges. But his argument does underscore how easily an astute *parlementaire* could graft the sale of offices to the principle of service to the nation and the king.

Bertaut concluded his book by arguing that the nobility of France should consider itself a homogeneous unit in society and that artificial categories should not distort the basic equality of all nobles. "It is easy to conclude from all that has been said," he wrote, "that the nobility that derives from military employment is not different from the nobility that derives from the magistrature. They both have their origin in the same principle, that is, virtue, which is the same for the one and the other."[87] This statement is rather surprising considering that Bertaut himself had dedicated his book to proving that the nobles of the robe should enjoy greater status, prestige, and prerogatives than the nobles of the sword. But his postscript is indicative of a trend that would develop fully in the eighteenth century: the coalescence of the high robe and high sword on issues of mutual interest and self-conception. Bertaut's conclusion stands as one of the first attempts by a *parlementaire* to transcend the judges' traditionally narrow approach to questions of status and to begin to identify with the nobility as a whole. Such attempts were, of course, at first rather limited, as Bertaut's seemingly contradictory dualism indicates. Yet it is important to note that the idea of the "equality of all the nobility" began to mature in the seventeenth century, but only late in the reign of Louis XIV.

Even the contemporaries of Bertaut who were not as favorable to the claims of the *parlementaires* indicated the persistence of magisterial self-esteem. The irascible Saint-Simon, for example, found it necessary to devote page after page of his memoirs to refute the social and political pretensions of the magistrates. His anger would not have been warranted if the *parlementaires* had not given him cause to be upset. Thus, his gloating over the victory of the peers in 1664 and his insistence that "the purely popular nature . . . of the magistrates has not changed up to the present, whatever efforts they have made to leave this essential lowness [*bassesse*], an idea which has long been present in their minds," has a hollow ring.[88] Saint-Simon's sentiments were shared by that famous critic of Louis XIV, Belesbat, though for different reasons. Belesbat attacked the *parlementaires* because he feared them; as members of the robe, they seemed to acquire an inordinate number of royal posts to the exclusion of the old sword nobility. The fact that Louis had trimmed the political prerogatives of the court did not prevent Belesbat from attesting to the high position that the *parlementaires* claimed for themselves in state and society.[89]

Despite the efforts of Saint-Simon, Belesbat, and others of their persuasion, the pretensions of the *parlementaires* continued to be widely recognized. Perhaps Paul Hay du Chastelet provides us with the most concise statement of how popular authors viewed Parlement. His *Traitté de la politique de France*, published in 1669, sums up widely read contemporary opinion of Parlement. "These *parlementaires* are chosen among the most honest and enlightened individuals in the state, and if republics are well ordered, one ordinarily prefers the rich to the poor and nobles to *roturiers* because it is assumed that they have more virtue and intelligence; consequently they are incapable of certain lownesses [*bassesses*], which [material] necessity and low birth would inflict upon them."[90] But even this author, who so willingly attested to the dignity of the judges, could not resist the temptation of pointing out how the *parlementaires'* social pretensions could be detrimental to royal authority. He continued: "Moreover, that which cannot be kept secret [is that] the parlements, which are a part of the Aristocratic Government of the state, are entirely opposed to Monarchial Government. The Senate, which was too powerful, ruined the First Monarchy of Rome."[91]

In the final analysis, the books of Bertaut, Chastelet, and others provide us with an indication of the sentiments of the *parlementaires* during the reign of Louis XIV. Their opinions reflected the judges' continued portrayal of themselves as a prestigious social and professional group. Bound together by their shared noble status, their membership in an eminent judicial institution, and their similar backgrounds and social contacts, the *parlementaires* never relinquished the view that as the highest members of the robe they were entitled to a privileged position in government and society. No matter how much changing conditions had altered their ability to interfere in "affairs of state," the high degree of magisterial self-esteem remained and continued to intensify during the Grand Siècle. Louis XIV was no more able to contain this mentality than he was able to recapture the appointment of judges or to change the composition of the court. With these developments in mind, it is hardly surprising that Parlement, like the ancient Phoenix, rose from the ashes to claim once again its prerogatives upon the Sun King's death in 1715.

CHAPTER THREE

Royal Policy and the Sources of Parlementaire Wealth

In the decades before the Fronde, the *parlementaires* naturally resented royal financial expedients that threatened the various sources of their wealth. Mazarin's plan in 1648 to postpone the renewal of the *droit annuel* and to suspend temporarily the payment of judicial salaries had provided the immediate pretext for the Parisian sovereign courts to meet at the Chambre Saint-Louis. Royal failures to pay interest on government bonds (*rentes*) more than once jeopardized the court's negotiations with the king. To be sure, few historians would maintain that the revolt of the judges hinged upon financial self-interest alone. There were simply too many other grievances and honest impulses for state reform to substantiate a crude economic interpretation of Parlement's participation in the Fronde.[1] Nevertheless, the *parlementaires*' concern for their fortunes played a significant, if not always predominant, role in their deteriorating relations with the monarchy. The administrations of Cardinal Mazarin and Louis XIV had to recognize that the judges would staunchly oppose any royal policies they perceived as detrimental to their prosperity.

The monarchy's attitudes toward the judges' economic interests, like its policies regarding the procedures of officeholding, bear directly on the issue of royal control of Parlement after the Fronde. A confident government, unconcerned with the prospect of judicial opposition, might have sought to subdue the judges by undermining the sources of their wealth. Neither Mazarin nor Louis XIV, however, proved to be so aggressive. Rather than threaten Parlement with economic sanctions, they favored the court's vested interests, even when this action jeopardized or modified their own programs. Such a moderate approach was not without value for the cardinal and the king, because it enabled them to avoid potentially volatile conflicts with the magistrates. Nevertheless, royal concessions never guaranteed Parlement's silence on other issues. Equally important, the government's willingness to compromise showed that even after the abortive Fronde the *parlementaires* retained sufficient influence to turn royal policy to their advantage.

The major portion of *parlementaire* wealth consisted of a combination of official income, land, investment returns on *rentes,* and the benefits obtained through royal patronage.[2] The judges differed considerably, however, in both the size of their fortunes and the relative weight of each of the above sources in them.[3] These wide financial variations, in addition to the lack of documentation on the total wealth of most magistrates in the mid–seventeenth century, make an evaluation of individual magisterial fortunes beyond the scope of this study. Instead, the following discussion concentrates on how the crown influenced the sources of *parlementaire* wealth as a matter of policy.

OFFICIAL INCOME

There were two major types of income a magistrate received by holding office in the Parlement of Paris. One was the salary the royal administration paid in quarterly payments from the royal treasury. The other was the fees (*épices*) litigants paid to the judges for their services. Although the crown did not itself pay these fees, it could pass legislation to regulate the official rates a magistrate could charge. There were two additional and minor sources of official income: fines (*amendes*) that litigants who lost suits paid to the court, and deposits (*consignations*) that litigants filed with the judges and subsequently forfeited. Parlement delegated special collectors for these funds, and they were divided among the judges every few months. Like the *épices,* fines and deposits were not direct financial obligations of the crown, but royal legislation could still regulate their administration.

In theory, judicial salaries were based on a percentage of the official value of a magistrate's office. For most of the seventeenth century, the rate was 5.5 percent annually. The account books of Parlement give the following yearly salaries between 1653 and 1673:[4]

Office	Salary (in *livres*)
Président à mortier	2,250
President of *enquêtes*	1,350
Maître des requêtes	1,300
President of *requêtes*	525
Lay councillor	416
Clerical councillor	339

At first glance, the judges' concern for their salaries might appear exaggerated. The amounts listed above are small, and because the official value of offices in the seventeenth century did not keep pace with market prices, the relative value of salaries declined through time. Mousnier estimates, for example, that the yearly salary of a lay councillor in 1597 amounted to 4.5 percent of the market value of his post, while by 1617 it had fallen to only 0.7 percent because of the rise in the market prices for parlementary offices.[5] Despite this general trend, however, the crown's frequent practice of selling salary increases (called *augmentations des gages*) to the judges easily compensated for this decline and made the payment of salaries a sensitive issue in the court. In return for a single contribution to the treasury, a magistrate received an increment in his yearly salary. A donation of 20,000 *livres*, for example, might bring the judge an additional 2,000 *livres* in salary each year.[6] Because of the long period of time necessary before a councillor could regain his investment, the judges viewed these salary increases as little more than forced loans, and they were consistently hostile to them. Moreover, salary increases followed the office, not the individual. Not only did this raise the market prices for offices in Parlement, but it also meant that the salaries due most of the judges were far higher than the base figures would indicate because their predecessors *en charge* had purchased one or more *augmentations des gages*.[7] Given these considerations, judicial salaries were not as inconsequential as historians have often assumed.

The potential for conflict between crown and Parlement was therefore inherent in the system of magisterial salaries on several levels. First, if the government refused to pay one or more quarters of salaries, the *parlementaires* could be expected to protest vigorously. The payment of salaries was habitually tardy, but a refusal to pay raised the ire of the most loyal magistrate. Second, if the royal administration attempted to engineer a forced salary increase, the magistrates were certain to oppose the policy. Finally, the judges were very sensitive to delays in the payments of raises acquired by previous holders of an office.

In the decades after the Fronde, few disagreements developed between Parlement and the royal administration on the issue of salaries. Parlement's own account books indicate that the annual base salaries of the court's members were paid in full.[8] In addition, the crown rarely placed *augmentations des gages* for sale, something it had done frequently in the past. Some surviving registers of the Parisian Chambre des Comptes for the years 1653–1673 do show that several million *livres* of salary increases were sold in 1652 and 1657.[9] But there is reason to suspect the accuracy of these entries. A report of some of the charges brought against Fouquet at the *Chambre de Justice* in 1662 asserts that the minister had intentionally fabricated the salary increase of 1652 in order to extort funds from the royal treasury. The document suggests that he might have used the same tactic in subsequent years.[10] The account books of Parlement further indicate that Fouquet failed to implement augmentations after the Fronde. A sample of the volumes for 1661, 1667, and 1673 lacks any entry for an increase of salaries created during the fifties or early sixties. The only successful raise in salaries in the immediate post-Fronde period occurred in January and December 1674 when Colbert decided to place a million *livres* of *augmentations des gages* for sale.[11] However, because all the sovereign courts were to participate in the purchase, an accurate assessment of how much the Parisian *parlementaires* actually contributed is impossible. At any rate, Parlement's registers, which normally expressed great interest in salaries, reveal no opposition to Colbert's policy in this instance.[12]

Only one aspect of judicial salaries generated controversy after the Fronde: the payments to magistrates for the salary increases that either they or their predecessors had purchased in the past. In 1659 and 1660 Fouquet had expressed an interest in reducing this royal debt. But his correspondence with Mazarin indicates that he never implemented such a plan, and several years later Colbert gave as the reason Fouquet's fear of stirring opposition in the sovereign courts.[13] After Louis XIV assumed personal rule the government acted less timidly. By a conciliar decree of October 1661 the crown reduced by one-third its payments on those *augmentations des gages* that royal officials had purchased since 1635.[14] This partial repudiation of the royal debt to their disadvantage infuriated the sovereign courts. The Cour des Aides issued several remonstrances against the reduction, and Parlement's protests on this matter continued well into the following year.[15] But the king remained firm, and in his memoirs he gloated over his own victory. "My affairs were in such a state that I had no reason to fear their [the sovereign courts'] anger," he stated, "and it was appropriate to let them know that I feared nothing, and that the times had changed."[16]

Louis's harsh words, however, should not lead one to exaggerate the impact of this decree on Parlement. The king neglected to add that Colbert bargained with several leading magistrates and continued to pay their salaries in full.[17] Moreover, the king accompanied his decree with other orders intended to facilitate the swift and accurate payment of the remaining portion of judicial salaries. Punctual payment of salaries easily compensated for the part that had been annulled.[18] Finally, the crown made no attempt to implement even a partial reduction of payments on those *augmentations des gages* sold to the judges before 1635. Throughout the period 1653–1673 the magistrates received payment on salary increases dating as early as 1614, 1622, 1625, and 1628.[19] In 1661, for example,

First President Lamoignon received 26,125 *livres* increment in his base salary owing to the payment of thirteen different salary increases his predecessors in office had purchased. Similarly, Guillaume de Flexelles received 3,365 *livres*, Nicolas le Prestre 2,625, Martin de Bermond 2,000, and René de Longueil 975.[20] No set of figures, of course, could fully establish if each councillor received all the raises due him. Nevertheless, the high frequency of entries dating to the early seventeenth century indicates that the crown intended only a partial reduction of this portion of magisterial salaries. And when compared to the financial exactions made on the *parlementaires* before the Fronde, these operations of 1661 appear relatively minor.[21]

The second major source of official income was *épices*, or judicial fees. These had evolved from the gifts that litigants gave to their judges. By the seventeenth century, *épices* had become institutionalized in the form of set fees that litigants paid to a common fund. The first president of the court periodically divided the fund among the judges.[22] Unfortunately, Parlement's archives lack exact figures on the *épices* for the years 1653–1673. Ford notes, however, that the fees were considerable. For example, the Parisian Chambre des Comptes received 39,418 *livres*, 15 *sous* in the first two months of 1696. Of this sum, the first president received 360 *livres*, each *maître* 240, each *correcteur* 168¾, and each auditor 150.[23]

The only serious threat to the flow of *épices* in the decades after the Fronde was a royal edict of March 1673 that threatened to revoke *épices* altogether at some future date when and if justice became free in France and magisterial salaries were increased to compensate for the loss of fees.[24] For a number of reasons, however, this edict did not signify a royal offensive against magisterial wealth. First, the edict states that Louis only intended to suppress *épices* after the salaries of the judges had been increased to compensate for the loss of revenue. Under this condition, the curtailment of *épices* posed no threat to the magistrates' income. Second, the king never executed his intent to revoke *épices*.[25] There is absolutely no indication that the administration of Louis XIV tampered with the *épices* of the magistrates at the Parlement of Paris. What scanty records have survived on *épices*, the *procès-verbaux* of *commissaires* of the court (those councillors sent on missions from Paris to research litigations) for the years 1635 to 1681, indicate that the judges received ample compensation for their services.[26] Even the codes for civil and criminal procedure that the crown issued in 1667 and 1670, while reducing the instances in which judges could collect fees, left the rates themselves to the discretion of the judges.[27]

The magistrates also received favorable consideration on matters dealing with the two minor sources of their official income, *amendes* and *consig-*

nations. The judges used these funds primarily to pay the debts and up-keep costs of the court; they divided among themselves any surplus. Records of fines are rare, but those which survive for the years 1665–1667 provide a rough estimate of their value in the mid–seventeenth century. In the period November 1665 to November 1666, Parlement received 24,613 *livres* from civil suits and 23,197 *livres* from criminal suits; from November 1666 to November 1667, the sums were 31,217 and 22,183 *livres* respectively.[28] Because approximately two hundred judges shared these sums, the paltry income provided by the fines generated little excitement in the court. The crown too showed little interest in *amendes*, and a single decree that the Privy Council issued on the subject in August 1658 benefited the magistrates. It stipulated that fines would remain within Parlement's jurisdiction and that the judges would have final jurisdiction over all appeals the receivers of fines might file. The stated intent of the decree was to ensure that Parlement continue to receive and divide the fines.[29]

The only issue of any consequence that involved *consignations* surfaced in 1666 upon the retirement of Jacques Le Tillier, the official receiver for those funds. When he retired, Le Tillier owed considerable sums to all the sovereign courts of Paris: 2,228,840 *livres*, 9 *sous*, 4 *deniers* to Parlement, 228,130 *livres* to the Privy Council, 443,432 *livres* to the Cour des Aides, and so on. The royal administration insisted that it knew nothing of Le Tillier's financial difficulties and, to show its support for magisterial claims, it established a board of directors including magistrates from all the courts involved to liquidate the debt through judicial litigation. The magistrates welcomed this solution, and they slowly set out to recover the lost funds.[30] In August 1669, Louis also issued a declaration establishing detailed regulations for the receiver of *consignations* in order to ensure the free flow of these funds in the future.[31] In this, as in most other areas of the magistrates' official income, the crown attempted to avoid threatening the judges' financial interests.

ROYAL DEMESNE AND PATRONAGE

Revenue from land, pensions, and royal patronage supplemented the *parlementaires'* official income. The judges shared the same passion for acquiring landed wealth as other nobles and many bourgeois in the *ancien régime*. In his brief, but illuminating study of landholding patterns in the vicinity of Paris in the seventeenth century, Marc Venard comments that "the milieu of the *parlementaires* seemed particularly attracted to the land; . . . a councillor ought to be a seigneur."[32] Bluche notes that in the eighteenth century most of the magistrates owned land, though in varying amounts, and that the *parlementaires* actively participated in the "feudal reaction."[33] A glance at a list of magistrates in the seventeenth century conveys the diversity and quantity of their landed titles. In assessing the relations between crown and Parlement, it should be emphasized that the judges normally acquired and managed their estates without royal supervision; the king's government was little inclined to interfere with purchases on the public market. In other respects, however, the influence of the monarchy on the landed wealth of the *parlementaires* could be considerable. First, the kings frequently attempted to supplement their income by selling portions of their own land, the royal demesne. The judges at Parlement had both a jurisdictional and a personal interest in these transactions because they registered the decrees of alienation and they purchased large quantities of royal land each time parcels of it were placed on the public market.[34] Second, the royal administration could increase the justice rights (referred to as high, medium, or low) that holders of royal demesne exercised. Royal grace could thereby raise a judge's income from seigneurial justice. Finally, the king alone had the authority to elevate the status of magisterial estates to the prestigious level of *vicomté, comté, marquisat,* and so on.

An examination of Parlement's registers for the period 1653–1673 indicates that the royal administration's activities in these areas benefited the judges. During these years, the *parlementaires* continued to purchase royal demesne and to receive generous grants of high, medium, and low justice privileges.[35] The crown also granted numerous rights of *châtellenie, foire, chauffage,* and *péage* on the seigneuries of the judges.[36] Not unexpectedly, the government treated First President Lamoignon generously. Between 1653 and 1673 he purchased a great deal of royal demesne at a low price and incorporated it into his extensive holdings in the county of Launay-Curson, the marquisate of Basville, and the barony of Saint-Yon.[37] The royal administration also did not hesitate to raise the official status of many *parlementaire* holdings. The lands of presidents Longueil, Bellièvre, Le Coigneux, and Bailleul and councillors Nointel, Estampes, and Briconnet attained the status of marquisates between 1653 and 1671.[38] The estates of councillors Brillac, Lavasseur, and Pithou were elevated to viscounties in the same period.[39] The crown also awarded the title of county to the lands of presidents Mesmes and Novion, councillors Bullion, Hodic, Fourcy and Sevin, and *Procureur Général* Harlay.[40]

The magistrates also benefited from royal patronage. In the period under consideration, many presidents and councillors of Parlement held prestigious posts in the royal household. François Le Roy, a councillor in Parlement, was the historian of the king, and Jérôme II Bignon, one of the *avocats généraux,* was the grand master of the royal library.[41] Octave de Périgny served as preceptor for the Dauphin, Jean de Longueil was chancellor for the queen mother, and Louis Fouquet, Bishop of Agde, headed the royal order of *l'Oratoire*. [42] Upon the death of the Duc d'Orléans, the king appointed Guillaume de Lamoignon, Claude Le Pelletier, and Nicolas Pinon as tutors to the deceased's daughter. [43] Other posts were venal, but because they were not subject to the *droit annuel*, the king ultimately decided who would fill them. Etienne Regnault was receiver of tolls at the port of Saint-Denis, President Novion exercised the post of *prévôt* of the *Ordres de Sa Majesté*, Louis Sevin was captain of the city of Chartres, and President Bailleul held the post of governor of Château-Gontier. [44] President Maisons enjoyed the prestigious and financially lucrative post of captain of the chase, governor, and concierge of Versailles and Saint-Germain-en-Laye. [45]

The royal administration also dispensed many benefices, abbeys, and prebends to those councillors who were members of the first estate, including Feydeau, Longueil, Prévost, Champlâtreux, and Bazoches. [46] Still other *parlementaires*, such as Nicolas Sevin, Jean Potier, Géraud Le Maistre, François de Bragleonne, Nicolas de Creil, Jean Hardy, Jacques Amelot, and Balthazar Phélypeaux, were among the chaplains (*aumôniers*) of the king. [47] Moreover, in 1668 and 1669 Louis took great pains to convince Pope Clement IX to restore the right of *indult*. This enabled officials in the high judiciary to occupy a vacant benefice in a bishopric or abbey if they were members of the clergy or to appoint an appropriate person if they were not. This prerogative was financially lucrative to the magistrates, and the king's successful negotiations to continue it were warmly received by the court. [48]

The royal administration was rather reluctant to grant permanent pensions to the *parlementaires*, no doubt because revocation could prove troublesome. The incomplete records of the Parisian Chambre des Comptes, which recorded pension payments, list permanent grants only to those magistrates who traditionally received them: the first president, the *gens du roi*, and those judges who had sat at the royalist Parlement of Pontoise during the Fronde. [49] Nevertheless, the royal administration often awarded judges in Parlement revokable yearly sums, which went under the nebulous title of "grants for services rendered." In 1653, for example, councillors Sevin and Champlâtreux received 1,500 *livres*, and Doujat, Baron, and Feydeau, 3,000 *livres*. [50] In 1663 Ferrand again received 3,000 *livres*, and even the personal secretary of Lamoignon, a sieur de Blanchard, received 2,000 *livres* " for services rendered."[51] For each year in the period 1653–1673, the account books show similar entries.

There is an additional financial matter that does not fit neatly into a specific category, but it reflects the royal administration's response to its financial obligations to the magistrates. The crown did not hesitate to solicit loans from its leading subjects, including the *parlementaires*. In June 1661, for example, Colbert obtained a large loan of 2,501,364 *livres*, of which the magistrates in Parlement contributed 130,000.[52] Earlier, in 1656, First President Bellièvre alone had lent the king 114,000 *livres* in two installments of 50,000 and 64,000 *livres*.[53] Requests for money, of course, hardly signified royal benevolence. Nevertheless, an attempt to repay such loans would at least indicate that the king and his ministers acknowledged their financial obligations to the court. Although contemporary sources make only sporadic mention of these loans, letters written during the administrations of both Mazarin and Louis XIV show that the crown made a serious attempt to repay them promptly.[54]

While considering the financial advantages Parlement enjoyed as a direct result of royal grace, the question arises whether the government was able to purchase the silence of the magistrates. The personal correspondence of individual judges would no doubt provide excellent clues to this difficult question. Unfortunately, few private papers of seventeenth-century magistrates survived the French Revolution. But enough indicators remain to permit guarded hypotheses. Certainly, the royal administration did not neglect the tactic of rewarding certain judges when their actions favored the interests of the crown. In a letter of May 25, 1657, for example, Mazarin reminded his *surintendants des finances* that "the king for several years now has made secret gifts to some councillors of Parlement and of the other sovereign courts," and, as noted above, many judges profited from temporary pensions.[55] Nevertheless, previous and subsequent chapters of this study should indicate that Parlement did not hesitate to oppose royal policies after the Fronde. Its continued recalcitrance clearly reveals that the judges withstood efforts to purchase their silence or to bribe them into submission. Cardinal Mazarin himself recognized this. In response to a request by Fouquet that the cardinal should see to the "interests" of several presidents of *enquêtes*, Mazarin replied angrily:

I have little inclination to counsel the king to make daily new graces to Parlement in general, particularly [because]... all that counts for nothing, and His Majesty does not receive greater marks of their [the *parlementaires'*] recognition and their submission to his will... especially in that which is needed to facilitate and assist in [financial] affairs.... One clearly sees that these messieurs are persuaded that all is due them, but that they owe nothing.[56]

After Mazarin's death, Louis XIV also recognized the limited value of financial rewards. When Colbert asked the king in May 1672 if he could reward several magistrates in Parlement for their recent good conduct, Louis consented, but he made it clear that he did not favor extensive reliance on this policy. Those rewarded, the king emphasized, should not view present gifts as a precedent for continued monetary rewards.[57] None of this should imply, however, that the royal administration's policy of favoring the financial vested interests of the judges was without consequence. Such a policy assuredly enabled the crown to avoid potentially volatile conflicts with the magistrates that the latter easily could have used to exacerbate other issues in contention between the royal administration and Parlement. But it did not render the judges docile receptors of all royal policies that came before the court.

RENTES ON THE HÔTEL DE VILLE

Of all the sources of *parlementaire* wealth, none created more friction between the crown and Parlement than the government bonds that the royal administration issued through the Hôtel de Ville of Paris. These bonds were initiated in 1522 when Francis I combined government and municipal securities both for the sake of simplicity and to establish a lower rate of interest. Similar to other *rentes* of the *ancien régime*, the bonds of the Hôtel de Ville offered the holder a perpetual right, or interest (*arréage*), on his investment, and they enjoyed the legal status of negotiable property. The kings normally set aside funds from income on royal demesne, taxes, and office creations to guarantee interest payments. The quantity of *rentes* increased through successive issues in the sixteenth and seventeenth centuries, and the bonds eventually developed into a major source of credit for the monarchy.[58] But the issuance of *rentes*, like the venality of offices, had both positive and negative results for the French kings. On one hand, *rentes* provided ready cash to a royal administration suffering the effects of foreign war, internal disorder, and the inadequacy of income from ordinary taxation. On the other hand, the monarchy commonly created more *rentes* than its revenues could support, and it further aggravated the situation by issuing them at an appealingly low price (referred to as *vil prix* or "dirt cheap" by contemporaries).[59] Whenever financial pressures dictated that the government temporarily suspend interest payments or lower the official rate of return, it was certain to meet the vehement resistance of the *rentiers*.

The judges had a dual interest in *rentes*. Most obvious was their heavy investment in them, a trend which began in the sixteenth century and continued to the end of the *ancien régime* itself.[60] Moreover, Parlement claimed the right to supervise the sale and interest payments of *rentes* under the aegis of its Parisian police powers. The result of this jurisdictional and individual self-interest was that *parlementaires* often stood at the center of *rentier* opposition to the royal administration. Protesting *rentiers* normally expected and received the support of Parlement whenever the government attempted to postpone interest payments or to lower the rate of interest.[61] One historian has asserted that the government's refusal to pay interest on *rentes* was one of the primary issues that sparked the parlementary Fronde.[62] The most recent historian of Parlement during the civil wars avoids drawing a direct causal relationship, but he nevertheless agrees that *rente* difficulties continuously aggravated relations between the crown and its leading court of law.[63] For example, many of the *frondeurs* of the high nobility repeatedly attempted to secure Parlement's support by magnifying the government's inability to provide full restitution on the *rentes*. Certainly much of the *parlementaires'* hostility toward tax farmers and intendants stemmed from the popular belief that these agents of the crown siphoned off funds earmarked for *rente* payments. Throughout the Fronde the magistrates issued a barrage of decrees to ensure the payment of annuities at a high rate of interest and to provide strict penalties for anyone who tampered with funds destined for the *rentes*.[64]

The conflicts between the crown and the judges over *rentes* also clearly raised serious political and constitutional issues. When Parlement challenged the royal administration's management of *rentes*, it unmistakably claimed an active role in the formulation of royal financial policy, an area over which the king and his councils increasingly demanded exclusive competence. Appropriately, therefore, a consideration of how Parlement influenced royal *rente* policy after the Fronde bridges this chapter on the financial interests of the judges with the next two, which deal with the court's political and administrative authority.

Not unexpectedly, the *rentier* disturbances, which had been frequent during the civil wars, began again when Mazarin and Fouquet continued their previous financial policies after 1653. On January 22 of that year, one of the *avocats généraux* at Parlement, Jérôme I Bignon, informed his colleagues that the *rentiers* were disturbed because the government was tardy in meeting interest payments on the bonds. The magistrates at first refused to receive these complaints, and the *grand' chambre* ordered that all illegal assemblies of *rentiers* in Paris cease immediately. The court instead delegated several councillors to visit the Hôtel de Ville and quietly investigate the situation.[65] Apparently the deputies were not pleased with what they discovered, because on January 30 one of Mazarin's spies informed him that the chambers of *enquêtes* had demanded that the entire Parlement hold a plenary session on the *rentes*.[66] A contemporary pamphlet indicated the magnitude of the royal debt on the bonds and helps to explain the agitation in Paris and the concern of the judges. According to the figures presented, the government owed 57 million *livres* on *rentes* guaranteed by the *gabelle*, 28 million by the *aides*, 891,000 by the clergy, 57,000 by the *taille*, and similar amounts by the *Cinq Grosses Fermes* and *entrées*.[67] Mazarin avoided immediate difficulty with the court by instructing the *prévôt des marchands* of the Hôtel de Ville (the mayor of Paris) to permit two councillors, Reffuge and Le Nain, to participate in deciding how the interest was to be paid.[68]

The temporary respite the government gained through concession quickly ended in the beginning of 1654. In January the Conseil d'Etat ordered that two and one-half quarters of *rente* be paid immediately.[69] Parlement was pleased, and once again it ordered a halt to illegal *rentier* assemblies. But Mazarin, desperate for funds, decided to rescind the council's decree and order that only two quarters of *rentes* be paid. Almost immediately the court held plenary sessions on the issue and illegal *rentier* assemblies, now attended by several councillors of Parlement, convened again. First President Bellièvre frantically urged the cardinal to restore full payment of interest, emphasizing that the trouble that would begin in Paris was not worth a mere one-half quarter of *rentes*.[70] The government's reflexive action, however, was to defend its decision. In a *lettre de cachet* dated January 19, 1654, the king informed Parlement that he suspected old *frondeurs* who were not even *rentiers* as the cause of disturbances. He asserted that despite the reduction of one-half quarter of *rentes*, the government promptly paid interest. He gave his "royal word" that no future suspension of payment was planned.[71] To show his good faith, he issued a decree in March intended to facilitate the payment of interest on *rentes* by reducing the number of receivers and payers of the bonds and streamlining the municipal bureaucracy.[72] Infuriated by this action, however, the receivers of *rentes* refused to surrender their account books.[73] As a result of this defiance, the judges, who had originally thanked the king for his decree in March, renewed their opposition and asked that the receivers and payers of *rentes* be reinstated, that *rentes* be paid in full, and that deputies among the *rentiers* be elected to supervise the officials at the Hôtel de Ville.

The extensive correspondence between Mazarin and his principal advisers indicates that the royal administration felt seriously threatened by these disturbances in Paris. Parlement and the *rentiers* had become closely allied; dissident *rentiers* met at the home of Bellièvre, while at the same time Parlement remonstrated "incessantly" that the king grant their demands.[74] Despite this activity, Mazarin held firm. One of his *surintendants des finances*, Abel Servien, had impressed upon him that the treasury simply could not afford to pay *rentes* in full; Mazarin echoed these sentiments to his close confidant, the Abbé Fouquet, and expressed the hope that the recent return of three exiled *parlementaires*—Machault, Le Boindre, and Le Clerc—would render the obtrusive court silent.[75] When this ploy failed, Mazarin, who had accompanied the young king on a campaign in Champagne, sent letters patent to Parlement demanding that the judges end their plenary sessions. The letters emphasized that despite the temporary suppression of one-half quarter of *rentes*, the interest nevertheless "was paid more punctually than ever, [and] that there was not the least justification to fear that an interruption of payment would occur [in the future]." The letters went on to insinuate that Parlement's participation in the Parisian disturbances encouraged the enemy to fight with greater tenacity on the battlefield.[76]

Unimpressed, Parlement continued to take advantage of the cardinal's absence to agitate for their demands. The *surintendants des finances*, Fouquet and Servien, remained in Paris desperately trying to calm a gathering storm.[77] They received the aid of the *prévôt des marchands*, Alexandre de Sève, who promised to take no action without the first minister's permission.[78] First President Bellièvre, "who acted with much prudence and affection in his court," used his influence to calm the magistrates and to moderate their demands. But the court rejected his overtures and decided to proceed without royal permission to elect the supervisory deputies.[79]

Affairs reached dangerous proportions in August. Mazarin's advisers informed him that agents of several old *frondeurs* of the nobility, notably Retz, Beaufort, and the Duc d'Orléans, actively exploited the tumultuous Parisian scene to further their rebellious plans. These *cabaleurs* had seen excellent opportunities opened by the absence of the king and the *rente* difficulties.[80] On August 4, Servien wrote a long letter to Mazarin in which he "frankly" assessed the gravity of the situation. He warned the cardinal that France was on the verge of another Fronde, especially since two other sovereign courts had also begun to hold assemblies on the *rente* issue. Such assemblies were "the same enterprises that had caused past disorders, and I fear that if a remedy is not provided soon, and with force, which was not done in the past, we will fall into the same situation." Even loyal *parlementaires*, continued Servien, refrained from defending the king's interests because they did not wish to offend their fellow magistrates, a tactic that he angrily likened "to those who kill for fear of dying." Not only were past *frondeurs* in Parlement active, such as Charton, Molé, Le Boindre, and Pointcarré, but even the royalist members of the Parlement of Pontoise, those twenty-five judges who had left Paris in 1652 to demonstrate their loyalty to the king, had joined with them in denouncing royal policy. Servien ended his letter with a suggestion that the cardinal not bend to every whim of the magistrates and that he deal with them "firmly."[81] It is likely that Mazarin was impressed by Servien's call to action, especially when one of his spies in Paris warned at the same time that Parlement's assemblies on *rentes* could easily develop into another Chambre Saint-Louis and a broader discussion of financial and "public" affairs in the court.[82] On August 14, Chancellor Séguier joined the chorus when he wrote the cardinal "that the troubles of the past did not have more powerful origins. . . . I fear that we may easily experience similar accidents if we do not oppose [Parlement] with firmness."[83]

Under the influence of such strong pleas, Mazarin finally decided to take action, but not the sort advocated by Servien, Séguier, and his other advisers. He did not carry the king to Paris and humble the court. Rather, he reluctantly decided to yield to Parlement's demands. In early September the government officially restored a full two and one-half quarters of *rente* payments and permitted Parlement to participate in selecting deputies to supervise their payment.[84] The judges graciously accepted these concessions and ended their plenary sessions, a move that greatly upset Retz's partisans, who had exploited the assemblies in favor of the *frondeur* in exile.[85] A timely victory of the royal armies in the siege of Arras helped further to bring the crisis to a close, although Mazarin himself recognized that "it would be quite imprudent to pretend that victories and conquests alone suffice to contain each in his duty."[86]

These difficulties over *rentes* in 1653 and 1654 provide an excellent indication of Parlement's motives and Mazarin's responses. If the cardinal had followed the counsel of his principal advisers, he would have rushed to Paris with the king and dramatically attempted to humble the court. But he reasoned that such a show of force would have been imprudent and might have aggravated an already dangerous situation. He chose compromise, and the settlement he proposed was clearly in accord with Parlement's demands. The conduct of the judges demonstrated that they too preferred compromise to open rebellion. Old *frondeurs* like Beaufort, Retz, and their agents immediately lost any advantages they had gained from the Parisian disturbances when Parlement ceased its plenary sessions upon the reception of royal concessions. In fact, the judges attempted to justify their actions after the settlement had been reached by stating that they had opposed the royal administration on the issue of *rentes* in order to prevent the *rentiers* and old *frondeurs* from pursuing rebellious activity that imprudent royal decisions would have inevitably produced.[87] In this fashion, Parlement legitimized its resistance on grounds of loyalty to the prince. As Moote has shown, Parlement continually adopted an aura of loyalty to justify its opposition to the crown during the Fronde.[88] The judges continually resurrected these tactics in the following decade, thereby effectively negating attempts by the royal administration to portray their actions as disobedient, or worse, treasonable.

Cardinal Mazarin and his advisers fully understood that difficulties with *rentiers* had their roots in the extraordinary financial policies they pursued. Successive creations of *rentes* were but expedients themselves to compensate for the inadequacy of income from ordinary sources of revenue.[89] As long as the government met its financial needs by extraordinary means, it could not help but fall back on a series of excuses to explain the postponement of its financial obligations. This in turn upset those who had an interest in the financial cul-de-sac. Mazarin made an attempt to pursue two policies at once: he allowed Fouquet to continue his financial wizardry, while at the same time striving to stave off the unending series of protests by the *rentiers*. In 1656, the cardinal even secured a personal loan of 100,000 *écus* from the financier Manmeulette to pay interest due on the *rentes*.[90] Such desperate policies, however, were hardly sufficient to pacify the *rentiers* for long. Fouquet increasingly found it necessary to issue new *rentes* to provide enough cash to pay the interest on existing bonds.[91] Throughout the years 1657 to 1659 the *surintendant des finances* created new *rentes* on *gabelles*, *tailles*, and *Cinq Grosses Fermes*, and he encouraged the cardinal to reduce the interest payments on existing bonds by one-half.[92] Understandably, these financial tactics were totally unsatisfactory to the *rentiers*. Not only did they fear a fifty percent devaluation of their bonds, but they also objected to new creations because they reasoned, perhaps correctly, that if the government was unable to pay interest on older *rentes*, it would inevitably forfeit interest on more recent creations.[93] Moreover, the flood of contraband salt into France in the late 1650s reduced the funds tax collectors were able to amass on the *gabelle*, thus removing a source of funds primarily used to pay the *rentiers*.[94]

The cumulative failures of Mazarin's financial policies of expediency resulted in more difficulties with the *rentiers* in 1659 and 1660.[95] On July 9, 1659, the secretary of state for war and close friend of Mazarin, Le Tellier, informed the cardinal that the *prévôt des marchands* had presented to the *grand' chambre* of Parlement a petition signed by sixty to eighty *rentiers* requesting that the judges protest Fouquet's *rente* creations on the *gabelle* and demand the full payment of interest. The *rentiers* considerably strengthened their protest by reminding the court that the recent peace treaty with Spain nullified any justification the royal administration might offer for additional expedients.[96] These demands disturbed Mazarin and Fouquet. They feared that Retz and Beaufort would again attempt to exploit Parisian disturbances as they had six years before and begin a "revolution." Mazarin even toyed with the idea of exiling the *prévôt des marchands* because of his "criminal" action in presenting the *rentiers'* petition to Parlement.[97]

Unfortunately, contemporary sources, though copious, do not describe fully the resolution of this issue. The correspondence of the cardinal, however, provides several strong clues that, as in previous years, the government was prepared to compromise with the judges. Fouquet, acting with the support of Mazarin, attempted to isolate Parlement from the dissident *rentiers*. First, he decided to restrict his planned curtailment of interest payments to those *rentes* created since 1657. This allowed him to sidestep parlementary resistance because the magistrates had invested heavily only in the older, or *anciennes rentes*, which were created before 1657. These the crown agreed to pay in full.[98] Acting upon the advice of his cunning minister, Mazarin also decided that priority be given the *parlementaires* in the payment of interest on the *rentes*. This tactic was geared to mollify the self-interest of the judges and to render their alignment with more vocal elements less likely.[99] Finally, Fouquet arranged to have one of his agents, a *rentier* named Pinon, head the delegation of the *rentiers*. Pinon convinced the *rentiers* to revoke their original protest from Parlement and instead to deliver it directly to the king.[100] Without the justification that they had been invited by the *rentiers*, Parlement lost its soundest legal basis for intervention in the conflict. Through this combination of tactics, Fouquet was successful, and he wrote Mazarin in April 1660 "that never has Parlement been so tranquil."[101] The crisis passed, therefore, "with sufficient calmness, . . . an affair in which many important individuals took interest."[102] Because it had received favored treatment, Parlement accepted these developments, and to ensure that *rentes* were paid, the judges issued a decree in January 1660 stipulating that interest continue to be paid promptly. When in September 1661 the government abolished the offices of seventy-two *secrétaires du roi*, Parlement registered the edict, but only with the modification that funds from the *gabelle* be used to reimburse the *secrétaires* only after the *rentes* and salaries of the magistrates were paid. The royal administration consented.[103]

After the death of the cardinal, it seemed that the new administration of Louis XIV and Colbert would repudiate the financial policies of the previous decades. In mid-1661 Louis simultaneously arrested Fouquet and established an extraordinary *Chambre de Justice* to punish those who had misused state funds during his minority. The commission included high-ranking members of the king's councils and many deputies of the provincial and Parisian sovereign courts, including several presidents and councillors of the Parlement of Paris.[104] It soon became apparent that several influential councillors of state in the *chambre* had advised the king that a full reformation of finances required that the *chambre* extend its activities beyond the crimes of individuals and into the realm of financial management itself. As early as 1662, *rentiers* were disturbed about rumors that a full reformation of *rentes* was in the making.[105] The *parlementaires*, who did not advocate premature action, issued a temporary injunction against the assemblies that the *rentiers* began to hold at the Hôtel de Ville.[106] But by mid-1662, the *avocat général* of Parlement and member of the *Chambre de*

Justice, Denis Talon, informed Chancellor Séguier that the commission had definitely decided to reform *rentes.* [107]

The impulse for reform came from Colbert. In a memoir dated 1663, the minister outlined his motives for encouraging the king to change royal *rente* policy. He assigned *rentes* a central place in the crown's recent financial and political problems. The rapid accumulation of interest due on successive bond issues had both consumed royal revenue and made prompt payment of interest virtually impossible. This in turn generated protests from the *rentiers* and thus, the sovereign courts. Colbert emphasized that before the time of Fouquet, tax farmers and financiers had purchased most of the bonds. But with the rise of Fouquet, *rentes* had become a particularly explosive issue since "most alienations [of taxes and royal demesne in the form of bonds] ended up in the hands of the *présidents à mortier,* other presidents and councillors of the sovereign courts, and all the persons of quality in the kingdom . . . and made it the interest of the courts and the persons of quality to preserve them." Only if the quantity of *rentes* and the interest paid on them were reduced, he asserted, could the monarchy improve its financial position and avoid the dangerous consequences of *rentier* disturbances. [108]

This reasoning appealed to the king. On March 13, 1662, the royal administration suppressed a million *livres* of *rente* established on the *taille.* On March 18, June 3, and June 30, the government ordered the repurchase of 600,000 *livres* on *gabelles,* 400,000 *livres* on the *Cinq Grosses Fermes,* and all *rentes* on *parties casuelles.* On April 3, 1663, the crown issued another decree that stipulated the liquidation of all *rentes* that had been established between 1656 and 1661 (including 120,000 *livres* on the *taille* established in 1659). The royal administration made arrangements to compensate the *rentiers,* but for many at a lower price than they had originally invested. [109] The *rentiers* were most upset, however, with a later edict of May 24, 1664, which ordered the liquidation of all *rentes* that had been crèated in the previous twenty-five years. [110] The principal due on *rentes* was reduced so that those who had purchased them at *vil prix* would not benefit from the suppression at the king's expense. Owing to the protests of the *rentiers,* Colbert eventually extended the period for the presentation of *rente* documents to three months, instead of the original one. But he remained firm in his plan to execute the declaration of May. [111]

As expected, the *rentiers* vigorously protested these ambitious reforms. In their remonstrances to the king, they stated their sympathy with Louis's intentions to suppress *rentes,* which were an unfortunate product of twenty-five years of war. But they emphasized that as the reforms stood, many families would suffer financial disaster. "Paris, the capital of the kingdom," they asserted, "subsists almost entirely on *rentes,* [and if they were liquidated], 100,000 families would have to leave France . . . and go to foreign lands." Asserting that "there are no more loyal subjects to the king than the *rentiers*," they pleaded with Louis to abandon his reform and leave the number of *rentes* at their present level and interest rates. If this was not done immediately, then "fathers will no longer be able to look at their children without tears in their eyes."[112] These passionate pleas were matched by vigorous activity. Ormesson reports in his *Journal* that throughout the month of June, *rentiers* flooded the Hôtel de Ville voicing their protests. This knowledgeable contemporary feared that open rebellion was imminent, and he hoped that Louis would moderate his program. But he recognized one problem that seemed insurmountable: "the character of Monsieur Colbert is too recalcitrant to profit from this occasion."[113]

Parlement's role in the tumultuous events that followed the council's decree of May defies simple explanation. Certainly the magistrates were upset, and the correspondence between Le Tellier and Séguier reveals that Parlement planned to call a plenary session on the issue of *rentes*.[114] The king ordered First President Lamoignon and *Avocat Général* Talon to refuse permission for the chambers to assemble, but at the insistence of the *enquêtes*, a plenary session did in fact meet on June 14.[115] The conduct of the judges at that session was strange indeed. At first, several members who had heavily invested in the *rentes*, among them President Le Coigneux and Councillor Tronchat, "spoke with anger" about the planned suppressions. But Lamoignon immediately calmed all tempers when he showed the court a mysterious letter from Le Tellier. Nicolas Foucault described the scene in the following terms to Colbert:

The first president heard all [complaints] without interrupting. Then, from his seat in the *grand' chambre*, having read the letter of Monsieur Le Tellier, those who were most disposed to harangue and to demand the plenary session remained silent and then concluded in their advice in favor of the king. Thus, Parlement undertook no resistance.[116]

Unfortunately, Le Tellier's letter to the court is neither in his papers nor in the records of Parlement. However, the royal administration's subsequent activity in the *rente* affair indicates that the adversaries decided to compromise. In a declaration of December 1664, the government modified its decrees of May and June, and instead of liquidating all *rentes* issued since 1639, it concentrated on those of recent creation (late 1650s).[117] The face value of other *rentes* was reduced by only one-fifth and the official interest rate from 6.8 percent to 5.5 percent annually. These alterations posed little threat to the judges' financial interests. Parlement had already shown in its quarrels with Fouquet in 1659 that it was unconcerned with the fate of bonds issued since 1657, those which Colbert now suppressed.

The *parlementaires* were more interested in the older issues, or *anciennes rentes*, and because many of these had been purchased originally at bargain rates (*vil prix*), the present reduction in their face value and interest did not seriously jeopardize past investments. Moreover, the government promised that it would not liquidate in the future any *rentes* held by royal officials and that subsequent bond redemptions would pay interest at 5.5 percent. The declaration of 1664 also stipulated that the supervision of *rentes* would be assumed jointly by the king's councils and the Hôtel de Ville, thus preserving Parlement's right to intervene through its police powers.

Even the great Colbert, therefore, had been forced to compromise as he did again in the following year on the issue of venality of offices and the *paulette*. Parlement was satisfied with the settlement because the *rentes* of most of its members had been preserved. In December 1664, a letter emanating from the *Chambre de Justice* testified "that the payments [of *rentes*] are not met as quickly, from year to year, as those held by the members of Parlement."[118] The royal administration further stabilized the situation when it restored, and made hereditary, the offices of the receivers and payers of *rentes* in January 1665.[119]

The history of *rentes* after 1664 confirms the thesis that the judges minimized their losses from the *rente* reforms. In a decree of June 1671, for example, Parlement reaffirmed the declaration of December 1664 and ordered the continued prompt payment of interest.[120] In the following year, the king issued a lengthy ordinance that defined in precise terms the functions of those officials at the Hôtel de Ville who handled *rentes* in order to ensure that they did not tamper with funds destined for interest payments.[121] Furthermore, when Colbert reduced the official rate of interest in December 1665 from 5.5 to 5 percent, he allowed many *rentiers* to collect the higher rate on the *rentes* they already held. He therefore kept his promise of December 1664.[122] All the more striking, however, is the fact that as Louis began to pursue the costly foreign policies that would mark the rest of his reign, Colbert was obliged to fall back on the expedients that had earned Fouquet his reputation. One by one, Colbert's *rente* reforms dissolved in the face of financial pressures. In 1672, for example, he raised the interest rates on *rentes* again to 5.5 percent and created 200,000 *livres* of *rentes* at this rate. In 1672 and 1673, he raised the amount of bonds an individual could purchase from 100 to 200 *livres*, and he even began to sell securities to foreigners.[123] The royal administration ordered successive *rente* issues in 1674, 1679, 1680, 1688, 1689, 1691, and 1702 to help finance Louis's foreign involvement, and interest rates as high as 7 percent were common.[124] The magistrates took advantage of these sales, and well into the eighteenth century government bonds constituted a solid portion of their fortunes.[125]

In the decades after the Fronde, therefore, the governments of both Cardinal Mazarin and Louis XIV had recognized the importance of *rentes* to the magistrates at Parlement. Frightened by the spectre of judicial resistance, Mazarin and Fouquet were content to compromise with the *parlementaires* and to assign high priority to fulfilling their *rente* obligations to the court. The aggressive policies of Colbert were certainly more responsive to the financial strains within France. But even his determination to reform *rentes* was tempered by a combination of parlementary recalcitrance and the needs created by royal foreign policy. The judges profited from the crown's difficulties. *Rentes* continued to play an important role in their fortunes, and the threat of Parlement's opposition hung like a Sword of Damocles over a royal administration with serious intent to reform the system of government bonds. Although the history of *rentes* in the seventeenth century has yet to be written, historians should not hesitate to doubt those who interpreted Colbert's operations in 1664 and 1665 as a sign of the advent of royal absolutism.[126]

In conclusion, the de-emphasis of economic sanctions against Parlement was a consistent feature of the policies pursued by both Mazarin and Louis XIV. Just as they failed to reform the procedures of officeholding and to change the composition and pretensions of the court, so they never attempted to control the judges by attacking the sources of their wealth. In this respect, the fate of the *parlementaires'* financial interests after the Fronde further underscores the expedient nature of Mazarin's policies and the limited scope and impact of the royal absolutism associated with the personal rule of Louis XIV: neither the king nor the cardinal created deep social or economic change within Parlement. This does not mean, however, that they did not strive to achieve a higher level of control over the judges' political and administrative activities. Parlement's response to this challenge is the subject of the following two chapters.

CHAPTER FOUR

Parlement in Opposition, 1653–1660

T he conflicts between the crown and the Parlement of Paris in the decades preceding the Fronde had raised a significant issue of constitutional importance: did the *parlementaires* have the right to transcend their primary function of judging litigation and participate with the king and his advisers in solving national problems and directing the course of royal policies? The affirmative response of most of the judges had animated their attack against the "governmental revolution" of Cardinals Richelieu and Mazarin in 1648, and five years of civil war had failed to cool the spirit of opposition in the court. Throughout the last decade of Mazarin's ministry, the judges remained determined both to assert their right to "mix in affairs of state," as contemporaries so aptly put it, and to defend their wealth, function, and prestige from the eroding influence of administrative centralization. That they often succeeded testifies not only to the continued political influence and administrative authority of Parlement, but also to the inability of Mazarin and his advisers to exploit fully the royal victory in the civil wars.

THE ADVERSARIES ON THE EVE OF RENEWED CONFLICT

The *parlementaires* justified a broad political role for their institution on the basis of both historical precedents and their own considerable responsibilities in the administration of the realm.[1] As regards Parlement's traditions of political influence, the historical record was sufficiently ambiguous to allow the judges wide latitude in asserting their claims. The Parlement of Paris, along with two other sovereign courts—the Chambre des Comptes and the Grand Conseil—as well as the king's councils had originated from the ancient Curia Regis of France. Over the centuries, the courts and councils had materialized and assumed their separate existence from the older judicial and deliberative body. But a fundamental problem of confusion of powers remained to plague these organs of the royal government. A general characteristic of French royal administration in the *ancien régime* was the absence of precise definitions of the proper spheres of activity for the crown's leading institutions. The kings had habitually amplified the jurisdictions of their highest officials according to particular circumstances, and Parlement had thereby come into frequent contact with many aspects of royal justice, finance, and administration. This eclectic delegation of authority might have enabled the monarchy to strengthen its position over the years, but it also bequeathed to all its courts and councils ample precedents to exercise functions the others considered part of their own competence. In the light of this legacy, the judges' opposition to the crown's extraordinary policies in the mid–seventeenth century was only a symptom of the more perennial problem of confusion of powers. The financial pressures and the "governmental revolution" generated by France's entrance in the Thirty Years' War had resurrected the fundamental issue of institutional authority.

When ambitious governments, like those of Richelieu and Mazarin, attempted to untangle the web of overlapping jurisdictions to the detriment of Parlement, the judges culled their voluminous archives to bring the weight of history to their defense. But the *parlementaires* did not call upon the cumulative experience of their predecessors solely for defensive purposes. Parlement boasted of its origins in the Curia Regis, and as the kings had consulted that older body, Parlement claimed that they should also consult its prestigious offspring. Indeed, the French kings had often done just that. On numerous occasions they had asked the court to give advice on important issues, to verify peace treaties, and to sanction regencies. Parlement was the court of peers, and thus claimed to represent the notables of the realm. The development of social cohesion and the concept of *noblesse de robe* in the court reenforced this sentiment of elitism. As the Estates General gradually disappeared from French life, Parlement claimed to assume its function of interceding between the king and his subjects. Moreover, as the leading court of law in an area two-thirds the size of the kingdom, Parlement judged hundreds of legal cases each year in the king's name. The magistrates' daily participation in litigation meant that a wide variety of matters came before them for definitive resolution.

Parlement also possessed powerful institutional machinery and broad administrative responsibilities that aggravated the confusion of powers and supported the judges' political aspirations. During the fifteenth and sixteenth centuries, Parlement had acquired the right to register many types of royal decrees. The court's participation in the legislative process undoubtedly offered advantages to the monarchy. Registration of decrees at Parlement provided an official sanction for royal policies and signified the willingness of the judges to enforce them. It also allowed the kings to publicize and keep a record of their legislative acts. In constitutional terms, moreover, registration did not make a decree "legal" because the monarch's will was theoretically supreme and not subject to the veto of his courts. The king's submission of a decree to the scrutiny of his highest judges was legally a voluntary act of royal grace. Nevertheless, by exercising the right of judicial review, Parlement necessarily nurtured a tradition of participating in the formulation and execution of royal policies. And whatever the legal status of registration actually was, for centuries jurists, judges, and subjects throughout the realm commonly equated registration of a decree with its legality and viewed Parlement's role in the promulgation of legislation as a check on royal despotism.

An integral feature of the registration process was the judges' right to remonstrate, or protest, the contents of decrees the crown placed before them. The judges frequently refused registration pending a favorable response to their complaints, and occasionally they even changed the meaning of decrees by adding their own "modifications" before proceeding to registration. Together, the practices of remonstrance and modification enhanced the formal political role of Parlement and armed the judges with powerful weapons to oppose royal policies. They also underscored the potential for conflict between crown and Parlement that was inherent in every act of judicial review.

Acting under the auspices of a vague "police power," the *parlementaires* were by definition administrators as well as judges. In addition to exercising important supervisory duties in Paris itself, Parlement was responsible for enforcing the decrees it registered within its area of jurisdiction. The magistrates could easily obstruct the implementation of royal acts either by benign neglect of enforcement or by actually issuing decrees contrary to the royal intent. Such tactics were often successful because Parlement also issued regulatory decrees (*arrêts de règlement*) that interpreted points of law, established administrative rules, and guided the conduct of the lesser courts in its area of jurisdiction. The hierarchic structure of the judiciary naturally favored close ties between Parlement and lesser officials, especially in instances when all viewed royal policy as a threat to their claimed rights and privileges.

Parlement also relied upon its judicial function to intervene in affairs of state. In the course of dispensing justice, the judges commonly handled litigation in which the government was the plaintiff, as when a defendant protested a royal tax. If the court found against the state, it could place royal policy in jeopardy because future litigants could oppose taxes citing Parlement's decision as a precedent. Even in religious affairs, the judges wielded considerable influence. Through the judicial procedure of *appel comme d'abus*, Parlement could evoke litigation from church tribunals if it considered that ecclesiastical judges had exceeded their powers, transgressed on secular jurisdiction, or violated the liberties of the Gallican church. As self-proclaimed defenders of the French church from papal interference, the judges further blurred the boundaries of secular and ecclesiastical jurisdiction and easily intervened in all sorts of religious affairs.

Finally, several of Parlement's internal procedures favored a united front against objectionable royal policies and further enhanced the court's political influence. Under pressure from deputies of the various chambers, the first president, with the approval of the three superior chambers, could call a plenary session to discuss "important issues" with all the magistrates present. Such unified pressure was often successful in bending the royal will because frequent plenary sessions at best meant a temporary cessation of judicial activity, and at worst a type of "judicial strike." Moreover, such plenary sessions were well publicized in Paris and in the provinces; the king and his ministers feared them because turmoil in Parlement gave other discontents a pretext to advance their own demands. Parlement also often used its annual (sometimes semiannual) *mercuriales*, meetings in which the court examined its internal procedures, to discuss national affairs and issues in contention between the court and the royal administration.

Confronted with Parlement's extensive duties, pretensions, and means of opposition, the crown undeniably had methods of coercion at its disposal. The most obvious, of course, was armed force. But because the judges carefully based their obstructionist tactics on legal precedents, the king and his ministers found it necessary to meet them on their own terms. One method of circumventing magisterial obstinance was through the issuance of *lettres de jussion*, which compelled the *parlementaires* to register a particular decree despite their remonstrances. A more certain method of control was the *lit de justice*, a ceremony whereby the king himself came to the court and personally supervised the registration of acts he felt Parlement might resist through the normal procedures. In more desperate moments, the king could exile recalcitrant *parlementaires* or establish extraordinary judicial commissions to handle matters in which he had grave concern. But none of these procedures, however impressive, could control the court in its daily conduct, nor could they ensure that the judges would enforce royal decrees or refrain from issuing their own decrees to block the royal administration's programs. They certainly did not resolve the basic issue of confusion of powers.

Excluding a redefinition of Parlement's many powers, two additional alternatives remained open to the crown to supervise the conduct of the judges. The first was simply careful management of the court. To achieve this, the king relied heavily upon the first president and the *gens du roi*, those *parlementaires* who were responsible for representing his interests at the court. The *avocats généraux* were often unreliable and unresponsive to royal needs; because their charges had become hereditary in fact if not in law, they could afford to act independently. The first president and the *procureur général* proved more reliable because their offices, though venal, were held on royal commission and not subject to the *droit annuel*. The first president exercised a very important post. As the presiding magistrate of the court, he enjoyed great prestige and influence with his colleagues. He could postpone a plenary session (though often not indefinitely) to prevent the court from voicing unified protest to royal policy. He also had the responsibility of wooing the judges to the royal point of view and deciding when to introduce legislation to ensure its registration. The *procureur général* also exercised influence along these lines, and equally important, he supervised the enforcement of royal decrees in the court's area of jurisdiction. It was imperative for the crown to cultivate the support of these officials—any breakdown of communication between them and the king and his ministers could prove disastrous for the royal programs before the court.

Another method of circumventing Parlement's opposition found favor with Richelieu and Mazarin: they avoided entirely the issue of confusion of powers and Parlement's arguments on behalf of participation in affairs of state. Instead, they resorted to programs of expediency they hoped the intendants and councils could enforce without recourse to the prestigious court of law. Rather than resolving the fundamental issues at hand, however, this approach had the opposite effect of generating Parlement's resistance to the crown and convincing the court to adopt the rebellious stance of 1648.

It should be readily apparent that so long as Parlement kept its administrative responsibilities and machinery intact, and so long as the confusion of powers remained a fundamental issue, the extraordinary policies of the royal administration would never escape the judicial review and resistance of the court. In this respect, the settlement of the Fronde had left an ambiguous legacy. The amnesty of 1652 exonerated all but a few of the most recalcitrant magistrates, and many of those whom the king had originally exiled were permitted to return. The crown had certainly made it clear in the declaration of amnesty that the judges should no longer "mix in affairs of state." But French kings had issued similar declarations in the past with little effect.[2] The prohibition from interference in affairs of state was all the more tenuous after 1653 because the crown had carefully avoided tampering with the administrative machinery Parlement relied upon to oppose royal policies. The right to register edicts, to remonstrate, to issue administrative and judicial decrees, and to hold plenary sessions remained intact after the Fronde. Parlement might not have won a victory during the civil wars to change the course of Mazarin's "governmental revolution," but when the smoke had cleared in 1653, the court emerged as the formidable body it had been before the wars with its prerogatives and pretensions remarkably well preserved.

The *parlementaires* felt they had good reason to oppose the royal administration after the Fronde. Under the supervision of Nicolas Fouquet, extraordinary financial policies remained the order of the day, and Mazarin reintroduced administrative practices to sustain them: the intendants slowly returned to their *généralités* under the name of *commissaires départis*, the king's councils continued to nullify Parlement's decrees and to evoke litigation, and ad hoc judicial tribunals transgressed upon the judges' jurisdiction. In this atmosphere of renewed crisis, however, it is important to recognize that the recent civil wars had wrought some basic changes in parlementary tactics. The court could not ignore the defeat of the insurgents by the royal armies: Mazarin's return to Paris and the fall of Bordeaux in 1653 testified to a royal victory. The Parlement that emerged from the Fronde was therefore decidedly on the defensive. This does not mean that the judges became the passive servants of Mazarin's reconstituted government. Quite the contrary, the following pages will reveal how vocally Parlement challenged many royal policies of national importance and frustrated their successful implementation. But the defeat of the Fronde did cause Parlement to turn within itself and concentrate its opposition on issues relating to its own prerogatives and jurisdiction; the ecumenicalism of the Fronde years disappeared. The judges made no attempt to encourage the broad reforms in the state that they had advanced so forcefully in 1648, nor did they interfere with the reestablishment of the provincial intendants, who threatened the jurisdiction of lesser courts far more than that of Parlement. The magistrates also expended little effort to establish a united front with other Parisian and provincial sovereign courts.[3]

The shift of Parlement's attention after 1653 meant that its major conflicts with the crown centered upon its relations with the king's councils. Most controversies about royal financial, religious, and administrative policies quickly boiled down to a confrontation between Parlement and council. Here lies the heart of the fundamental problem of confusion of powers. Recent scholarship has emphasized that the king's use of his councils, and consequently the authority these bodies claimed for themselves, increased simultaneously with Richelieu's and Mazarin's policies of expediency. Under the supervision of these two first ministers, the councils became more specialized and the perennial duplication and overlap of their administrative activities decreased through time. Membership in the councils was restricted to administrative specialists, which increased efficiency.[4] As the government relied upon the councils to enforce its policies, the opposition of Parlement to these bodies, which was inherent in the confusion of powers, reached its highest intensity in the post-Fronde decade.

In 1653, therefore, the crown and Parlement were on a collision course. On one hand, Mazarin and Fouquet were prepared to continue their extraordinary policies; on the other, Parlement stood ready to oppose them, keeping its administrative machinery and its pretensions to a role of participation in affairs of state intact. In the years that followed, the strength of each would be put to a thorough test.

PARLEMENT AND ROYAL FINANCIAL POLICY

Parlement opposed royal financial policies after the Fronde on several grounds. Aside from objecting to expedients that threatened their economic self-interest, the judges resented the imposition of taxes in their area of jurisdiction without prior registration at the court. Almost all direct and indirect taxes (except the *taille* and the *aides*, which were handled by other sovereign courts) easily fell into this group. Closely related to this protest was the court's opposition to conciliar decrees ordering taxes. The crown often turned to its councils to issue financial decrees in order to avoid sending them to Parlement for registration. The judges had voiced their objections to all these practices at the Chambre Saint-Louis in 1648, and the reform articles of that body had prohibited them.[5]

As early as the end of 1652, however, it became clear that the government intended to ignore the protests of 1648 and to continue its extraordinary taxation. In December, Louis XIV held a *lit de justice* at Parlement and forced the court to register thirteen financial edicts. Among them were many of the financial expedients the judges had protested before the Fronde, including taxes on royal demesne, salary augmentations, and office creations.[6] The *lit de justice* coincided with *rentier* disturbances in Paris and the continued agitation of the partisans of Condé and Retz. The result was a highly inflammable situation. The magistrates pressed Mazarin to allow them to discuss the edicts despite the fact that they had already registered them in the king's presence. The cardinal refused, and his correspondence indicates that only the threat of exile had forced the judges to submit.[7] Nevertheless, the agitation in Paris and the recalcitrance of other sovereign courts, especially the Parisian Chambre des Comptes, eventually convinced Mazarin to suspend some of the most objectionable edicts.[8]

Far more serious threats to royal financial policy emerged during the *rentier* crisis of 1654. Throughout that year, the king's councils had issued decrees creating new taxes and extending established levies within Parlement's jurisdictional area without the judges' approval. Understandably, Parlement responded unfavorably to these tactics which were intended to circumvent its interference. While the court aided the *rentiers* in their call for full restitution of interest on bonds and the election of deputies to supervise payment at the Hôtel de Ville, members of the *enquêtes* chambers called on the entire court to establish a committee of *police générale* in conjunction with other Parisian sovereign courts.[9] Mazarin's advisers quickly realized that although the formation of such a committee was ostensibly intended to discuss *rentes*, the judges would inevitably proceed to the examination of "affairs of state," particularly "the new impositions that have been ordered."[10] Throughout the month of August, Chancellor Séguier pleaded with Mazarin to prevent such a committee from meeting. His letter of August 14 is highly instructive because it testifies not only to Parlement's determination to participate in affairs of state, but also to its intention to obstruct royal financial policies, especially those ordered by the king's councils without its consent.

The last movements [the Fronde] and unjust enterprises that produced such evil did not have more powerful beginnings. They [the judges] try to appear as the protector of the public, accusing the king's councils of [unjust] impositions and claiming to act on behalf of the people so as to win their affection and become the master of all.... After having surveyed all these public ills, I fear that we may easily fall into similar accidents [again, an allusion to the Fronde] if we do not oppose them with firmness. The council is weakened by all this, not having the authority to act against this court [Parlement], and I fear that all the orders we [the council] give will only provide Parlement with the excuse to oppose their execution and to render all our deliberations utterly useless.[11]

It is difficult to determine if the committee for *police générale* ever met; there is no trace of it in Parlement's archives. Nevertheless, the intent of the court was clear, and the cardinal's advisers were attentive to the implications of such a group ever assembling. No doubt the possibility of such a meeting helped to persuade Mazarin to accord Parlement's desires on the issue of *rentes*: the crown promised full restitution on the bonds and permitted the election of deputies.[12] The *rente* settlement made no mention of the taxes the council had imposed, but without the issue of *rentes* to protest, the court temporarily lost the justification to assemble a committee. As a result, both sides compromised, but the basic issue of Parlement's right to interfere in royal financial policies and its authority vis-à-vis the king's councils remained unresolved. This became clear in the disagreements between the crown and Parlement over royal financial policy in the following years.

Under continual financial pressure owing to the war, Louis held a *lit de justice* on March 20, 1655, at which he presented fourteen fiscal edicts to

Parlement for registration. As in 1653, many of the edicts contained extraordinary taxes, fees, and office creations that offended the judges.[13] Chancellor Séguier spoke eloquently to the judges of the king's financial needs and how all subjects "could not refuse to their country what each individual owes to his family." Until the war ended, he said, all must accommodate themselves to extraordinary financial policies.[14] Parlement registered the edicts, but several days later decided to reexamine them.[15] This action violated the very nature of the *lit de justice*, which supposedly ensured the court's obedience.

The situation was very similar to the *lit de justice* of January 15, 1648, that had led to the Fronde. In order to prevent further discussion of the edicts, Louis himself entered the court unannounced on April 13 and expressly ordered the assembled judges to cease their discussion of the edicts. It was at this ceremony that Louis supposedly uttered the words, "L'état, c'est moi," but despite the splendid show of royal will, the magistrates remained obstinate. The court sent deputies to speak with Mazarin about the issue, but the cardinal remained firm. He did tell the deputies, however, that the king "was no longer dissatisfied with his Parlement... [and] that the king approved of the court assembling for other affairs."[16] Apparently, the deputies deliberately twisted Mazarin's words in their official report to the court, because Colbert informed Mazarin on April 16 that when the deputies appeared before Parlement, they told the judges that the cardinal approved of their discussing the edicts. "Even all the presidents reported very falsely, and to the disadvantage of Your Eminence, the conference you held with them," complained Colbert.[17] The magistrates used the reports of the deputies as an excuse to continue discussion of the edicts, to issue remonstrances, and to send additional delegations to the cardinal throughout April and May.

Mazarin and First President Bellièvre remained in close contact and apparently planned to frighten the court into submission, for on May 12 Bellièvre reported to Parlement that an informant had awakened him at one o'clock in the morning and told him that the king planned "to bring a storm upon those who should enter the *grand' chambre* to demand a plenary session."[18] But such tactics only gained the government several weeks respite, because on May 28 the court finally secured a general meeting and ordered the continuation of remonstrances to the king "to approve that the court deliberate the edicts in the accustomed fashion."[19] Mazarin stiffened his resistance and again prohibited Parlement from continuing its discussion of the edicts. At this point the judges suddenly ceased their opposition, and most historians assume that Mazarin won a sound victory.[20] However, there are indications that the adversaries had again compromised. In a letter of June 3, Servien informed Mazarin that Parlement still continued to discuss several of the edicts, and the biographer of Fouquet reports that the *procureur général* eventually modified some of them.[21]

In late 1655 another serious conflict developed between the crown and Parlement over royal monetary policy. In December, the Cour des Monnaies registered legislation that ordered the minting of new coins, the ultimate effect of which was to depreciate the value of most other coins in circulation. As *surintendant des finances*, Fouquet hoped that this devaluation would reduce the royal debt, especially the interest due on *rentes*. Parlement immediately objected to the edict. In several memoranda dated late 1655 and early 1656, the magistrates asserted that their court, and not the Cour des Monnaies, should register monetary edicts under the auspices of its "police powers." The question was not purely jurisdictional, however, because the judges also opposed the devaluation as harmful to national interests: while individual taxpayers and creditors would incur losses as the value of money declined, the public at large would suffer from an erosion of purchasing power and a decline in the value of French currency on the international market.[22] In a long and detailed "Escrit touchant les monnoyes qui prouve que la cognoissance en appartient au Parlement," an anonymous author supported these assertions and insisted that the right to participate in monetary policy belonged to Parlement, "which by the administration of justice has a clear and certain knowledge of the public necessity." The monarchy, continued the author, could not change monetary values without some form of "consent," which was best expressed in France by Parlement. "Our kings have never authorized their acts by force [alone], but by justice and the laws of state, desiring that they are neither received, recognized nor obeyed as the truth without free and legitimate verification by their Parlement, which is the throne of their justice."[23]

Resting on what they believed to be firm theoretical support for their intervention, the judges began to hold plenary sessions and to issue remonstrances against the edict in January 1656. Over the next four months, relations between the crown and Parlement degenerated to an exchange of hostile decrees and mutual recriminations.[24] To their plenary sessions and remonstrances the magistrates added a full scale "judicial strike" by postponing the judgment of all litigation until they reached a favorable settlement with the government. At the same time, they ordered the lesser courts in their jurisdiction to ignore royal decrees, and they welcomed to the court delegations of *rentiers*, merchants, and army officers who saw their own financial interests threatened by the proposed devaluation. On its part, the government at first refused to compromise with the judges. Mazarin had the royal councils issue a barrage of decrees condemning

Parlement's activity, and in late January he exiled five of the most recalcitrant *parlementaires*, including one of the *avocats généraux*, Denis Talon.[25] In
early May, the king sent an angry letter to Parlement stating that the
court's obstructionist tactics had renewed the ferocity of the Spanish army
on the battlefield and had provided Condé and Retz the opportunity to
continue their cabals.[26] But these barely concealed charges of treason and
the young king's bold defense of divine-right monarchy failed to silence
the judges. The *parlementaires* also dismissed as mere rhetoric Fouquet's
assurances that the king "wishes to conserve [the court] in all the rights and
privileges that properly belong to it," especially since the *procureur général*'s
only defense for royal monetary policy was that the king "had much more
knowledge [about the need to devalue coinage] than reason permits him to
divulge."[27]

As the struggle intensified, Paris seemed to be on the verge of open
rebellion. As early as February, Colbert told Mazarin that he feared
Parlement's opposition would provoke an uprising in the city, and he
urged the cardinal to end forcibly the court's plenary sessions, even if that
required the exile of all the judges.[28] In subsequent months, other Parisian
sovereign courts joined in protest against the edict, and provincial resistance began to emerge.[29] A judge in the *grand' chambre* sympathetic to
Mazarin informed the cardinal at the end of May that the spirit of opposition in the court had changed little since the crisis had begun.[30]

A break in the stalemate appeared at the end of June. Fouquet informed
Mazarin that he intended to send to Parlement a new declaration on
coinage which he hoped would end the court's jurisdictional conflict with
the Cour des Monnaies. But because Fouquet still feared that Parlement
would protest the change of monetary values, he suggested that a clause be
added to the declaration to the effect that the king would restore the
previous values to coins as soon as "the condition of affairs permits it."[31]
Apparently, his request was granted, because a few days later one of
Mazarin's agents, Bartet, informed the cardinal that a new edict on coinage had been sent to the court, "the articles of which rule in favor of
Parlement's jurisdiction."[32] To seal the compromise, Mazarin then permitted the exiled councillors, including Talon, to return to their posts.[33]

The edict Parlement registered did indeed contain a clause that gave the
judges jurisdiction over its enforcement; but it still contained provisions
for devaluing coins in circulation, and the minting of new pieces proceeded on schedule.[34] For this reason, it is hardly surprising that the most
recent reference to this issue by a historian indicates that Mazarin had won a
victory over Parlement.[35] However, the correspondence of the cardinal
offers evidence to the contrary. Fouquet erred if he thought that the
judges would tolerate the devaluation once they won their jurisdictional

conflict with the Cour des Monnaies. In August 1656, Mazarin complained to Colbert that the financial relief the king hoped to obtain through the edict had not materialized; he was "quite distressed that this affair is still undecided." Obviously, Parlement had not gone to great lengths to enforce the edict, because Mazarin instructed Colbert to meet with First President Bellièvre and discover which clauses of the edict upset the court, after which the first president could "change them and add to the edict all restrictions and modifications he believes are warranted in order to cut short the length and difficulties [in this matter]."[36] But even these adjustments failed to deter judicial resistance. Parlement received appeals on the edict and often found in favor of litigants who opposed it. Several times the judges also exonerated parties whom the Cour des Monnaies had jailed for violating specific clauses. As regards the newly minted coins, the public simply refused to accept them at the values the crown had established, and the entire operation failed dismally.[37] Two years later, when Fouquet renewed his attempts to tamper with coinage values, he again encountered opposition at Parlement. The *surintendant des finances* sought to reduce the value of *liards* (a copper coin of little value, worth one-quarter of a *sou*) from three to two *deniers*. When Denis Talon, the *avocat général* who had been so recalcitrant in 1656, threatened that Parlement would hold plenary sessions on the reduction, Fouquet decided not to provoke a confrontation and deferred the execution of his plans.[38]

The *affaire des monnaies* proves to be highly instructive in defining Parlement's motives and tactics in resisting royal policies. That the court felt its opposition was justified is obvious: its memoranda of 1655 and 1656 and its prolonged resistance to the monetary edict confirms that the magistrates believed they possessed the right to involve the court in public affairs, particularly in matters dealing with royal finances. Their opposition to the crown was far more than a jurisdictional conflict with the Cour des Monnaies, for even after the king and his ministers formulated an edict in favor of their jurisdiction, they continued to oppose monetary devaluation. Parlement also demonstrated the persuasive power of its administrative machinery: judicial and administrative decrees, remonstrances, plenary sessions, and judicial strikes had together contributed to convince the government that a compromise solution was the only way to break the deadlock.

But Parlement's success had another dimension: the inability of Mazarin and his advisers to control a deteriorating situation. Much of their problem resided in their poor communication with the *gens du roi* of the court. Talon was openly hostile to royal monetary policy and had to be exiled. Even Bellièvre frequently assumed an antiroyalist posture and did little to help postpone plenary sessions. It was a well-known fact that the relations between Bellièvre and Fouquet were in a constant state of turmoil.[39] In the middle of June 1656, when Mazarin and Fouquet tried to engineer their compromise edict through the court, the cardinal had confided to Colbert that "the secrets [of my plans] are kept very poorly when it is a question of matters that regard Parlement. This experience necessitates that [we] take better precautions in the future."[40]

Fouquet's willingness to compromise with the court and his influence with the cardinal likewise benefited the bargaining position of the magistrates. It is curious indeed to observe the man most responsible for extraordinary financial policies constantly changing those policies to pacify the judges. Fouquet's dilemma lay in the difficulty of effectively exercising both his ministerial post of *surintendant des finances* and his parlementary post of *procureur général*. He knew that if he firmly opposed Parlement, he would alienate the judges and lose much of his influence in the court. Moreover, recognizing that his financial policies were extremely unpopular, he feared that forceful action against Parlement could provoke an uprising in the capital city. As a result, Fouquet's proclivity to seek short-range expedients in financial affairs was correspondingly exhibited in his relations with Parlement. These problems were exacerbated by Mazarin's confidence in Fouquet and his reliance upon that minister's ability to control both financial and parlementary affairs. Time and again the first minister rejected the counsel of advisers like Séguier, Colbert, and Le Tellier who emphasized the need to take a firm stand against the recalcitrant court of law as an alternative to Fouquet's continual retreat to compromise. The resulting instability that surrounded royal policy-making held two important implications for Parlement. First, the court's resistance to the crown was considerably strengthened when it faced a first minister and influential *surintendant des finances* who consistently vacillated in their resolve to execute their policies. There can be little doubt that much of Parlement's strength, influence, and confidence in the 1650s lay in the position Fouquet enjoyed in the high circles of the royal administration. Second, the fact that Fouquet continually modified his financial policies meant that he had to seek additional extraordinary ones to replace them, thus ensuring the prolonged resistance of Parlement. Exhilarated by their victories, the judges were prepared to oppose each successive policy they disliked. The resultant war of attrition between the crown and Parlement was remarkably similar to that which had produced the Fronde, and it has prompted more than one historian to refer to the 1650s as a "miniature Fronde."[41]

Further conflict over royal financial policy occurred at the end of 1659 when a simple conciliar decree established a monopoly and a tax on all imported whale oil. The tax farm was granted to the Duchesse de Chevreuse and the Duc de Guise, but there is reason to suspect that both Mazarin and Fouquet had a personal interest in the monopoly.[42] Parlement immediately protested the extraordinary taxation and ordered the incarceration of the tax farmer in charge of collection. The council responded with a decree that ordered his release and the arrest of the local officials who interfered with the collection of the tax. For several months a war of decrees ensued between Parlement and the king's council, each nullifying the decrees of the other and demanding that their own be enforced.[43] Parlement's resistance was effective enough to prevent temporarily the collection of the tax and to ensure the distribution of oil in its area of jurisdiction without difficulty.[44]

After a series of plenary sessions and remonstrances failed to move the first minister, Parlement issued a definitive decree against the collection of the tax upon the request of two local officials.[45] Surprisingly, two of the king's own *gens du roi*, the *avocats généraux* Talon and Bignon, led the opposition. In a series of letters to the king, Mazarin, and Le Tellier, they attempted to justify the court's resistance to the tax. As in the *affaire des monnaies*, they cited jurisdictional considerations (Parlement never registered the conciliar decree) and the negative effect the tax would have on French commerce. Acting as if Parlement had an undeniable right to oppose royal financial programs, Talon and Bignon expressed the hope that the king would be "too just to reverse by this single example all the policies and fundamental laws of state and bring this injury to the first court [*compagnie*] of his kingdom."[46]

The issue of the tax on whale oil illustrates how dangerous it was when the king's own *gens du roi* opposed his policies and the communication between the crown and its representatives at the court disintegrated. In a letter to Mazarin, Fouquet expressed his hostility to Talon and noted how the actions of the *avocat général* disrupted his plans: "The first president knew well how to defer the affair [by postponing a plenary session] yesterday, but when those who speak in the king's name [the *avocats généraux*] demand things . . . where the king has interest, it [Parlement] can hardly refuse them."[47] He was furious that Talon had received the request of the two local officials against the tax; this was a clear violation of the authority of the *procureur général*, who alone was empowered to receive such requests. "Your Eminence can see by all of this," wrote Fouquet, "that everyone knows that Monsieur Talon only pays attention to what he wishes, and that neither the council, its decrees, nor the orders of the king hold him to his duty."[48] Even Mazarin, always prone to mediate conflicts between his advisers, noted that Talon "is sadly mistaken if he pretends to erect himself as a tribune of the people."[49] To the biographer of Fouquet, such episodes serve to illustrate that "anarchy was complete at the *parquet* [collectively, the *gens du roi*] and that the authority of Fouquet... [was] entirely disregarded [in the court]."[50]

In a rare display of determination, Mazarin decided to remain firm on this issue. In September 1660, the council issued a decree that nullified all those of Parlement and again ordered the arrest of local officials who interfered with the collection of the tax.[51] Nevertheless, the opposition to the tax that Parlement had fostered in the provinces was so great that by 1663 the tax farm on whale oil had begun to fail miserably.[52]

Not all of Parlement's opposition to royal financial policies was as glamorous or as well publicized as that which surrounded the famous *lits de justice* of 1652 and 1655, the *police générale* of 1654, and the conflicts over coinage and taxes on whale oil. Nevertheless, the registers of the court reveal that the judges' interference in all sorts of financial questions was continuous and often successful throughout the decade after the Fronde. In April and May 1657, for example, Parlement successfully remonstrated and eventually modified two royal edicts on *francs-fiefs* and mortgages, lowering the taxes that individuals paid and limiting the physical force royal agents could use in collecting the fees.[53] In September 1657, when the *procureur général* introduced a declaration increasing the sale of royal demesne, the chambers of *enquêtes* and *requêtes* actually held a plenary session without the consent of the first president and eventually convinced the crown to sell the lands through a special commission composed of officials from the Parisian sovereign courts. The commission then placed limits on both the amount and type of land to be sold.[54] In all these instances Mazarin and Fouquet made considerable concessions; they had originally forbidden the court to discuss the issues.

Upon the conclusion of the war with Spain in 1659, Parlement increased its resistance to royal financial policies since the magistrates believed the crown had now lost its excuse to pursue extraordinary financial activity. The court began to receive litigation on royal taxation and to absolve parties of future payments on taxes instituted during the war.[55] This was done, for example, upon the requests of the *échevins* of Bourges in 1659 and the *échevins* and merchants of Amiens, Abbéville, Château-Thierry, Le Mans, and Troyes in 1660.[56] The court also protected the *greffiers* of the kingdom from taxes in 1660 and 1661, and they successfully defended the *péage* jurisdiction of the *trésoriers de France* in 1660.[57] This opposition necessarily involved Parlement in serious conflict with the king's councils, which continued to issue decrees ordering the payment of all royal taxes. Fouquet exacerbated the situation by insisting to Mazarin that the crown could not yet afford to abandon extraordinary financial measures despite the end of the war.[58]

Parlement's opposition to postwar taxation created a notable crisis early in 1660. Following the advice of Fouquet, Mazarin had the Grand Conseil register a decree that taxed all individuals who had purchased alienated ecclesiastical property. A royal commission immediately began to execute the edict at the Augustinian monastery in Paris. Parlement protested both the tax and the execution of an edict within its jurisdictional area without prior registration at the court. When the council again ordered the enforcement of the tax, Parlement nullified the decree, ordered the suspension of the tax, and instructed the lesser courts in its jurisdiction to ignore the measure.[59] The council responded by arresting Huby, the *huissier* of Parlement who had posted the judges' decree throughout Paris.[60]

Curiously enough, Fouquet was in no hurry to levy the tax on ecclesiastical land. He had hoped to use the tax as a threat to force the General Assembly of the Clergy, which was soon to convene, to grant a high *don gratuit*.[61] Parlement's decree, however, frustrated his plans. As on previous occasions, moreover, *Avocat Général* Talon had acted contrary to royal interests because the judges had issued their decree upon his suggestion, without consulting *Procureur Général* Fouquet. In several letters to Le Tellier, Chancellor Séguier fumed over Parlement's pretensions. He urged the minister of war to punish severely the *huissier* Huby, who became a symbol of the conflict, and he emphasized that if the king did not nullify Parlement's decree, "the royal councils will remain in such a state that they will no longer be able to serve, and public affairs will no longer be sustained."[62] Several weeks later, Séguier continued to warn Le Tellier that "I foresee that the king's council will suffer great scorn and that Parlement will not hesitate to take great advantage [of this]."[63] For the moment, Le Tellier and Colbert supported Séguier's opinions and encouraged the first minister to take a firm stand against the judges.[64]

As he had done so often in the past, however, Cardinal Mazarin turned to his *surintendant des finances* for a solution. On February 5, 1660, Fouquet advised him that there were two possible solutions to the problem. One was to follow the advice of Séguier, Colbert, and Le Tellier and "push the situation with firmness [*avec hauteur*]." The other was to compromise with the court. He advocated the latter course of action, suggesting that the council nullify Parlement's decree and forbid its envoy in the provinces. In return, he would postpone the execution of the tax edict, at least until after the assembly of the clergy had met. As for Huby, Fouquet believed that Parlement should punish him, and if the punishment was light, the king could always increase the penalty later.[65] Mazarin responded that he would follow his minister's advice.[66] At the end of February, the council issued a decree nullifying those of the law court. But it also suspended the tax indefinitely and dissolved the royal commission at the Augustinian monastery. Parlement judged Huby for the sake of appearances, but restricted the punishment to a moderate fine and a prohibition from exercising his charge for three months.[67] Chancellor Séguier remained quite distressed about the conclusion of this affair; he wrote Le Tellier that he would adhere to Mazarin's decision, but he insisted "that I was not mistaken in the judgment I made in this affair and that [Parlement will continue] to evade the good resolutions that we undertake."[68] Le Tellier found it necessary to reassure the chancellor that if Parlement continued to resist the crown's programs, he would not be blamed.[69] The royal administration's policy of compromise had changed little since 1653.

The royal victory in the Fronde, therefore, had not spelled defeat for Parlement. Quite the contrary, the powerful court of law had proved itself a worthy opponent to the crown's financial expedients in the decade after the civil wars. Although Parlement remained unable to prevent the government's reliance on extraordinary financial policies, it nevertheless reduced the benefits Mazarin and Fouquet hoped to derive from them. In part, the magistrates' frequent success stemmed from the considerable administrative machinery they could mobilize to frustrate the royal will. But their resistance was all the more effective owing to the royal administration's poor management of the court, the unpopularity of its financial policies, and the willingness of Mazarin and Fouquet to compromise with the recalcitrant judges. In February 1660, only a year before Mazarin's death, Séguier testified to the popularity and effectiveness of Parlement's opposition. "The public considers Parlement its protector," he wrote the cardinal, "because it receives comfort by the cessation of taxes that we have ordered through the councils, which without a doubt now suffer great contempt; [the councils] are powerless to sustain and execute what they judge necessary for the king's service."[70]

Judicial Administration: Parlement and the Royal Councils

The conflict between the Parlement of Paris and the royal councils over financial policy also extended into the realm of judicial administration.[71] Just as Cardinals Richelieu and Mazarin hoped to avoid Parlement's interference with their financial policies by using the councils to issue fiscal decrees, so they encouraged the councils to evoke litigation from the law court whenever it seemed that the magistrates might judge a case contrary to royal interests. The councils used a variety of procedures to infringe upon Parlement's jurisdiction. Most often they withdrew a case from the court (*évocation*), nullified a verdict the judges had rendered on a particular case (*cassation*), or suspended the execution of a judicial decision while the council reviewed its validity (*surséance*). By the time of the Fronde, the Conseil d'En haut, the highest of the royal councils composed of the king and his ministers, had occasionally resorted to these procedures with little resistance from Parlement. However, when the lesser councils, particularly the Privy Council, aspired to the same privilege, Parlement vehemently resisted encroachment upon its judicial functions.

There were certainly instances when the king's councils could legitimately intervene in litigation before Parlement. For example, they could suspend the execution of a judicial decision if a litigant filed either a petition that claimed an error in fact or a *requête civile* founded upon the fraud or personal interest of a judge in a particular case. If the councils found in favor of the request, they had the authority to send the case to another court. The councils had the same option if a litigant proved that an opposing party had family ties to a number of the *parlementaires* (*évocation de justice*). A change of venue was also justified if two courts claimed jurisdiction over a particular case. The appropriate council then issued a *règlement de juges*, stipulating which court was to judge the case. These procedures were clearly stated in the great ordinances of the sixteenth and early seventeenth centuries, and Parlement did not object to the councils' interference when it was within these specific confines.

The conflict between the councils and Parlement developed when a council attempted to extend its jurisdiction by evoking cases not specified by the ordinances and judging them itself without sending them to another court. This procedure, called *évocation de propre mouvement*, or evocation on the council's own initiative, was defensible on the grounds that the king had the right to judge any case he pleased. But it was onerous to the judges because it directly threatened their judicial function, especially when the king or his councillors of state chose to exercise it frequently. Parlement also objected when the councils evoked cases involving individuals in which none of the parties concerned had filed for a change of venue, a procedure called *évocation des affaires contentieuses*. In addition, the judges protested when a council granted a "general evocation," which entitled an individual or corporation to evade Parlement's jurisdiction on all matters that concerned them, regardless of the legal questions involved. Finally, Parlement objected to the councils' practice of nullifying or suspending the court's judicial decisions in instances not specifically mentioned in the old ordinances. The judges had protested extraordinary conciliar activity before the Fronde, and in the royal declaration of October 22, 1648, the king promised to curtail the attacks of his councils on the court's judicial authority.[72]

Not unexpectedly, the royal administration's reliance on extraordinary financial policy after the Fronde entailed the continuation of conciliar evocations. Parlement decided to protest these transgressions formally in 1656, no doubt because at that time the judges were also involved in serious conflict with the crown over the coinage edict and the terms of renewal for the *droit annuel*. The conflict over evocations held serious constitutional implications for both Parlement and the council because each began to question seriously the authority of the other. At the heart of their disagreement lay the crucial issue of confusion of powers. The voluminous correspondence exchanged between Mazarin and his advisers on this affair demonstrates that they were gravely concerned about the outcome of the council-Parlement contentions.

In May 1656, deputies from the chambers of *enquêtes* and *requêtes* asked First President Bellièvre to grant a plenary session to discuss the excessive number of conciliar evocations.[73] One *parlementaire* wrote Bellièvre that if not rectified "this affair . . . will bring entire ruin upon the court."[74] Dissidents circulated anonymous pamphlets in the court attacking the councils, and within a month both Parisian and provincial sovereign courts attentively followed the course of events.[75] Having decided at a *mercuriale* on August 5 to protest officially against conciliar evocations, the magistrates issued a harsh decree on August 18 stating that they would henceforth ignore conciliar evocations that were not expressly permitted by past ordinances.[76]

To support their position, the judges prepared several memoranda outlining the extent of the councils' transgression on Parlement's judicial function. Four of the memoranda together list nearly two hundred conciliar evocations between 1645 and 1656, eighty-one of them after 1651.[77] The magistrates had taken great care to list only those evocations in violation of the ordinances. A careful reading of the memoranda reveals that the councils had indeed evoked many cases in which the king and his ministers had a vested interest, involving either personal friends or litigation that pertained to royal policy. Several cases, for example, dealt with protests against royal taxation, *rente* policies, or financial sanctions levied on lesser judicial officials. Many other evocations dealt with criminal cases in which the crown obviously hoped to exonerate certain influential nobles whom Parlement was certain to find guilty. The councils had also issued numerous general evocations on matters involving influential individuals and controversial issues, such as Jansenism. In all these instances, the councils had clearly intended to deny Parlement jurisdiction when the court's judgment of a case might have nullified or reduced the effectiveness of a royal policy. For the councils, the demands of the moment took precedence over legal formalities. In order to emphasize that their memoranda contained only those evocations that violated past ordinances, the magistrates had several pamphlets published listing articles from the edicts and ordinances of Blois, Moulins, Orléans, Bourdaiz, Chantalon, and the declaration of 1648 that the councils had supposedly violated.[78] Parlement's memoranda and supporting documents were indeed impressive. The magistrates had carefully substantiated their protest against conciliar evocations with historical and legal precedents, and even Colbert, who was normally hostile to the judges, recognized the validity of some of their points.[79]

The *parlementaires*, however, were not content to restrict their opposition to the preparation of memoranda and pamphlets. They broadened the scope of conflict considerably when they decided to attack the functions of the *maîtres des requêtes* and the chancellor of France. The magistrates were particularly distressed whenever the councils evoked cases from Parlement and sent them to the court of Requêtes de l'Hôtel, which was staffed exclusively by the *maîtres des requêtes*. Besides their duties at that court, the *maîtres des requêtes* also prepared the work that went before the councils. The *parlementaires* saw the collusion between the council and the Requêtes de l'Hôtel, which the *maîtres des requêtes* provided by their association with both bodies, as a threat to their own jurisdiction. In order to prevent such collusion, Parlement decreed that *maîtres des requêtes* could be called before the court at any time to explain their conduct in signing decrees of evocation. Some of the judges insisted that the chancellor of France himself, as chief of the judiciary, could also be called before Parlement to explain his conduct. If the judges had successfully enforced these orders, they would have introduced a rudimentary system of "ministerial responsibility" into the royal administration by subjecting both the councils and the chancellor to the judicial review of Parlement. As it happened, however, a *cause célèbre* developed around two *maîtres des requêtes*, Gaulmin and Laffemas, who had recently signed a conciliar decree suspending Parlement's verdict in the case of a Marquis de La Porte, whom the court had found guilty of violating one of the queen's ladies-in-waiting. Parlement ordered the two to appear before a plenary session to explain their reasons for signing the decree; they refused, and the court removed them from their functions in Parlement.[80]

Several of Mazarin's advisers vehemently denounced Parlement's protest against evocations and its attack on the *maîtres des requêtes* and the chancellor. Colbert urged the cardinal not to compromise with the judges, insisting that even in the matter of evocations, where Parlement had the soundest legal claims, the king could ignore past legislation on the subject because these acts had been granted by weak monarchs "in times of trouble."[81] While Chancellor Séguier shared Colbert's total disregard for legal precedent, he chose to emphasize the implications of Parlement's activity for conciliar authority. On August 23, he wrote Mazarin that "Parlement has taken a route of authority as if it were superior to the council and had the right to correct [conciliar] judgments." To the chancellor, Parlement's pretensions symbolized an attempt "to change the established order" and "to erode the councils' jurisdiction, to raise the parlements above [them], and to constitute [Parlement] the judge of the First Court of the kingdom." He reminded the cardinal that during the Fronde, Parlement had attempted to veto the councils' financial policies, and that the judges would now gain this right if they were able to hold the *maîtres des requêtes* accountable for their actions. Without a broad mandate from the cardinal to continue evocations from Parlement, he concluded, those who oppose royal taxes "would carry their complaints to Parlement, which would assume jurisdiction and prohibit the collection [of taxes]."[82]

These and other letters Séguier wrote to Mazarin and Le Tellier are highly instructive in two respects.[83] On one hand, they clearly reveal that it was common practice in the councils to evoke cases from Parlement when unfavorable judgments at the court might disrupt the execution of royal policies, particularly in financial matters. On the other hand, the need the councils felt to evoke large numbers of cases indicates that the judges had, in fact, used their judicial function to frustrate the implementation of Mazarin's programs, and that they had often done so successfully.

While the cardinal sifted through the opinions of his advisers, Parlement's protests became all the more threatening when Bellièvre and Talon openly supported the pretensions of the court. Colbert denounced Bellièvre, who willingly permitted plenary sessions to meet "in the hope of raising his court higher than it was before him, and thereby to become its master by the credit he acquires by all sorts of activity [against royal policy]."[84] Mazarin himself expressed similar sentiments to Colbert concerning the conduct of Talon, "who . . . [is] persuaded that Parlement cannot fail; in this respect he is more inflexible than his father [Omer, *avocat général* of Parlement during the Fronde] had been."[85] Once again, communication between the ministers and the royal agents in Parlement had deteriorated. The judges easily continued their opposition with little interference.

Throughout the months of August and September 1656, Parlement continued to reiterate its decree against conciliar evocations and to order Gaulmin and Laffemas to appear before the court. Following the orders of Séguier and the ministers, the *maîtres des requêtes* refused to obey.[86] Both Parlement and the *maîtres des requêtes* then remonstrated and sent a stream of delegates to the king and Mazarin to justify their jurisdictional claims.[87] Throughout the turmoil, Colbert, Servien, and Séguier continued to urge Mazarin to subdue the court forcefully. Among them, Servien was particularly angry. Now was the time to strike, he asserted, for "circumstances will never be more favorable, the public not being interested at all in this affair."[88] Mazarin apparently agreed with his advisers, for on October 19 the Conseil d'Etat nullified Parlement's decree of August 18 and held that the *maîtres des requêtes* were not required to appear before the court to explain their conduct. In its registers, the council spoke of "this enterprise of Parlement that tends to establish for itself an unlimited authority and to raise itself above the king's councils, sending for the officials who have the pleasure to sit there to render account of what passes in the councils." If Parlement succeeded in calling these officials before the court, the decree continued, "this not only would ruin entirely the function of their [the *maîtres des requêtes'*] charges and the authority of the king, but would also destroy the order of the monarchy that previous kings have established." The decree also reinstated Gaulmin and Laffemas in their functions.[89]

In the months following the council's October decree, Parlement abruptly ended its opposition, indicating that perhaps the judges had accepted defeat on the evocation issue. Fortunately, Talon wrote a lengthy memoir about this affair, and his words provide an altogether different explanation of the judges' silence at the end of 1656.[90] Talon attributed Parlement's·moderation to a series of royal compromises, principally Mazarin's.concessions on the coinage edict in August and his promises to renew the *droit annuel* in December. Talon also noted that even after the council issued its stern decree, Fouquet promised the judges that he would continue to intercede on their behalf to Mazarin and the king.

That the judges' submission was only temporary became clear in January 1657 when they renewed their complaints about conciliar evocations. They officially rejected the council's decree of October and reiterated their own decree of August 18. Faced with the spectre of a continuation of the events of 1656, Mazarin reluctantly had the Conseil d'Etat issue another decree on January 11 that returned to Parlement several cases the councils had evoked.[91] In a letter accompanying the decree, Louis promised that in the future the councils would obey the ordinances on the subject of evocation.[92] In return, the judges dropped their demand that the *maîtres des requêtes* and the chancellor report to the court, but they insisted on keeping in force their decree of August 18 which prohibited extraordinary conciliar evocations. The crown demonstrated its resignation on the affair by issuing similar decrees returning cases to several provincial parlements and other Parisian sovereign courts.[93]

This compromise of 1657 was extremely tenuous. The crown had certainly made concessions, for among the cases returned to the court were several involving royal taxes, financial demands on officials, and general evocations for some influential individuals. Nevertheless, no more than twenty-one specific cases and two broad issues of litigation were included in the council's decree of January 11. This number certainly did not approach the some two hundred evocations about which Parlement had originally complained. The compromise had therefore resolved neither the issue of evocations nor the broader question of confusion of powers. The crown further complicated matters when in a *règlement* of May 4, 1657, it referred to the Conseil d'Etat et des Finances, the Conseil des Finances, and the Privy Council collectively as the "first company of the kingdom," while it continued to accord the same honor to Parlement.[94] By the end of the year, Parlement and the Cour des Aides again agitated for the return of more cases from the councils.[95]

The evocation issue surfaced again in the summer of 1658, when Parlement claimed that despite the decrees of August 18, 1656, and January 11, 1657, the councils had continued to evoke cases on their own initiative (*de propre mouvement*) and to judge them themselves. The judges chose a propitious moment to press their complaints. The young king was quite ill, the government was preoccupied with military matters in the north after the siege of Dunkirk, and nobles of various provinces, particularly Normandy and Poitou, were in rebellion.[96] On August 6, Talon delivered a stirring speech denouncing conciliar evocations as a threat to Parlement's judicial function and jurisdiction.[97] Faced with so many internal difficulties, Mazarin decided to compromise with the judges, and on August 20 Parlement registered a conciliar decree returning additional cases to the court. The judges appended an order prohibiting under penalty of a heavy fine all *procureurs* and advocates from pleading any cases the council evoked.[98]

An anonymous account of the court's proceedings that day exists in Mazarin's papers. It testifies to Parlement's desire to remain firm, yet moderate, in its demands. When an old *frondeur*, Le Clerc de Courcelles, urged the judges to resurrect the attempt to bring before the court *maîtres des requêtes* who signed evocations, his fellow magistrates rejected the proposal by a vote of eighty to twenty-four. All the judges agreed, however, that conciliar evocations *de propre mouvement* should cease, and they readily accepted President Mesmes's proposal that the entire court should assemble every three months to discuss evocations.[99]

The correspondence between Séguier and the cardinal indicates that the royal administration compromised with the court only because of the uncertainty of affairs created by the king's illness, the siege of Dunkirk, and the rebellions of provincial nobles. While advisers such as Colbert and Servien encouraged Mazarin to take "firm action" against the court, Séguier attempted to moderate the cardinal's passion and convince him to grant temporarily Parlement's demands until the situation improved in France. The chancellor condemned the judges' pretensions, but he recognized that a temporary truce would end the crown's contest with Parlement, which "would eventually open propositions of greater consequence" if it continued.[100] Mazarin remained distressed about Parlement's activity, but he decided to follow Séguier's advice and let matters stand as they were.[101]

At this time, the royal administration's management of the court was at its lowest ebb. Talon's opposition was exacerbated by the absence of a first president at the court since Bellièvre's death in 1657. *Président à Mortier* Nesmond had been appointed to the post temporarily, but he was not competent enough to control the plenary sessions.[102] Fouquet emphasized to Mazarin several times that a loyal first president was necessary to control the court on the issue of conciliar evocations.[103] In October 1658, the king officially appointed Guillaume de Lamoignon to the post. A descendant of a long line of *parlementaires*, Lamoignon was at this time only a *maître des requêtes*. However, he had performed useful service in the provinces, and Mazarin's advisers hoped that his previous service to the king had conditioned him to support royal policies. Both Fouquet and Le Tellier, who were often at odds with each other, actively supported his candidacy.[104]

The appointment of a first president may have been necessary, but it did not suffice to silence the court. As Séguier had forewarned Mazarin, the councils had neither ceased their evocations from Parlement nor returned to the court all the cases included in the decree of August 20. By January 1659, Parlement remonstrated about both violations.[105] Even Colbert and Lamoignon agreed that more cases should be returned to the court.[106] The councils, however, were in no more hurry to accord Parlement's desires than were the magistrates prepared to cease their opposition. As a result, conciliar evocations remained a hotly contested and unresolved issue throughout the closing years of Mazarin's ministry.[107]

Two evocations in the final years of the cardinal's administration received a great deal of publicity and occupied considerable space in ministerial correspondence. At one and the same time, they exemplify the motives behind conciliar evocations and illustrate why the judges so opposed them. In September 1658, Parlement accepted a request by a monk who wanted the court to investigate scandalous conduct at the Augustinian monastery in Paris. Under pressure from the clergy, who saw the court's intervention in the affair as an attack on their privileges, the Conseil d'Etat evoked the case from Parlement.[108] The magistrates immediately protested on the grounds that the council had ordered the evocation simply to pacify the clergy. Colbert reported that a councillor named Tambonneau had "said three times today [December 17] that the court should not expose itself to the council and that they [the judges] should take action if they wished to conserve the honor and dignity [of the court]."[109] Following the advice of Lamoignon, Mazarin decided to transfer the case from the council to the head of the Augustinian order in France. This certainly withdrew the case from Parlement's jurisdiction, but it also prevented the council from directly supervising the reform of the monastery.[110]

Another conflict between Parlement and the council centered upon the case of René de L'Hôpital, Marquis de Choisy. This reckless individual had quarreled with a curé and had him murdered. Upon the complaints of the clergy, several provincial courts had sentenced him to death. When his case arrived at Parlement by appeal, the magistrates were also disposed to find him guilty. Fearing for his life, the marquis appealed to the council, which evoked the case and sent it to the Grand Conseil (another sovereign court in Paris not to be confused with the king's councils). The king then sent letters of absolution to the Grand Conseil as a favor to the influential relative of the marquis, Maréchal L'Hôpital.[111] The judges vigorously protested the evocation, which was based solely on the king's desire to accord a favor to a marshal of France; they ordered that the marquis be placed in the Bastille until the king replied to their remonstrances.[112] Denis Talon was particularly contentious: Le Tellier informed Mazarin that in a plenary session the *avocat général* "discussed [not only this case, but] also the maxims of the council by which it judges evocations."[113] Mazarin was so angered with Talon's conduct that he ordered the minister of war to speak to him "and moderate his impetuosity [or] he will suffer some punishment [*malheur*]."[114] But Talon paid no heed to the threat, and he pressed the court to continue its remonstrances. Finally, on July 16 the king received three deputies of the court who officially brought Parlement's written objections to the evocation.[115]

This session clearly resulted in a compromise. The king firmly insisted that the case of the marquis pass over to the Grand Conseil and that the letters of absolution remain in force.[116] But in return Louis agreed not to send such letters to the Grand Conseil in the future, promising the deputies that that court's jurisdiction in this affair would not set a precedent for future evocations. To demonstrate further his desire for an accommodation with the judges, the king sent to Parlement a duelling case the council had evoked in the previous year.[117] Surprisingly, Talon advised the court to reject this compromise and to issue additional remonstrances. Desperately trying to maintain a moderate stance, however, the judges overrode the protests of their *avocat général* and officially sanctioned the transfer of the marquis's case. On September 2, 1659, Le Tellier was able to inform Mazarin that Parlement's conduct "was very respectful and conforming to the order of justice."[118]

Several conclusions emerge from this survey of Parlement's opposition to conciliar evocations. That the quarrel between the court and the councils continued unabated until the death of Mazarin shows that neither side won a clear victory. The royal compromises of 1657 and 1658 had failed to deter the councils from evoking cases from Parlement in instances that were not specified in past ordinances. In 1659, Chancellor Séguier himself admitted "that of the two hundred cases the *gens du roi* have pretended to be in Parlement's jurisdiction, . . . only eighty have been returned to them, the rest having been judged in the councils."[119] But conciliar successes do not imply, as one historian has asserted, that Parlement's protests "were in vain."[120] On many occasions the opposition of the magistrates had compelled the royal administration to grant significant concessions. The judges had managed to secure the return of many cases, and several times they received the king's promises that conciliar evocations would cease. To the judges, these royal compromises confirmed what they had long asserted: evocations were a highly irregular and extraordinary method of circumventing Parlement's rightful jurisdiction. The judges' fundamental belief in the legitimacy of their resistance strengthened their resolve to oppose the councils and limited much of the relief the royal administration hoped to gain from evocations. Chancellor Séguier expressed this point in a letter to Minister of War Le Tellier in September 1659:

I am able to tell you that the patience of the councils encourages the enterprises of Parlement in all occasions. They [the judges] nullify the decrees of the councils upon the request of parties without even ascertaining the cause involved, as if we [the councils] were inferior judges. This is a new jurisprudence . . . and if it continues, it will be impossible to sustain the affairs of the king, which will doubtless suffer much prejudice if we do not take action to stop the course of these procedures that cause a great deal of difficulty [*bruit*].[121]

Thus, just as Parlement had opposed royal financial policies in defense of its claimed prerogative to participate in affairs of state, so the court resisted conciliar evocations as a violation of its legal jurisdiction. If in both instances the judges failed to curtail the extraordinary policies of Mazarin and his advisers, they at least reduced their effectiveness.

POLITICAL TRIALS

In addition to using the royal councils to circumvent the jurisdiction of Parlement, the government occasionally established special commissions to judge criminal cases in which it had a vested interest. Viewing these handpicked tribunals as an extension of the councils rather than of Parlement, the judges objected to them as a violation of their own judicial function. In October 1653, for example, the king established a temporary tribunal at the Paris Arsenal to judge the cases of several *frondeurs* who had not benefited from the amnesty. The members of this court included the chancellor and a select group of loyal councillors of state and *maîtres des requêtes*; not a single *parlementaire* was included.[122] Mazarin admitted to Chancellor Séguier that his intention in establishing the court was to ensure that those accused would be found guilty, because "it is very difficult to secure justice by ordinary means."[123]

One of the defendants scheduled to appear before the tribunal was a *maître des eaux et forêts* named Bertaut. Fearing for his life, he filed an appeal at Parlement. The judges welcomed this opportunity to intervene, and they immediately remonstrated to the king that the Arsenal court was illegal because Parlement alone had cognizance of treason cases. The court requested that the king dissolve the commission.[124] Mazarin decided to stand firm, and he refused to recognize the validity of Parlement's claims. The crown eventually dissolved the commission, but only after it had finished its work: Bertaut and several others were judged and executed.[125] The royal administration had clearly been successful in this instance. But Parlement's subsequent response to extraordinary judicial commissions demonstrates that its relative passivity regarding the Arsenal court, like its docile reception of royal fiscal edicts in the same year, stemmed more from the proximity of the civil wars than from an abrogation of its jurisdictional claims. The trial of Antoine Fouquet, sieur de Croissy, later in the same year made this quite evident.

Croissy-Fouquet (no relation to Nicolas Fouquet) was a councillor at Parlement who had been an active *frondeur* and confidant of the rebellious Prince of Condé. Mazarin had ordered his arrest on the charge of treason and had delegated several councillors from the royal councils to judge his case and render a verdict of guilty.[126] Parlement vehemently protested the commission, claiming both jurisdiction over treason cases and the right to judge its own members. The cardinal compromised to the extent of permitting two *parlementaires* to gather information and evidence for the case. But this only exacerbated the contest because under the protection of Parlement, the two refused to turn over their evidence to the commissioners whom Mazarin had delegated to judge the case.[127]

Mazarin's advisers urged him not to tolerate Parlement's resistance. One of his informants, Bluet, wrote that a favorable decision in Croissy-Fouquet's case "would produce advantageous results not only for the reestablishment of royal authority, but also for the interests of Your Eminence," and Fouquet's fellow *surintendant des finances*, Servien, warned that if Croissy-Fouquet went unpunished, he would become a symbol of successful rebellion and "it would be impossible to preserve royal authority, and in consequence, the tranquillity of the state."[128] In an attempt to demonstrate the resurgence of royal authority, the cardinal inflamed the situation by exiling several of his most vocal opponents in Parlement.[129]

Nicolas Fouquet, however, saw the affair in a different light. Fearing that the issue would mature into a crisis, he convinced a reluctant Mazarin to compromise with Parlement. The king permitted the return of the exiles and transferred Croissy-Fouquet's case to Parlement. The *procureur général* then prevented the court from exonerating the *frondeur* by allowing him to escape to Italy before Parlement finished the case.[130] In this fashion, Fouquet allowed the government to save face, but Mazarin lost the opportunity to implement his original plan of punishing Croissy-Fouquet as a symbol of rebellion. Parlement's resistance and Fouquet's willingness to compromise combined to frustrate the first minister's plan to engineer a well-publicized political trial.

The *procureur général* was even less successful in his management of the trial of Claude Vallée in 1657. Vallée, like Croissy-Fouquet a councillor at Parlement and old *frondeur*, was arrested and accused of treason for aiding the Spaniards. Hoping to avoid a conflict with the magistrates over the jurisdiction of the case, Mazarin permitted Parlement to judge Vallée late in December 1656.[131] It was understood, however, that Fouquet would ensure that Vallée be convicted and sentenced to death. The trial lasted until April 1657, and all the while Fouquet actively encouraged the judges to vote the death penalty. The court did indeed find Vallée guilty of treason, but by a vote of sixty-one to forty-three the judges decided to spare his life and simply banish him from the kingdom and confiscate his property.[132] A rare voting list shows that Fouquet had been successful in convincing all but one of the *présidents à mortier* (Le Coigneux) to vote the death penalty; it had been the younger, more rebellious judges who ultimately frustrated his plans.[133] Cardinal Mazarin was furious with the court's decision and felt humiliated that Vallée had been let off so lightly. In the eyes of all, Parlement had made a fool of the first minister.[134] Once again, the judges had demonstrated their ability to disrupt the government's plans.

JUDGES AND JANSENISTS

Several times during the 1650s Parlement challenged royal religious policies, especially those intended to suppress Jansenism. Why the French followers of Cornelius Jansen provoked the hostility of the monarchy, the papacy, and the majority of the French clergy is well known.[135] Even before the posthumous publication of the Bishop of Ypres's *Augustinus* in 1640, a deeply moral tradition of the Catholic Reformation despaired over the secular concerns of the French church, the interference of the state in religious affairs, and the ever widening gap between the mass of the faithful and the remote and aristocratic episcopal hierarchy. The Jansenists accepted these opinions and raised issues of theological consequence as a result of their proclaimed adherence to Saint Augustine's view that the grace necessary for salvation was a gift of God not contingent upon the efforts of men. In the eyes of their contemporaries, the Jansenists were engaging in dangerous flirtation with the doctrines of justification by faith alone and predestination. The Jansenist tragic world view that society and man were absolutely corrupt and sinful led the sect to reduce the importance of the church as the mediator between man and God, to reject the casuistic theology of the Jesuits as frivolous "modernism," and to question the theory of papal monarchy expressed at Trent. Despite their assertions of loyalty to Rome and the monarchy, the proclivity of the Jansenists to disregard the authority of earthly institutions, be they secular or clerical, ensured them the enmity of influential authorities in church and state. Although only a few Jansenists had opposed the crown during the civil wars, the administrations of Cardinal Mazarin and Louis XIV associated Jansenism with civil as well as religious insubordination. Sparks of anti-Jansenist sentiment, fanned by the Jesuits in the decades preceding the Fronde, ignited into flames of earnest persecution in 1653.

The Parlement of Paris was deeply involved in the Jansenist controversy. Throughout the 1650s, the judges opposed anti-Jansenist legislation while leading figures in the sect rushed to the court for protection from their enemies. Scholars who have attempted to explain this apparently cordial association between Parlement and the Jansenists fall into two principal groups. Those influenced by Marxist theory see Jansenism as the ideology of a social group threatened by material adversity. Noting that many judges and Jansenists shared common backgrounds in the robe, they assert that the decline in wealth, function, and prestige magisterial families suffered as a result of royal centralization generated robe opposition to the crown on two levels: the political resistance of the judges in the sovereign courts and the spiritual rebellion of Jansenism. By mid-century, both of these strands merged in a tight braid of reciprocal reenforcement. As many *parlementaires* accepted the pessimism and tragic world view so characteristic in early Jansenism, they naturally defended the sect from their enemies.[136] Other historians have rejected the view that Jansenism was a "social heresy," but without necessarily severing the bonds between Parlement and the Jansenists.[137] They retain the Marxist assumption that the relations between the judges and the sect were positive and mutually reenforcing, but they see the reasons for this collusion in the respect both groups had for tradition and their shared opposition to modernism. The appeal of Jansenism in Parlement stemmed more from the tendency of both Jansenist and magistrate to seek in the golden past a panacea for contemporary ills than from their common membership in a harassed social group.[138]

It is beyond the scope of this study to elaborate and evaluate all aspects of these arguments.[139] For our purposes, let it suffice to point out that a fundamental weakness exists at the core of both these widely accepted interpretations: the assumption that many *parlementaires* adopted the religious beliefs of the Jansenists and that the court was unequivocally committed to defending the sect. There is much evidence to the contrary. An examination of Parlement's response to Jansenism reveals that the judges were reluctant allies of the sect. They opposed royal policies not because of religious sympathy with the Jansenists, but rather because when the enemies of Jansenism—the crown, the clergy, and the papacy—joined forced to eradicate the sect, they threatened Parlement's conception of the liberties of the Gallican church and jeopardized the court's asserted authority in religious affairs. Understanding these motives behind parlementary resistance will underscore the nature of the tension between crown and Parlement in this period and clarify the court's place in the history of early Jansenism.

The magistrates' conception of themselves as the defenders of the Gallican church provided an important touchstone for their relations with the Jansenists. Defined simply, Gallicanism was a complex set of institutional arrangements designed to protect the French church from papal influence. The kings, the judges, and the episcopacy all had a stake in minimizing Rome's intrusion in church affairs. Nevertheless, they seldom agreed on the best means to achieve this goal. It was upon this disagreement that the conflicts between the crown and Parlement over religious policies so often hinged.[140]

To the episcopacy, Gallicanism signified the independence of the church from both Rome and the king's secular courts. The *cause célèbre* of the clergy was the judicial procedure called the *appel comme d'abus*, whereby the *grand' chambre* of the parlements received appeals on cases filed within or decisions rendered by ecclesiastical jurisdictions. The clergy viewed the *appel comme d'abus* as an attack on their ancient judicial prerogatives, and they continually complained about it in their general assemblies.[141] But Parlement defined Gallicanism differently. The judges saw their institution as the bulwark of Gallican liberties. In their view, those liberties provided for the exclusion of the pope from affairs regard-

ing the French church, but they did not grant the episcopacy independence from secular authorities within the kingdom. For centuries Parlement had encroached upon ecclesiastical jurisdiction and had worked with
the crown to bring the church progressively under royal control. The
judges were also skeptical of pronouncements from Rome about religious
affairs in France. To them, the pope was simply another foreign prince,
and they maintained that doctrinal conflicts should be resolved not in
Rome, but in a council of French bishops. The opinions of the magistrates
were all the more crucial for the resolution of religious problems because
in addition to the right to receive *appels comme d'abus*, the judges supervised
the University of Paris, including the faculty of theology, by virtue of
their Parisian police powers. They also registered papal bulls to give them
the force of law in the realm.

Between these "two Gallicanisms" stood the kings. Although they continually vacillated between the two theories, the kings most often supported Parlement's point of view as a method of controlling the church. At
times, however, political expediency drove the kings into the arms of both
pope and clergy. At such a juncture, Parlement could be "more Gallican
than the king" and left alone to uphold its traditional views. The court's
administrative privileges in religious affairs, which the crown so often
encouraged, then became barriers to the execution of royal policy. Such
was the case in the 1650s.

A recent study of Mazarin's diplomacy with Rome after the Fronde has
shown that the cardinal, who himself intensely disliked the Jansenists,
attempted to placate the pope's hostility to his anti-Spanish foreign policy
by siding with the clerical enemies of the Jansenists.[142] In 1653, the rare
alliance of king, pope, and clergy resulted in the publication in France of
Innocent X's bull, *Cum occasione*, which condemned five propositions supposedly taken from Jansen's *Augustinus*. A group of anti-Jansenist bishops,
headed by Archbishop Pierre de Marca of Toulouse, requested all bishops
and archbishops in the kingdom to publish the bull in their dioceses.
All the prelates agreed to do so, but not without protests from the
Archbishop of Sens and the bishops of Angers, Beauvais, and Com-
minges. These four reasoned that the bull had no validity in France on the
grounds that the papacy could not decide spiritual questions without consulting a general Roman church council, that a council of French bishops
had not been convened, and that the work of Jansen did not contain the
five propositions. They added that together these irregularities violated
the liberties of the Gallican church. These disagreements inevitably involved Parlement in the controversy because the judges, who were always
sensitive to issues that involved Gallican liberties, had not registered the
bull, and because the Archbishop of Sens filed an *appel comme d'abus* at the

court to protect himself from possible retribution by Marca and his associates.[143]

The judges so opposed the bull that Mazarin never attempted its registration at Parlement. The Jansenists thereby gained temporary respite because the bull lacked legal status in France without Parlement's approval. Nevertheless, Mazarin's correspondence with Marca indicates that the judges' reaction to the bull and their willingness to accept the *appel comme d'abus* did not signify Jansenist sympathy within the court. As Mazarin's principal adviser on Jansenism and a former president of a provincial parlement, Marca was well informed about both the tactics the harried Jansenists employed to protect themselves and the reasons for judicial opposition to the cardinal's Jansenist policy. In a memorandum to Mazarin dated January 1654, Marca stated that the magistrates based their resistance upon the desire to preserve Gallican liberties and not upon religious sympathy with the Jansenists. He emphasized that the Jansenists had secured the support of only "two or three councillors in the court," but that this small faction had successfully incited the others to protest royal and episcopal encouragement of Rome's interference in affairs regarding the French church.[144] The Jansenists had thereby attached their cause to Parlement's traditional hostility toward Rome.[145]

Between 1654 and 1657 the Jansenist issue subsided somewhat because the recalcitrant prelates submitted to the pleas of their peers and agreed to accept the principles of the bull. They did so, however, only with the qualification that a distinction between *droit* (right) and *fait* (fact) existed in the pope's action of 1653. The Jansenists granted that the pope had the right to condemn the five propositions, but they insisted that the *Augustinus* did not contain them. This circumvention of the bull infuriated the anti-Jansenist bishops. They continued their polemics and convinced Mazarin and Alexander VII (who succeeded Innocent X in January 1655) to end the temporary truce. Their plans to crush the Jansenists culminated in the bull *Ad sanctam*, which the pope sent to France in March 1657. The bull reiterated the condemnation of the five propositions, this time "in the sense of Jansen." It also ordered the entire French clergy to sign a formulary, which the General Assembly of the Clergy had drawn up a year earlier, stating their submission. Those who refused to sign would be susceptible to charges of heresy and judged by a commission of French bishops appointed by the pope.[146]

Because the bull of 1657 nullified the distinction between *droit* and *fait*, the small group of Jansenists in Parlement renewed their agitation. They again used the argument that the pope could not judge spiritual questions without consultation with a Roman church council or a general session of French bishops, and that the five propositions were not in Jansen's treatise. They further charged that Rome desired to establish an inquisition in France and that the clergy aspired to limit Parlement's jurisdiction in religious affairs by encouraging the king to revoke the judges' right to receive *appels comme d'abus*.[147] Colbert informed the cardinal that registration of the bull would be difficult because "the Jansenists have inflamed spirits in Parlement . . . against the bull."[148]

Two interesting letters written to Mazarin in May 1657 explained why Parlement opposed anti-Jansenist activity. Chancellor Séguier, a friend of the Jesuits who disliked Jansenism perhaps even more than he detested the pretensions of Parlement, wrote that the court "is convinced that the bull establishes an inquisition in France, [and] it believes the king wishes to take away the *appel comme d'abus* and that the clergy has requested this." He dismissed as absurd the idea that the crown supported an inquisition, but he confessed that "it is true that the [General] Assembly of the Clergy hoped that the *appel comme d'abus* would no longer be permitted when it proceeds against heretics." Séguier concluded that "the opposition that forms there [in Parlement] is only the work of a faction that takes advantage of [the court's] plenary sessions."[149]

Archbishop Marca expressed similar sentiments. This most adamant enemy of the Jansenists emphasized that Parlement opposed Jansenism but refused to act against the sect because the Jansenists had raised the sensitive issues of Gallican liberties and Parlement's jurisdiction. He concluded that

there is reason to believe that the judges in Parlement will be more disposed to register [the bull] when they see the desire of the king to abolish this sect. . . . Things are reduced to such a state that we cannot retreat without giving advantage to the Jansenists, as if one believed that Parlement favored their heresy, and without stigmatizing with this proposition, although false, the reputation of the court, which is absolutely opposed to heresy. The officials who compose [Parlement] have not lost the zeal and piety of their predecessors . . . who registered the bull against Luther.[150]

Heeding the counsel of his advisers, Mazarin postponed registration of the bull until a *lit de justice* in December. However, even then he had to placate Parlement's Gallican sympathies by convincing the papal nuncio to add a provision to the letters accompanying the bull stating that "no new jurisdiction is attributed to the bishops and archbishops in our kingdom, beyond that which they already possess."[151] As might well be expected, it was Fouquet who pressed the cardinal to accord this concession to Parlement. To ensure that no one missed their point, the magistrates delegated *Avocat Général* Talon to deliver a discourse at the *lit de justice* that defended the independence of the Gallican church and warned the pope not to consider the bull as a precedent for interfering in French religious affairs. In his conclusion, that "the bulls against Jansen should be administered through the authority of the king, who is the arbiter in these matters," Talon revealed a significant feature of Parlement's response to Jansenism: persecution of Jansenists was acceptable so long as the secular authorities within the kingdom retained ultimate control.[152] Although Parlement's defense of secular jurisdiction in religious affairs was favorable to royal authority, Mazarin was reluctant to support the judges because of his delicate relations with Rome. He even convinced young Louis to write a letter of apology to the pope for Talon's conduct.[153]

The registration of the bull, which proceeded without a word in defense of the Jansenists, did not ensure victory for the anti-Jansenist forces because it only exacerbated the jurisdictional question of Parlement's right to receive *appels comme d'abus*. Marca had warned Mazarin on several occasions that effective enforcement of the bull required that the royal administration curtail Parlement's exercise of this privilege. His protests revealed not so much the fear that the judges would decide cases in favor of the Jansenists as the clergy's hostility to both the secular court's interference in religious affairs and the opportunity the appeal would provide the Jansenists to use Parlement as a forum for their ideas.[154] The issue flared in mid-1659 when the Cathedral Chapter of Beauvais ignored the authority of their bishop and ordered all clergy in the diocese to sign the formulary of 1657. The Jansenist bishop, Choart de Buzenval, filed an *appel comme d'abus* that Parlement readily accepted. Following the advice of Marca and his colleagues, Mazarin directed the council to evoke the case, presumably to pass it on to a group of anti-Jansenist bishops for final judgment.[155]

This action further inflamed the magistrates by aggravating the perennial jurisdictional conflict between the council and Parlement. First President Lamoignon pleaded with Mazarin to allow the case to remain at his court. Lamoignon had a personal interest in the case because Buzenval was his cousin, and he was "particularly indebted to his family, his mother having reared my wife." But more important, he predicted that the cardinal's decision would generate a renewal of the conflict between the councils and Parlement. The Jansenists, he emphasized, would be the major beneficiaries of such a struggle, although the judges did not share their religious convictions, "and thus, a perpetual conflict will form, in which it seems that Parlement will support their [the Jansenists'] cause in general, although it is far removed from their sentiments."[156] Mazarin reluctantly compromised with the judges by convincing the young king to evoke the case directly to himself, thus preserving, at least theoretically, Parlement's right to receive *appels comme d'abus*.[157] The king remained within the bounds of legality and also denied jurisdiction to both the council and a group of bishops. Although Mazarin ultimately secured the evocation of the case with these concessions, however, the passion generated by the Beauvais affair convinced him to postpone definitive judgment.[158] As a result, the formulary—that principal weapon against the Jansenists— remained a dead letter in France for the remainder of his ministry.

An interesting way to illustrate that Parlement's protection of the Jansenists in the 1650s was politically motivated is to trace briefly the judges' response to the sect after Louis XIV assumed personal rule. In April 1661, just a few weeks after the death of Mazarin, the king and his advisers again considered how they might enforce the dormant formulary. As might be expected, Marca believed that a decree of council would suffice to accomplish this. He also reiterated his advice that the king should strip Parlement of its right to receive *appels comme d'abus*. Both Fouquet and Le Tellier, however, were skeptical of the archbishop's proposed solution. They wished to take advantage of Parlement's hostility to Jansenism by having the judges register the conciliar decree. The problem remained the *appel comme d'abus*, and on this point Fouquet was particularly perceptive about the reasons why the Jansenists had been able to solicit Parlement's support in the previous decade. While elaborating upon his disagreement with Marca, Fouquet emphasized that

we should consider the interests of Parlement, whose authority would suffer if a public controversy were resolved by virtue of a [conciliar] decree without the *appel comme d'abus*. . . . It is to be feared that this extraordinary procedure [of denying *appels comme d'abus*] would give the Jansenists a pretext to protest a contravention against all form. The offended parlements would join them, the lesser officials would follow their example, and all would fortify the Jansenist party.[159]

Louis agreed with his ministers. He sent a conciliar decree to Parlement that maintained the compromise of 1659 by preserving the court's right to receive *appels comme d'abus* except in cases involving the formulary, which the king would judge personally. As in 1659, the judges were not totally satisfied, but they did welcome the opportunity both to register a decree of council and to preserve theoretically their asserted prerogatives in religious affairs. More important, the king's decision denied both the pope and the episcopacy judgment of the Jansenists, which accorded with Parlement's Gallican sympathies.[160]

This compromise, settling as it did Parlement's grievances of the previous decade, helps to explain why the judges, who had supported the Jansenists in the 1650s, actually joined the sect's enemies in the following decade. Parlement remained aloof from the dispersal of some of the nuns of Port-Royal in 1664 despite the pleas of leading Jansenists for the court to intervene. In April 1664 and 1665, the court registered without complaint a papal bull and a royal declaration that condemned once again the five propositions "in the sense of Jansen" and ordered the entire French clergy to sign the formulary of 1657. In all these actions, the crown avoided parlementary opposition because Louis XIV, unlike Mazarin, respected the judges' jurisdiction and aligned himself with *parlementaire* Gallicanism by attempting to keep the pope's involvement in the Jansenist affair at a minimum. This change in royal policy broke the tenuous bonds between the judges and the sect.[161] Indeed, if the Jansenists subsequently escaped the renewed attacks against them, this was due far more to a growing rift between the monarchy and the papacy after 1661, which made the resolution of religious problems (including Jansenism) extremely difficult, than to any action in the sect's favor at the Parlement of Paris.[162]

This summary account of the relations between the judges and the Jansenists is, of course, incomplete because the events of the 1650s were only a brief episode in a religious controversy that spanned two centuries of French history. But the present analysis is sufficient to demonstrate that in another crucial area of "affairs of state" Parlement retained the ability after the Fronde to influence the course of royal policies and to impede the successful implementation of those they opposed. It also exposes the reasons for the judges' frequent defense of the Jansenists. But these reasons do not substantiate the views of those scholars who have interpreted Parlement's opposition to royal religious policies as a sign of an extensive spread of Jansenist ideas among the judges. Neither supportive nor benevolently neutral, all but a small faction of the *parlementaires* remained hostile to the sect. Parlement became a rallying point for the Jansenists only when their cause became inextricably bound to the judges' desire to defend the Gallican church from papal interference, to protect their jurisdiction in ecclesiastical affairs (in this case, the *appel comme d'abus*), and to prevent the royal councils from intervening in matters the magistrates considered to be in their own area of competence. Although the Jansenists showed great skill in exploiting these issues to their advantage, they converted few judges in the process. Judicial support for the sect faded quickly whenever royal policy became compatible with the magistrates' sensitivity for Gallican liberties and Parlement's jurisdiction.

The royal victory in the Fronde had neither diminished the magistrates' desire to preserve their political influence and administrative powers nor reduced their determination to oppose the extraordinary policies of Mazarin's administration. The results of Parlement's opposition were mixed. The court had certainly not prevented the government's reliance on policies of expediency. Throughout the 1650s, Mazarin and Fouquet continued to procure funds through financial expedients, the royal councils achieved more than nominal success in removing litigation relating to royal policies from the court, and the king and his ministers remained determined to eradicate Jansenism. Furthermore, the judges were hardly revolutionaries. They conducted their opposition without offering broad reforms in the state or establishing sustained alliances with other discontented groups. Parlement preferred compromise to revolt, and perhaps this moderation helps to explain why the tumultuous events of the 1650s did not result in a new Fronde. Nevertheless, despite these limited royal gains and the judges' defensive stance, Parlement remained more than a minor irritant to the royal administration. The foregoing survey of the court's challenge to royal financial, judicial, and religious policies reveals how frequently the judges intervened in affairs of state and modified, if not totally dismantled, the government's programs. Upon Mazarin's death in March 1661, the question of Parlement's political authority, its relations with the king's councils, and indeed the entire issue of confusion of powers remained unresolved.

In retrospect, Parlement's strength in the 1650s rested on two foundations. One was a legacy of the Fronde. The crown had not curtailed the effectiveness of the administrative machinery the judges relied upon to oppose royal policies. The magistrates used singly or in combination judicial and administrative decrees, remonstrances, plenary sessions, and judicial "strikes" to frustrate the royal administration. The second source of *parlementaire* strength lay in the government's weakness. The unpopularity of royal policies, particularly financial ones, generated a great deal of public support for the judges: to silence the court with force might have provoked rebellion in Paris and elsewhere. In addition, Parlement's effective and coordinated use of its duties and powers stands in sharp contrast to Mazarin's inability to manage even the royal representatives in the court. The first president and the *gens du roi* quarreled with each other and with the royal ministers, thereby leaving Parlement virtually unsupervised. Finally, Mazarin, under the influence of Fouquet, consistently chose to compromise with the judges rather than provoke a major confrontation. To be sure, royal concessions dovetailed with Parlement's own reluctance to pursue open rebellion, thus contributing to prevent a repetition of the events of 1648. Nevertheless, the continual modification of royal policies reduced their intended impact. Indecisiveness and confusion at the highest levels of the royal administration only encouraged the judges to continue their frequently successful opposition. When young Louis XIV surprised everyone and announced upon Mazarin's death that he would assume personal rule, he had to recognize that Parlement's vitality rested on a combination of that institution's own strength and the government's weakness if he was to silence his recalcitrant court of law.

CHAPTER FIVE

Parlement in Submission, 1661–1673

The preceding chapters of this study have emphasized the continuity in relations between the crown and Parlement during the final years of Mazarin's ministry and the first decade of Louis XIV's personal rule. This continuity, however, was rooted more in the limits to royal control of the court than in the advent of absolutism. Neither the king nor the cardinal attempted to control the *parlementaires* by threatening their economic vested interests, by recapturing magisterial appointment, or by undermining Parlement's status as a social corporation. But in the matter of Parlement's political activities, Louis was determined to reverse the trends of previous decades, and during the 1660s and 1670s he successfully reduced the court's ability to oppose royal policies and intervene at will in affairs of state. When viewed in contrast to the judges' conduct in previous years, Louis's accomplishment deserves recognition. Nevertheless, while he achieved better political control of Parlement than Mazarin had attained, he introduced few lasting innovations in the court's duties and powers, and he never fully excluded the magistrates from participating in affairs of state. The political decline of Parlement, although striking to contemporaries and historians alike, was neither complete nor irreversible, as the Sun King's successors learned in the following century.

NEW DIRECTIONS IN ROYAL POLICY

For Louis XIV to diminish the political role of Parlement, he had to strike at both foundations of the court's successful opposition in the previous decade. On one hand, this required direct action against the judges' extensive administrative responsibilities and means of opposition. On the other hand, the king had to rectify the weaknesses in Cardinal Mazarin's administration that had left the government so vulnerable to judicial opposition. Beginning in 1661, Louis began to erode both sources of Parlement's political power. An examination of the ways he eliminated the weak spots in the government's relations with the judges will provide a context for the more direct actions he took against the court.

One of the principal weaknesses of Cardinal Mazarin's administration was the unpopularity of its extraordinary financial policies. By repudiating these policies in the years immediately following the cardinal's death, Louis XIV both improved the crown's relations with the judges and removed one of the pretexts for their opposition. In November 1661, for example, Louis established a *Chambre de Justice* to punish those who had mishandled royal finances during the administration of Mazarin.[1] The chamber was an extraordinary commission composed of councillors of state, *maîtres des requêtes,* and presidents and councillors of the Parisian and provincial parlements.[2] In theory, Parlement had much to object to in the creation of the chamber. The judges had opposed extraordinary judicial commissions in the past, but the initiation of this Chamber of Justice placed them in an awkward position. The stated intent of the body was the punishment of those who had abused and been responsible for the financial policies of expediency Parlement had so vehemently protested in the past. The culprits included not only Nicolas Fouquet, the *surintendant des finances,* but also many tax farmers whom the court had denounced as recently as 1659. Furthermore, *parlementaires* were to hold key posts in the chamber. The king chose First President Lamoignon to preside over the commission and named *Avocat Général* Talon as its *procureur général.* In addition, *Président à Mortier* Nesmond and councillors Catinat, Brillac, Renard, and Fayet were given seats. Any resistance on the part of Parlement to the chamber, therefore, would have seemed incongruous with the desire of the magistrates both to secure and to participate in a reformation of financial administration. Indeed, when the chamber was established, Parlement addressed a note to Chancellor Séguier stating that it would be impossible

to exaggerate our joy about the establishment of a Chamber of Justice for the investigation of financiers and tax farmers, which has been to the present the wish of the people, the hope of the intelligent, the terror of the evil, and the hope of all who are oppressed. . . . It is by this means that the king and his council undertake a war against the gravest plague of the state . . . [namely] the avarice of some ministers, officials, tax farmers, and financiers, who have forgotten all [morality] in their pursuit to satisfy their passion.[3]

Similarly, at the first session of the chamber, both Lamoignon and Talon praised the commission and "these works of reformation."[4]

Certainly, all did not run smoothly at the chamber, which met continually until 1665 and was officially disbanded in 1669. Many tax farmers escaped punishment, and when Louis included in his declaration of December 1665 a grant of amnesty to the tax farmers and a provision that their relatives could enter the judiciary, Parlement was indeed upset.

Moreover, when Colbert used the chamber to issue his *rente* reforms, this also inflamed the crown's relations with the court. Nevertheless, the chamber proved to be a useful, if not totally effective, tool for exposing and punishing the financial abuses of previous decades. Many tax farmers were called before the commission and their records examined carefully. The judges ordered the death penalty for some and heavy fines for others.[5] In all, the crown recovered 110 million *livres* from the tax farmers. Allotments on tax farms were reduced to 4 percent instead of rates as high as 25 percent when Fouquet was *surintendant des finances*. If the crown did not dispense totally with tax farmers, it at least brought them under a greater degree of control. Their accounts were rigorously supervised in the future, and Colbert was able to increase revenue from the farms through better collection procedures.[6] If it is also recalled that the two issues that angered Parlement about the chamber—the permission for tax farmers to enter the court and the *rente* reforms—were eventually resolved in favor of the judges, the Chamber of Justice stands as a royal success in pleasing the court and correcting and punishing some of the financial abuses that had generated conflict between the crown and Parlement in the past.

The impulse to reform finances was not limited to punishing tax farmers. In order to render the collection of taxes more efficient, Louis abolished the office of *surintendant des finances* late in 1661 and placed financial affairs in the hands of Colbert, who was aided by several *intendants des finances*. At the same time, Louis created a separate Conseil royal des Finances in order to centralize financial administration in a single body, which was preferable to the dispersion of financial affairs among several councils as had been the case before 1661.[7] If not in theory, then at least in practice this reorganization gave Colbert as much authority in the realm of finances as Fouquet had enjoyed before him. But Colbert used his authority differently. Recognizing that *rentes* were a drain on the royal treasury, he aspired to curtail them. As noted previously, he was not altogether successful: he had to modify his original plan of liquidating all the *rentes* that had been issued since 1639 and make concessions to the *parlementaires*. Nevertheless, his *rente* reforms resulted in annual savings of 4 million *livres*. Colbert was also determined to alleviate a major cause of provincial popular unrest by reducing the *taille personnelle* (direct tax on individuals, not property) from 42 to 34 million *livres* between 1661 and 1671.[8] A declaration of May 6, 1662, discharged all debts due on royal taxation for the years 1647 to 1656.[9] In addition, the *brevet* for the *taille* in 1663 reduced the weight of this tax by 4 million *livres*.[10] Colbert achieved further economy by repurchasing one-quarter of the offices the crown had created and sold since 1630, thus securing annual savings of 2 million *livres* in salary payments. He was even able to increase the revenue from royal demesne to 5 million *livres* a year by 1671, while in 1661 such income was negligible. In all, during the first decade of Louis's personal rule, net royal income doubled, and except for a brief period during the War of Devolution, income exceeded expenditure. The king was proud of this achievement, and the royalist *Gazette de France* did not miss the opportunity to boast in 1663 that "the people will no longer be able to doubt that they are the most happy subjects in the world, because they have a sovereign whose only object . . . is their good fortune."[11]

Another notable feature of the 1660s that provides a context for Colbert's financial reforms was that except for brief wars against England and the United Provinces, the first decade of Louis's personal rule was a time of peace. After twenty-five years of continual warfare, the nation enjoyed a temporary respite in which to recuperate. The government was able to shift from the seemingly perennial wartime economy and temporarily avoid the extraordinary financial policies of Mazarin and Fouquet. To be sure, this condition did not last much longer than 1672 when the king embarked upon an aggressive and expensive foreign policy that proved burdensome to the populace and disastrous to many of Colbert's financial reforms. But while peace lasted, Louis intended to make good use of it. He was able to turn his attention to domestic affairs, and the first decade of his personal rule witnessed the host of administrative, judicial, financial, military, and economic reforms for which he is remembered. As Louis himself noted in his memoirs to the Dauphin, in the 1660s "all was calm everywhere; neither unrest [*mouvement*] nor fear or appearance of rebellion was able to interrupt me or oppose my projects; peace had been established with my neighbors."[12] Paul Pellisson, who wrote these words for the king, noted in his own history of the first eighteen years of Louis's personal rule that "one saw in France six years of peace, when the interior of the state took on an entirely new face, [and gained] such a reputation outside that jealousy filled all neighboring nations."[13] Even the Venetian ambassador to France reported to his superiors in 1663 that Louis was not likely to undertake war in the near future, though he might have desired to do so, because it would disrupt his financial reforms and upset the stability he had nurtured in domestic affairs.[14]

Colbert's financial reforms and the peace which marked the 1660s had a significant impact on the crown's relations with Parlement. In the first place, Louis removed from the court an issue that had consistently antagonized the judges in the past. The *parlementaires* had long called for reform in the royal financial administration. When Louis himself undertook such a project, Parlement could do little but approve. Moreover, by taking the additional care to modify those reforms that directly affected the judges, such as those pertaining to *rentes*, in such a way that the magistrates barely felt their effect, the king further removed the wind from the sails of Parlement's opposition to royal financial policies. Contrary to the 1650s, Parlement's registers were virtually silent on financial affairs in the sixties. In part, this was owing to the fact that during the first decade of his personal rule the king began to reduce Parlement's ability to resist his policies. But in large measure, it also resulted from the determination of Louis and Colbert to remove the obvious abuses that troubled the king's subjects.

Second, by removing such a major source of discontent, Louis was able to erode the public support the judges received by their opposition and channel it to himself. In the 1650s, Parlement had easily asserted that its resistance was in the common interest of all the king's subjects, and any attempt by Mazarin and Fouquet to trim the court's political influence might have provoked a rebellion. In the 1660s, however, the pretexts for judicial opposition gradually diminished. For the first time in several decades, Parlement was isolated and vulnerable to a redefinition of its political authority.

Finally, a decade of peace reenforced these implications of Louis's financial reforms. For if war had originally turned the government to financial expedients, it had also led the crown to favor compromise with its sovereign courts because the king and his ministers feared that internal dissension would bring disaster both on the battlefield and at the negotiating table. With the pressures of war gone, the king could turn his attention to redefining the privileges and prerogatives of his often recalcitrant magistrates.

Certainly, events after 1672 destroyed the peace and helped to erase many of the achievements of Colbert's financial policies. As Louis embarked upon the costly foreign policy that was to mark the rest of his reign, Colbert and his successors often had to have recourse to the very financial expedients that had earned Fouquet his notoriety. As French armies took to the field, *rentes* flourished at high interest rates, tax farmers again became a keystone of finances, and both direct and indirect taxation increased. Nevertheless, the waste and misery that marked the France of Louis's later years should not obscure the achievements of his earlier years. If Parlement accepted the very financial policies later in the reign that it had opposed before 1661, it was because the king used his first decade of peace to limit some of the powers that the court relied upon to sustain its opposition.

Another weak point in the crown's relations with Parlement in the 1650s was the influence of Nicolas Fouquet in Cardinal Mazarin's advisory circles. Not only was Fouquet largely responsible for the financial measures that had so often generated Parlement's opposition, but he was also the prime mover behind the cardinal's policy of compromising with the court. The arrest of Fouquet and his subsequent trial enabled the crown to remove both of these obstacles.

For most contemporaries and historians alike, the trial of Fouquet symbolized the dawning of a new era in French history. When the young king attacked Fouquet, he not only audaciously challenged a powerful and influential minister, but also repudiated the financial policies of the previous decades that were permeated by inefficiency, corruption, and expediency. The punishment of the ex-minister and *procureur général* was the perfect complement to the financial reforms Louis and Colbert simultaneously pursued. The events surrounding the fall of Fouquet are well known.[15] Louis had been content to keep Fouquet in his posts after Mazarin died because he had been a talented and loyal servant, despite his personal aggrandizement through royal funds. Nevertheless, Fouquet quickly became an anachronism among Louis's advisers. The end of the war rendered his extraordinary financial policies less necessary and his personal corruption and ambition less tolerable. At the same time, Colbert, who had always disapproved of Fouquet's financial policies, encouraged the king to dispose of the powerful minister.[16] In September 1661, Louis sealed Fouquet's fate with charges of financial mismanagement and treason. The agonizing and dramatic trial that followed lasted over two years, from mid-1662 until the end of 1664. Royal attorneys presented literally thousands of documents to prove Fouquet's guilt, and the ex-minister himself wrote countless memoranda in his own defense. When the members of the Chamber of Justice ultimately found him guilty as charged, however, they ordered only the confiscation of his property and banished him from the kingdom. Louis, who had clearly indicated that he desired the death penalty, was so angered that he reversed the decision and instead sentenced him to perpetual incarceration. The king was determined to destroy ruthlessly this symbol of the government of the past.

While planning the arrest of Fouquet, Louis had ensured that the Parlement of Paris would not interfere in the trial. Remembering that the *parlementaires* claimed the right to be judged by their peers in a plenary session, Louis had persuaded Fouquet to sell his charge of *procureur général* before he ordered his arrest. In this fashion, the king prevented a recurrence of the events which had marked the trials of Croissy-Fouquet in 1653 and Claude Vallée in 1657, when the magistrates used their privilege of judging their peers to oppose the royal administration. Fouquet did petition the court to accept his case in July 1662, and Parlement sent delegates to the king to request the transfer of his case to their jurisdiction. Louis, however, was under no legal obligation to consent to their request, and Parlement could do little but defer to his decision.[17]

Nevertheless, several *parlementaires* sat in the Chamber of Justice and their role in the trial is somewhat controversial. Lamoignon and Talon, for example, were responsible for many delays in the opening stages of the trial. The king and his advisers complained about this frequently, and several times they ordered the two judges to hasten the proceedings.[18] Apparently, the *parlementaires* paid little heed to the royal reprimands, and Louis finally removed Lamoignon from the chamber in December 1662 and relieved Talon of his duties in November 1663.[19] The question naturally arises whether the two magistrates actively supported Fouquet's cause and sought to protect him by extending the length of the trial.

Nothing indicates that Talon sympathized with Fouquet's plight. He was a known enemy of the ex-minister and most contemporary accounts of the trial agree that his procrastination was due far more to a time-consuming love affair with the widow of Marshal L'Hôpital than to any deep-seated political motives. Lamoignon's role is more complex. Several times in the early stages of the trial, the first president seemed to act openly in favor of Fouquet. It was upon his request, for example, that the king appointed the councillors Renard and Fayet to the commission—they subsequently voted for Fouquet's banishment instead of death. Lamoignon also helped Fouquet to secure benefit of counsel despite the strong protests of Séguier and Colbert. The first president's complicity with Fouquet is given additional credibility by a document Fouquet drew up in 1657 or 1658, which outlined a plan his supporters were to follow if he were arrested. In it he spoke highly of several *parlementaires* whom he trusted and considered his clients. Among them he included Lamoignon, "who is entirely obligated to me for the post he now holds [in Parlement], which he never would have received, whatever his merits, if I had not conceived the idea . . . [and] cultivated and took charge of everything with unbelievable . . . care." Fouquet confidently wrote that "he will make every effort in my behalf . . . and he would sooner relinquish his charge than cease solicitation for me."[20] Perhaps to Fouquet's consternation, Lamoignon refused to sacrifice his post for the former *procureur général*. In fact, there is reason to believe that the first president's temporization in 1662 was not intended to further Fouquet's cause, although delays in the trial did enable the ex-minister to prepare his defense, but rather to show his dissatisfaction with the chamber's other activities, such as the *rente* reforms and the recent reduction in judicial salaries. After the king had rejected his solicitations on these issues, Lamoignon visibly expressed his displeasure by decreasing his efforts in the chamber, and thus Louis felt obliged to relieve him of his duties.[21] This interpretation of Lamoignon's conduct is more plausible because the royal administration was well aware of Fouquet's implicating document before the king chose the first president to preside over the chamber.[22] Apparently, Louis believed that Lamoignon would not risk his career to defend Fouquet and events proved him correct.

The removal of Fouquet from his important posts in the ministry and Parlement had significant implications for the crown's relations with its leading court of law. The punishment of the *procureur général* confirmed Colbert's and Louis's intention to repudiate the extraordinary financial policies that had generated much of the conflict between the crown and Parlement. But equally important for the judges, Fouquet was the last representative in high governmental circles who consistently advocated a policy of compromise with the *parlementaires*. With his passing, Louis's remaining advisers were individuals who were exceedingly hostile to the pretensions of Parlement. In the first decade of his personal rule, Louis relied heavily upon a "Council of Three" to advise him: Lionne, Le Tellier, and after the removal of Fouquet, Colbert.[23] In the 1650s, Le Tellier and Colbert had encouraged Mazarin to take vigorous action against the court, but Mazarin had continually adopted Fouquet's more moderate approach. With the death of the cardinal and the arrest of Fouquet, however, the path was cleared for a firmer stand against judicial opposition. Without question, the policy of compromise did not totally disappear, as is evident from the many concessions the judges enjoyed on issues touching their social and economic interests in the period of Louis XIV's personal rule. Nevertheless, in the all-important matter of Parlement's political influence and its ability to oppose royal policy, the sentiments of the king and his leading advisers dovetailed perfectly: they were of one mind to curtail Parlement's ability to participate in affairs of state. Thus the fall of Fouquet, like the financial reforms of Colbert and the king's maintenance of peace, created an atmosphere conducive to a major redefinition of the privileges and prerogatives of Parlement.

The poor relations between the royal administration and the king's representatives in Parlement had constituted another weakness in the crown's position against the judges in the 1650s. First President Bellièvre and *Avocat Général* Talon often resisted royal policies and used their influence and duties in the court to incite the magistrates to opposition. *Avocat Général* Bignon was most often swept along by the more aggressive Talon. Fouquet, in his dual role of *surintendant des finances* and *procureur général*, could please no one. The *avocats généraux* frequently usurped his administrative duties, and personal disagreements exacerbated the hostility to his financial policies. The appointment of Lamoignon as first president in

1658 had helped to ease tensions somewhat, but it was hardly sufficient to rectify what Fouquet's biographer has called "the complete anarchy of the *parquet* [collectively, the *gens du roi*]."[24] In the 1660s, Louis improved this situation considerably.

In the first place, the government abandoned the belief that an effective way to manage the court was to have a *procureur général* who was also a minister. The experience of Fouquet had clearly shown that such an individual was extremely vulnerable. In many respects, the simultaneous exercise of posts in the ministry and Parlement represented a rudimentary form of ministerial responsibility. While the judges certainly could not topple a minister, they could pressure him to modify his policies if he hoped to retain influence in the court and satisfactory relations with them. Louis may not have been cognizant of these implications when he approved as Fouquet's successor Achille II de Harlay, but the choice turned out to be a wise one. Harlay, who served as *procureur général* from 1661 to his death in 1667, came from a long line of *parlementaires*. He was a *maître des requêtes* before he became *procureur général*.[25] Unlike Fouquet, Harlay did not enjoy a prestigious position in high governmental circles. The king severed all ties between the ministry and Parlement. Contemporary sources rarely mention Harlay, and his tenure in office seems to have been unexciting. But apparently he loyally served the crown, for the king allowed his son, Achille III, to succeed him. Even Louis recognized the extraordinary nature of this privilege because the office of *procureur général* was not subject to the *droit annuel*.[26]

Louis was no less satisfied with Achille III. Like his father, the younger Harlay served the king faithfully. As noted previously, it was he who complained when the royal administration failed to enforce its edicts on the abolition of age dispensations to the judges. What little survives of his correspondence for the period under consideration indicates that he enjoyed cordial relations with Colbert. The minister often sent him royal decrees that he intended Parlement to register for preliminary examination and comment. Harlay also strove to supervise the enforcement of royal decrees in Parlement's jurisdiction.[27] Even his own writing reflected his desire to bend to the royal will. While he was *procureur général*, for example, he drew up a short compendium on Parlement's internal organization and authority. In it he stated categorically that "Parlement ought only to have cognizance of particular affairs of justice," and he listed many historical precedents to substantiate the view that French kings had forbidden the court to "mix in affairs of state."[28] Louis was apparently so pleased with his performance that he appointed Harlay to the post of first president later in the century. Saint-Simon recalled in his memoirs that as first president, Harlay "knew above all how to govern his court with an authority that does not suffer repetition, and that no other first president was able to achieve before him. . . . Besides, sustained in all by the crown [*Cour*] . . . he was the slave and the very humble servant of whatever was in its favor."[29]

Louis also successfully maintained good relations with the first president and the *gens du roi* he had inherited from Mazarin. Although historians have yet to uncover the personal papers of these *parlementaires*, certain conclusions may be drawn about their relations with the crown. When Mazarin consented to the appointment of Guillaume de Lamoignon as first president in 1658, he shared the hope of his advisers that the *maître des requêtes* would be a docile servant of the crown. Lamoignon, of course, never developed into the passive official Mazarin had expected. Nevertheless, his appointment proved to be a wise one. Lamoignon was a forceful, ambitious, and independent individual. He rarely hesitated to intercede on behalf of his court to the king. He vigorously opposed Colbert's policies on *rentes* and magisterial salaries, and repeatedly attempted to change the king's opinions on the edicts that stabilized the prices of offices in the court and allowed the relatives of tax farmers to enter the judiciary.[30] The first president also took an active role in guiding the course of Louis's judicial reforms of 1667 and 1670, defending Parlement's jurisdiction and even formulating his own plans for a reformation of judicial administration.[31] Despite this streak of independence, however, Lamoignon never sought to incite Parlement to active opposition against the crown. Rather, he preferred to deal directly with the king, and while he often remonstrated about royal policies, he consistently exhorted the judges to defer to Louis's final decision.[32] Unlike Bellièvre, Lamoignon never turned to Parlement to oppose the royal policies with which he disagreed. Even Colbert, who was often at odds with Lamoignon, noted in a memorandum of 1663 that "although the first president is persuaded that his esteem and his service ought to bring him all he desires, [he nevertheless is] a man of great merit, incapable of plots, who never relinquishes his service in favor of the king."[33]

As *avocat général* Jérôme II Bignon (who replaced his father, Jérôme I, in 1656) had rarely taken any initiative in the 1650s and he exhibited this same quality after 1661. Talon, on the other hand, had often urged the magistrates to oppose royal policies after the Fronde. To the consternation of Mazarin, Séguier, and Fouquet, Talon proved to be one of the most recalcitrant foes of the government in Parlement. Often he was more adamant in opposing royal judicial, financial, and religious policies than the judges themselves, urging them on several occasions to reject royal compromises that were quite acceptable to the majority of the magistrates. On one occasion, Mazarin had even ordered his exile. Mysteriously, however, contemporary sources rarely mention the contentious Talon after 1661. His speeches no longer cluttered the court's registers, and not once in the 1660s did he seriously oppose royal policies. It is almost impossible to explain this sudden change in conduct without access to his missing papers. A single clue that survives are several letters Colbert wrote to Mazarin in 1656. On September 7, Colbert, who was at that time the personal intendant of the cardinal, reported to Mazarin that Talon had visited him to express his good intentions and his desire to serve the first minister. Colbert believed him and requested that Mazarin "cultivate the good disposition of . . . Talon."[34] The cardinal, however, was extremely skeptical of Talon's protestations of fidelity (subsequent events proved him correct), and he warned Colbert not to be so gullible in the future about Talon, "who only seeks to acquire credit in his court, which can only be done at our expense."[35] Colbert replied, "I do not believe that he is a man we should abandon entirely, but only to manage him and avoid his [extreme conduct] in a pressing occasion; and finally, I feel that he is one of [the king's] lukewarm [*tièdes*] servants, who during the reestablishment of royal authority does not merit to be excluded, but used to our advantage."[36] The details surrounding Colbert's role in Talon's sudden conversion in 1661 unhappily remain obscure. As early as 1656, however, Colbert claimed to have the ability to change the *avocat général*'s conduct, and after becoming Louis's most trusted adviser, Colbert was able to fulfill his prophecy to Mazarin.

In considering the ways Louis XIV reduced Parlement's ability to oppose royal policies, therefore, a survey of the direct actions he took against the court would be insufficient. Colbert's financial reforms in an era of peace, the removal of Fouquet from the court and the ministry, and improved relations with the first president and the *gens du roi* did not alter the functions or pretensions of the judges. But together they were of considerable consequence to Parlement's authority because they rectified weaknesses that had left the crown vulnerable to judicial opposition in previous decades.

REDEFINING THE "NATURAL LIMITS" OF PARLEMENT'S AUTHORITY

The conflicts between the crown and Parlement in the 1650s revealed that weaknesses in Mazarin's government were only partially responsible for the magistrates' often successful opposition to royal policies. Effective parlementary resistance also rested on the court's extensive administrative duties and machinery. The right to register and remonstrate royal decrees, to hold plenary sessions, and to issue judicial and administrative decrees all proved to be formidable obstacles to a government that desired the submission of the judges. Royal control of Parlement depended in large measure upon the successful redefinition and supervision of these powerful privileges.

Perhaps Parlement's most successful weapons of opposition in the 1650s were the judicial and administrative decrees it issued to prevent the implementation of royal policy. The court exonerated litigants from paying extraordinary taxes and prohibited the lesser courts in its area of jurisdiction from executing the royal decrees it opposed. Parlement's practice of issuing decrees in this fashion set in bold relief the confusion of powers that had involved the judges in protracted struggles with the king's councils and had considerably diminished the impact of royal programs. On July 8, 1661, Louis issued a decree he hoped would rectify the problem of confusion of powers and clarify the relationship between his councils and the sovereign courts. It ordered that in the future all sovereign courts would "defer to the decrees of his councils, forbidding them [the courts] to take cognizance of affairs and proceedings that His Majesty retains and reserves to himself and his councils." The decree also required the *gens du roi* to consult with the chancellor before they offered any advice on legislation before Parlement. If at any time they or the judges had any reservations about conciliar decrees, they were to deliver their complaints directly to the king rather than take independent action.

In the preface to the decree, Louis addressed the problem of confusion of powers, noting how the sovereign courts, "to which His Majesty has given the power to judge in last resort, have [frequently] contested his authority and issued orders contrary to those of his councils." He had especially harsh words for the *gens du roi*: "It has been even more strange that those who carry the title of *gens du roi*, ... who were established principally to maintain his [the king's] authority, and who ought always to see to the conservation of his interests, have been guilty of such enterprises, and that some have abused the name and word of His Majesty to oppose his policies."[37] Although the decree applied to all the sovereign courts, one cannot help but get the impression that these words were directed specifically to *Avocat Général* Talon.

The decree not only dealt a severe blow to the court's ability to oppose royal policies, but theoretically threatened Parlement's entire judicial and administrative jurisdiction. In the first place, the king's action limited Parlement's right of judicial review. The councils were now legally free to issue royal policies through their decrees, and the king was under no obligation to submit conciliar decisions to the scrutiny of his Parlement. Thus, even if the judges retained the right of remonstrance, they could only delay or suspend the implementation of legislation which the king formally presented to the court for registration. Any pretense on the part of the judges to extend this power over the actions of the councils was swept away by the decree. Moreover, because the new regulations failed to specify the limits of the councils' authority, they jeopardized Parlement's judicial function by sanctioning a virtual *carte blanche* for conciliar evocations. Finally, by officially establishing the councils as superior bodies over the law courts, the king indirectly but clearly challenged Parlement's asserted privilege of participating with the king and his ministers in the resolution of "affairs of state."

Whether Louis developed these implications to their fullest extent is an issue that requires examination. But in July 1661, the *parlementaires* immediately saw the decree as a threat to their authority, jurisdiction, and prestige. A week after the Conseil d'En haut issued the decree, Talon and Bignon sent a lengthy memorandum to Chancellor Séguier protesting against the decree, "which seems to condemn the conduct of all the sovereign courts of the kingdom." They denied that Parlement had ever intended to oppose the king. Rather, it had been extraordinary conciliar activity that had provoked the court's resistance to royal policies. In fact, they emphasized "the moderation with which we [the *parlementaires*] have suffered, without a murmur, all the novelties the Council of Finances has introduced against the jurisdiction of the parlements and the liberty of the king's subjects." If the decree were sent to the lesser courts in Parlement's jurisdiction in its present form, they asserted, it would injure the honor, dignity, and function of the court.[38]

Louis refused to give satisfaction to his *avocats généraux*. On July 21, deputies from the *enquêtes* and *requêtes* chambers requested a plenary session to discuss the decree.[39] For two weeks, First President Lamoignon refused to grant a general session, but the persistent requests of the deputies finally convinced him to allow one on August 5. When the judges assembled, Talon delivered a long speech urging the judges to accept the decree without opposition. His words not only confirmed his own submission to the royal will, but underlined the potential impact of the decree on Parlement's authority.[40]

He began by noting that when he had first seen the council's decree he had shared "the common opinion" of the judges that it was "contrary to the ordinances and liberty of the king's subjects . . . and fatal to the dignity of the sovereign courts; that [the king] wished to destroy and reverse legitimate authority and despoil [the judges'] functions." But he added that a second reading of the text convinced him that this was not the king's intention. He then advanced three principal arguments in favor of the decree.

The first was that the decree represented the initial act of a "universal reformation in all parts of the state that we [the judges] will welcome." Talon thus exposed a weak point in the opposition of the magistrates: they

had always called for such a reformation, and the king was simply re-
sponding to their desires. Talon noted that during the war years, royal
authority had suffered "some sort of eclipse," and the king simply wanted
to reestablish in the courts "the rules of prudence [and] the limits of their
authority, . . . [in order to] strike a just equilibrium." Second, the *avocat
général* admitted that the decree gave the councils a veritable free hand in
evocations, and as he had done in the past, he stated that frequent evocations were indeed an abuse. But he assured the judges that the king also
intended to regulate the activity of his councils and to limit their excur-
sions into Parlement's jurisdiction. Finally, Talon reminded his colleagues
that the source of conflict between their court and the councils had been
extraordinary financial policies: royal policies of expediency had provoked
Parlement's opposition, which had in turn generated the councils' policy
of nullifying Parlement's decrees and evoking cases from the court. He
admitted that if the July decree had been issued during the war, "we could
have been . . . [justifiably] angered . . . considering the prohibitions it contains as an attempt to establish all sorts of impositions without consent."
But Talon hastened again to reassure the judges that with the onset of
peace, Louis intended to curtail financial expedients, thus removing the
cause of Parlement's opposition as well as the councils' pretext for evoking
cases from the court.

As might be expected, the judges were not entirely pleased with Talon's
reasoning. His assurance of the king's beneficence toward the court did
not obscure the fact that the decree elevated the councils as a superior
body over the sovereign courts and empowered them to issue decrees and
evoke cases without the approval of the magistrates. Talon's assertion that
the decree did not represent a threat to Parlement because the court's
conflict with the councils would diminish on its own account owing to the
end of the war likewise offered little consolation to the offended judges. As
a result, the plenary session delegated Lamoignon to visit the king and
request the revocation of the decree. On September 2, he reported on his
conversation with Louis. He told the judges that the king "did not intend
to diminish the court's authority, but only to regulate its functions as well
as those of the councils." The king had assured the first president that if
the decree seemed "troublesome," it did not concern the Parlement of
Paris, "but only the other sovereign courts, which in troubled times took
extraordinary actions" against the royal will.[41] This minor concession to
the judges, however, did nothing to change the terms of the decree or to
reduce its implications for Parlement's authority.

Most historians of Parlement agree that the conciliar decree of July
1661 seriously threatened the jurisdictional authority of Parlement and its
pretension to participate in affairs of state.[42] This assumption, if based
solely on the text of the decree, is correct. Nevertheless, in assessing the

impact of the decree as it was actually implemented, it is important to draw a distinction between Parlement's judicial function and its practice of opposing royal policies and participating in affairs of state. This is necessary because it seems that the royal administration itself seriously attempted to distinguish between the two areas of the court's activity.

After 1661, the tensions between Parlement and the royal councils subsided considerably, not because the latter completely dominated and usurped the functions of the former, but because Talon's prophecy that Louis intended to prevent the councils from abusing their officially recognized superiority was correct. In his memoirs to the Dauphin that dealt with the year 1661, Louis recognized that the conflicts between the councils and Parlement were not solely the fault of the magistrates. "Even my council," he wrote, "instead of regulating other jurisdictions, often added only confusion by a strange quantity of contradictory decrees... issued under my name as if by myself, which rendered the disorder all the more shameful."[43] Only two weeks after he issued the decree of July 8, Louis had informed a group of his highest advisers that "he desires that nothing happens in the council which will give the sovereign courts subject to remonstrate to him about the execution of the decree that prohibits them from making enterprises against his authority or the decrees of the council.... [Tomorrow the king will tell the councillors of state] that his intention is that no order will emerge from his council that is contrary to past ordinances."[44] Louis desired, therefore, to regulate both his sovereign courts and his councils. It was not his intention to deprive the courts of their judicial function, but to prevent them from opposing his policies and assuming an exaggerated role in affairs of state.

Both the administrative correspondence of the period and the registers of Parlement and the councils indicate that the king intended to preserve the judicial competence of the court. When in June 1671, for example, a Madame de Villancourt attempted to secure a conciliar evocation of her case before Parlement for reasons that had little legal foundation, Talon protested to Le Tellier, who replied that the council would refuse her request. Le Tellier stated that the king did not wish "to authorize any decree contrary to the order that must be maintained in justice."[45] Not long after he became chancellor of France in 1677, Le Tellier assured *Procureur Général* Harlay that "I will let nothing pass [before me] that could be prejudicial to the authority of Parlement."[46] One historian of the royal councils has also noted that as chancellor, Le Tellier carefully scrutinized petitions for *cassation* of Parlement's decrees and rejected many that lacked sound legal foundation.[47]

An examination of conciliar records for the period 1661 to 1673 reveals that the amount of litigation the councils evoked from Parlement and the number of the court's decrees they nullified decreased sharply after the

issuance of the decree of July 1661.[48] On one hand, as Talon had predicted, this resulted from Louis's financial reforms. As the crown resorted
less frequently to extraordinary financial policies and fewer litigants came
before the court to protest royal taxation, the degree of Parlement's opposition and the need for evocations diminished. This was especially true
after 1663 when almost all conflict between Parlement and the councils
over royal financial policies disappeared from the registers of both bodies.
On the other hand, the royal administration simultaneously dissuaded the
councils from evoking cases from Parlement except in instances that were
specifically mentioned in past ordinances. It seems that Louis made a
concerted effort to fulfill the promises Mazarin had made in his name in
the compromises with Parlement of 1657 and 1658 on the subject of
evocations. Many times in the 1660s the *parlementaires* successfully protested conciliar evocations and secured the return of cases to their court.[49]
Occasionally, the councils even returned cases that involved royal financial policies if Parlement proved that it was legally entitled to jurisdiction.[50] Conciliar records also indicate that the crown favored Parlement in
its jurisdictional conflicts with other sovereign courts. All but a few of the
règlements de juges the councils issued favored the Parlement of Paris.[51] In
addition, almost all of the cases the councils evoked from provincial courts
were sent to the Parlement of Paris for definitive judgment.[52] In fact, the
councils seemed to have evoked far more cases from provincial parlements
than from their Parisian counterpart. Thus, if the crown by its decree of
July 8, 1661, in theory granted the councils the authority to sap Parlement
of its judicial duties, it did not attempt in practice to exploit this potential.

The king and his ministers pursued a similar policy in reference to
Parlement's authority in Paris itself. Over the centuries, Parlement had
acquired formidable administrative and police duties in the capital city.
The magistrates supervised the upkeep of highways and streets, and they
issued regulations that concerned public hygiene, the functioning of trade
guilds, and the provision of bread and wood to the citizenry. The court
also maintained public order, punishing vagrants, thieves, and prostitutes.
The judges supervised the Châtelet, which was the criminal tribunal of
the *prévôté* of Paris, and they worked closely with the lieutenant civil of the
prévôté, a judicial official who was charged with preserving public order.
Parlement also supervised municipal elections and finances, which, as has
been noted, involved the court in affairs that dealt with *rentes*. The university and educational system of Paris also fell under the supervision of
Parlement, and its power of censorship was considerable.[53]

There were two notable events during the first decade of Louis XIV's
personal rule that affected Parlement's municipal authority. The first was
a royal edict of March 1667 that abolished the post of lieutenant civil and

replaced it with two distinct offices, a new lieutenant civil and a lieutenant general of police. The edict stated that the motive behind the reorganization was that "the functions of justice and police are often incompatible and of too great a magnitude to be exercised efficiently by a single official in Paris."[54] At this time, Colbert was alarmed at the increasing crime rate in Paris, and he believed that only an official who had specific police powers could rectify the situation.[55] The duties of the lieutenant civil remained those of the past, primarily judicial obligations at the Châtelet. The lieutenant general of police, however, was given wide-ranging powers. He was responsible for maintaining order in the city, provisioning the citizens, lighting the streets, regulating the guilds, and supervising prisons, markets, and hospitals.

Without question, the authority delegated to the lieutenant general overlapped the traditional municipal jurisdiction of Parlement. Nevertheless, Parlement's registers and the correspondence of the first lieutenant general, Nicolas La Reynie, with Colbert indicate that the new official and the judges cooperated and that no serious jurisdictional friction developed between them. In a letter to Colbert dated December 14, 1670, for example, La Reynie reported that he, Lamoignon, Talon, and Harlay had joined forces to confiscate the mass of libelous literature that had flooded Paris and to punish those who had distributed it.[56] On May 23, 1671, the lieutenant general entered Parlement to request that the lighting of city streets be improved. Although this was within his competence, La Reynie told the magistrates that he believed "it belongs only to Parlement to order this and to raise the funds [for this project] if it judges my request reasonable."[57] In fact, one historian has emphasized that the lieutenant general "was an extension of Parlement . . . [who] always exercised his powers jointly with the court. . . . Often his instructions, when they did not come from [Colbert], were given to him by the first president of Parlement or more often by the *procureur général.*"[58] Moreover, even after the creation of the lieutenant general, Parlement continued to register royal legislation and to issue decrees of its own that established markets, regulated guilds, and supervised the operation of Parisian prisons and hospitals.[59] In April and May 1668, when a plague raged near Paris, it was Parlement in conjunction with the Hôtel de Ville that controlled the flow of merchandise along rivers in order to prevent the spread of disease. The judges delegated one of their own colleagues, Lamoignon's son Chrétien, to travel to Laon, Château-Thierry, Reims, and other towns to set up health facilities and to enforce the decisions of the court.[60] Thus, although the establishment of a lieutenant general of police made inroads into the municipal authority of Parlement, there is ample evidence that the two institutions complemented rather than antagonized one another. La Reynie enjoyed cordial relations with the *parlementaires*, and Parlement continued to exercise the bulk of its police powers.

The other notable event that concerned Parlement's municipal authority was a series of meetings Colbert held with several councillors of state and *maîtres des requêtes* in late 1666 to organize a "reformation of the police of Paris." The group was concerned primarily with curtailing crime in the city and improving standards of hygiene. Most discussions concentrated on the need to regulate the right of citizens to bear arms, to control the influx of vagabonds into the city, and to clean up the highways, streets, and rivers in the Parisian area.[61] Although the committee did not include any *parlementaires*, its members kept in close touch with the court of law.[62] On December 2, for example, the group decided to send a delegation to Parlement in order to give the judges an account of its sessions.[63] At the meeting of December 24, it was reported that another delegation had visited Lamoignon for advice on the problem of cleanliness in the city and that the first president had suggested that the committee formulate a decree on the subject and send it to Parlement for registration.[64] At the same session, Councillor of State Boucherat reported that *Président à Mortier* Nesmond had volunteered to inspect prisons. Moreover, at several sessions Colbert emphasized the need to enforce the exemplary regulations Parlement had issued on the cleaning of streets.[65] In fact, the most notable work of the committee, an edict of December 1666 that dealt with the cleaning and lighting of Parisian streets, was based upon a decree Parlement had issued on April 30, 1663.[66] In planning for a reformation of police in 1666, therefore, Colbert both consulted Parlement and used its previous regulations as the basis for his own plans.

The crown also pursued a policy of moderation in defining the relationship between Parlement and the provincial arms of the councils, the intendants. The intendants were the heirs of a variety of royal emissaries who in the sixteenth century were sent with temporary commissions to the provinces to rectify local judicial and financial abuse.[67] The entrance of France in the Thirty Years' War generated a great spurt in the evolution of these officials. Cardinals Richelieu and Mazarin saw them as a means of meeting the financial needs of war by circumventing the established financial officials, whose cumbersome procedures and resistance to royal policies had combined to restrict the flow of funds the crown needed so desperately to maintain the war effort.[68] The intendants, who were most often *maîtres des requêtes* responsible to the crown, operated through a commission that broadly outlined their duties, but they received detailed instructions from the royal council. They entered the *bureaux des finances* at the *généralité* level of the financial administration and had the authority to supervise the *trésoriers de France* and their subordinates, the *élus*, in all matters regarding the assessment, collection, and litigation of the *taille*. [69] However, the ambiguous nature of their commissions and the proclivity of the government to seek expedient solutions to problems meant that the intendants often interfered in judicial affairs. Their commissions were registered by presidial courts as well as by the *bureaux des finances*, and they often intervened in litigation before the presidial, bailliage, and seneschal courts. Such intrusion not only generated the opposition of financial officials, who resented the usurpation of their duties, but also upset the Parisian and provincial sovereign courts, which viewed the intendants as a threat to their appellate jurisdiction. [70] At the beginning of the Fronde, the representatives of the sovereign courts in the Chambre Saint-Louis denounced the intendants and secured their revocation in all but a few frontier provinces by the royal declaration of October 22, 1648. [71]

The relations between the intendants and the Parlement of Paris had always been ambiguous. Many intendants had previously held offices in the sovereign courts (including Parlement), and in practice they only marginally encroached upon the jurisdiction of the *parlementaires*. Indeed, there is reason to believe that the court joined the chorus of opposition to them in 1648 primarily because it resented their collusion with tax farmers (who deprived the judges of the revenue for *rente* and salary payments), and because it wanted to demonstrate its solidarity with other royal officials. Parlement disliked the intendants far more as symbols of the "governmental revolution" than as a direct threat to its own jurisdiction. [72] This is an important point for assessing Parlement's attitude toward the intendants after the Fronde.

Both during and after the civil wars, the royal administration blatantly violated its declaration of 1648 and reestablished the intendants under the title of *commissaires départis*. They once again worked their way into the financial administration, and Mazarin simultaneously attacked the privileges and prerogatives of the financial officials (*trésoriers de France* and *élus*) who opposed them. [73] Historians have properly emphasized the importance of the intendants in the changing patterns of administration in seventeenth-century France. By supporting these officials, the crown did not remove the established venal bureaucracy, but it added another layer upon it that was directly responsible to the king and his councils. Nevertheless, the rapid evolution of the intendants did not necessarily limit the jurisdictions of the judicial courts, particularly the Parlement of Paris. The primary task of an intendant was financial administration, and thus their destructive effect on the functions of royal financial officials is understandable. After the Fronde, however, there seems to have been a marked reluctance on the part of the crown to have the intendants interfere in nonfinancial jurisdictions. [74] During the 1650s, when Parlement relinquished its drive to protect all venal officials, its registers were silent about the intendants, and not once in the post-Fronde decade did the Parisian *parlementaires* complain about them. Because Parlement was so vocal during these years on all other issues that touched upon its privileges and prerogatives, one is led to conclude that its silence on the intendants stemmed simply from the fact that they gave the judges little reason to complain. This also seems to have been the case during the first decades of Louis's personal rule.

The intendants undeniably acquired a great deal of authority after 1661. Their jurisdiction over regional finances became virtually complete, and they performed useful service as royal investigators, as is evident from the many reports they sent to Colbert on a wide variety of administrative and economic issues.[75] However, just as the king attempted to ensure that his councils did not abuse their authority and usurp the judicial functions of the sovereign courts, so Colbert likewise moderated the conduct of the intendants. During his ministry, Colbert frequently moved the intendants from one area to another, ostensibly to give them more extensive knowledge of the kingdom, but also to prevent them from becoming entrenched in a particular locality. He also attempted to limit the number and authority of the subdelegates of the indendants.[76] According to the eminent historian Georges Pagès, "nothing indicates that the judicial courts, bailliages, and parlements lost any of their competence in administrative [*police*] affairs in the time of Colbert."[77]

An excellent indication of Colbert's attitude toward the relations between the judicial courts and the intendants is a letter he wrote to Le Vayer, the intendant of Soissons, in October 1682. Le Vayer had apparently attempted to interfere in a local court's handling of procedures regarding judicial documents. Colbert curtly informed the intendant that the Parlement of Paris had registered a declaration on the subject and that therefore "the cognizance of it [the edict] belongs to the ordinary judges." He continued:

You therefore are not supposed to be able to have cognizance of it without the express orders [of the king]; . . . this is the true maxim of universal justice of the kingdom, and particularly that which is observed presently in financial affairs, which tends to maintain the magistrates in the jurisdiction that belongs to them by their functions unless they abuse it. The duty of the intendants of the provinces consists only in seeing that the judges do their duty and execute the laws and ordinances established by the Prince, and not to have direct authority over any affair in which they do not have the precise authority [given by] the king.[78]

The registers of the council do record numerous instances when the council sent litigation that had come to it by appeal back to the intendants for definitive judgment. Virtually all of the cases, however, dealt with financial matters, and few involved the Parlement of Paris.[79]

It would be a mistake, therefore, to overstate the effects of the decree of July 1661, the creation of a lieutenant general of police, and the reestablishment of the intendants on the jurisdiction of Parlement. Louis XIV had no intention of striking away the judicial and municipal authority of the court. This would have been beyond his means and quite unwise because Parlement exercised a legitimate and necessary function for the crown. What he did desire was the reduction of Parlement's ability to oppose royal policies and to participate at will in the solution of affairs of state, which he believed beyond the capacity and function of a judicial body. In a revealing section of his memoirs, Louis reviewed each segment of society and its role in the state. The peasants supplied food, the artisans and merchants met material needs, the clergy taught morality and religion. The judges, he noted, expedite justice. "This is why," he continued, "instead of slighting any of these conditions or favoring one at the expense of the others, we ought . . . to bring each . . . to the perfection due to it."[80] Later in the memoirs, Louis elaborated this view as it applied to the parlements.

The elevation of the parlements . . . had been dangerous to the entire kingdom during my minority: it was necessary to humble them, not for the evil they had done, but for that which they might do in the future. Their authority, [which was] so great that it was opposed to mine, . . . produced very bad effects in the state. . . . [It was necessary to reduce things] to their natural and legitimate order. . . . It was necessary to take away from these bodies a part of that which had been given them in previous reigns, as the painter has no difficulty in erasing that which he could make even more brilliant and more beautiful whenever he sees that there is room for improvement and some visible disproportion with the rest of his work.[81]

That the king here had a perspective on the future is also important. As noted previously, Louis's financial policies, peaceful approach to foreign affairs, and better management of the court removed many of the pretexts for Parlement's opposition and improved relations with the judges. Still, he saw the need to redefine Parlement's authority, not as punishment for past deeds, but to ensure that his later policies did not provoke the court to regress to its pre-1661 recalcitrance and successfully frustrate his will.

If it has been necessary to qualify the impact of some of Louis's reforms on the judicial competence of Parlement, it is nevertheless essential to recognize that the king retained the option of interfering with the judicial business before the court when he deemed such intervention necessary. For example, despite the fact that conciliar evocations tapered off in the 1660s, the councils did resort to them occasionally when Parlement's de-

crees contradicted royal policies or dealt with matters the king wished to
handle personally. This was most often the case in instances involving
royal taxation, the Protestants, and the enforcement of the judicial ordinances that appeared after 1667.[82] Moreover, Louis could always turn to
his intendants to intervene in the judicial business before his regular
courts. In March 1664, for example, he ordered the council to evoke the
cases of several tax farmers from the Parlement of Toulouse and send them
to the local intendant for definitive judgment. While admitting that this
violated normal procedure, the king claimed the right to such evocations
"as the occasion might require."[83] Louis's main preoccupation, therefore,
was with Parlement's political authority. In practice, he rarely utilized the
power inherent in the decree of July 1661 to usurp the judicial functions of
the court. But if conditions warranted occasional interference, the king did
not hesitate to resort to his councils and intendants; and because he kept
incursions into Parlement's jurisdiction at a minimum, the judges were
more tolerant about them than in previous decades.

Louis XIV was not content simply to regulate the relations between
Parlement and the councils. His goal of reducing Parlement's political
activities led to further attacks on the court's privileges and prerogatives
later in the decade. On April 20, 1667, Louis entered Parlement and
supervised the registration of the famous ordinance on civil procedure, the
first title of which, "On the Observation of Ordinances," severely limited
the sovereign courts' exercise of judicial review by the rights of registration and remonstrance. The opening articles of the title ordered the courts
to begin registration procedures as soon as they received royal decrees.
Unless the king personally delivered legislation or sent it with his "express
command," the judges could still issue remonstrances before registering it.
But the utility of remonstrances as a means of opposition was considerably
reduced because the judges could issue them only within a limited time
period. The Parisian sovereign courts, for example, had only eight days to
remonstrate after they received legislation. After that time, royal decrees
were to be considered registered and published, and in consequence, they
had to be enforced and dispatched to the lesser courts of the realm. Under
such stringent conditions, remonstrances became a mere formality.
Another provision reduced the judges' independence of action in interpreting royal decrees for the lesser judiciary. The *parlementaires* had frequently
used their *arrêts de règlement*, which had the force of law in their area of
jurisdiction, to modify the terms of royal decrees. Henceforth, if questions arose about the execution of a decree, the magistrates were to consult
the king before taking any independent action, and in no instance could
their judicial decisions or orders to lesser courts contradict royal policies.
The title concluded with a threat to the judges' financial interests by

permitting litigants to sue for damages any magistrates who violated royal legislation in the judgment of a case.[84]

The thirty-four titles that followed dealt with the details of procedure in civil litigation. Because they necessarily touched upon Parlement's judicial methods and jurisdiction, they are analyzed in the following chapter. The first title, however, did not deal with civil procedure. It was an entity in itself, an appendage directed specifically at curtailing the influence of the sovereign courts in affairs of state.[85] Nevertheless, if the title may be divorced from the rest of the ordinance for separate analysis, it must still be considered within the context of Louis's and Colbert's intention to reform the administration of justice in the kingdom. Only then can the origins and intent of these harsh restrictions be fully appreciated.

As early as 1661, Louis had publicly stated in the decree of July 8 his intention to reform judicial administration in France. As noted previously, Colbert addressed a memorandum to the king in early 1665 in which he elaborated a proposal to have royal deputies visit the courts of the realm and draw up reports on the judicial abuses they discovered. From these reports, a committee of councillors of state would formulate a series of ordinances to regularize judicial procedure throughout the kingdom and reduce the length and cost of litigation.[86] On September 25, 1665, Louis and Colbert began to organize the machinery of reform. They established an eighteen-member Council of Justice and divided it into commissions to study particular problems. The group decided to send *maîtres des requêtes* to Paris and the provinces to draw up reports and submit them to the commissions, which would then distill the information and formulate the ordinances. The most striking feature of the ad hoc council was that it did not include any members of the sovereign courts. Colbert had seen to it that the ordinances would be a product of conciliar representatives, *maîtres des requêtes*, ministers, and advocates, but not the judges themselves. For Colbert, judicial administration became an "affair of state." The sovereign courts would expedite justice, but not formulate the precepts of its operation.[87] Only two years later, in January 1667, did First President Lamoignon convince the king to allow a delegation of *parlementaires* to meet with representatives of the Council of Justice and discuss each provision in the rough draft of the ordinance. But between 1665 and 1667, while the Council of Justice prepared the ordinance on civil procedure, the *parlementaires* had little knowledge of the council's work and no voice whatsoever in determining its content.

Title 1 of the 1667 ordinance was the first task the Council of Justice completed. The members of the council discussed a rough draft of its articles in the king's presence as early as October 25, 1665, two years before the entire ordinance was put before the magistrates for examination. The minutes of the council's deliberations indicate that the men Louis had chosen to formulate the ordinance intended the first title to frame whatever else might be accomplished in judicial reform; it was to be the base for all that was to come.[88] A councillor of state (and Colbert's uncle), Henri Pussort, noted that the first title "was the most considerable and most indispensable part of the ordinance," because it would correct the "abuses of the past." By this, he was not merely referring to specific abuses in civil procedure. Rather, he wished to impress upon the king that the successful implementation of *any* reform depended upon the submission of the sovereign courts. Pussort never stated categorically that these courts would always oppose reform. But he did emphasize that they had often done so in the past and that the restrictions in the first title would therefore serve a useful preventive function. "There is presently the need to take away all pretext [of opposition]," he advised, "and to hold the courts and the authority that has been given them within legitimate limits."

The discussion among the members on the articles of the first title centered on three questions, all of which were ultimately resolved against the pretensions of the sovereign courts. The first was whether the king should use the word "successors" in the first article of the title to indicate that the ordinance would be binding on future kings and, added Pussort, to ensure that "even the most perpetual and indissoluble of courts [including Parlement] and all the subjects of the king" did not modify the king's labor in the future. The council conveniently forgot that future kings would not be bound by the actions of their predecessors and voted thirteen to five to make the ordinance an inalienable legacy for future generations. The second question was whether the sovereign courts should, in fact, be referred to as "sovereign." All the councillors agreed that only the king was sovereign and that his authority suffered when judicial courts shared the same honor. At best, the courts were only "superior." Councillor of State Verthamon noted that "the word 'sovereign' did not signify independence, but only superiority," and Colbert agreed that to apply the dignity of "sovereign" to certain courts was "vain and useless." The council voted to avoid the term, and the final draft of the articles in the first title simply stated "our courts of Parlement, Grand Conseil, [etc.]."

The last question, and the most important for the authority of Parlement, concerned remonstrances. The councillors all emphasized how the magistrates had used remonstrances in the past to frustrate royal policies. Colbert held the view that remonstrances should not even be mentioned in the ordinance, not because he approved of judicial review, but because "it was useless and dangerous to accord such an express liberty by the law, the example of previous times having made us all aware that too great a liberty of remonstrance authorized rebellion and resistance." The wording of Colbert's comments does not make it clear whether he wanted to preserve the right of remonstrance, but simply not mention it in the ordinance, or whether he wanted the king to suppress it altogether. At any rate, Louis reassured Colbert that "during my lifetime, remonstrances will not prejudice [my] authority, because I will know well how to prevent [their] needless and tumultuous results and give consideration to those that are reasonable and respectful." When the votes were tabulated, the councillors had voted twelve to six to keep remonstrances in the edict, but only under the harsh restrictions that emerged in the final version.

The views expressed in the Council of Justice about the first title of the 1667 ordinance paralleled the royal administration's policy regarding the decree of July 1661 and the authority of the intendants. Neither the members of the council nor the king spoke against Parlement's legitimate right to judge litigation. Even Pussort, who was hostile to the pretensions of the magistrates, only spoke of reducing the sovereign courts "to their legitimate limits," and Louis himself decided to preserve the traditional right of remonstrance. Far more important to Louis and his advisers was the sovereign courts' ability to oppose royal policies and their asserted right to participate in the decision-making process for affairs of state as a matter of course. It was exactly these traditions that Louis sought to repudiate. The king felt that a redefinition of the prerogatives of the sovereign courts was absolutely necessary if his future reforms were to be executed without magisterial interference. In this respect, Louis's remark in his memoirs that he limited the authority of his leading courts not as revenge for their opposition in the past, but as insurance that they would undertake no successful resistance in the future, can be appreciated. This point is especially pertinent because Parlement had issued only six remonstrances between 1661 and 1667, and these were on minor issues.[89]

From January to March 1667, representatives from the Parlement of Paris and the Council of Justice held fifteen conferences to discuss the rough draft of the ordinance on civil procedure.[90] Curiously, the magistrates hardly mentioned the first title at these sessions, and thus they failed to modify any of its articles. Because of its general content, the deputies had postponed discussion of the title until the last conference. At that time, First President Lamoignon did make several broad observations. He said that the first title was "one of the most severe against the judges, . . . [and] it begins with menace to the parlements and all the sovereign courts: especially because the courts and all the officials of the kingdom never before have been in such perfect submission to the wishes of the king."[91] As Lamoignon elaborated his views, however, he concentrated only on the seventh and eighth articles of the title, which dealt with the judges' right to interpret decrees and the financial penalties to which the magistrates were subject if they violated a royal decree in judging litigation.[92] Nothing was said on the subjects of registration and remonstrances. Why the magistrates avoided discussion of such crucial issues is not clear. Even Francis Monnier, the historian of the conferences, offers no explanation. Perhaps the magistrates recognized that nothing would be gained in a struggle with the Council of Justice. Previous conferences had shown the reluctance of the councillors of state to modify any of the other titles and articles of the ordinance. Moreover, it is possible that the king ordered Lamoignon to avoid the controversial subject of judicial review. It should be recalled that after Parlement registered the ordinance, Louis dispensed lucrative land grants to the first president "for services rendered" in his association with the ordinance.[93]

The registration of the ordinance on April 20, 1667, was uneventful. Nevertheless, as the magistrates had done so often in the past, a few days later several *parlementaires* requested that the court reexamine the ordinance in a plenary session. Louis reacted quickly and severely. He not only exiled the most recalcitrant judges, but ordered three of them, President La Grange and councillors Miron and Le Bret, to relinquish their seats in the court and to sell their offices.[94] Parlement protested, but Louis held firm.

On February 24, 1673, Louis issued letters patent that further curtailed Parlement's right to remonstrate by ordering that only after the court registered decrees and sent them to lesser jurisdictions could the judges issue remonstrances.[95] By this time, such a prohibition was entirely symbolic because Parlement had not issued a formal remonstrance since 1667. This, of course, raises the question why Louis saw the necessity to deal this humiliating *coup de grâce* to the magistrates. Indeed, in April 1672 Parlement had registered six financial edicts with absolutely no opposition.[96] Ormesson remarked in his journal that Louis would be pleased, "because he [the king] feared that he would be obliged to come to Parlement to make it register them in his presence."[97] Despite the submission of the court, however, Louis still decided to issue the letters. The most plausible explanation of the king's action has been presented by Shennan in his recent survey of the history of Parlement. He notes that at this time royal armies had just begun the campaigns of the Dutch War. Realizing that this might require extraordinary financial policies, Louis desired to ensure that Parlement did not oppose such policies as it had done so readily in the past.[98] Shennan's view is credible because immediately after Louis issued the letters, he ordered the court to register several edicts in late February and March that created new offices and *rentes*, alienated royal demesne, and clarified particular points of his procedural codes.[99] In fact, the crown's relapse to extraordinary financial policies and the slow erosion of Colbert's reforms dates from this period. That Louis wished to exclude the court from participation in state affairs is all the more obvious because the preface of the letters stated that their intent was to curtail remonstrances "on public affairs of finance and justice."

In addition to restricting the right of remonstrance in 1667 and 1673, Louis made two symbolic gestures in 1665 and 1668 which, while not threatening Parlement's jurisdiction, underscored his determination to make it clear to the magistrates that he did not sanction their unsolicited participation in affairs of state. In October 1665, Louis began the practice of referring to his Parlement as a "superior" rather than a "sovereign" court. He did this to emphasize that he alone was sovereign in the state and, as such, he was not obliged to share this honor with a judicial court.[100] In January 1668, Louis informed the judges that he wanted all of the court's registers for the years 1648 to 1652 destroyed because "there are several things in the registers of Parlement [that are] contrary to [my] service and [my] state."[101] First President Lamoignon visited the king and complained that such action was "contrary to form," but Louis held firm, stating that he wanted to obliterate all memory of his tumultuous minority and the Fronde.[102]

In addition to all these acts against Parlement, the king was also determined to reduce the frequency of the court's plenary sessions. Parlement's opposition to the crown in the 1650s had almost always begun in the general sessions of the court. With all members present, the *parlementaires* found it easier to build a united front against royal policies. First President Bellièvre, who had often opposed Mazarin's government, was quite liberal in granting plenary sessions. But this was less true for his successor. For example, Lamoignon postponed a plenary session to discuss the conciliar decree of July 1661 for two weeks, and he refused to call one at all on the ordinance of 1667 on civil procedure. An excellent example of the first president's superb skill in maneuvering occurred in 1662 and 1663 when many magistrates wanted to assemble and protest a royal tax on court clerks. Time and again Lamoignon turned away the deputies of the chambers of *enquêtes* and *requêtes*, telling them that he would speak to the king personally because "one can do more directly with the king than by a general assembly of the chambers."[103] When the deputies persisted in their requests, he would agree to call a plenary session and then postpone it at the last possible moment.[104] In 1665, Colbert noted the beneficial results of the first president's efforts. While reflecting upon the means by which the crown had silenced Parlement, he remarked that the royal administration had not suppressed the court's legitimate right to hold plenary sessions, but that it had "worked by all sorts of means to avoid and postpone [them]." In parenthesis, he added that "it was in this time [1661–1665] that . . . the most consummate policies [*politique*] and most important services to the state [were accomplished], and for which we required the grace, which we have merited only too much, of postponing plenary sessions for eight or ten days."[105]

During the first decade of Louis XIV's personal rule, therefore, a number of royal policies converged to enable the crown to achieve substantial control of the Parlement of Paris. By initiating financial reform and pursuing a policy of peace, the king improved his relations with the judges and removed the pretexts for their opposition. He also managed the court more effectively than had his cardinal-minister through better control of the first president and the *gens du roi*. At the same time, he took advantage of this period of domestic tranquility to redefine Parlement's powerful administrative privileges and duties. In the course of a single decade, he sanctioned the superiority of conciliar decrees over those of Parlement, curtailed the effectiveness of remonstrances, supervised the content of the court's judicial and administrative decrees, and reduced the frequency and obstructiveness of plenary sessions. Louis XIV's restrictions on the court's authority and activity were neither absolute nor unlimited, as shown by his temperance in restraining the incursion of his councils and intendants into Parlement's judicial and municipal jurisdiction, and by his decision to allow registration, remonstrances, and plenary sessions to remain integral parts of the court's duties. Nevertheless, they were sufficient to limit severely Parlement's political influence for the remainder of the reign.

PARLEMENT AND AFFAIRS OF STATE AFTER 1661

The prohibitive legislation of the 1660s and early 1670s did not absolutely exclude Parlement from involvement in affairs of state. The court's extrajudicial activity was especially evident in religious affairs, a continuing influence which stemmed primarily from the king's deteriorating relations with Rome after the death of Mazarin. During the 1650s, the judges had opposed the cardinal's religious policies because they believed he had disregarded their jurisdiction and sacrificed Gallican liberties by aligning with the pope and the clergy against the Jansenists. Parlement interpreted Mazarin's desire to placate the Holy See concerning his anti-Spanish foreign policies as an invitation for increased papal interference in French religious affairs. But the conflict between crown and Parlement began to subside after 1661. On one hand, Louis confirmed the court's right to receive *appels comme d'abus* and he assured the judges that his anti-Jansenist policies would not entail increased papal influence in France. On the other hand, the issues of religious controversy began to change significantly after Louis assumed personal rule. Although Jansenism remained a perplexing problem, a growing conflict between the monarchy and the papacy dominated the crown's religious policies. As the struggle materialized, the king's Gallicanism gradually aligned with that of his principal magistrates. Unlike the situation in the 1650s, Parlement's traditional hostility toward both Rome and the jurisdictional claims of the French clergy became more a support than a hindrance to the king. Because Louis and his judges agreed on fundamental issues, the way opened for the *parlementaires* to participate in affairs of state despite the king's legislation to the contrary.

Both the crown and Parlement profited from this cooperation. For the king, Parlement's continuing involvement in religious affairs added considerable support to his antipapal policies. It also confirmed his control of the judges' political activity for it was he, not they, who determined both the extent and direction of the court's participation in affairs of state. As in other areas of Parlement's administrative and judicial duties, Louis may have preserved many of the court's traditional privileges, but he effectively controlled them and ensured that they did not work contrary to his interests. In short, the court assumed an active role because the king permitted it to do so. But the judges also benefited because the resurgence of royal authority in the second half of the seventeenth century did not entail a thorough repudiation of their political role. Parlement preserved its traditional view of itself as a corporate body endowed with the prerogative of influencing the direction of royal policy. Continued contact with affairs of state, however limited, provided the judges with a precedent for reasserting their claimed privileges after the king's death in 1715.[106]

The sour relations between the monarchy and the papacy during most of Louis's reign have been chronicled many times.[107] Let it suffice to underscore their impact on Parlement. Most historians agree that Louis attempted to reduce Rome's spiritual and temporal influence in France and Europe. Immediately after he assumed personal rule, the king demanded satisfaction from the pope on a number of volatile issues: the deposition of Cardinal de Retz, the *frondeur* archbishop of Paris; a grant of *indult* for the three bishoprics ceded to France by Spain in 1659; and a settlement of a nasty diplomatic incident known as the Créqui Affair. Parlement joined the fray on another front in 1663. Exercising their Parisian police powers, the judges urged the faculty of theology at the Sorbonne to condemn a thesis written by a student named Gabriel Drouet de Villeneuve that exalted the pope's spiritual authority and hinted at his infallibility and superiority over church councils. In a rage, *Avocat Général* Talon told deputies of the faculty that a thesis promoting these views threatened the liberties of the Gallican church and undermined the temporal authority of the king. "Those who are the authors [of such theses]," he stormed, "will not fail to extend this maximum authority [of the pope] on the temporal [authority of the king], and . . . undermine the supports of the monarchy. To tell the truth, if the infallibility of the pope is approved just one time, this would open the door to an infinite number of other seditious propositions, prejudicial to the sovereign authority of the king, to the rights of the crown, to his royal person, and to the welfare of his state."[108]

The faculty delayed condemnation of the thesis, not because a majority of its members approved of its ultramontane propositions, but because it felt that the secular court lacked the authority to decide doctrinal issues.[109] For several months, delegates of Parlement and the faculty discussed and debated both the thesis and the magisterial right of intervention. By the end of May, Parlement grew weary of the haggling and ordered the faculty to condemn the thesis without further discussion and to register the famous Six Articles of the Sorbonne. These articles, which a group of faculty members had drawn up to avert royal displeasure, condemned the doctrine of papal infallibility, defended the king's temporal authority, and reasserted the independence of the Gallican church from Rome.[110]

It is essential to note that the king was well aware of Parlement's activity at the Sorbonne, and he approved of the court's conduct. On September 26, the council issued a decree that sanctioned the Six Articles and commanded the faculty's submission to them. Furthermore, supported by Colbert, Le Tellier, and Lionne, the king actively encouraged the faculty to accept Parlement's dictums without question.[111] By 1663, therefore, the king became aligned more closely with Parlement's Gallican views. He resented the ultramontane thesis as an indication of papal encroachment in the affairs of the French church. The shift in the king's position gave Parlement the freedom to participate in this area of state affairs, even to the extent of recognizing the court's cognizance of doctrinal issues. According to one historian of these events, "Parlement was no longer trapped by the king and the council. Its doctrines seemed to emerge triumphant. In effect, the times had changed. The policy of abstention and silence was no longer the order of the day."[112] During the years 1664 and 1665, Parlement condemned two additional theses written by Jacques Vernant and Amadius Guimenius. In both, the judges believed that they had discovered the ultramontane proposition that the pope was infallible and superior to church councils.[113]

While the controversy over ultramontane theses raged, Louis still attempted to strike a delicate equilibrium in his relations with the papacy. He did not favor a break with Rome. While he encouraged Parlement to condemn the ultramontane theses, he continued his pursuit of the Jansenists, which certainly pleased the Holy See. On April 29, 1664, Louis held a *lit de justice* at Parlement and supervised the registration of a declaration that again ordered the clergy to sign the formulary of 1657 which condemned the five propositions of Jansen. Because several recalcitrant bishops maintained that the orders did not apply to them, Louis presented a papal bull at another *lit de justice* a year later stipulating that the bishops had to sign the formulary.[114] On both occasions, Parlement, which did not favor the Jansenists, registered the declaration and bull without opposition. Talon spoke in favor of their sanctions, and Lamoignon told the king that the judges approved of anti-Jansenist legislation as long as it did not offend the liberties of the French church.[115]

This reconciliation of king, pope, and Parlement was superficial, however, because the anti-Jansenist legislation raised more questions than it resolved. Agreement about suppression of the Jansenists did not ensure that all parties would agree on how to accomplish it. But this problem lay in the future, and for the moment it seemed that the monarchy and the papacy could still cooperate on issues of mutual concern. The duration of this cooperation, however, proved to be very short indeed because Louis's pursuit of the Jansenists had failed to pacify the pope regarding the condemned theses. In mid-1665, after he had secured the registration of the anti-Jansenist legislation, Pope Alexander VII felt confident enough to issue a brief and a bull that censured the faculty's condemnation of the theses of Vernant and Guimenius.[116] Interpreting these actions as a violation of Gallican liberties and a papal assertion of infallibility, Parlement responded immediately with a decree condemning the bull and ordering the faculty's censures to stand as they were.[117] The *gens du roi* urged the king to support his court's decision.[118] The General Assembly of the Clergy, which was then in session, at first denounced Parlement's action because it resented the secular court's interference in doctrinal matters (as had the faculty in 1663). But two weeks later the assembly joined with Parlement against the bull because it too believed that certain clauses violated Gallican liberties. The prelates were particularly upset with the bull's implication that the pope alone could judge the merit of theological works.[119] Despite the advice of his leading magistrates and clergy, however, Louis felt that the issue did not warrant a break with Rome. He decided to allow the judges to keep their decree in the court's registers, but he prohibited its publication and distribution in the kingdom. The existence of Parlement's decree served as a warning to the pope, but Alexander's bull remained in force "because . . . the decree of the *grand' chambre* slept in the minutes of the *Conseil Secret* [that is, the court's registers]."[120]

Louis's decision in this matter is of utmost importance for determining the nature of Parlement's participation in affairs of state. In 1663, the king had permitted Parlement to condemn ultramontane theses. In 1665, however, he did not wish to precipitate a break with Rome and he checked the enthusiasm of his judges. A recent historian of these events has noted that "Parlement and the Sorbonne, which had quarreled in 1663 over the frontiers of their jurisdictions, had united with the General Assembly of 1665 in protest against the pope. That protest proved abortive only because the king, for political reasons, chose not to force the issue."[121] The king's action in this encounter indicates that although he permitted Parlement to participate in this area of state affairs, he carefully supervised this participation and kept it within limits that suited his policies, which at the moment happened to include not offending the pope. Parlement was hardly a free agent that acted independently. Quite the contrary, the king found the court a useful tool in pursuing his policies.

In 1666, Louis settled two issues of conflict between Parlement and the General Assembly of the Clergy that again demonstrated his flexibility in adapting the court's participation in affairs of state to his own particular needs. On December 12, 1664, Talon had delivered a speech to Parlement in which he denounced Jansenism but alluded to the king's rather than the pope's authority to suppress the sect. Although the speech was hostile to Jansenism, the General Assembly of the Clergy and the papal nuncio demanded a retraction because they felt Talon had advocated secular control of the church.[122] Late in 1665, the prelates added another complaint to their grievances against the court. Earlier in the year, the king had delegated a group of *parlementaires* to hold an extraordinary court of assize, called *Grands Jours*, in the province of Auvergne. Ostensibly intended to correct judicial abuses in lesser courts and to punish the lawless nobility of the region, the tribunal soon dealt with religious affairs. In two decrees of November 1665, the magistrates transgressed upon the authority of the local bishop by issuing regulations on monastic discipline and by ordering local judges to visit churches and supervise the administration of the sacraments.[123] At the end of 1665, the prelates remonstrated to the king that both Talon's speech and the decrees of the *Grands Jours* violated their ecclesiastical prerogatives and jurisdiction. In order to settle the dispute, Louis ordered the assembly to submit memoranda detailing its complaints.

The king's responses to these protests in January 1666 favored the *parlementaires*. After consulting with the *Grands Jours*, the council rescinded the objectionable decrees but continued to enforce the judges' regulations under its own authority. The clergy protested this devious solution, but to no avail.[124] In fact, for the remainder of his reign Louis strove to bring the episcopacy under further secular supervision with the cooperation of his judges, and so long as Parlement's intervention in ecclesiastical affairs buttressed royal policies, the councils left the judges wide latitude for vigorous activity.[125] As regards Talon's speech, the king was content to have the *avocat général* report to him personally that he had not intended to insult the clergy. Louis then proclaimed that he was satisfied with Talon's apology and therefore saw no need to strike his words from Parlement's registers.[126]

In the 1670s, Parlement increased the tempo of its participation in religious affairs, but again this was possible only because the king felt that the court's activity benefited his policies. In the 1660s the king had stood between pope and Parlement. While he cooperated with the papacy against the Jansenists and remained equivocal on the infallibility issue, he also permitted Parlement to assert periodically its Gallican spirit and to encroach upon ecclesiastical jurisdiction. In this fashion, Parlement served a useful purpose for the king, but Louis was careful both to check the court's attacks on the pope and to avoid a break with Rome. In the following decade, however, the monarchy headed on a collision course with the papacy. As a break between the two materialized, Louis was able to unleash his Parlement and to exploit its traditional respect for his temporal authority and hostility toward Rome.

One indication that the crown's relations with Rome would worsen before they improved was the failure of Louis and Alexander VII to cooperate on the Jansenist question. As noted above, by 1665 the enemies of Jansenism possessed the weapons necessary to suppress the sect: several bulls and a formulary, registered by Parlement and supported by king, pope, and clergy. But in subsequent years, Louis and Alexander were unable to agree on how to enforce them. Diplomatic exchange had failed to resolve under whose auspices the Jansenists would be prosecuted, the king's or the pope's.[127] By late 1668, this stalemate had resulted in a compromise between Louis and Clement IX (who succeeded Alexander in 1667) known as the Peace of the Church. It provided that the formulary remain in effect, but the Jansenists could sign without relinquishing their cherished distinction between *droit* and *fait*. This compromise obviously benefited the Jansenists. Once again disagreement among their enemies had prevented concerted action against the sect: in the 1650s Parlement protected the Jansenists from king, pope, and clergy; in the 1660s Louis's conflicts with Rome hindered settlement of the issue. As regards the king's relations with Rome, however, the breakdown of communication between king and pope on a matter they both wished to resolve testified to the growing rift between the monarchy and the Holy See.

In the 1670s, the rift grew wider. In 1673 and 1675, Louis issued two edicts claiming that the crown was entitled to the right of *régale* throughout the kingdom. This privilege enabled the king to collect revenue on vacant bishoprics. The papacy contended that several provinces, notably

Brittany, Languedoc, Guyenne, Lyonnais, Dauphiné, and Provence were exempt from this royal privilege. As early as 1608, the Parlement of Paris had encouraged the king to ignore these exemptions, and in 1660 Chancellor Séguier had spoken of the *régale* as a "right of the crown that cannot be compromised."[128] By his two edicts, Louis officially brushed aside all restrictions to his right of *régale*. This clearly antipapal stance received the approbation of the judges, and throughout the decade Parlement supported the king: it willingly registered the edicts of 1673 and 1675 and issued a host of supporting decrees to ensure their enforcement.[129] The *gens du roi* collaborated with the ministers, delivered inflammatory speeches in Parlement, and worked diligently to guarantee their court's support of the king.[130] When Louis precipitated a break with Rome in 1682, Parlement swiftly registered the famous Four Gallican Articles that gave the king the unrestricted right of *régale* and asserted his independence from Rome.[131] The Gallicanism of the king had united with that of his Parlement.

This brief sketch of Parlement's role in religious affairs after 1661 is far from complete because the judges continued to voice their opinions on religious issues in the following decades. In fact, the first clear opposition of the court to Louis XIV in the closing years of the reign involved a religious issue: the registration of the anti-Jansenist bull *Unigenitus*, which the *parlementaires* interpreted as prejudicial to the liberties of the Gallican church. Nevertheless, the pattern of Parlement's activity for all but the last few years of the reign had been established by 1682. The king was quite willing to allow his Parlement to participate in this realm of affairs of state, and the judges enthusiastically welcomed the opportunity to do so. But as the events of the 1660s and 1670s clearly demonstrated, Louis XIV regulated the court's intervention and channeled it along lines that favored his own policies toward both Rome and the French clergy.

Louis XIV's management of Parlement's influence in religious affairs paralleled his policies regarding the court's judicial and administrative authority. The king's legislation in the 1660s and early 1670s was not intended to curtail Parlement's duties as a court of law, either in judging litigation or supervising the lesser courts in its area of jurisdiction. Nor did Louis desire to exclude Parlement from participating in affairs of state when it supported his policies. What the king did desire was to prevent the magistrates from opposing his policies, especially in an era of great reform. The course of Parlement's conduct in the first decade of his personal rule indicates that in this he had succeeded.

Considering Parlement's prominent place in the judicial opposition to the crown in previous decades, Louis's success in trimming the court's political role testifies to the growth of royal authority during his personal rule. Nevertheless, recognizing the king's achievement should not obscure the limits of his control. These limits not only reveal more precisely how the "absolutism" associated with his reign actually worked, but they also help to explain why the *parlementaires* reasserted their political claims so rapidly after the king's death.

Without question, Louis could have reduced Parlement to a mere ornament of the royal administration if he had been able to capture the control of magisterial appointment, break the social bonds between the judges, diminish their conception of themselves as a privileged elite in state and society, or erode the basis of their wealth. He did none of these things, however, and his control of the court was restricted to redefining its political authority. But even in this aspect of his relations with Parlement, the king relied more upon supervision and management of the judges than upon instituting permanent changes in the court's privileges and duties. Despite royal restrictions, Parlement retained the right to register and remonstrate royal legislation, to issue judicial and administrative decrees, and to hold plenary sessions. The judges preserved, again despite restrictions, some influence in affairs of state. Moreover, although conciliar supremacy was firmly established in 1661, the king's councils normally refrained from interfering with Parlement's traditional judicial function. The new lieutenant general of police cooperated with the judges rather than antagonized them, and the intervention of the provincial intendants in the judicial business before the court remained a rare exception rather than the rule.

Not only were the methods Louis XIV employed to control Parlement limited, but the success he enjoyed was superficial in the sense that it was not deeply rooted enough to bequeath to his successors. Because it did not entail lasting innovation, royal control of Parlement ultimately depended upon the king's remarkable skill in balancing his interests with those of the judges and pursuing a pragmatic policy that combined compromise with coercion. Without his personal supervision, the submission of Parlement was not ensured. In 1715, Parlement was still a tightly knit social corporation with extensive judicial and administrative authority and a tradition of political involvement. All that was necessary was the opportunity to mobilize these sentiments, precedents, and duties to reclaim its heritage of participating with the crown in the resolution of national problems and exerting an influence that extended beyond judicial administration. Not unlike events in 1643, a child-king and a compromising regent provided this opportunity to Parlement upon the Sun King's death.

Given both the limits and the legacy of Louis XIV's control of the Parlement of Paris, one should take care not to exaggerate the changes within traditional institutions that accompanied the resurgence of royal authority after 1661. But in another sense, Louis still deserves his reputation as an effective ruler because the implications of the limits to his control lay in the future and not in his reign. During the period of his personal rule, Parlement was unable to exploit the shortcomings of the king's policies. By simultaneously rectifying the weaknesses of Cardinal Mazarin's administration and curtailing Parlement's means of opposition, Louis effectively neutralized a potential challenge to his policies. If in this process the court retained much of its traditional authority, the king ensured that the judges did not mobilize it against his interests. Furthermore, if many royal programs were frustrated in subsequent decades, the Parlement of Paris, once the center of opposition to the crown, shared none of the credit. It can certainly be demonstrated, for example, that Louis's control of some provincial parlements was less than absolute. They often refused to enforce royal decrees, added modifications to legislation before registration, and in some areas, particularly Brittany, even lent their support to local rebellions against the crown's post-1672 extraordinary financial policies.[132] But the Parlement of Paris was not the Parlement of Rennes, and provincial opposition to Louis XIV does not automatically imply or require a Parisian counterpart.[133] The degree of royal control of the judiciary obviously differed from area to area. Louis's control of his most prestigious court of law might have indeed lacked deep roots, but it was effective enough to submit the judges to the royal will while he lived.[134]

CHAPTER SIX

Parlement and Louis XIV's "Reformation of Justice"

J udicial administration was Parlement's primary and legitimate function. Each year the *parlementaires* judged hundreds of cases in first instance and on appeal, and they supervised the conduct of the lesser courts in their area of jurisdiction. From these activities, members of Parlement derived not only a portion of their wealth through official income, but also some of the administrative powers that enabled them to oppose royal policies on the national and local level. In addition, they were beneficiaries of a great prestige, which, like sentiments of social elitism in the court, reenforced their desire for political influence and participation in affairs of state. Parlement's daily operation as a court of law has been the subject of little historical scholarship, primarily because in most periods of French history the judges conducted their judicial business without serious interference from the monarchy. During the opening decades of Louis XIV's personal rule, however, the king and his advisers took an active interest in judicial affairs. In the 1660s and 1670s they undertook what they and their contemporaries referred to as a "reformation of justice" in order to eliminate abuses in the judicial administration of the realm. An analysis of this reforming activity has an important place in this study, because it will reveal whether Louis's attempts to control the judges included significant modification of their judicial powers and practices.

The most famous and lasting of the king's reforms were two ordinances of April 1667 and August 1670 that established the procedures royal and seigneurial courts were to follow in judging civil and criminal litigation. This chapter traces the formulation and implementation of this legislation and assesses its impact on Parlement's judicial methods and authority. It must be emphasized, however, that the two great codes were only a part of the monarchy's plans to reform judicial administration. The king and his advisers recognized that the causes of judicial abuse extended far beyond just procedural matters into the complex organization of the judiciary and the conduct of the magistrates themselves—the way they acquired and bequeathed their posts, their familial ties with one another, and their age and education upon assuming office. The extent to which the crown eliminated the nonprocedural abuses in the judiciary constitutes a second theme of this chapter because it provides further insight into the impact of the "reformation of justice" on the Parlement of Paris.[1]

The chronology of reform is well known.[2] In the conciliar decree of July 1661 the king announced his intention to eliminate "abuses" in judicial administration. Colbert had advocated judicial reform while Mazarin was alive, but the cardinal's obsession with other problems precluded serious consideration of such an ambitious project.[3] In the early 1660s, Colbert renewed his efforts and prepared a memorandum for the king that listed all royal ordinances on judicial matters that had appeared between 1303 and 1626, indicating that he might have had some type of codification in mind.[4] In 1661, Henri Pussort indicated in a note to his nephew that he too had begun "to scratch the surface" in an examination of past judicial ordinances.[5] Direct action on reform slumbered, however, until 1665. In that year, Colbert had several councillors of state and other advisers submit memoirs describing abuses in the judiciary, he wrote his famous memorandum of May 15 on the direction reform should take, and he worked with the king to establish a Council of Justice.[6] As noted earlier, although the minutes for only three sessions of this ad hoc council are extant (extending from September 25 to October 25, 1665), that body met regularly from mid-1665 until January 1667 and produced the code of civil procedure.[7] After this ordinance was issued in April, the council, reduced in size, continued its labors until early 1670 and formulated the code on criminal procedure. Throughout the entire process of preparing the ordinances, the magistrates in Parlement were excluded from the council's sessions. Only several months before the issuance of each piece of legislation did the king allow them to examine its contents and debate the various titles and articles with deputies from the Council of Justice.[8] While the council concentrated on procedural matters with the very limited participation of the *parlementaires*, the king issued several decrees concerning age requirements for judicial office, the prices of posts in the high judiciary, and the familial ties between judges in the same court. In the following decade, the monarchy issued other regulations aimed at improving the quality of legal training in French universities. Together, these ordinances and decrees constituted the major portion of the royal attempt to enact a "reformation of justice." An evaluation of the impact of this legislation requires an examination of each stage of reform with particular attention to the abuses the king and his advisers perceived in judicial administration, the methods they adopted to rectify them, and the implications of their decisions for the judicial authority of Parlement.

THE ABUSES IN JUDICIAL ADMINISTRATION

Even before he became a close confidant of the king, Colbert had expressed an interest in reforming the judiciary. In his famous memorandum to Mazarin of October 1659, in which he frankly criticized the cardinal's and Fouquet's financial policies, Colbert also noted what he believed were the principal abuses in judicial administration and his motives for correcting them. In keeping with the tenor of his memorandum, he stressed the economic advantages of judicial reform. The major abuses he cited were the excessive length and cost of litigation. Estimating that each year the king's subjects spent the exorbitant sum of 20 million *livres* to secure justice, he urged Mazarin to search for ways "to take this load from the people and allow them the means to furnish funds to the state."[9] For Colbert, judicial reform dovetailed perfectly with the financial reforms he promoted when Louis XIV began his personal rule. If justice could be dispensed swiftly and inexpensively, all segments of the populace would have more funds at their disposal to develop the economy and to place in the service of the monarchy. Although later, when royal legislation began to appear, the king understandably emphasized its humanitarian consequences, the national economy was obviously foremost in Colbert's mind.

From 1659 to 1665 Colbert may have recognized the principal abuses in judicial administration and developed strong sentiments about correcting them, but as yet he had not clearly established their causes or formulated a definite plan of action.[10] The magnitude of the task that lay before him became evident only in 1665 when reform began in earnest. Throughout that year, Colbert solicited memoirs on the subject of judicial abuse from a handpicked group of advisers who had expertise in legal matters. The most famous of these reports were filed by several councillors of state, and one historian of French criminal procedure has analyzed them cursorily.[11] But among the minister's papers are many additional reports indicating that he did not rely solely upon the personnel of the royal councils for advice. Most of these memoirs are anonymous, but some bear the signatures of eminent advocates, professors of law, and in one instance, a practicing magistrate—*Procureur Général* Achille II de Harlay.[12]

The considerable body of information assembled for Colbert constitutes an invaluable source for the historian in several respects. First, the memoirs provide a detailed description of judicial abuse, analyze its causes, and offer suggestions for reform. By comparing the memoirs to the legislation the crown ultimately issued, one can determine to what extent Louis and Colbert adopted the suggestions of their advisers and attacked the major abuses they cited. Second, excluding Harlay's report, none of the memoirs were written by judges in the royal courts. Free of magisterial bias or vested interests, the memoirs candidly reveal abuses at all levels of the judiciary. Third, the memoirs are numerous enough (over twenty-five were submitted) to account for individual differences of opinion without sacrificing the consensus on major issues. Finally, both the government and the Council of Justice probably relied quite heavily on these reports when they prepared the legislation that appeared in subsequent years. The surviving minutes of the Council of Justice indicate that the group decided in 1665 to send *maîtres des requêtes* to the various provincial parlements to prepare supplementary memoirs on abuses particular to each locality.[13] But contemporary documents lack any reference that this work was ever accomplished; at any rate, reports of the *maîtres des requêtes* have not survived in major archival collections.[14]

The memoirs confirmed Colbert's belief that the principal abuses in judicial administration were the great length and cost of litigation in the kingdom's courts. The authors repeatedly emphasized, however, that the causes of these abuses were deeply rooted not only in the confusing quantity and variety of civil and criminal procedures, but also in the complex organization of the judiciary and the conduct of the magistrates themselves. The message to Colbert was clear: effective royal reform required serious changes in all these aspects of judicial administration.[15]

When they considered the conduct of judges, the memoirs almost always spoke negatively about the venality of offices and the *droit annuel.* Magistrates were secure in their posts and virtually independent of royal control because they owned their offices as negotiable property and enjoyed the right to choose their successors. Such freedom, the authors argued, sanctioned laziness and corruption. Moreover, because family, social group, and financial considerations often were foremost in the mind of a judge who wished to dispose of his post, many talented and able candidates for office never entered the judiciary.[16] The memoirs also deplored the high prices that judicial offices commanded on the public market. Not only did these further limit the quantity of eligible candidates for office, but they tempted the judges to extend the length and cost of litigation as compensation for their sizeable investment in a post. Litigants stood helpless before irremovable judges who were determined to make each case financially rewarding.[17]

Many of the memoirs related the oppressive cost of litigation to the personal fees, or *épices*, that the judges charged for their services. According to Councillor of State Barillon de Morangis, "the greatest evil that has been introduced [in the judiciary] and that supports and nourishes chicanery and litigation is the petty and sordid gain of *épices*, which grow daily; they are a poison that spreads insensibly in the most notable individuals, and in the end they smother what remains of the spirit of justice."[18] To many authors, the high fees were an inevitable outgrowth of the venality of offices. Because magistrates paid dearly for their posts and received low salaries, they naturally viewed *épices* as a legitimate way to make their profession profitable. Litigants, of course, suffered the financial consequences of subsidizing the operation of the judicial system in this fashion. The memoirs associated venality to still another cause for the length and cost of litigation: the overabundance of judicial officials in the kingdom. Desperately searching for new sources of revenue, generations of kings had created and sold more offices than the efficient rendering of justice required. This had both increased the number of courts in the realm, and thus the jurisdictional conflicts between them, and inflated the ranks of avaricious magistrates who were determined to profit from each case that came before them.

The memoirs insisted that these problems called for major changes in royal policy. Many authors urged the king to curtail the venality of offices, revoke the *droit annuel*, reduce the number of judicial officials and limit, if not abolish, the *épices* that judges collected.[19] Several others added that if the total suppression of venality proved impossible, the king should at least reduce or stabilize the prices magistrates paid for their posts. This would allow more competent men to compete for entrance into the judiciary and perhaps relieve the necessity judges felt to charge high fees as compensation for their investment.[20]

While on the subject of magisterial conduct, several memoirs also complained that many judges lacked the proper age and legal education to exercise their functions properly. They condemned the age dispensations that magistrates purchased from the crown to allow younger relatives to enter the judiciary before they had attained the legal age. Youthful judges, the authors asserted, rarely possessed sufficient maturity and training to decide the fate of a litigant's life or property. The authors also forcefully denounced the quality of legal education in the universities, emphasizing that curricula were frequently outdated and law faculties understaffed. Moreover, they complained that student attendance was highly irregular, that some judges did not possess the mandatory advocate's diploma to hold a judicial post, and that a variety of dispensations allowed young men to cut short their legal training. Not surprisingly, therefore, many memoirs encouraged the strict enforcement of age and education requirements for officeholding and advised the king to include in his program of judicial reform a thorough investigation of legal education in France.[21]

Complaints about the familial ties between judges in the same court also figured prominently in the reports to Colbert. When judges were extensively interrelated through birth and marriage, they were frequently called upon to decide cases involving the friends of their ever-expanding family circles. This in turn generated a flood of appeals and the time-consuming and expensive process of evoking cases from one court to another. The memoirs noted that favoritism on the part of judges was particularly widespread in criminal proceedings, with the result that wealthy and influential defendants often went unpunished. Few authors offered specific advice on how to dissolve the familial bonds between judges, but some did suggest that magistrates be prohibited both from entering a court where their relatives sat and from marrying into the families of their colleagues.[22]

In addition to their comments on the conduct of judges, the majority of authors advocated structural change in the judiciary as a necessary ingredient of effective reform. Most complained that there were simply too many jurisdictions. This, of course, was related to the problems associated with the venality of offices and the abundance of judicial officials in the kingdom. Both had resulted in perennial jurisdictional conflicts among courts and in great expense to litigants who faced a vast judicial hierarchy if they were entitled to appeal a decision from a lower court. The suggestions the authors offered to alleviate this situation varied. Some urged the king to increase the types of cases presidial courts could judge in last resort and thereby reduce the number of appeals that traveled through the entire judiciary.[23] One author reached the radical conclusion that the only viable solution to organizational problems was to abolish the provincial parlements and replace them with a unified and central hierarchy of courts under the Parlement of Paris.[24] At any rate, the counsel of the memoirs to streamline the judiciary did not threaten the Parlement of Paris because most of the authors' hostility in this matter was directed against seigneurial and lesser royal courts.[25]

Finally, the memoirs to Colbert treated procedural questions at great length. The authors agreed that the methods of receiving, documenting, and deciding cases had to be changed in order to abbreviate the length and cost of litigation. Although an occasional memoir spoke of the need to establish a single code of law in the kingdom, most authors rejected the idea either because they held the various provincial customs in high esteem or because they believed them far too entrenched to be rooted out.[26] They did advocate, however, the formulation of procedural codes that would apply uniformly to all royal and seigneurial courts.

The authors found much to complain about in both civil and criminal procedures.[27] Civil procedure in the seventeenth century consisted of many complicated, lengthy, and expensive steps from the reception of a case to final judgment.[28] Even before actual litigation began, summons had to be issued, *procureurs* established, and documents registered at the court and exchanged between contesting parties. Proceedings were often delayed while defendants challenged the jurisdiction of the court or a prospective judge or questioned the validity of a claimant's evidence. When the case came before the magistrate(s), litigants had to secure the services of an advocate. Each of these steps was expensive because numerous documents had to be filed and because the fees of the many lesser officials involved in litigation—*procureurs*, *greffiers*, and advocates—were high and often unregulated. Even after these preliminaries, cases often languished on full and poorly organized dockets. Moreover, the judges' decision about how a case would be heard frequently exacerbated the length and cost of litigation. In most jurisdictions, judges could decide a case orally and summarily (*sur-le-champ*, *à l'audience*), but more often they channeled litigation through additional written procedures (*procès par escript*, of which there were at least four varieties in the seventeenth century) because they did not receive *épices* on cases decided by the briefer oral and summary procedures. The written procedures were lucrative for judicial officials but burdensome to litigants because of the additional fees, delays, and paperwork involved. Finally, if judicial sentences were subject to appeal, the whole process might begin anew in a higher court.

The memoirs focused on those aspects of civil procedure that noticeably increased the length and cost of litigation. They counseled the king to reduce both the delay periods available to defendants and the number of documents necessary to judge a case. They also believed that more types of cases should be heard mandatorily by oral instead of written procedures.[29] Reiterating that judges' fees were too high, the memoirs were especially critical of the conduct of minor judicial officials. Advocates, *procureurs*, and *greffiers*, for example, often encouraged a presiding magistrate to extend the hearing of a suit and to apply written procedures so that they could preserve their own role in a case and extract higher fees from the contestants. All of these lesser officials, noted the memoirs to Colbert, had to be carefully supervised and their avariciousness checked by new regulations.[30] Most authors also agreed that both the length and cost of litigation could be reduced if appellate procedures were modified. Two suggestions were popular among the authors. The first was to give presidial courts the capacity to judge more cases in last resort, thus reducing the volume of appeals that flooded into superior courts and greatly delayed the final judgment of a case.[31] The second was to establish fines for appellants who lost their appeals. The authors hoped that this would discourage parties from appealing decisions unless they were relatively certain that their appeals had a sound legal basis.[32] If enacted, both suggestions threatened to reduce the number of cases that came before the sovereign courts, including Parlement.

Criminal procedure before and after the ordinance of 1670 was both rigorous and harsh.[33] Because there was no uniform criminal code in France, judges in conjunction with *procureurs généraux* had great latitude in deciding what constituted a crime and its appropriate punishment. Many individuals withered in prison for months before their cases were heard, and upon the decision of the presiding magistrate prisoners were denied counsel and subjected to torture. Often cases moved toward completion before a defendant knew the full nature of the charges against him because both his interrogation and the testimony of witnesses were secret until the final stages of a trial. Most of these procedures had been established by the royal ordinance of 1539, and the authors of the memoirs saw little need to change them. Only the reports submitted by the councillors of state dealt with criminal procedure in any depth, and they were far less concerned with modifying the procedure than with compelling the judges to enforce vigorously what already existed. Particularly vexing for these authors, especially Pussort, was the favoritism that judges often accorded wealthy and influential parties.[34] Another problem was that courts were often lax in prosecuting to the fullest extent of the law if *épices* and court costs were not forthcoming. In French criminal procedure, the plaintiff frequently had to bear the costs of prosecution. Oftentimes, however, private parties could not afford to prosecute, and royal tax collectors balked at diverting their funds to pay for criminal litigation when the state served as plaintiff. With little prospect of income, therefore, judges dismissed many cases, and serious crimes often went unpunished. The other complaints about criminal procedure in the memoirs paralleled those made about civil procedure: judicial fees were excessive, and there were too many delaying tactics and documents to permit swift and inexpensive justice.

While elaborating on all these abuses in judicial administration, most of the authors did not single out the Parlement of Paris for special consideration. This was not because they felt that the *parlementaires* were above reproach, but rather because the problems they cited applied to all levels of the judiciary. Occasionally, however, a few authors did isolate specific practices in Parlement for criticism. Several memoirs, for example, denounced the supremacy of the *grand' chambre*, which promoted lengthy and costly litigation because it alone possessed the authority to distribute cases to the other chambers. It was suggested that appellate cases proceed directly to the *enquêtes* without the approval of the senior judges.[35] Other memoirs urged the king to reduce the quantity of cases Parlement received on appeal and to require that the oral and summary procedures be applied to most of those that did reach the court.[36] Several authors suggested that the right of *committimus*, which entitled a variety of nobles and royal officials to have their cases heard in first instance by the chambers of *requêtes*, be restricted in order to alleviate the backlog of suits before Parlement.[37] More than one memoir called for the suppression of the *chambre de l'édit*, that chamber of Parlement established by the Edict of

Nantes in 1598 to decide cases involving Protestants. This suggestion stemmed less from religious hostility than from the length and expense Protestants added to litigation by having their cases transferred from lesser jurisdictions to the special chamber.[38] Pussort provided the most radical suggestion that applied specifically to Parlement. Not only did he advise the termination of the venality of offices, the *droit annuel*, and the *épices* of the magistrates, but he also urged Colbert and the king to reduce the number of judges and chambers in the court.[39]

With candor and precision, therefore, the memoirs to Colbert exposed the many reasons why litigation was so costly and time-consuming. They also emphasized that the elimination of abuses in judicial administration required significant alteration in the organization, composition, and operation of the entire judiciary. The prospect of the full implementation of the authors' suggestions threatened the vested interests of all judicial officials, including the Parisian *parlementaires*. Serious modification of intracourt and appellate procedures could have jeopardized the financial emoluments the magistrates received and disrupted Parlement's jurisdictional competence and methods of judgment. Proposals to reduce the number of judicial officials, to curtail the venality of offices and the *paulette*, and to regulate the age and family ties of the judges posed a more serious threat to the *parlementaire*. They endangered not only the post he held, but also the very procedures that guaranteed his position in society and ensured him freedom of action in his relations with the monarchy.

After Colbert received most of the memoirs in the summer of 1665, he prepared an abstract of their major points for the king.[40] Soon after, Louis established the Council of Justice and reforming activity began in earnest. Of all the reports he received, Colbert was most captivated by Pussort's. Not only was the minister's abstract of this memoir more extensive than the others, but Pussort expressed many opinions that Colbert had included in his own memoir to the king on judicial matters, dated May 15, 1665.[41] In retrospect, Pussort made four major contributions to the reformation of justice. First, the councillor of state echoed the sentiments of the other memoirs by advocating a broad approach to reform that would encompass the office, age, education, and family ties of a judge as well as procedural and organizational matters. In his memoir, Colbert had offered similar advice, and the following years witnessed a number of decrees that dealt with the many aspects of judicial administration. Second, Pussort urged the creation of a Council of Justice and its division into subcommittees to examine past ordinances on justice and formulate procedural codes. Such was the body that Colbert had also suggested to the king and that was established in September 1665. Third, Pussort was one of the few authors who encouraged the king to exclude the magistrates of the sovereign courts from the council's sessions. Several councillors of state, among them Barillon de Morangis, Sève, Estampes, and Aligre, felt that royal judicial officials should have a voice in the reform.[42] But Colbert agreed with his uncle that the reformation be directed by a small, handpicked Council of Justice composed principally of faithful councillors of state. That the *parlementaires* ultimately received permission to debate the codes with members of the Council of Justice before registration owed more to the intercession of First President Lamoignon before the king than to the advice of Pussort and Colbert. Finally, Pussort emphasized that adequate procedural reform did not require a slate of new procedures. French juris-prudence already had an overabundance of these, he asserted, and the king should concentrate on distilling the best ones from past ordinances and bringing them together into comprehensive codes. Louis need then only ensure that the resulting legislation was enforced uniformly in all royal and seigneurial courts. In these suggestions, one sees the origins of both the format of the ordinances of 1667 and 1670, which codified existing procedures rather than formulated new ones, and the first title of the ordinance of 1667, which restricted the right of courts to remonstrate and prohibited magistrates from interpreting sections of the codes without prior consultation with the royal councils.

According to the plans of Pussort and Colbert, the king channeled the reforming activity that began in mid-1665 along two paths. On one hand, the Council of Justice worked diligently to prepare ordinances on civil and criminal procedure. On the other hand, Louis issued several decrees con-cerning the prices of high judicial offices, the age and education of magis-trates, and the familial ties between judges of the same court. In order to evaluate the impact of these reforms on Parlement, we must examine the royal legislation and determine to what extent the king and Colbert rec-tified the many abuses cited by the memoirs. Such analysis will be more informative, however, if it takes into account Parlement's own approach to judicial reform. Historians have traditionally ignored this subject, first, because Parlement's attempts to correct abuses in judicial administration were overshadowed by the more extensive reforming activity of the crown, and second, because the most remembered facts about the judges' role in the "reformation of justice" were their exclusion from the Council of Justice and their only last-minute cognizance of the codes. To be sure, Parlement's efforts at reform were less ambitious than those of Louis and Colbert. Nevertheless, the court's registers reveal that for several decades the *parlementaires* had taken steps on their own initiative to eliminate abuses in judicial administration, particularly in the realm of procedure. This reforming spirit becomes important when assessing Parlement's re-sponse to the royal codes.

PARLEMENT AND PROCEDURAL REFORM BEFORE THE CODES

That the magistrates of Parlement desired to reduce the length and cost of litigation is evident from the regulations they issued from *mercuriales*, the annual sessions the court held after autumn recess to monitor the internal discipline of Parlement and the conduct of the lesser courts in its area of jurisdiction.[43] As noted previously, the judges frequently used a *mercuriale* as they would a plenary session to discuss affairs of political importance and to coordinate opposition to royal policies. Most often, however, the sessions concentrated on preparing regulatory decrees (*arrêts de règlement*) aimed at suppressing procedural abuses.

Records for all of Parlement's *mercuriales* are not extant, but enough survive to reveal the magistrates' reforming impulse. On January 29, 1658, for example, Parlement issued a lengthy decree that shortened appellate procedures.[44] In order to reduce the backlog of appeals before royal courts, the decree provided lesser judges with a list of cases on which they could execute sentences despite appeals. It also transferred many categories of litigation from the written procedures to the oral, and it established fines for *greffiers* and *procureurs* who fattened their fees.[45] Moreover, the *parlementaires* delegated several presidents to examine the registers of *greffiers* and punish any fraud they discovered.[46] In addition, the decree ordered judges in both Parlement and the lesser courts to decide criminal cases even if the contestants could not afford court costs and fees.

Another *mercuriale* of March 1658 reiterated and supplemented these provisions.[47] The *parlementaires* established the goal of finishing cases within two weeks after litigation began "in order to avoid the vexation that litigants suffer by the prolongation of processes." They also stipulated that a councillor have two years' experience in the court before he participated in criminal litigation in the *chambre de la tournelle*, because a criminal trial "often concerned the life and death of the king's subjects." As a way to reduce incidents of favoritism, the regulations prohibited judges from soliciting cases from litigants. Moreover, the fees that *huissiers* and *procureurs* charged for their services were further regularized "so as to remedy the abuses present in court costs." Parlement issued similar regulations at a *mercuriale* on April 23, 1659, which further monitored the fees of lesser officials and reduced the quantity of official documents necessary to hear a case.[48]

Although they were justifiably proud of their achievement, many *parlementaires* felt that the *mercuriales* of the late 1650s symbolized the beginning rather than the completion of reform. A councillor in the *grand' chambre* named Séguin clearly expressed this sentiment in a letter to First President Lamoignon dated October 29, 1659. "Until now," he wrote, "you have done all that is possible, not only to abbreviate the length of litigation, but also to work for the relief of the public by suppressing . . . a great multitude of abuses [*chicanes*]. Nevertheless, it is necessary . . . to bring still more exactness to the reformation of procedure."[49] The magistrates did indeed continue to promote procedural reform in their *mercuriales*. As late as July 10, 1665, while Colbert was in the midst of formulating his own plans on the reformation of justice, Parlement issued a significant decree that set forth civil and criminal procedures for bailliage, seneschal, and presidial courts within its jurisdiction.[50] The decree covered a broad range of procedural questions: how cases were to proceed within and between courts; the form, content, and registration of documents by *greffiers* and *procureurs;* the assessment of court costs and *épices* by judges and lesser judicial officials; and the delays permissible during each stage of litigation. It also created uniform procedures for cases of *saisies-réelles* (the seizure and auction of real property to pay debts) and succession to lay benefices, which were subject to extreme procedural variations among regional courts.

The decree sought to rectify procedural abuses in several ways. In order to reduce the varying procedural criteria judges employed to expedite litigation, it forbade lesser judges to interpret questions concerning procedure without recourse to the opinions of Parlement. The judges hoped that this would diminish jurisdictional conflicts and the quantity of evocations. For similar reasons, the *parlementaires* also ordered that all litigation commence at the court nearest the scene of a civil contest or crime. Several articles reiterated previous *mercuriale* decisions that increased the volume of litigation subject to oral and summary procedures and ordered judges to decide all types of cases even in the absence of court costs and *épices*. As regards the imposition of *épices*, the decree stipulated that judges levy them on the amount of written evidence in a case rather than on the litigant's ability to pay.

Nearly a third of the decree dealt with the conduct of *greffiers* and *procureurs* in preparing, registering, and exchanging judicial documents. All officials who participated in a case were required to sign documents involved in litigation and to record the fees they collected. The presiding judge had the responsibility of placing documents in a public repository to serve as an archive for future inspection and reference. So that litigation might come before courts in an orderly fashion without inordinate delays, the decree provided detailed instructions for the preparation of civil and criminal dockets. Other articles reduced the length of delay periods that interrupted each stage of litigation and made these changes binding upon the judges. Finally, Parlement established fines for officials who violated any of these provisions.

The important point to notice about this decree is that the *parlementaires* adhered to the same principles that guided the Council of Justice when it prepared the royal ordinances in subsequent years. Like the codes of 1667 and 1670, Parlement's decree of July 1665 both reduced the length and cost of litigation and assembled regulations from past legislation into a procedural code that applied uniformly to all royal courts in its area of jurisdiction. Indeed, the decree contained so many worthwhile provisions that much of it found a place in royal legislation.[51] Parlement's commitment to serious reform is further confirmed by the resistance its regulations encountered in several lesser courts, particularly the presidial and bailliage courts of Poitiers, which refused to implement the decree and issued a circular letter calling upon other tribunals to do the same. The *parlementaires* removed at least three of these judges from their posts as punishment for this opposition.[52]

Parlement did not restrict its reforming activities to *mercuriales* alone. Often the judges devoted their plenary sessions to the preparation of procedural regulations. Between 1661 and 1665, for example, Parlement issued no less than eight decrees that further regulated the conduct and fees of lesser judicial officials, established guidelines for the preparation of judicial documents, reorganized dockets to facilitate the swift and orderly judgment of litigation, and encouraged judges to reduce their *épices* and decide cases even if litigants could not afford these fees.[53] In a plenary session on August 28, 1665, just one month after they issued the decree on procedures for lesser royal courts, the *parlementaires* unveiled a significant decree of nearly two hundred articles establishing the maximum amounts litigants had to pay for various procedural actions and the preparation of documents.[54] By setting these uniform rates, the judges hoped to reduce both the court costs "that consume litigants" and the surfeit of appeals in the judiciary generated by the multiplicity of local practices. These regulations had the additional advantage of applying to all the courts in Parlement's jurisdiction—seigneurial and municipal as well as royal. Moreover, like the procedural decree of July, many of these rates were incorporated in subsequent royal legislation. In fact, the ordinance of 1667 sanctioned Parlement's decree, and well into the eighteenth century the court costs it established remained in force.[55]

The *parlementaires* also exhibited their reforming spirit by sponsoring conferences for the advocates attached to the court. These sessions have gone unnoticed by historians, but contemporary documents indicate that parlementary advocates assembled twenty times between August 1661 and May 1665 to discuss the procedural aspects of their role in litigation.[56] The meetings were very productive, resulting in regulations on the communication of documents, the preparation of dockets, the collection of fees, and other matters that could save litigants considerable time and money. That Parlement supported this activity is obvious because the advocates frequently based their decisions on advice they had solicited from senior judges in the court.[57]

Parlement received an excellent opportunity to attack judicial abuse on the local level in 1665 when Louis XIV delegated some of the magistrates to hold a *Grands Jours* tribunal in the province of Auvergne. These tribunals were specially constituted courts of assize that the monarchy periodically established on temporary commission to concentrate the judicial authority of Parlement on a troublesome locality (the most recent had assembled in Poitiers in 1634).[58] The king's motives for sending *parlementaires* to south-eastern France in 1665 no doubt reflected his desire to demonstrate his stern approach to internal disorder, particularly in an area that was notorious for its oppressive nobility and disregard for law.[59]

Twenty officials from the Parlement of Paris made up the tribunal. In addition to sixteen councillors, a *maître des requêtes*, and a *greffier*, *Président à Mortier* Nicolas Potier de Novion served as presiding magistrate and *Avocat Général* Denis Talon assumed the duties of *procureur général*. The royal decree establishing the tribunal gave the judges extensive judicial and administrative authority.[60] They could revise the sentences of local magistrates, institute criminal proceedings, judge civil matters, and in fact override the normal judicial machinery in their area of jurisdiction, which included Auvergne and the surrounding regions of Nivernais, Lyonnais, Marche, and Berry. All decrees and decisions of the tribunal had the legal force of Parlement's own decrees, and local officials were ordered to cooperate with the visiting magistrates. The judges therefore received wide latitude for independent activity although the original impetus for the *Grands Jours* came from the king and Colbert.

The tribunal met regularly in the town of Clermont from September 26, 1665, until January 31, 1666. Its most glamorous and well-publicized activity was the arrest and prosecution of some of the local nobility, a lawless lot who either ignored or controlled local judicial bodies and terrorized the peasantry of the region.[61] As noted previously, the magistrates also became involved in local religious affairs, and their decrees on monastic discipline and the administration of sacraments upset the General Assembly of the Clergy.[62] Judicial affairs too occupied the tribunal. Immediately upon their arrival in Clermont, the *parlementaires* became aware of abuses in the administration of justice. In October, President Novion informed Colbert that "we are discovering here as much ignorance and abuse... among the judges as violence among the nobility; all the cases that have been brought before us have been poorly prepared and judged [by local magistrates]."[63] A month later, he complained again to the minister about the poor conduct of local judicial officials, "which is worse than one can imagine."[64]

Novion and his colleagues attacked judicial abuse from two directions. The first was to punish local officials who had either ignored procedural regulations in the judgment of litigation or had overcharged parties for their services. Throughout their tenure in Clermont, the *parlementaires* summoned judges before the bar, examined their accounts, and levied stiff fines.[65] Far more significant, however, were the detailed regulations the tribunal issued to define the procedural methods local judges were to adopt in deciding civil and criminal litigation. The *Grands Jours* ordered local courts to implement Parlement's decrees of July 10 and August 28, 1665, on procedures and court costs. It then formulated a set of regulations on December 10, 1665, that clarified and expanded upon these two earlier decrees, particularly on matters regarding the handling of judicial documents.[66] In addition to providing detailed instructions on the preparation and exchange of documents, this decree listed severe fines (up to 300 *livres*) for disobedience, often with the provision that successive violations would result in the removal from office of a *greffier* or indolent judge.[67] At the same time, the *parlementaires* ordered *greffiers* throughout Auvergne to submit their registers for examination by the court.[68] It is worthy of note that the tribunal prepared this decree on its own initiative. On November 17, 1665, Novion notified Colbert that his colleagues had already drawn up the regulations.[69] Apparently the minister and the king did not object, because the *Grands Jours* registered and distributed the decree less than a month later.

In January 1666, the *Grands Jours* continued its legislative activity. Acting on a request by Talon, the judges issued a lengthy procedural decree of eighty-four paragraphs "in order to correct some particular abuses other than those expressed [by the decrees of July 10, August 28, and December 10], to reduce further the cases pending in the judicial seats in the *Grands Jours'* resort, and to revoke and abolish superfluous procedures that cause litigants time, money, and embarrassment."[70] Detailed regulations followed that simplified the recording, copying, and distribution of documents, ordered improvements in the upkeep and management of prisons, demanded strict adherence to delay periods in the course of litigation, and outlined the fees judicial officials could charge for their services.[71]

What lasting effect the *Grands Jours* had upon judicial administration in the region of Auvergne will only be ascertained by a thorough examination of local archives. But the importance of the tribunal for determining Parlement's attitudes toward judicial reform is clear. The magistrates had already demonstrated their interest in rectifying judicial abuses through the regulations they issued from their *mercuriales* and plenary sessions.

The legislative activity of the *parlementaires* in Clermont was an expression on the local level of the broader consensus in Parlement that the quality of judicial administration should be improved and that the most respected magistrates in France were able to initiate reform.

A final indication of Parlement's involvement in judicial reform was the work of its first president to bring about a partial codification of French law. In a letter to an anonymous friend dated December 1669, the advocate Barthélemy Auzanet, who earned distinction by serving both Lamoignon and the Council of Justice, told of the first president's enterprise.[72] Lamoignon was dissatisfied with the inconsistencies in customary law on a number of important legal questions. He felt that these variations, like procedural abuses, caused confusion among judges as to what decisions were appropriate in a given legal situation and added length and cost to litigation by generating numerous appeals and changes in venue. He aspired to improve judicial administration not by dispensing with customary law, but by formulating uniform laws on matters where custom was silent or contradictory, such as the condition of persons, the preparation of wills, the succession to property, and so on.[73] In one sense, Lamoignon's plans were even more ambitious than those of the crown, going beyond procedural matters to deal with the laws themselves. Nevertheless, he did not contemplate a codification of all law, but simply a clarification of particular topics of confusion.

Auzanet informs us that at the same time the Council of Justice conducted its work, the first president assembled both advocates and *parlementaires* to discuss conflicting points of law and to draw up articles for a future ordinance. The sessions, which met at Lamoignon's home, passed "with little satisfaction" (Auzanet does not elaborate) and they soon ended. Nevertheless, for two years, probably between 1665 and 1667, the first president continued to work on his project with a smaller group of aides including advocates Auzanet and Fourcroi, Councillor Brillac, and President Le Pelletier. The results of their combined efforts have been published in many editions under the title, *Arrestez de M. le p[remier] p[résident] de L[amoignon]*. In keeping with the goals of his project, the work is a compilation of articles from customary law dealing with specific legal questions, such as debts, mortgages, seigneurial rights, succession to fiefs, and so on.[74]

The importance of Lamoignon's efforts reside not in these articles themselves, which were never implemented because of the subsequent appearance of the royal codes, but in the fact that the first president was concerned about judicial reform and that he took definite steps to translate this concern into a polished piece of work. In this sense, his efforts to streamline customary law complemented Parlement's own work in the field of civil and criminal procedure.

In the years before Louis XIV's "reformation of justice," therefore, Parlement demonstrated that the royal administration did not have a monopoly on the desire to eliminate abuses in the administration of justice. Like the authors who addressed memoirs to Colbert, the magistrates recognized the need to reduce the length and cost of litigation. Understandably, however, there were significant limits on both the scope and the success of Parlement's regulations, and these help to explain why the king and his advisers decided that effective judicial reform required centralized direction.

In the first place, Parlement legislated only for its area of jurisdiction. No matter what efforts the judges expended to regularize procedure in their own domain, their work could never have eliminated the diversity of procedures throughout the kingdom. Through no fault of the *parlementaires*, the geographical limits of their authority reduced the impact of their decrees. Second, the magistrates did not approach the problem of reform with a complete plan of action. Particular abuses were handled as they arose, usually upon the request of the *procureur général*. The results of *parlementaire* reform, therefore, never approached the comprehensive quality of the royal procedural reforms that followed in 1667 and 1670. Third, there was the related problem that much of Parlement's legislation, however well intended, was redundant and simply called for the enforcement of existing regulations. This could confuse as much as improve judicial administration by piling more and more decrees, often no more than bits and pieces from the past, upon an already imposing bed of legislative precedents. Both Parlement and the lesser courts found it difficult to keep track of the successive waves of legislation and to understand fully what regulations were in force at any given time. Moreover, unlike the crown, Parlement had no intendants to enforce its decrees and to supervise the lesser jurisdictions. At the impressive *mercuriale* of 1658, a councillor named Sève recognized this problem when he told his colleagues that "the greatest abuse today in justice is that all our regulations remain unenforced and in consequence their duration is short."[75] Finally, Parlement restricted its reforms solely to the realm of procedure. The magistrates lacked both the authority and the inclination to undertake reform in other equally crucial aspects of judicial administration.

Considering these shortcomings of Parlement's activity, the crown's attitude that it alone had the resources and power to bring about effective judicial reform on the national level is understandable. Nevertheless, Parlement had shown a willingness to promote reform on its own initiative, even if only in the realm of procedure. Yet the king and his advisers chose to exclude the judges from participating in the formulation of the civil and criminal codes, even though these too dealt solely with procedural matters. Like ships passing in the night, the crown and Parlement were unable to pool their talents for a common cause. The reason, of course, was the monarchy's lack of confidence in Parlement, its belief that this court would never be able to put aside entirely its vested interests and work for a thorough reformation of judicial administration. The years of strife and conflict between the crown and the judges had left such an adverse impression on the king and his advisers that they could not even bring themselves to trust Parlement to participate fully in what it supposedly knew best, judicial administration. This view was evident not only in Pussort's influential memoir, but also in Louis's and Colbert's decision to exclude the magistrates from the Council of Justice.

What effect the crown's refusal to include the judges among its confidants actually had upon the reformation of justice is difficult to determine. Lamoignon's son, Chrétien, for example, once remarked that the members of the Council of Justice lacked the legal expertise of the *parlementaires* and thus "they fell into a thousand errors, which forced them to give the public a very imperfect work."[76] Nevertheless, if we consider Parlement's dogged defense of its interests in the past and the disagreements that would develop between the delegates of Parlement and the Council of Justice when they assembled to discuss each code before its issuance, there is no reason to suspect that the relations between the two groups would have been entirely cordial, or the reforms more effective.

The king and his advisers thus felt that Parlement and other judicial bodies could neither promote nor adequately enforce a broad range of reforms. For this reason, Louis's reformation was both centrally directed and carried on with only the limited participation of the kingdom's most prestigious judicial officials. It was in such an atmosphere that reform began in earnest in 1665. The memoirs on judicial abuse had been submitted to Colbert, and the royal administration now possessed a detailed analysis of the nature of abuses in judicial administration and recommendations to correct them. On the basis of this information, the Council of Justice worked on procedural questions and the crown issued decrees that affected the conduct and composition of the magistracy.

ROYAL LEGISLATION ON CIVIL PROCEDURE

The Council of Justice completed a rough draft of the ordinance on civil procedure by January 1667.[77] Fearing that it would be issued without prior consultation with his court, First President Lamoignon secured the king's permission for a group of *parlementaires* to meet with deputies of the Council of Justice and discuss the provisions of the ordinance before Parlement registered it.[78] Most scholars agree that had not Lamoignon stepped in, the code would have arrived at Parlement for registration without the prior cognizance of the judges.[79] The delegates of Parlement and the Council of Justice held fifteen sessions between January and March 1667 to examine the titles and articles of the ordinance and to debate whether certain provisions of the rough draft warranted revision. An understanding of how the *parlementaires* reacted in these sessions and an evaluation of the impact of the code on Parlement require a brief description of the ordinance and its major provisions. The final form in which the ordinance appeared in April 1667 will suit this purpose because the judges enjoyed little success in making any major revisions in the rough draft. Except for minor alterations, the draft of the ordinance and the official edition were identical.

The ordinance on civil procedure was indeed impressive.[80] As stated in the preface, the aim of its thirty-five titles and several hundred articles was the abbreviation of the length and cost of litigation. Equally important, these regulations applied to *all* royal and seigneurial courts in the realm. The crown intended that its ordinance sweep away the multitude of local practices and replace them with a single, uniform set of procedures. The structure of the ordinance reflected the Council of Justice's attempt to include all the major stages of civil procedure and to describe in a detailed fashion how judicial officials were to process litigation from its reception to final judgment. Thus, the second title dealt with preliminary summons and the last title with appellate procedures after sentencing. A dozen titles indicated how litigants and lesser judicial officials were to prepare and file suits even before these came before the magistrate(s) who would hear them. Other provisions defined delay periods, the quantity and format of documents presented as evidence, and the methods of judging by oral or written testimony. The eleventh title dealt specifically with the procedures that sovereign courts were to apply to various types of litigation. The code also reviewed other practices that normally accompanied the pleading of a case, such as the investigation of evidence, the summons and testimony of witnesses, the solicitation of expert opinions, and the assessment of court costs. The various options of preparing and executing verdicts as well as appellate procedures received detailed treatment. Several procedures that were particularly open to abuse, such as the sequestering and seizure of property, the detainment of defendants during litigation, and the methods of judging cases involving benefices and *régales*, received special consideration.

A careful reading of the code indicates that the Council of Justice made a serious effort to eliminate those procedural abuses that the memoirs to Colbert had described so lucidly. Many provisions of the ordinance converted what had been several procedures in the past into single procedural steps.[81] This reduction and combination of procedure produced a corresponding decline in both the participation of lesser officials in litigation and the fees they collected.[82] While the code combined some procedures, it simply abolished others that served no useful purpose except to increase court costs.[83] The establishment of specific time periods for delays, which judges could no longer extend, earned the praise of later commentators on the code.[84] Still other articles forbade judges to collect *épices* on certain types of procedure.[85] One of the most notable features of the ordinance was its encouragement of judgment by the oral and summary procedures, which most certainly reduced the length and cost of litigation because these required fewer documents and no *épices* to the magistrates. Reflecting upon the seventeenth title of the code, which enlarged the scope of cases subject to the less expensive procedure, the noted eighteenth-century jurist, Daniel Jousse, remarked that "this title is the most important in the ordinance, because its observation can contribute more than any other to simplify the administration of justice."[86]

The Council of Justice also attempted to streamline appellate procedure. Titles 11 and 35, which outlined how courts were to receive and judge appeals, reduced procedural steps by an impressive two-thirds.[87] Other provisions sought to diminish the quantity of appeals in the judiciary. Presidial courts gained the right to hear more cases in last resort, and litigants who lost appellate contests were subject to fines.[88] In addition, several articles in title 35 increased the types of cases for which verdicts could be implemented despite appeals, and an article in the sixth title prohibited all courts from evoking cases from a lesser jurisdiction unless they adopted summary procedures.[89]

Finally, throughout the ordinance articles stipulated that if a judge violated the code and caused a litigant unjustifiable expense or delay, the judge's verdict was nullified and the offended party could file against him for damages.[90] The obvious intent of the Council of Justice in this instance was to coerce the judiciary to enforce the code in an exact fashion by leaving magistrates susceptible to civil suits and forfeited *épices*.

The civil code of 1667 was an important part of Louis XIV's reformation of justice. Certainly, the very magnitude of the task that confronted the Council of Justice meant that the ordinance was neither definitive nor complete, and in subsequent years the king supplemented the work of his advisers with additional decrees. Furthermore, being largely a compilation of articles from previous ordinances and decrees, the code introduced few novel procedures. What was striking about the code, however, and herein lies its importance, was that the Council of Justice had sifted through a voluminous number of confusing precedents and had combined the most useful into a single set of regulations that applied uniformly throughout the kingdom. With skillful eclecticism the Council of Justice had compensated for its lack of originality. Moreover, the ordinance did not deal with the composition of the magistracy or the organization of the judiciary. By not attempting to tackle all the problems involved in judicial administration, the Council of Justice concentrated efficiently on a specific task—procedure.[91]

The *parlementaires* had their first opportunity to examine the rough draft of the code at the fifteen sessions they held with delegates from the Council of Justice in early 1667. The minutes of the conversations in these meetings, drawn up by its recorder Nicolas Foucault and subsequently published, reveal that the confrontation between the two groups quickly boiled down to a personal contest between First President Lamoignon and Councillor of State Pussort. Those historians who have analyzed the dialogue between the two men usually consider their debate symbolic of the broader issues at stake in the mid-seventeenth century between the crown and its judicial officials.[92] On one hand, Lamoignon is portrayed as the spokesman of the conservative magistrates who, in defense of their vested interests, resisted any royal attempt to tamper with judicial administration. On the other hand, Pussort, who gained notoriety in the Chamber of Justice that judged Fouquet, in the Council of Justice that produced the code, and with his influential memoir to Colbert on judicial abuse, emerges as the representative of an aggressive royal administration that was willing to sacrifice the self-interest of the judges in favor of both reform and the assertion of royal authority.

Although this interpretation ignores Parlement's own considerable reforming activities, the fact that Lamoignon and Pussort frequently clashed on broader issues than the details of civil procedure justifies ascribing a symbolic quality to their confrontation. The agenda that the two delegations adopted for their sessions was to take up each article of the code in turn, discuss its merits, and vote upon its inclusion in the final draft of the ordinance. Lamoignon and Pussort dominated the debates and had something to say on nearly every article. Throughout the discussion, Pussort based his arguments on a single precept he revealed early in the sessions. He told the assembled delegates that "the principal aim that we [the Council of Justice] have adopted in preparing the articles for the reformation of justice is the abbreviation of litigation and the reduction of costs [to parties]: this is the universal spirit of the articles."[93] He emphasized repeatedly that all procedures that violated this principle had to be abandoned despite the vested interests of the judicial officials who might seek to preserve them. When Lamoignon protested some of the code's provisions that reduced delay periods, for example, Pussort defended the action because the king's "intention is to shorten litigation, whose length ruins his subjects."[94] The first president received a similar reply when he objected to the elimination of written procedures in certain instances. Pussort noted that the less expensive summary procedure was "the straightest canal for justice," and he added curtly that "if the usage of Parlement is contrary to this provision, it will be necessary to annul it."[95]

Despite these forays on the curtailment of procedure, however, the *cause célèbre* that dominated the debates between Lamoignon and Pussort concerned the articles that made magistrates who violated the code in the course of litigation liable to prosecution by litigants. Lamoignon asserted that such condemnation "is pronounced eight or nine times in the articles . . . and the ordinances in force at present do not contain similar resolutions."[96] He objected to these articles for several reasons. The first president identified the magistrates with the law; to attack the judiciary was to attack justice itself. "The dignity of judges," he noted, "particularly those of the sovereign tribunals, cannot be distinguished from justice itself."[97] He warned that "to insert in all the articles penalties against the judges, to expose them to prosecution by parties, and to menace them with damages and costs was not becoming either to their character or to the welfare of justice. In arming the ordinance against the judges, the judges would arm themselves against it and destroy it."[98] Lamoignon felt that a magistrate's conscience was sufficient to guide his conduct. "In effect," he emphasized, "honor and dignity are the principal attributes of a judge [and] . . . the interior law of a judge is stronger than all others to retain him in honest moderation."[99] The first president also defended the judges on practical grounds. He noted that the new ordinance would be unfamiliar to most judges (after all, magistrates had not formulated it) and that it would be unfair to punish them for honest mistakes they would inevitably commit while enforcing it.[100]

As he pursued these points further, Lamoignon revealed that he was particularly distressed that the penalties in the code applied to the magistrates of the sovereign courts, particularly Parlement. He insisted that "the prosecution of judges by litigants only regards the lesser judges; the sovereign courts had always been exempt from such attacks."[101] By ignoring the special status that sovereign courts enjoyed in past legislation, the Council of Justice had acted "contrary to the sovereign justice of the king, of which these courts are the repositories."[102] The first president was also anxious to defend the preeminent position that the Parlement of Paris occupied in judicial affairs, and in this respect he displayed the *parlementaires*' traditionally narrow perspective of their relations with the rest of the judiciary. He stressed that Parlement could discipline itself in its *mercuriales* without outside interference, and he pointed with pride to his court's decree of July 1665 that not only regulated the conduct of presidial, bailliage, and seneschal courts, but provided fines for lesser judges who violated parlementary decrees.[103] At one point in the discussion, Lamoignon was clearly agitated, and he testified to the *parlementaires'* conception of themselves as a privileged elite among royal officials:

The first president, raising his voice . . . so as to be heard by the entire session, said that the competence of Parlement was general for all sorts of affairs, . . . and that it was in the king's power to give judicial competence to judges, but that all the particular attributes that had been given to other courts did not remove from Parlement this general competence, which came from its origins [*institution*].[104]

In a later session, he snapped at Pussort "that Parlement had received sufficient authority from the king for things that concerned the administration of justice, and it has no need of further confirmation in this regard."[105]

Pussort did not need lofty reasoning to counter the first president's assertions. The whole issue was quite simple for him. He granted that a good many judges were upright and honest individuals, but he added that a susceptibility to penalties would make them more so. "Without a doubt," he noted, "it was religion, conscience, and honor that motivated magistrates; nevertheless, the truth is that the most poorly enforced ordinances were those that depended upon their honor and conscience. What is at stake here is to make all judges in the kingdom act in a just fashion."[106] At another session, he reiterated that "the threat of penalties is more effective than honor and conscience" in regulating the conduct of judges.[107]

Pussort also attempted to refute the first president's position by citing precedents from past ordinances that justified penalties for judges. This reasoning faltered somewhat when Lamoignon retorted that such precedents were valid, but only for lesser judges.[108] Undaunted, the councillor of state simply changed his tactics and asserted that the king was not bound by the actions of his predecessors, even in matters regarding the Parlement of Paris. If Louis wished to place the sovereign courts (which, of course, Pussort consistently referred to as "superior" courts) along with lesser tribunals under a uniform code of procedure that included penalties for disobedience, the *parlementaires* would have to adjust to their new status without complaint. The royal response to conservative magisterial attitudes could have found no better expression than the words Pussort spoke to Lamoignon on this occasion:

If all the old laws would be contrary to the new ordinance that the king proposes, that is no reason to prevent its execution . . . because a prince has no need of antiquity to compose new laws for his state; it would suffice for me to say with the Apostle, *serviamus in novitate spiritus; et non in vetustate litterae.*[109]

Frustrated at every turn, Lamoignon failed to secure major revisions in the ordinance. Monnier, the historian of the conferences, does note that the first president obtained modifications in many articles, but that these added clarity to the code rather than changed the intent of its authors.[110] The ordinance Parlement registered in April was essentially the same one its delegates had examined in the beginning of the year.

One perplexing aspect of the debates was that the *parlementaires* enjoyed majority representation at the conferences and yet they had voted down, along with the delegates of the Council of Justice, most of the proposals for revision offered by their first president. One might infer from this that Lamoignon's colleagues disagreed with him. Such a conclusion, however, fails to account for the very tenor of the debates and the limited participation of the magistrates in the whole process of judicial reform. The *parlementaires* easily recognized from the outset of the sessions, and especially from Pussort's remarks, that the ordinance in its original form pleased the king and that he would not have tolerated major revisions. Each time the two groups did deadlock on a particular point, for example, Pussort referred the issue to Louis, who consistently opted for the opinions of the delegates from the Council of Justice.[111] The magistrates understood, then, that if they had attempted to destroy the code, Colbert and Pussort would have advised the king to intervene. As a result, the delegates from Parlement viewed the sessions more as a forum for their views than as an opportunity to secure major revisions in the code. They voted in favor of the articles in the ordinance, but only after their first president had ample time to air his grievances.

Lamoignon's objections, it should be noted, were not based solely upon the material interests of the judges. Certainly, the topic that had generated most controversy dealt with the provisions of the ordinance that left judges susceptible to financial penalties if they violated the code. But the first president had little to say on other features of the code that potentially reduced a judge's income, such as the many provisions that diminished the instances when *épices* could be collected. Behind Lamoignon's arguments about the articles that provided penalties for judges were more significant issues which involved the theoretical status of his court. In the first place, he opposed regulations that treated Parlement the same as lesser courts. To Lamoignon, Parlement stood apart from and above the rest of the judiciary, and in consequence it deserved special dispensations. The king had attacked this pretension in the code. Second, the first president's words with Pussort revealed Parlement's resentment at being excluded from all but last-minute participation in the formulation of the ordinance. Lamoignon believed that Parlement had the authority and the desire to supervise its own conduct as well as that of the lesser courts in its area of jurisdiction. The crown had insulted the *parlementaires* by failing to give them a greater role in the reformation of justice.

In addition to providing procedural reform, therefore, the code marked another stage in Louis XIV's attempt to reduce the independence of his highest judicial officials and their ability to oppose his policies. As regards the Parlement of Paris, the monarchy at one and the same time formulated a major judicial ordinance with only the limited participation of its most prestigious court of law and included it, along with other courts, under a uniform code of procedure. As the conciliar decree of July 1661 sought to obliterate Parlement's claimed supremacy over the royal councils, the code of 1667 attacked the *parlementaires'* conception of themselves as a body too privileged to be subject to regulations that applied to the entire judiciary.

Soon after the issuance of the ordinance, the royal administration, recognizing both difficulties in its execution and omissions that still exacerbated the length and cost of litigation, issued subsidiary legislation to expand and clarify it. The additional legislation was intended to eliminate these problems, and, like the code, it applied uniformly to all royal and seigneurial courts of the realm. One decree of August 1669, partially entitled "a continuation of the ordinance of 1667," attempted to reduce friction between courts by defining procedures for evocation and *committimus*. It also established methods for issuing and implementing the variety of royal letters that postponed the summons of a litigant before a court or delayed the execution of a judicial sentence.[112] In subsequent years, at least four other decrees reiterated and further explained provisions in the code that judges had either misunderstood or enforced poorly, particularly on matters concerning judgment by written evidence, the preparation of documents, and the filing of appeals.[113]

Several royal decrees applied specifically to the Parlement of Paris. By letters patent of February 5, 1669, the crown suppressed the *chambres de l'édit* at the parlements of Paris and Rouen.[114] Although those cases that were still pending at these courts were to remain there until final judgment, litigation of Protestants was thereafter subject to the cognizance of lesser judges. Louis's motives in suppressing the chambers might have well included his dislike of Protestants, but the preface of the letters stated that the action was a response to the length and cost Protestants added to litigation by having their cases transferred to the parlements for judgment. If Louis abolished one chamber, he created another. By the terms of an edict of August 13, 1669, a chamber of *tournelle civile* would meet several times each week and judge suits involving up to 3,000 *livres*. Composed of presidents of the *enquêtes* and councillors of the *grand' chambre* on a rotating basis, the new chamber enabled Parlement to decide more cases in a given period of time, which certainly benefited litigants by unclogging the court's full dockets.[115] The king had previously set up such a chamber on a temporary basis in 1667, and the edict of 1669 simply formalized it and provided it with "an augmentation of authority."[116] At the same time, Louis issued another edict regulating Parlement's *chambre des vacations*, the interim chamber that sat when the court was in recess each autumn. The edict noted that the effectiveness of this group often suffered because its membership had never been defined precisely and because "its authority had expanded far beyond the limits of its natural competence." To correct these problems, the edict both specified which *parlementaires* were to sit in the chamber and limited their jurisdiction to cases involving less than a thousand *livres*. Litigation entailing more than that amount was to be put aside until Parlement reconvened in regular session.[117]

In the early 1670s the crown continued to supplement the code. The most important legislation was an edict of March 1673 concerning the judges' *épices*.[118] The decree neither suppressed the fees (though it announced the king's intention to do so in the future) nor revised the monetary sums the judges could levy. It did specify, however, those procedures for which magistrates could collect *épices* and those which were to be accomplished gratuitously. The intent of the edict was both to reduce the number of procedures subject to fees and to exclude all but the judges who actually decided a case from collecting them. Other edicts of March 24 and July 10, 1673, ordered Parlement to prepare special dockets for appellate cases and established the format that all courts were to adopt in drawing up judicial documents. Both sought to standardize bookkeeping and thereby facilitate the inexpensive and swift judgment of litigation.[119]

The registers of the king's councils testify to the royal administration's determination to enforce the code and its subsidiary legislation. Throughout the years after 1667 the councils issued many decrees that ordered judges at all levels to enforce the code and nullified their verdicts if they violated its provisions. On September 23, 1668, for example, the council sent instructions to the seneschal court and Parlement of Toulouse and the presidial court of Bourg explaining how several cases then before them were to be judged according to the ordinance.[120] In the same year the council nullified several judgments of the Parlement of Grenoble that violated the procedure for sending cases on appeal to the Parlement of Paris.[121] Acting on the complaints of the *greffiers* of Moulins, the council on February 21, 1672, ordered all *procureurs* to obey the provisions of the code on matters dealing with the form and registration of documents.[122] The king did not hesitate to punish judges who violated the code. Ormesson reports that in 1668 Councillor L'Escuyer of the Parisian Chambre des Comptes and councillors Perrot and Canaye of Parlement's *grand' chambre* were suspended from their posts for three months for "violation of the code," while President Nicolai of the Chambre des Comptes, who had disobeyed the ordinance "three or four times," was threatened with the loss of his post.[123]

The council also used its authority to enforce the code in the Parlement of Paris. On September 28, 1668, a conciliar decree nullified a judgment rendered by the *chambre de l'édit* which violated several articles of the code limiting the procedures used in judging cases on the basis of written evidence.[124] In April 1669, the council evoked the case of a professor of theology at the Sorbonne from the court because royal legislation did not include him in a *committimus* category that permitted the *grand' chambre* to hear his case in first instance.[125] In his commentary on the code published in 1755, Philippe Bornier included an appendix listing many of the decrees the council issued to enforce the code and to nullify the verdicts of courts that violated it; sixteen among them applied to the Parlement of Paris in the three years after the appearance of the code.[126]

Understandably, the council supported the *parlementaires* when they obeyed the ordinance. Thus, on December 22, 1669, it upheld the judges' decision to combine several appeals on the same case into a single judgment, a procedure the code had sanctioned.[127] In fact, the royal administration kept in close contact with *Procureur Général* Harlay, answering his queries about how the king wanted particular articles of the code interpreted. On June 13, 1669, for example, Chancellor Séguier sent him a written explanation of articles 22, 37, and 40 of the last title of the code that dealt with appellate procedures.[128] Harlay enjoyed especially cordial relations with Le Tellier after the latter became chancellor in 1677. Much of their correspondence dealt with the interpretation and enforcement of the code.[129] In February 1676, Colbert informed the *procureur général* that he approved of his writing to the king and his ministers for advice on the ordinance. "You may use this application [that is, writing for advice]," he noted, "so as to know the wishes of His Majesty in all occasions that might arise [concerning the code.]"[130]

PARLEMENT AND THE ROYAL LEGISLATION ON CIVIL PROCEDURE

If the code is viewed only in terms of the combative spirit of the Council of Justice that formulated it and the determination of the royal councils that strove to enforce it, one might infer that the new regulations threatened Parlement's judicial authority and methods. The failure of the *parlementaires* to secure exemption from the royal legislation and their limited participation in the process of reform might indeed reenforce this impression. Nevertheless, a closer look at the code and its subsidiary

legislation as they applied to the Parlement of Paris reveals that the judges
had little to fear from this aspect of Louis XIV's "reformation of justice."

One obvious point to emphasize is that despite their good intentions,
the king and his councils were never able to enforce all the provisions of
the code. The judiciary was simply too large to permit flawless supervision, and many of the abuses the Council of Justice hoped to eliminate
persisted well into the eighteenth century.[131] The flood of conciliar decrees and subsidiary legislation itself testifies both to the difficulty the
crown had in implementing the code and to the confusion among the
judges in observing all its provisions. Indeed, violations were so common
during the early years of reform that on January 31, 1669, the council
pardoned all judges for any contravention of the new regulations that had
occurred since 1667.[132]

While it is important to recognize the problems involved in enforcing
the code, one should not exaggerate their significance. Eventually, most of
the king's program became a permanent feature of judicial administration,
some aspects even surviving the French Revolution. Far more important
reasons why the code and its supporting decrees did not affect Parlement
adversely are to be found not in enforcement, but in the provisions themselves. For example, several sections in the code actually extended the
length and cost of litigation to the advantage of judicial officials, a circum-
stance that the Council of Justice neither desired nor anticipated. Thus the
tenth title permitted litigants to request the interrogation of opposing
parties on specific points of evidence any time during the case; the twen-
tieth title not only increased the types of written evidence that were
acceptable in civil litigation, but required that oral testimony be accompanied by substantial (and expensive) documentation.[133] Also, if a litigant
wished to challenge the authenticity of a document his opponent presented as proof, this required a separate and costly criminal procedure.[134]
To be sure, these shortcomings do not negate the value of the new regulations. When compared to previous practices, the simplified procedure of
1667 unquestionably benefited litigants, even if it contained imperfec-
tions. Nevertheless, the code's positive contributions to judicial administration should not obscure its failure to provide a panacea for all the
procedural abuses in civil litigation.

Other provisions on the royal legislation favored Parlement more directly, either by ignoring certain subjects altogether or by respecting the
judges' traditional practices. One must remember, for example, that the
code and its subsidiary decrees dealt almost exclusively with procedure
and thus represented only a part of Louis XIV's "reformation of justice."
The Council of Justice had clearly established how litigation would pass
through and among individual courts, but it had not stipulated which

cases magistrates were entitled to judge. Stated simply, the king's legislation on civil procedure did not reorganize Parlement's jurisdiction. The eleventh and thirty-fifth titles of the code, which pertained directly to Parlement's method of civil procedure and judgment of appellate cases, in no way reduced the quantity or type of litigation that came before the court. In fact, these titles benefited the *parlementaires* by ensuring that appeals flowed smoothly into their court from lesser jurisdictions. Likewise, the edict of August 1669 preserved Parlement's traditional rights in litigation involving *committimus*. The first title of the same edict, which dealt with evocations, simply restated the provisions of past ordinances concerning those evocations that arose from familial ties between judges and litigants. As noted earlier, even during their tumultuous conflicts with the royal councils in the 1650s the *parlementaires* never objected to evocations on these grounds, which they considered perfectly legitimate.[135] The first article did mention general evocations, to which Parlement had objected, but emphasized that the councils would grant them only in "great and important occasions."

The code and its subsidiary legislation also did not alter the internal structure of Parlement to the disadvantage of the magistrates. The number of councillors and presidents remained the same as before, and the organization of the *grand' chambre* and the chambers of *enquêtes* and *requêtes* likewise escaped innovation. In fact, the *parlementaires* profited from the structural changes that were enacted. If the king suppressed the *chambre de l'édit*, he replaced it with a more substantial chamber of *tournelle civile* that gave the magistrates an opportunity to hear more cases and to earn additional fees and salaries. A contemporary document notes that the members of this chamber handled at least twenty cases per session, and that they assembled four times a week.[136] The influx of cases into the court was so great that a royal edict of July 1683 reestablished the judgment of litigation by delegates of the presiding judge, a practice that a decree of 1673 had prohibited.[137] Moreover, many of the edicts of 1669 and 1673 that increased the types of dockets in each of Parlement's chambers were a response to the great quantity of litigation that came before the *parlementaires*.[138]

Equally important, neither the king nor the Council of Justice attempted to change the laws that magistrates used to resolve litigation. It remained a magistrate's prerogative to interpret the law and to formulate new precedents and procedures if customary law, royal edicts, or Parlement's decrees did not provide a basis for adjudication. Several seventeenth- and eighteenth-century jurists who published compendia of "notable questions of law," such as Jean Dufresne and Claude Le Prestre, testified to Parlement's ongoing activity and interest in these matters.

Their works contain many parlementary decrees from the 1660s and 1670s that interpreted customary law and established jurisprudence on particular points of law that the customs had either ignored or were at variance with.[139]

Furthermore, it is worthy of note that the royal councils did not monopolize either the interpretation or the enforcement of the code. Using their regulatory powers over lesser courts, the *parlementaires* continued after the issuance of royal legislation both to guide the conduct of lesser judges and oftentimes to aid the crown in implementing the new regulations. Between 1667 and 1670, Parlement issued no less than seven *arrêts de règlement* explaining the procedures judges were to follow for specific types of litigation and conveying additional information about fees and court costs. In preparing these regulations, the court adhered to the principles and guidelines of the code.[140] The *parlementaires* also regulated their own conduct in the spirit of the ordinance. In May 1669, for example, they decided to eliminate *épices* for appeals that did not have written reports attached.[141] Later in the year they set up an ad hoc committee to monitor the fees that *procureurs, greffiers,* and *huissiers* collected and to punish those who violated recent decrees on this matter.[142] In a *mercuriale* of 1673, the magistrates ordered the enforcement in Parlement of all royal legislation concerning written procedures. At the same session they adopted the *tournelle civile*'s practice of preparing special dockets for specific categories of litigation.[143]

Not only did Parlement retain the ability to interpret and enforce the new regulations, but it had also helped to determine their contents. Many provisions in the code and its supporting decrees were taken directly from the *parlementaires*' own practices and regulations, which further illustrates the lack of dramatic change that royal procedural reform caused in Parlement. As noted previously, Parlement had demonstrated in a variety of ways its willingness to attack the major abuses associated with civil procedure. The members of the Council of Justice apparently thought highly of this reforming activity because they borrowed heavily from the judges with whom they disputed publicly. Thus, large portions of Parlement's decrees of July and August 1665, which dealt with procedures in lesser tribunals and the establishment of court costs, appeared in the code and in the royal edict of 1673 on *épices*.[144] In addition, the twenty-seventh title of the code, which set forth procedures for implementing sentences, simply extended to other courts what Parlement had practiced all along.[145] In fact, throughout the ordinance articles restated Parlement's legislation, often in similar wording, particularly on matters that had priority in the court's *mercuriales* and plenary sessions: the conduct of lesser judicial officials, documentation, delays in litigation, *saisies-réelles*, the abolition of superfluous procedure, and the encouragement of the briefer oral and summary procedures. Rather than change Parlement's methods, therefore, royal legislation often adopted the court's procedures and applied them to the rest of the judiciary.[146] This explains why First President Lamoignon concentrated on issues other than the details of civil procedure when he debated the code with Pussort.

The question of the financial impact of procedural reform on the *parlementaires* is difficult to resolve. The code potentially threatened their official income in two respects: by reducing superfluous procedures and those instances when judges could collect *épices*, and by making a magistrate susceptible to prosecution by litigants if he violated the new regulations. On the issue of *épices*, although contemporary records of these fees have not survived, a few guarded hypotheses may be proposed. It seems that a number of features of royal reform combined to reduce the spectre of financial loss to individual judges. First, most of the articles of the code that limited fees applied to lesser judicial officials—advocates, *procureurs*, *greffiers*, and *huissiers*—and not to the judges who actually decided a case. Second, although the code expanded the category of litigation that was eligible for summary and oral procedures not subject to *épices*, the more costly written procedures remained the principal course of justice in civil cases.[147] Third, the simplified procedure provided by the code and the creation of a new chamber presumably allowed the *parlementaires* to hear additional cases. Quite possibly, therefore, royal legislation benefited individual litigants without jeopardizing a judge's overall income. Fourth, the code and the royal edict of March 1673 limited the instances when judges could collect *épices*, but they did not restrict the magistrate's privilege of setting the monetary amounts that litigants would pay; the king never executed his threat to abolish *épices* altogether. Finally, the *parlementaires* seemed unconcerned about the code's effect on their fees. They seldom discussed this topic at the sessions with the Council of Justice, and in the years prior and subsequent to 1667 they frequently reduced *épices* on their own initiative.[148]

As for the provisions of the ordinance that allowed litigants to sue a judge for damages incurred by violation of the code, which Lamoignon had protested in the sessions with the Council of Justice, there is no indication that such a practice was widespread, at least at the Parlement of Paris. An examination of the decrees of the Privy Council, presumably where such charges would have been filed against magistrates of a court of last resort like Parlement, does not reveal a single case of a litigant filing suit against a *parlementaire*. Such prosecutions might have indeed occurred, but they are certainly not prevalent in the conciliar records.[149]

For a number of reasons, therefore, royal reform of civil procedure neither diminished Parlement's jurisdiction nor changed judicial methods to the disadvantage of the magistrates. To be sure, the *parlementaires* found some aspects of reform humiliating. They suffered a blow to their pride because they had not assisted the Council of Justice in preparing the code and because they had exercised little influence in the sessions of 1667. They also resented the inclusion of Parlement in regulations that applied to the humblest of royal and seigneurial courts. In practice, however, royal legislation of the 1660s and 1670s not only respected Parlement's traditional judicial authority, but frequently incorporated the court's own reform decrees and gave them wider application.

PARLEMENT AND ROYAL REFORM OF CRIMINAL PROCEDURE

Like the civil code of 1667, the criminal code that the Council of Justice completed in early 1670 provided a single procedure that applied uniformly to all royal and seigneurial courts.[150] It simplified and regularized procedures in the courts and in the appellate hierarchy, reducing the length and cost of litigation. The first of the code's twenty-eight titles dealt with the jurisdictional competence of courts, establishing the general principle that the tribunal nearest the commission of a crime would initially hear a case. Subsequent titles set forth precise rules for the summons, arrest, and imprisonment of a defendant, the interrogation of witnesses, the establishment of proof, delay periods, and the methods of preparing and filing trial documents. Other provisions considered the right of the accused to confront hostile witnesses and elaborated on the procedures for reviewing evidence. The code also outlined how the presiding judge in a case and the *procureur général* of a court were to draw up and implement verdicts, whether these involved acquittal, imprisonment, corporal punishment, or the collection of additional evidence. Appellate procedures received detailed attention, and one title concentrated specifically on procedures for those lesser criminal judges who were notorious for poor conduct, such as *prévôts des maréchaux*, *vice-baillis* and *sénéchaux*, and *lieutenants-criminels de robe courte.*

The code unquestionably eliminated many of the abuses that had crept into the administration of criminal justice. Shorter trials meant that many accused individuals did not have to suffer the torments of prison for long periods of time; one of the most praiseworthy features of the code was its insistence that all accused persons be interrogated within twenty-four hours of their arrest.[151] Likewise, the requirement that judges, and not their subordinates, interrogate defendants and take testimony from witnesses shortened the preliminary stages of prosecution and reduced the quantity of appeals that arose from inaccurate records.[152] Those titles that regulated the treatment of prisoners and the fees they paid to their judges and jailers during incarceration also improved the lot of those who found themselves behind bars.[153] In similar fashion, the provisions that dealt with the preparation of documents and the fees of *greffiers* swept away many complicated, expensive, and useless procedures that caused defendants and plaintiffs alike financial hardship.[154] As in the code of 1667, moreover, many articles established penalties for judges who decided cases contrary to the provisions of the ordinance.[155] Equally important, the code ordered magistrates at every level to process litigation even in the absence of court costs and fees.

Like its counterpart for civil procedure, the criminal code of 1670 eliminated many superfluous procedures and had humanitarian consequences. Nevertheless, once again the judicial authority and methods of the Parlement of Paris escaped substantial change. In large measure this statement applies to the entire judiciary, and the reasons stem primarily from the monarchy's own approach to the punishment of crime and to the role of judges in promoting public order. Despite their occasional bursts of hostility against the magistrates, the king and his advisers saw a powerful judiciary as the most important source of the rigorous criminal justice they hoped to maintain in France. As noted previously, even the authors who submitted memoirs on judicial abuse to Colbert had recommended few innovations in the strict criminal procedure sanctioned by the ordinance of 1539. Both they and the Council of Justice that reviewed their suggestions for reform were concerned far more with coercing a judge to prosecute suspected criminals than with limiting his powers to do so. As a consequence of this climate of opinion, the authority of judges received higher consideration in the code than the rights of the accused. Criminal judges continued to decide with little outside interference such crucial issues as the granting of counsel to defendants, the nature of proof, and the application of torture. Most important, royal judges and *procureurs généraux* retained great discretionary power in determining what constituted a crime and its appropriate punishment.[156] The ordinance established only very broad categories of crimes and punishments, and in almost all instances a presiding judge could increase or reduce a sentence given in a lesser court or set forth in the code itself.[157] Such a system, according to the historian of French criminal procedure, Adhémar Esmein, meant that even after royal reform "the judge in a manner played Providence."[158] Superior judges, moreover, actually gained in jurisdictional competence, because while the code preserved a judicial abuse by maintaining the criminal jurisdiction of seigneurial and *prévôts des maréchaux* courts, it stipulated that all capital verdicts and appeals from these tribunals were subject to review and verification by the sovereign courts.[159]

All of these points, of course, apply to the Parisian *parlementaires*. There were several other implications of the code that were peculiar to the king-

dom's most prestigious court of law. By the terms of the code, the Parlement of Paris remained the supreme criminal tribunal of the land, with the
exception of the king in his council. Parlement retained its status as the
court of last resort for criminal litigation on appeal, and the privilege of
certain individuals to have their cases brought before the *parlementaires* in
first instance remained intact.[160] Six years after the code's appearance, for
example, Colbert wrote to *Procureur Général* Harlay to confirm that "the
king has decided . . . to give you [Parlement] the liberty to judge . . . in the
grand' chambre the criminal cases of all sorts of persons who have only you
for judges."[161] Furthermore, the *parlementaires* had attempted to improve
criminal procedure long before reform began on the national level and, as
in 1667, their work influenced the content of royal legislation. This was
especially true in the field of prison reform. As recently as 1659, the king
had officially reiterated Parlement's jurisdiction in matters dealing with
royal prisons.[162] Between 1660 and 1667 the magistrates put this authority
to good use, issuing numerous regulations on the upkeep of prisons and
the conduct of the officials who managed them, particularly on matters
regarding bookkeeping, the collection of fees, and the sustenance of prisoners.[163] Perhaps the most humane provisions of the entire code were
those that dealt with incarceration, and much of what the Council of
Justice unveiled in 1670 originated directly from these earlier parlementary decrees.[164]

For all these reasons, the seven sessions that representatives from
Parlement and the Council of Justice held in early 1670 to discuss the
rough draft of the code were more subdued and marked by fewer hostile
exchanges than the meetings of 1667.[165] The *parlementaires* still resented
their exclusion from the Council of Justice and their inclusion in regulations that applied to the humblest criminal tribunals. But the code's
basic respect for their authority removed the grounds for heated opposition. Consequently, the debate between Lamoignon and Pussort, who
again dominated the sessions, is far more interesting to the student of
contemporary attitudes toward criminality than to the historian of
Parlement's relations with the crown. Free from the need to wrangle over
a judge's powers, the two spokesmen concentrated on issues concerning
the rights of suspected criminals, such as the application of torture, the
right of a defendant to counsel, and the requirement that the accused take
an oath to tell the truth and suffer penalties if he lied.[166] When issues did
arise that dealt with a magistrate's authority or financial emoluments, the
first president often defended successfully his point of view. Although he
failed to remove those provisions that left judges susceptible to financial
penalties, he convinced the delegates to preserve the jurisdiction of the
notorious seigneurial courts, claiming that for a lord, justice was a finan-

cial benefit he received by his patrimony.[167] On similar grounds, he secured modification of some articles that reduced the fees of *greffiers, procureurs,* and jailers.[168] He also preserved a magistrate's privilege to establish court costs for witnesses.[169] In all these instances, Lamoignon helped to perpetuate abuses in criminal justice in defense of the vested interests of judicial officials.

In the years following the issuance of the code, the *parlementaires* (and most other judges) also benefited from notable omissions among its articles and the lack of adequate enforcement. The code failed to modify superior judges' fees in a significant way, for example, and despite provisions to the contrary, magistrates often refrained from prosecuting suspected criminals unless those who filed charges financed the proceedings.[170] According to Esmein, "the question of money not only hampered prosecutions, it often vitiated them."[171] Perhaps the greatest abuse that survived royal reform was the effect of influence and money on the course of criminal justice. Bribery remained a prominent feature of judicial administration and wealthy individuals easily obtained trial documents, which were supposedly secret.[172] Furthermore, judges and their subordinates frequently ignored the code's praiseworthy provisions on the handling of judicial documents. Especially in lesser criminal tribunals, these remained costly, poorly written, badly recorded, and subject to falsification.[173] The result of these limitations to the code's effectiveness was not only that judges retained their judicial power and financial gain, but that poor individuals found it difficult to prosecute anyone while the rich were able to secure the favor of a judge. Finally, because courts at every level continued to rely heavily on customary laws and their attendant procedures in deciding criminal litigation, the provision in the civil code of 1667 that prohibited magistrates from interpreting law contrary to royal decrees was, in the words of Esmein, "bound to be in vain."[174]

The Parlement of Paris therefore emerged from another round of royal reform with its judicial authority and methods largely intact. As in 1667, the *parlementaires* had some justification to resent the new regulations. Once again, they had access to legislation only after the Council of Justice had already completed it, and Parlement did not enjoy exemption from reform because of its preeminent status among judicial institutions. Nevertheless, as was the case with royal reform of civil procedure, the actual contents of the code preserved Parlement's extensive authority in criminal affairs. Not only had the judges influenced many provisions with their own regulations, but they subsequently evaded those sanctions that contradicted their traditional practices. Most important, the monarchy's motives behind the reform of criminal procedure benefited Parlement, for while the king and his advisers intended to reduce the length and cost of litigation, they were determined to do so without sacrificing either the harsh procedures of the past or the judges' powers to prosecute suspected criminals.

PARLEMENT AND THE NONPROCEDURAL ASPECTS OF JUDICIAL REFORM

French historians of law have unfortunately stopped short of a thorough analysis of Louis XIV's "reformation of justice" because they have evaluated royal judicial reform in terms of the codes alone. But the memoirs Colbert solicited on judicial affairs clearly indicated that changes in civil and criminal procedure were in themselves not sufficient to improve the quality of judicial administration. The authors of the memoirs saw procedural problems as only the sunlit tip of a submerged iceberg of judicial abuse, and they firmly believed that the crown had to probe deeper than judicial methods if reform was to be complete and effective. More specifically, two nonprocedural aspects of justice captured their attention. First, they felt that reform should encompass the organization of the judiciary—the number of courts, their jurisdictional competence, and their relations with one another. Second, they encouraged the king to focus on the magistrates themselves—their number in the kingdom, the way they acquired their posts and the prices they paid for them, and their education and familial ties with one another.

Louis XIV and Colbert did share their advisers' concern that the two procedural codes would provide only a partial solution to judicial abuse. Yet, as previous chapters have shown, their plans to extend judicial reform beyond the realm of procedure were either abandoned, poorly enforced, or unsuited to rectify the problems cited in the memoirs. The crown's failure to deal adequately with the nonprocedural abuses in judicial administration further reduced the impact of the "reformation of justice" on royal courts, including the Parlement of Paris.

In the first place, the king failed to adopt the memoirs' almost unanimous call for the abolition of the venality of offices and the *droit annuel*. [175] Not only could the crown not afford to repurchase offices on a large scale, but their sale remained a lucrative source of royal revenue. Moreover, a substantial and influential segment of the population, almost all of the monarchy's own officials, derived social status and income from the sale of offices and the *droit annuel*. To have curtailed them altogether might have provoked a constitutional crisis that even Louis XIV was not prepared to risk. The preservation of the two practices, of course, had a detrimental effect on judicial administration. Continued ownership of office as negotiable property not only ensured judges a basis of independence from the crown, but precluded a reduction in either the number of judges or the size of the judiciary. Equally important, because judges normally used criteria of wealth and social standing to choose their successors, the survival of the *droit annuel* severely restricted the number of men who could rise to judicial office on the basis of talent alone. Finally, the office of magistrate remained a considerable investment on the part of an individual or family, and judges continued to expect a return on this investment, often at the financial expense of litigants.

Second, the crown enacted few organizational changes in the judiciary. Even the seigneurial and *prévôts des maréchaux* courts, which the memoirs had condemned, were simply regulated by the codes, not abolished. In Parlement, the *grand' chambre* retained its authority to direct the court, and the new chamber of *tournelle civile* might have actually increased the volume of litigation that came before the judges. Although the two codes raised the jurisdictional competence of some courts in certain instances, for example, the increased capacity of presidial courts to judge more cases in last resort, the judiciary remained as large and complex as before royal reform. Thus, even if procedural legislation reduced the length and cost of litigation in individual courts, litigants continued to face years of court contests and appeals in the vast judicial hierarchy to bring a case to completion.

Third, although royal decrees of 1665 and 1669 stabilized the prices of offices in the high judiciary by 1683, the reform neither harmed the judges at Parlement nor improved the administration of justice.[176] The *parlementaires* did not suffer financial ruin, either because they added the *pot de vin* to the sale price of their posts, or because previous family members had purchased the office at a price below the level established in 1665. Nor did a stable market value for a *parlementaire's* charge diminish his conception of himself as a member of a prestigious judicial institution that conferred high social status and attendant political influence. As regards the administration of justice, so long as judges purchased their posts and controlled recruitment through the *droit annuel*, the reduction of office prices failed to throw open the judiciary to talent. Office prices remained high (either 90,000 or 100,000 *livres* for a councillorship in Parlement) and judges had considerations other than a candidate's merit in mind when they transferred or sold their posts.

Fourth, royal legislation aimed at curtailing age dispensations and breaking the familial ties between judges remained a dead letter.[177] The crown's financial needs largely accounted for this failure. As Chancellor Le Tellier explained to *Procureur Général* Harlay in 1678, the king's involvement in a foreign war required the continued sale of age dispensations to candidates for judicial office as one way of increasing royal revenue. As the demands of the treasury therefore took precedence over reform, young and inexperienced magistrates remained a permanent feature of the judiciary. A similar fate awaited the edict of 1669 that prohibited judges from entering a court where their relatives sat or from marrying into their colleagues' families. The king lacked the authority to annul marriages, and by the 1670s the government awarded dispensations for parental ties to those magistrates willing to pay for them. In just the five years after the issuance of this edict, ten *parlementaires* married the daughters of other officials in the court, and the council's records of evocations demonstrate how extensively the judges were related to one another through birth and marriage. Thus, despite the wise counsel of the memoirs to Colbert, the judicial abuses that arose from familial bonds between judges persisted throughout the reign of Louis XIV.

Finally, the crown achieved only limited success in its efforts to improve the quality of legal education in France; the authors on judicial abuse were thus frustrated on still another front. In April 1679, the king issued a significant declaration on the subject of legal education.[178] It ordered that candidates for legal degrees pursue three years of study, that students attend classes and register several times a year to certify their attendance, that universities keep records on student progress, and that documents attesting to these facts as well as an advocate's diploma be required of all candidates for a magisterial post. The declaration also contained two notable innovations. In order to provide prospective judges with more secular education, the king reestablished the study of civil law at the University of Paris. He also initiated a program of French law, which would be taught in French (not Latin) and focus upon the study of customary law, royal ordinances, Parlement's decrees, municipal charters and statutes, and so on. The aim of this program, which students were to integrate into their third year of study, was to provide future judges with practical training for the courtroom.[179]

In subsequent years, the crown issued subsidiary legislation. A conciliar decree of March 23, 1680, added twelve *docteurs agrégés* to each law faculty in order to offer students additional courses.[180] Another royal declaration of August 1682 reiterated the provisions of the declaration of 1679, provided details on the professorship of French law, and outlined the procedures that students were to follow in registering and attending this course.[181]

It is worthy of note that the *parlementaires* recognized the inadequacies of legal training and had taken steps to eliminate them on their own initiative before the king issued his legislation. In September 1655, for example, Parlement added twenty-four honorary professors to the faculty of law at the Sorbonne to compensate for the dearth of qualified instructors.[182]

First President Bellièvre, whom one historian of the University of Paris refers to as "a tireless defender of the faculty," had encouraged the study of civil law at the university in the early 1650s in order to enhance the legal knowledge of students.[183] Acting on a request of *Procureur Général* Fouquet, Parlement issued three decrees in 1657 on the subject of legal education. Two repeated past legislation that prohibited the sale of "blank" diplomas and required an advocate's degree from all candidates for judicial office; the other instructed students to register at their university four times a year in order to certify their attendance in writing.[184] The king acknowledged Parlement's expertise in this aspect of judicial administration. Not only did he incorporate provisions from the court's decrees in his own reforms, but when he established a commission in 1667 to examine the curriculum of the University of Paris and propose changes, he included several *parlementaires* in the group.[185]

Despite the efforts of both crown and Parlement, however, many of the reforms were unsuccessful. Often the vested interests of the faculties and the liberties they enjoyed as corporations frustrated the new regulations, especially in the provinces.[186] Louis also may have dethroned canon law and replaced it with civil law as the preeminent basis of legal instruction, but he failed to establish fully the more practical program of French law in university curricula.[187] Another significant shortcoming of the reforms arose from the monarchy's refusal to enforce some of its own legislation. For example, the king continued to grant dispensations from attendance requirements to influential individuals. Many future judges thereby acquired a diploma without attending university for the required three years. *Parlementaires* did not hesitate to secure this royal favor for their relatives. The son of First President Lamoignon, Chrétien, and Louis-Achille de Harlay, a younger relative of the *procureur général*, received such dispensations as did many other judges in the court.[188] "It is curious to establish undeniably," wrote one historian of the University of Paris, "that Louis XIV, the great reformer of the faculty [of law], introduced... a pernicious principle of dissolution [in his reforms] by propagating a profusion of exceptions [to the new regulations]."[189]

The judicial reforms of Louis XIV, therefore, failed to deal adequately with the nonprocedural aspects of judicial administration. This shortcoming bears directly on a general assessment of the effectiveness of his "reformation of justice." Although the two codes of 1667 and 1670 unquestionably improved procedures, the more fundamental causes of judicial abuse survived the king's legislation. Contemporaries recognized the deficiencies of royal reform. Isaac de Larrey, in his history of Louis's reign published in 1718, noted that despite the partial success of the codes, "chicanery [in judicial administration] is no less stubborn, litigation is not expedited any swifter, and except for some useless procedures that [the codes] abolished or abridged, evil is no less great than it once was. . . . [The fault resides] in general in the nation itself, and in particular in this vast multitude of judicial officials who do not wish to remain without occupation, and who love, so to speak, to fish in troubled waters."[190] In his biography of Colbert published in 1696, Sandras de Courtilz was equally skeptical about the king's achievement. "In order to see the little utility of the new ordinance [of 1667], it is necessary to establish that chicanery comes from four causes: the diverse degrees of jurisdiction, the conflicts between courts, the useless procedures, and [the poor application of the law]."[191] Even *Avocat Général* Talon provided a telling analysis of the king's reforms. Sometime after the issuance of the codes (since he mentions the royal legislation of 1667, 1669, and 1670) he wrote a report for Louis on justice, police, and ecclesiastical discipline. On the subject of justice, he stressed that the more basic problems of judicial administration had escaped reform: the venality of offices, the *droit annuel*, the number of judges and courts, age dispensations, and so on. "The ordinances that have been formulated since 1667," he stated candidly, "have for the most part a need to be improved."[192]

Effective reform in the administration of justice in seventeenth-century France ultimately required three distinct, but related legislative actions: simplification of the procedures used in courts, organizational changes in the judiciary, and changes in the methods of a judge's tenure in office. Louis and Colbert actively pursued only the first possibility, with the result that the reforms they produced had only a limited impact on the quality of judicial administration. The son of First President Lamoignon, Chrétien, once remarked about the preparation of the royal codes of 1667 and 1670 that "the genius of those who worked for the reformation of justice was not extensive, [for] they stopped their work at that which was the least part, which is procedure."[193] If Chrétien's statement is qualified to allow that even the procedural reforms did not significantly alter the *parlementaires'* judicial authority and methods, it constitutes an accurate assessment of the impact of Louis XIV's "reformation of justice" on the Parlement of Paris.

The fate of Parlement's judicial authority after the Fronde further underscores the lack of dramatic change that accompanied Louis XIV's control of the judges. Like Mazarin, the king had not attempted to submit Parlement to his will by disrupting the judges' control over their offices, by threatening their economic vested interests, or by undermining the court's status as a social corporation. In the realm of judicial administration, the restricted scope and limited impact of the "reformation of justice" ensured the preservation of Parlement's traditional functions as a court of law. In his relations with Parlement Louis was concerned primarily with reducing the *parlementaires'* political activities, and in this respect he enjoyed considerable success. But even here, his accomplishment rested more on careful supervision of the judges and compromise with them than on the abolition of the duties and powers they relied upon to participate in affairs of state. All the elements were present, therefore, to allow Parlement to reassert its claimed privileges and prerogatives after the king died.

Conclusion

$\mathbf{B}$ecause the Parlement of Paris had emerged from the Fronde with its membership, powers, and pretensions remarkably well intact, the problem of controlling the judges remained a matter of crucial importance to the monarchy in subsequent decades. This study has attempted to determine the means of control that were available to the crown, to isolate those the administrations of Cardinal Mazarin and Louis XIV decided to pursue, and to assess their impact on Parlement's development in the second half of the seventeenth century. When written around these themes, the history of Parlement after the Fronde reveals in microcosm the methods, achievements, and limitations of royal absolutism. It also provides the background for the role the magistrates were to play in eighteenth-century state and society.

There were several ways the crown might have attempted to control Parlement. Perhaps the most effective would have been to abolish the procedures whereby the judges purchased their offices on the public market and chose their successors in return for an annual tax. Together, the *vénalité des offices* and the *droit annuel* had political and social consequences in Parlement that were detrimental to royal authority. Because the *parlementaires* owned their posts as negotiable property and were free from royal appointment, they enjoyed a security in office that enabled them to assert their claims and grievances against the monarchy with remarkable independence. Equally important, their control over office transmission allowed them to recruit Parlement's membership along family and social group lines, which enhanced the court's status as a social corporation. *Parlementaires* commonly shared similar social and professional backgrounds, and families in the court frequently intermarried and built dynasties. As these social and familial ties in Parlement proliferated, the judges increasingly thought of themselves as a social elite, a belief that both intensified and reenforced their desire to participate with the crown in affairs of state. Thus, had either the cardinal or the king drastically changed the procedures of officeholding, they could have dissolved the social bonds between the judges and reduced Parlement's independence by staffing it with more docile officials.

The monarchy's capacity to influence important sources of magisterial wealth provided a second possible method for control. Despite variations among individual judges, a significant portion of their fortunes consisted of official income, interest on *rentes*, investment return on royal demesne, and the benefits of crown patronage. Royal policy could have taken two directions. The government might have sought to secure the judges' support by facilitating their access to these funds. On the other hand, Mazarin and Louis might have pursued a more stringent course of action by undermining *parlementaire* wealth through a variety of economic penalties.

The royal administration might have also attempted to submit the magistrates to the royal will by redefining the institutional duties and privileges that they employed to oppose the crown on the national and local level. In this respect, Parlement's right to register and remonstrate royal legislation, to issue judicial and administrative decrees, and to hold plenary sessions and *mercuriales* constituted prime targets for change because without them the judges lacked the means to translate their opinions into action. Mazarin and the king might have complemented reform along these lines by improving their relations with the first president and the *gens du roi*. These officials possessed considerable power and influence to guide royal programs through the court. During the successive conflicts resulting in the Fronde, however, they had frequently supported judicial opposition to the crown and voiced the grievances of the *parlementaires*.

Finally, Parlement's activities as a court of law provided still other means to control the judges. Despite their social, economic, and political interests, the *parlementaires'* primary responsibility was judicial administration. From their continual contact with civil and criminal litigation, they derived not only a portion of their wealth through official income, but also many of the legal procedures that enabled them to frustrate the execution of royal policies. The traditional preeminence of the court in legal affairs also enhanced the magistrates' position in society. Had Mazarin or the king boldly reduced Parlement's judicial functions and jurisdiction, they could have denied the judges their fundamental source of power and prestige.

Clearly, then, the monarchy had at its disposal a variety of methods to control Parlement, all of which reflected the complex interaction between the procedures of officeholding, the court's judicial and administrative traditions and authority, and the judges' political and financial interests. The only alternatives to aggressive royal action were compromise with the judges or full consent to their demand for a participatory role in affairs of state. Full consent, of course, was out of the question for the governments of Mazarin and Louis XIV, given their objectives. Compromise, which had always occupied an important place in the crown's relations with Parlement, unquestionably had the advantage of enabling the royal administration to avoid potentially volatile conflicts with the magistrates. Nevertheless, it also implied a reduction in the intended effects of royal policies and rarely resolved other issues in contention.

The turbulent relations between Parlement and the administration of Mazarin after the Fronde revealed the cardinal's reluctance to adopt the methods available to him to control the judges. Rather than opening an era of the consolidation of royal authority, the 1650s stand as a postscript to the conflicts of previous decades. The royal victory in the civil wars had neither ensured the *parlementaires'* acceptance of administrative centralization nor diminished their ability to oppose royal policies effectively.

Throughout the post-Fronde decade, the crown and Parlement remained on a collision course. Obsessed with raising funds to continue the war with Spain, Mazarin and his financial adviser Fouquet continued the "governmental revolution" of previous years. They introduced new taxes and extended older levies, tampered with coinage values, created and sold new offices, and attempted to reduce interest payment on *rentes*. The cardinal and Chancellor Séguier sought to avoid judicial opposition to these practices by using the royal councils to issue decrees without formal registration and to evoke from Parlement litigation that concerned royal policies.

The *parlementaires*, offended by the attempt to circumvent their asserted privilege of participating in affairs of state, and fearful that the cardinal's financial policies and the conciliar activity would threaten their wealth, function, and prestige, opposed the royal administration with fervor and often with great success. Encouraged by the king's own representatives in the court, the judges combined their administrative duties and privileges to block new taxes and to defeat planned reductions in salaries and *rentes*. They issued countless remonstrances against royal expedients and delayed registering legislation placed before them. They also resorted to administrative and judicial decrees that instructed lesser courts to ignore the government's orders and exonerated litigants who protested royal taxation. Parlement battled with the royal councils, nullifying their decrees and protesting their practice of evoking controversial cases. Even in the realm of religious affairs, the *parlementaires* obstructed Mazarin's campaign to eradicate Jansenism, not because they shared the sect's convictions, but because they believed that the cardinal's alliance with Rome and the French clergy violated the liberties of the Gallican church as well as their own jurisdiction.

These clashes between the crown and Parlement were similar to those which had produced the Fronde. To be sure, some major elements of the judicial revolt of 1648 were missing in Parlement's opposition during the following decade. The court no longer promoted a broad program of state reform or attempted to forge lasting alliances with other discontented groups. Despite this shift in Parlement's approach to its conflicts with the royal administration, however, Mazarin and Fouquet still feared the wrath of the judges. They recognized that their policies were unpopular in Paris and the provinces, and they had no guarantee that turmoil in Parlement would not spark another round of domestic strife. As a result, they responded to the court's recalcitrance by consistently modifying or abandoning their programs. But while this spirit of compromise enabled the government to weather successive crises, it failed to resolve the basic issues in contention. Each time the crown yielded to the judges, it only raised Parlement's expectations and diminished the impact of royal policies, thus opening the door to future expedients and renewed judicial opposition. The administration of Cardinal Mazarin failed to break this vicious circle.

If Mazarin and his advisers enjoyed little success in controlling Parlement's political activities, they also took no action to curtail the sale of offices and the *droit annuel*, to restrict the sources of magisterial wealth, or to break the social bonds between the judges. Instead of viewing these as means of control, Mazarin and Fouquet saw them as vehicles for compromise. On their part, the *parlementaires*, who were concerned primarily with their own vested interests, habitually ceased their opposition when the royal administration offered a satisfactory compromise; indeed, they often frustrated old *frondeurs* who hoped that the court's strident protests would incite internal disorder. Thus, armed with timely concessions, Mazarin kept the judges from open rebellion. But he did so at considerable cost to his own policies and without enacting change in Parlement's judicial and administrative authority, social composition, and asserted privilege of participating with the crown in affairs of state.

New directions in the relations between the crown and Parlement occurred only during the personal rule of Louis XIV. Yet a careful examination of the methods Louis employed to secure the submission of the judges reveals that he took only limited advantage of the methods available to control the court and that he had not forsaken the policies of compromise so dear to Mazarin and Fouquet. As a result, the absolutism associated with his reign did not entail permanent institutional change at Parlement.

Because of both financial pressures and the possibility of stirring the kingdom's officials to unified opposition to the crown, the royal administration never implemented proposals to curtail the venality of offices or the *droit annuel*. For similar reasons, the king and his advisers abandoned their attempts to end the sale of age dispensations and to prevent judges from marrying into the families of their colleagues. This benign neglect ensured that the magistrates would retain their posts as negotiable property and thereby preserve a basis of independence from the crown. They also continued to choose their successors along family and social group lines, as is evident from a study of the genealogies of the councillors who entered the court after 1661. Social solidarity developed in Parlement throughout Louis's reign and the *parlementaires* held fast to the contention that they deserved a political influence that was fitting to their elite social status and to the traditions of the court.

The government of Louis XIV also refrained from jeopardizing the sources of *parlementaire* wealth; in fact, Louis and his advisers made more of an effort to satisfy the economic interests of the judges than had Mazarin and Fouquet. Royal demesne and patronage remained available to members of Parlement, and the crown ensured that the *parlementaires* received favored treatment on matters that concerned their salaries and *rentes*. Even the reduction and stabilization of office prices in 1665 was not as damaging to the judges' interests as might first appear. Although the new official values fell below contemporary market values, they were nevertheless higher than most of the judges had originally paid for their posts, and many councillors evaded the regulations altogether by adding a supplementary fee to the sale price of their charges. Moreover, the reduction of office prices had beneficial consequences for the social cohesion among the judges. With prices lowered, a *parlementaire* no longer felt the temptation to sell his post to a high bidder who was socially unacceptable. Increasingly, lesser robe and official families gained access to Parlement and fewer judges moved on to higher bureaucratic positions. These trends probably intensified the magistrates' identification with the concept of "nobility of the robe" and the attendant privileges and prerogatives they associated with it.

It is also clear that Louis XIV's "reformation of justice" did not threaten Parlement's functions as a court of law. Because the royal legislation was limited in scope and dealt primarily with procedural matters, it failed to eliminate the deeply rooted causes for abuse in judicial administration. Moreover, although the two codes of 1667 and 1670 abolished superfluous procedures and reduced the length and cost of litigation, they left intact Parlement's organization and jurisdiction, and the judges retained their traditional rights to interpret the law and to supervise the conduct of lesser tribunals. In fact, the codes frequently incorporated Parlement's own reform decrees and extended throughout France judicial methods that the *parlementaires* had practiced all along.

In his relations with Parlement, Louis was concerned primarily with reducing the judges' political influence and their ability to oppose royal policies. While he was willing to respect their economic and social interests and to maintain them in their traditional judicial functions, he was determined to curtail their unsolicited participation in affairs of state. The decline in Parlement's political activity during his personal rule attests to Louis's success in pursuing this goal. Nevertheless, an accurate evaluation of this transformation must recognize that the king's achievement did not result from the imposition of dramatic change either in the court's duties and privileges or in the administrative mechanisms that the judges used to resist the crown. The key to royal control lay in management rather than innovation, in supervision rather than reorganization.

Each direct action that the king took to limit Parlement's ability to interfere with his policies had compensating features for the judges. For example, although the decree of July 1661 gave conciliar decrees supremacy over those of Parlement, the king simultaneously restricted the intrusion of his councils and intendants in the court's judicial and administrative jurisdiction. It was not in response to force and threats that Parlement gradually ceased its opposition to the councils after 1661; rather it was owing to the king's wise policy of removing a source of irritation and of reserving conciliar intervention for only the most important occasions. Likewise, although the king reduced Parlement's right to remonstrate royal decrees to a mere formality, even Colbert recognized this as only a temporary expedient that could be, and was, abandoned after Louis died. At any rate, the right of remonstrance was only the most visible means of Parlement's opposition, and the crown made no attempt to dispense with the other, equally important procedures the judges had used effectively in the past to oppose royal policies. Plenary sessions, *mercuriales*, the registration of legislation, and the right to issue judicial and administrative decrees remained integral parts of Parlement's privileges and tradition.

If Parlement rarely interfered with the execution of royal policy in the provinces, it was not because it had lost the ability to do so, but because the king improved the royal administration's management of the court and had recourse to policies more palatable to the judges than those of Mazarin. By disposing of Fouquet and establishing close ties with the first president and the *gens du roi*, the king kept abreast with affairs in the court and used his representatives to supervise Parlement's institutional procedures without abolishing them. He also abandoned many of the policies that had provoked judicial opposition during the ministry of Mazarin. In the first decade of his personal rule, Louis pursued a policy of peace in foreign affairs and thus could afford to dispense with many of the extraordinary financial policies promoted by the cardinal and Fouquet. Parlement approved of Colbert's financial reforms and the minister himself was careful to modify his programs on matters of particular concern to the judges, such as the rate of interest and payment of *rentes*.

Louis XIV's relations with Parlement reveal some characteristics of the royal absolutism of the era and open additional perspectives for assessing the impact of his reign on other traditional institutions. In the first place, Louis's absolutism was limited in scope. His administration did not utilize methods of control that resulted in deeply rooted change in Parlement's membership, social composition, structural organization, or judicial and administrative authority. Second, Louis's absolutism was primarily political in the sense that he concentrated on reducing Parlement's opposition to royal policies. The king was undeniably successful in this respect. Once the center of resistance to the crown, Parlement did not actively support nor participate in the opposition to Louis XIV, which grew as his reign progressed. Nevertheless, Louis accomplished this more through management and supervision of the magistrates' activity, compromise on issues that concerned them, and recourse to policies less susceptible to their opposition than through the introduction of permanent innovations. Parlement retained a significant, though restricted, tradition of participation in affairs of state, and except for the right of remonstrance, the institutional procedures it relied upon to resist the crown remained intact.

Finally, these features of Louis XIV's control of Parlement indicate that the absolutism associated with his reign was highly personal and did not possess qualities that he could bequeath to his successors. The quiescence of Parlement after 1661 underscores the king's remarkable ability to work through rather than destroy traditional institutions. But because permanent innovations occupied such a minor place in his control of the judges, the Parlement that faced a child-king and compromising regent in 1715 was similar to the one that had confronted Mazarin and the young Louis XIV in 1653: a tightly knit social corporation with extensive judicial and administrative authority and pretensions to participate with the crown in affairs of state. The central role of Parlement in the aristocratic resurgence in later reigns testifies to Louis XIV's limited use of the means available to bend the court to the royal will.

NOTES · BIBLIOGRAPHY · INDEX

Abbreviations

AAE	Archives des Affaires Étrangères, Mémoires et Documents, France
AMG	Archives du Ministère de la Guerre
AN	Archives Nationales
BA	Bibliothèque de l'Arsenal
BI	Bibliothèque de l'Institut de France
BM	British Museum
B. Maz.	Bibliothèque Mazarine
BN	Bibliothèque Nationale
BN, MSS. Fr.	Bibliothèque Nationale, manuscrits français
BN, n.a.f.	Bibliothèque Nationale, manuscrits nouvelles acquisitions françaises
BS	Bibliothèque du Sénat

All translations in the text and notes are by the author.

Notes

Introduction

1. On the lack of historical research on traditional institutions after the Fronde, see the essays by John B. Wolf, "The Reign of Louis XIV: A Selected Bibliography of Writings Since the War of 1914–1918," *Journal of Modern History*, XXXVI (1964), 127–44, and Ragnhild M. Hatton, "Louis XIV: Recent Gains in Historical Knowledge," *Journal of Modern History*, XLV (1973), 277–91, as well as the excellent bibliographies in P. Guiral, R. Pillorget, and M. Agulhon, *Guide de l'étudiant en histoire moderne et contemporaine* (Paris, 1971), and John C. Rule, ed., *Louis XIV and the Craft of Kingship* (Columbus, 1969).

2. Only the first president and the *gens du roi* did not benefit from the *droit annuel*. They purchased their posts like the other judges, but held them on revokable royal commission. The king thereby retained direct control over the appointment of these officials.

3. The sovereign courts included the Parisian Parlement, Chambre des Comptes, Cour des Aides, Grand Conseil, and Cour des Monnaies as well as their counterparts, if any, in the provinces.

4. A. Lloyd Moote, *The Revolt of the Judges: The Parlement of Paris and the Fronde, 1643–1652* (Princeton, 1971). A complete listing of historical works that deal with the origins of the Fronde and Parlement's role in it would expand a footnote into a small volume. Fortunately, Moote's recent study of Parlement during the Fronde skillfully reviews the major historiographical trends on these subjects; the reader interested in books and scholarly articles on the subjects treated in this introduction should refer to his study and to the bibliography at the end of this volume. Moreover, many of the themes discussed here recur in greater detail in following chapters, and I will make reference to particular historical interpretations as the need arises.

Chapter 1. The Office of Councillor at Parlement in the Reign of Louis XIV

1. Roland Mousnier, *La Vénalité des offices sous Henri IV et Louis XIII* (Rouen, 1945); Martin Göhring, *Die Ämterkäuflichkeit im Ancien régime* (Berlin, 1938).

2. In addition to Mousnier, see Georges Pagès, "La Vénalité des offices dans l'ancienne France," *Revue Historique*, CLXIX (1932), 477–95, and Franklin Ford, *Robe and Sword: The Regrouping of the French Aristocracy After Louis XIV* (Cambridge, Mass., 1953), chap. 6, *passim*.

3. Ford, *Robe and Sword*, p. 108; Mousnier, *La Vénalité*, bk. II, chap. 4, *passim*.

4. Mousnier, *La Vénalité*, pp. 23, 43–45, 215–16, 309–11, 398–404, 561–62; Koenraad Swart, *The Sale of Offices in the Seventeenth Century* (The Hague, 1949), pp. 11–12; Victor-L. Tapié, *La France de Louis XIII et de Richelieu* (Paris, 1967), pp. 49–50; J. Russell Major, "The

Crown and the Aristocracy in Renaissance France," *American Historical Review*, LXIX (1964), 644; Christopher Stocker, "Office as Maintenance in Renaissance France," *Canadian Journal of History*, VI (1971), 42–43.

5. Mousnier, *La Vénalité*, pp. 550–51.

6. This is the theme of ibid., bk. III, chap. 4, *passim*.

7. For sensitive treatments of this subject, see Georges Pagès, "Essai sur l'évolution des institutions administratives en France du commencement du XVIe siècle à la fin du XVIIe," *Revue d'Histoire Moderne*, VII (1932), 8–57, and Moote, *Revolt of the Judges*, chaps. 2–3, *passim*. In his *La Bourgeoisie française au XVIIe siècle* (Paris, 1908), pp. 18, 35–40, Charles Normand also noted the disadvantages of the *paulette* for royal authority, but he so overstated them that historians have long since ignored his opinions.

8. Moote, *Revolt of the Judges*, p. 119 ff. Moote's careful investigation of how royal-official clashes over the procedures of officeholding contributed to Parlement's participation in the Fronde serves as a corrective to Mousnier's absolutist thesis.

9. Of the sixty officials who entered Parlement during the reign of Charles VIII, eleven were appointed by the king, twenty-one were elected by the judges, and twenty-five were received *in favorem*. On three there is no information. Christopher Stocker, "Offices and Officers in the Parlement of Paris, 1483–1515" (Ph.D. dissertation, Cornell University, 1965), p. 40.

10. Ibid., pp. 277–81.

11. Phrase is Stocker's. Ibid., p. 79.

12. Edouard Maugis, *Histoire du Parlement de Paris de l'avènement des rois Valois à la mort d'Henri IV* (Paris, 1913–1916), I, 214–18, 237.

13. Ibid., II, 236–41.

14. Mousnier, *La Vénalité*, p. 509.

15. For standard treatments of the cardinal's domestic policies in this period, see Gabriel Hanotaux and Duc de La Force, *Histoire du Cardinal de Richelieu* (Paris, 1933–1947), IV, 275–398, and Tapié, *La France*, bk. III, chap. 3. Moote provides a concise analysis in *Revolt of the Judges*, chap. 2.

16. On this affair, see AN, U 2094, fols. 234–77; E 1685, fols. 379, 393. As late as 1641, however, the *parlementaires* refused to allow those councillors who had gained entrance into the court the privilege of collecting judicial fees on litigation. Mousnier, *La Vénalité*, pp. 186–88.

17. Surprisingly, Isambert has not included this edict in his collection of French laws. A complete copy, however, is in the Ormesson family papers, AN, 144AP, 152, fols. 69–84v. It is referred to there as "the principal edict of its kind" (fol. 68). A memoir on the *droit annuel* in BN, n.a.f. 9807, fols. 11–25v refers to it as the "touchstone" for all future legislation on the subject.

18. The official evaluations are scattered throughout BN, MSS. Fr. 11110 and 18230.

19. Mousnier, *La Vénalité*, pp. 336–37.

20. Memoir on the *droit annuel*, BN, MSS. Fr. 21016, fols. 875–78v.

21. Moote, *Revolt of the Judges*, p. 119 ff.

22. The duties of the *procureur général*, like those of the other *gens du roi*, were to represent the king's interests in the court, to decide when to introduce legislation for registration, and to see that decrees were properly enforced.

23. AAE, 900, fols. 168–70. First President Pomponne II de Bellièvre agreed with Fouquet. See his letter to Mazarin of July 1656 in Jules Mazarin, *Lettres*, ed. A. Chéruel (Paris, 1872–1906), II, 38–39.

24. "Mémoire sur le droict annuel," AN, U 939, fol. 4; "Mémoire sur la paulette," BA,

MS. 672, fols. 351–53v. See also the letters exchanged between Fouquet and Mazarin on July 3, 19, and 21, 1657, in AAE, 900, fols. 185–87v; 901, fols. 98, 160.

25. See below, p. 96. In a letter to Mazarin dated June 27, 1657, Fouquet complained that Parlement had not registered several financial edicts "in exchange for the *droit annuel*" as he had hoped. AAE, 902, no fol.

26. These events are discussed in detail below in chapter 5.

27. Jean-Baptiste Colbert, *Lettres, instructions et mémoires,* ed. P. Clément (Paris, 1861–1882), VII, 164–83.

28. Ibid., VI, 5–12.

29. The reports submitted to Colbert on the subject of judicial abuse and the impact on Parlement of the procedural codes the crown issued in 1667 and 1670 are analyzed below in chapter 6.

30. In a letter to the king dated October 22, 1664, Colbert had earlier stated his views on age requirements. Colbert, VI, 4.

31. Ibid., pp. 247–48.

32. Ibid., pp. 15–17.

33. James D. Hardy, *Judicial Politics in the Old Regime: The Parlement of Paris During the Regency* (Baton Rouge, 1967), p. 19.

34. In this connection, it is interesting that Le Tellier, who firmly opposed Parlement in the 1650s, was a force for moderation with the judges after Louis XIV became involved in foreign war. See below, pp. 79, 133.

35. AN, X¹a 8664, fols. 438–41; E 1728, fol. 265; and F.-A. Isambert, *et al.,* eds., *Recueil général des anciennes lois françaises* (Paris, 1822–1833), XVIII, 66–69.

36. For the dates of renewal to 1709, see Isambert, XVIII, 204; BN, MSS. Fr. 21016, fols. 875–78v; 15533, fols. 675–90.

37. For a list of these officials, see the memoir on the *paulette* in AN, 144AP, 152, fols. 84v–86.

38. In the beginning of the eighteenth century, the historian Isaac de Larrey reflected on the edict of 1665 and concluded that the king had been wise to renew the *paulette* because "nothing [had] upset the parlements and the other courts of justice [in the past] more than the suppression of the *paulette,* which the crown [periodically] threatened." He saw the renewal of the fee as a victory for the officials. *Histoire de France sous le règne de Louis XIV* (Rotterdam, 1718), II, 392.

39. Jean Meyer, *La Noblesse bretonne au XVIIIe siècle* (Paris, 1966), II, 943–46; John J. Hurt, "The Parlement of Brittany and the Crown, 1665–1675," *French Historical Studies,* IV (1966), 414–15, 422–26, 433.

40. Mousnier, *La Vénalité,* pp. 336–37.

41. Mme. Cubells, "Le Parlement de Paris pendant la Fronde," *XVIIe Siècle,* no. 35 (1957), pp. 171–201.

42. BN, Cinq Cents Colbert MS. 260, fol. 66; Félix Joubleau, *Etudes sur Colbert, ou exposition du système d'économie politique suivi en France de 1661 à 1683* (Paris, 1856), II, 261–63. The 1638 figures in BN, MSS. Fr. 11110, fol. 97 and 18230, fols. 1–2v vary slightly from those presented here, but only by a few thousand *livres.* The market value of all posts in Parlement in 1665 was estimated to be 50,723,000 *livres.*

43. BN, Cinq Cents Colbert MS. 260, fols. 38–81, and estimations throughout vols. 257–260; Meyer, *La Noblesse bretonne,* II, 930–31; Hurt, "The Parlement of Brittany and the Crown," p. 425.

44. Mousnier, *La Vénalité,* p. 342.

45. Meyer, *La Noblesse bretonne,* II, 944.

46. Abbé Charles-Irénée Castel de Saint-Pierre, *Annales politiques, 1658–1740*, ed. J. Drouet (Paris, 1912), pp. 106–07.

47. An excellent analysis of the financier's desire to gain access for his children in the sovereign courts is in Julian Dent, *Crisis in Finance: Crown, Financiers and Society in Seventeenth-Century France* (New York, 1973), chap. 9, *passim*.

48. Cited in Cubells, "Le Parlement de Paris," p. 180. Cubells provides a concise explanation of the motives behind the *parlementaires'* hostility to tax farmers and financiers. It is true, as Daniel Dessert has recently shown ("Finances et société au XVIIe siècle: A Propos de la Chambre de Justice de 1661," *Annales: Economies, Sociétés, Civilisations* [juillet-août 1974], pp. 847–82), that many financiers and tax farmers in the mid-seventeenth century were legally nobles, not bourgeois. But it must be remembered that most of them were nobles of recent extraction, normally by virtue of the expensive post of *secrétaire du roi*, which conferred hereditary nobility on the incumbent. Judges at the Parlement of Paris were hostile to the men who rose quickly in this fashion, whatever their legal status. Because the *parlementaires* consistently referred to financiers and tax farmers as "bourgeois," I have followed their lead and employed similar language for the remainder of this section.

49. Ibid., p. 183. See also Dent, *Crisis in Finance*, chaps. 2–3, *passim*; Ernst Kossmann, *La Fronde* (Leiden, 1954), pp. 53–54; Germain Martin and Marcel Besançon, *L'Histoire du crédit en France sous le règne de Louis XIV* (Paris, 1913), p. 134.

50. A memoir on the decree is in BN, MSS. Fr. 14029, fols. i–xx.

51. AN, X^{1}a 8391, fols. 56, 58.

52. Ibid., fols. 91v–92, 293.

53. Ibid., fols. 297–305.

54. Letter dated December 1658, BN, MSS. Fr. 17395, fols. 19–21v. The informant's fears were soundly based because Parlement also approved the letters of admission for the *maîtres des requêtes* and the councillors of the lesser courts in its area of jurisdiction. For example, on December 12, 1659, *Avocat Général* Denis Talon encouraged the judges to reject the candidacy of a Monsieur L'Avocat for a post of *maître des requêtes* because his father had been interested "in finances." AN, X^{1}a 8392, fols. 11–12v; Mazarin to Fouquet, January 27, 1660, AAE, 284, fols. 86–90, 93.

55. AN, U 2108, fols. 255v–68 (Talon); BN, n.a.f. 2431, fols. 88–91v (Miron).

56. Garnier's name does not appear on any list of councillors received by the court. However, he is mentioned in a notable dictionary of nobility as having been a president at the Parlement of Metz in 1674. François-Alexandre Aubert de La Chesnaye Des Bois, *Dictionnaire de la noblesse* (Paris, 1863–1876), VIII, 185.

57. The decrees were issued in January 1659. AN, X^{1}a 8391, fol. 325v; 8299 *bis*, fol. 15v. For a summary of the decrees Parlement issued against tax farmers between 1648 and 1659, see BN, MSS. Fr. 14029, fols. i–xx.

58. BN, Morel de Thoisy MS. 50, fol. 254 (Cour des Aides); AN, P 2603, fols. 190v–91 (Chambre des Comptes).

59. The procedures used to draw up the genealogies of the judges are discussed below, pp. 38–39.

60. AN, K 695, no. 38; X^{1}a 8391, fols. 413, 416v; 8392, fol. 62v. Parlement did accept a younger son, Anne Hervart, in 1674. Ibid., 8397, no fol. That the judges did desire to enforce the decrees of 1659 is evident from the notations "père de..." and "mère de..." before each candidate's name in the court's registers after 1659.

61. Compiled from Isambert, XVIII, 66–69 and from BN, Cinq Cents Colbert MS. 260, fol. 66.

62. Olivier Lefèvre d'Ormesson, *Journal*, ed. A. Chéruel (Paris, 1860–1861), II, 332, 423.

63. Ibid., pp. 428–31; AN, U 2114, fols. 40v–42.

64. AN, X¹a 8394, fols. 40–41. Adolphe Chéruel discusses this issue in his *Histoire de l'administration monarchique en France depuis l'avènement de Philippe-Auguste jusqu'à la mort de Louis XIV* (Paris, 1855), II, 100–06, and in his *De L'Administration de Louis XIV (1661–1672) d'après des mémoires inédits d'Olivier d'Ormesson* (Paris, 1850), pp. 49–50.

65. Charles Dreyss, ed., *Mémoires de Louis XIV pour l'instruction du Dauphin* (Paris, 1860), I, 125–27.

66. See for example, the anonymous *Vie de M. le premier président de Lamoignon* (Paris, 1781), p. xxxv. Ormesson also states that Louis was "determined to exile the first [judge] who spoke" and that this placed Lamoignon in a difficult position. *Journal*, II, 428–31, 434–37.

67. François Bluche, *Les Magistrats du Parlement de Paris au XVIIIe siècle* (Paris, 1960), p. 167. The government intended to enforce this edict. Between 1689 and 1704, Louis planned to create a sixth chamber of *enquêtes*, and the prices he decided to charge for the new posts conformed to the guidelines of 1665. Although the new chamber was never created, the royal intent is clear. On these plans, see BN, MSS. Fr. 16524, fols. 66, 175–76v.

68. *Journal*, II, 522. Examples of others who did this are on pp. 506–07.

69. Gatien Sandras de Courtilz, *La Vie de Jean-Baptiste Colbert, ministre d'état sous Louis XIV* (Cologne, 1696), pp. 147–48.

70. Indeed, the prices established in the edict were well *above* the levels proposed by Colbert earlier in the year: *président à mortier*, 300,000 *livres;* president of *enquêtes*, 75,000 *livres;* lay councillor, 40,000 *livres;* and clerical councillor, 75,000 *livres.* Colbert, VI, 5–12.

71. Ormesson reports such an edict in 1671 (*Journal*, II, 615) and Isambert mentions one dated October 18, 1678 (XIX, 180). The prohibition of *pots de vin* could be highly effective because while they were legal, a councillor who sold his office for an additional fee could take legal action against the purchaser who failed to pay it. If they were illegal, however, a councillor had no recourse to recover a forfeited *pot de vin.*

72. Bluche, *Les Magistrats*, pp. 81, 85.

73. Meyer, *La Noblesse bretonne*, II, 930–31.

74. AN, X¹a 8394, fols. 27v–28v.

75. Ibid., 8395, fols. 207–10; Bluche, *Les Magistrats*, pp. 76–77.

76. Paul Pellisson, *Histoire de Louis XIV, depuis la mort du Cardinal Mazarin en 1661 jusqu'à la paix de Nimègue en 1678* (Paris, 1749), I, 34–35.

77. In his essay on Louis XIV's reign, Voltaire noted how Fouquet sold his post of *procureur général* in 1661 for 1,400,000 *livres* and added that "the exorbitant amounts paid for seats in Parlement prove that this body still commanded considerable respect even in its decline." *Siècle de Louis XIV* (Paris, 1903), p. 458.

78. On this point, see Bluche, *Les Magistrats*, pp. 163–68; Meyer, *La Noblesse bretonne*, I, 937–46; and Michel Antoine, *Le Conseil du roi sous le règne de Louis XV* (Genève, 1970), pp. 234–35.

79. AN, X¹a 8393, fol. 56v. The letters were drawn up in November 1661. The stipulation of age requirements for entrance into the judiciary was not new. The crown had issued edicts to this effect in the past, but the judges had evaded them. For example, see the edict of December 29, 1638, in ibid., 8653, fols. 324–25v.

80. Ibid., 8393, fol. 271v–72. An anonymous memoir dated January 1663 describing Parlement's views on this subject, "Observations sur la déclaration du roy sur l'aage et les habits des messieurs du Parlement," is in BA, MS. 672, fols. 17–20.

81. Isambert, XVIII, 66–69; AN, X¹a 8664, fols. 438–41.

82. Isambert, XVIII, 325–29 (1669); AN, X¹a 8669, fols. 220–22v (1672). The edict of 1669 also reiterated the office prices established in 1665.

83. Compiled from BN, n.a.f. 8385, fols. 212–13 and references in the following volumes at AN: X¹a 8392, 8397, 8668, 8670; U 2112–14, 2117. See also the manuscript table compiled

by Alphonse Grün, "Table des lettres de provision, de dispenses et de vétérans, et des réceptions... au Parlement de Paris de Septembre 1669–1790," which is located in the reference room of the Archives Nationales.

84. See Grün's table cited in the previous note.

85. Bluche, *Les Magistrats*, p. 57.

86. BN, MSS. Fr. 17414, fol. 170. Le Tellier reached similar conclusions in other letters to the *procureur général*. See ibid., fol. 171; 21118, fols. 15–16.

87. Isambert, XIX, 121–22. Clément (Colbert, VI, 4, n.1) dates it in 1674 and Sandras de Courtilz, *Vie de Colbert*, pp. 289–90, mentions a similar edict of 1683. Ormesson (*Journal*, II, 615–16) charges that Colbert himself ignored his own regulations when age dispensations involved his friends and supporters. Colbert's toleration of age dispensations and the continuing award of these grants is also mentioned in a letter from Servien to Lionne, April 1671, in AAE, Savoie 62, fol. 123.

88. The reports submitted to Colbert and the response of both crown and Parlement to judicial malpractice is the subject of chapter 6 below.

89. See above, nn. 27, 28, 31, 32.

90. Isambert, XVIII, 325–29; AN, X¹a 8667, fols. 225–29.

91. Lamoignon emphasized that *parlementaires* had the right "contracter des marriages égaux entre leurs enfants, pour conserver une qualité sans tache, que la magistrature demande plus que toutes les autres professions." BN, n.a.f. 2429, fols. 587–88. Ormesson (*Journal*, II, 565–66) reports that Lamoignon protested so vigorously that "he received the universal applause [of his colleagues]," and that his action "reestablished his reputation in Parlement, because one thought him incapable of such vigorous action."

92. AN, X¹a 8668, fols. 415–16v. Parlement's registers for the years 1653–1673 contain references to eighteen grants of officeholding in the court *en concurrence*.

93. See François Bluche, "L'Origine des magistrats du Parlement de Paris au XVIIIe siècle," *Paris et Ile-de-France: Mémoires*, V–VI (1953–1954), 60 (Amelot), 88 (Berthier), 319 (Monthullé); La Chesnaye Des Bois, *Dictionnaire*, VIII, 986–87 (Caumartin), XIV, 514–15 (Morant), XIX, 662–64 (Vialart); BN, MSS. Fr. 32138, fols. 219–20 (Boucher), 375 (Chauvelin); 32785, fol. 489 (Maignart); 32786, fol. 777 (Bazin de Bezons).

94. Ford, *Robe and Sword*, p. 111; Isambert, XIX, 121–22.

95. Bluche, *Les Magistrats*, pp. 128–30.

96. AN, V⁶ 563, March 18, 1670.

97. Ibid., 488, no. 62.

98. Ibid., 493, no. 28.

99. AN, O¹2, fols. 216–17v (copy of a decree of the Conseil d'Etat).

100. Louis Moréri, *Le Grand Dictionnaire historique* (Paris, 1759), V, 526–27; AN, MM 821, fols. 103v–04.

101. Bluche, "L'Origine des magistrats," pp. 177–78.

102. Ibid., pp. 234–35.

103. BN, Cabinet des Titres, *dossiers bleus*, 314.

104. Ibid., 518.

105. The records are those of the Parisian Chambre des Comptes, which contain references to office transmissions (*quittances*). I consulted twenty-eight volumes for the years 1653–1673: AN, P 3231–35, 3239, 3242, 3246, 3252, 3258, 3259, 3270, 3271, 3273–85, 3287, 3430. These records are not complete, thus only 116 transfers are available. Some transfers are also listed in BN, Clairambault MS. 756, fols. 38–67, but these too are incomplete.

106. AN, P 3246, fols. 36, 55; 3284, fol. 17.

107. The councillor is Paul Payen. The king sold his post of clerical councillor to Jacques Gaudart for 80,000 *livres*. Ibid., 3277, fol. 39, February 11, 1667.

108. *Journal*, II, 472–73, mentions Le Pelletier's reluctance to purchase the post.

109. Ibid., pp. 423–24.

110. Colbert, II, 222–23, shows the list of candidates and Ormesson, *Journal*, II, 417, relates Colbert's desire to get a post in the court for one of his relatives at the same time.

111. Adolphe Chéruel, *Histoire de France sous le ministère de Mazarin (1651–1661)* (Paris, 1882), I, 361–62; Isambert, XVII, 299–301.

112. Moote, *Revolt of the Judges*, pp. 361–62.

113. AN, X¹b 8858.

CHAPTER 2. THE SOCIAL COMPOSITION OF PARLEMENT AND THE CONCEPT OF NOBLESSE DE ROBE

1. François Bluche and Pierre Durye, *L'Anoblissement par charges avant 1789* (Paris, 1962), II, 23–24.

2. Although Bacquet published treatises as early as 1580, his first book on the nobility, *Droit d'anoblissement*, appeared in 1608. This paragraph is based upon Jean Bacquet, *Oeuvres* (Lyon, 1744), II, 363–64; Charles Loyseau, *Traité des ordres et simples dignitez* (Paris, 1613), p. 55; and Gilles-André La Rocque de La Lontière, *Traité de la noblesse, de ses différentes espèces* (Rouen, 1710), p. 138.

3. Loyseau summed up the distinction in these terms: "We must realize that [in France] we have simply the nobility which originates from the ancient race [*ancienne race*] and that which stems from dignities. The first is without origins, the second has its beginnings. The one is inherent [*native*], the other can be traced in time [*dative*]." *Traité*, p. 55. For a similar definition, see Paul Hay du Chastelet, *Traitté de la politique de France* (Cologne, 1669), p. 43.

4. Bacquet, *Oeuvres*, II, 363–64.

5. Ford, *Robe and Sword*, pp. 59–66; Mousnier, *La Vénalité*, p. 504; and the latter's *Les Hiérarchies sociales de 1450 à nos jours* (Paris, 1969), p. 67.

6. Charles Loyseau, *Cinq Livres du droict des offices* (Paris, 1613), chap. 9, pp. 130–31.

7. Ibid., pp. 133–34; see also his *Traité*, p. 69.

8. Loyseau, *Cinq Livres*, chap. 9, pp. 128, 132. For Loyseau's opinions on this matter, see Mousnier, *Les Hiérarchies sociales*, pp. 76–79, and Cornelius Sipple, "The *Noblesse de la Robe* in Early Seventeenth-Century France: A Study in Social Mobility" (Ph.D. dissertation, University of Michigan, 1963), pp. 200–02. On pp. 197–202 Sipple describes how the *parlementaires* were fond of the view that a noble office blessed its holder and his family with nobility. In a speech before Parlement (date unknown) First President Lamoignon expressed this idea perfectly. He noted that the judges were noble because "ils la [noblesse] reçoivent d'eux [les rois] par réflexion et par la communication de leur employ." BN, n.a.f. 2429, fol. 585.

9. Loyseau, *Cinq Livres*, chap. 9, pp. 128, 131–32. For a discussion of *nobles hommes*, see J. Trévédy, "Sur le titre 'noble homme,'" *Revue Morbihannaise* (1902).

10. La Rocque, *Traité*, pp. 139, 255.

11. Bluche, *Les Magistrats*, p. 134; J. H. Shennan, *The Parlement of Paris* (Ithaca, 1968), p. 121.

12. Ford, *Robe and Sword*, pp. 66–67.

13. By the terms of an edict of September 4, 1657. AN, X¹a 8660, fols. 320–22v.

14. La Rocque, *Traité*, p. 256. Ford cites a similar decision in a special *taille* law for Dauphiné in 1639 whereby the principle of *patre et avo consulibus* was to apply to the Grenoble Parlement, Chambre des Comptes, and Cour des Aides. *Robe and Sword*, p. 63.

15. Louis Nicolas Henri Chérin, ed., *Abrégé chronologique d'édits, déclarations... et lettres patentes des rois de France de la troisième race concernant le fait de noblesse* (Paris, 1788), p. 109.

16. AN, X¹a 8660, fols. 291–92v.

17. Ford, *Robe and Sword*, p. 64. Bluche and Durye, *L'Anoblissement*, II, 23–24 do not mention the edict of 1715.

18. François-C. Desmaisons, ed., *Nouveau Recueil d'arrêts et règlements du Parlement de Paris* (Paris, 1667), pp. 409–10.

19. Laurent Jovet, ed., *La Bibliothèque des arrests de tous les parlemens de France* (Paris, 1669), pt. II, pp. 4–6.

20. See the memoir on the office creations of 1690 and the nobility of the *parlementaires* in BN, n.a.f. 7981, fols. 209v–10v.

21. For similar conclusions, see Ford, *Robe and Sword*, p. 64; Bluche, *Les Magistrats*, p. 371; and Meyer, *La Noblesse bretonne*, II, 935.

22. Bluche, *Les Magistrats*, pt. III, chaps. 3 and 5.

23. Ibid., pp. 82–85.

24. Sipple's dissertation provides a provocative analysis, based upon an examination of literary sources, of the *parlementaires'* struggle to justify their elite status in the face of sword hostility. On the resentment of the *ancienne noblesse* toward the magistrates in the seventeenth century, see also Mousnier, *Les Hiérarchies sociales*, pp. 70–72; Normand, *La Bourgeoisie*, pp. 47–51, 73–75; and Jean-Pierre Brancourt, *Le Duc de Saint-Simon et la monarchie* (Paris, 1971), pp. 222–23.

25. The list of *parlementaires* who entered the court was culled from Parlement's registers in series X¹a at the Archives Nationales, where the entrance of new judges into the court was recorded. Other partial listings, especially those in BN, MSS. Fr. 22728, 32933, and AN, P (Chambre des Comptes) were helpful for checking the accuracy of Parlement's registers. In drawing up the genealogies, the most useful published sources were Bluche, "L'Origine des magistrats," La Chesnaye Des Bois, *Dictionnaire*, and the relevant volumes of the *Dictionnaire de biographie française*. The principal manuscript sources consulted were the collections that comprise BN, Cabinet des Titres: *dossiers bleus, cabinet d'Hozier, nouveau d'Hozier, carrés d'Hozier, pièces originales*, and *Chérin*. Each collection lists many hundreds of families in alphabetical order, and several hundred volumes were consulted to yield accurate genealogies. The following volumes in BN, MSS. Fr. also contained useful genealogical information: 14018, 22728, 32138, 32139, 32353, 32354, 32464, 32484, 32785, 32786, 32987. The following volumes in AN contained information not found elsewhere: M 271; MM 404, 700ᴮ, 703, and 818¹. An attempt was made to check each genealogy in at least three different sources to ensure accuracy.

26. Those families which contributed three members were the Foucaults, Pinons, Le Pelletiers, and Phélypeaux.

27. Whenever a councillor's father or grandfather exercised several positions in his lifetime, the post he held at the time of the councillor's reception is used; if they were deceased at the time of reception, the last position occupied is given.

28. Most positions fit easily and obviously into one of the six categories. But in a few instances, some explanation may be necessary. Secretaries and councillors of state are included in the high judiciary, despite the fact that these were not magisterial posts, because the individuals concerned were often members of prestigious magisterial families and because most among them had exercised a judicial post before proceeding to a higher charge. Similarly, advocates in the sovereign courts and secretaries in the royal councils are included in the category of lesser judiciary because although they might have never occupied a judicial post, they were in constant contact and identified with the judiciary throughout their careers. *Trésoriers de France*, who could have been placed in the nonjudicial official group, are here included in the lesser judiciary because they frequently exercised a judicial function and

because they associated themselves with the robe. Councillors of provincial sovereign courts have been placed in the lesser judicial category rather than in the high judiciary because their prestige, though considerable, was often primarily local.

29. *Secrétaires du roi* are here included with the bourgeoisie because although these posts legally conferred hereditary nobility upon the holder (Loyseau, *Cinq Livres*, p. 131; La Rocque, *Traité*, p. 201), they were purchased most often by wealthy bourgeois who sought rapid ascension in the social hierarchy. Nobles of both the robe and the sword were hostile to these opulent upstarts, whom they considered to be "bourgeois" despite their legal nobility. See Pierre Robin, *La Compagnie des secrétaires du roi (1351–1791)* (Paris, 1933).

30. Bluche, *Les Magistrats*, pt. I, chap. 5.

31. Bluche, "L'Origine des magistrats," p. 324.

32. Ibid., pp. 273–74; BN, MSS. Fr. 32139, fols. 403–04.

33. La Chesnaye Des Bois, *Dictionnaire*, XV, 732–35; BN, MSS. Fr. 32139, fols. 421–24; 32354, fol. 807.

34. Bluche, "L'Origine des magistrats," p. 60; BN, MSS. Fr. 32138, fol. 5.

35. BN, MSS. Fr. 32484, fol. 168v; 32785, fols. 424–25; AN, MM 818[1], fol. 329.

36. Bluche, "L'Origine des magistrats," pp. 116–17.

37. *Dictionnaire de biographie française*, V, 943; BN, MSS. Fr. 32484, fol. 59v.

38. In a recent study of the councillors of state during the reign of Louis XIV, Mousnier has arrived at similar conclusions regarding the *maîtres des requêtes*. Of those who assumed their posts in 1658, 98 percent had previously held a post in a sovereign court, 79 percent from those in Paris. In 1663, 90 percent had the same experience, 83 percent in a Parisian sovereign court. Mousnier notes that "the normal route to become a *maître des requêtes* was therefore to pass through the superior judicial courts, above all else those in Paris," a trend, he asserts, that intensified as the seventeenth century progressed. Many *maîtres des requêtes*, and therefore former magistrates, went on to assume the higher posts of councillor of state and intendant. Roland Mousnier *et al.*, *Le Conseil du roi, de Louis XII à la Révolution* (Paris, 1970), pp. 23–31, 56–63. For a similar analysis of the eighteenth-century *maîtres des requêtes*, see Antoine, *Le Conseil du roi*, pp. 188–90, 249–50.

39. For example, Julien Brodeau married Madelaine Becheser of the "ancienne noblesse de campagne," Jacques Boutillier married the daughter of the first *écuyer* of a royal order, and Claude Le Rebours married Jeanne Pantin, daughter of Gilles, a captain in the royal cavalry (La Chesnaye Des Bois, *Dictionnaire*, III, 889–93; XIII, 739; XV, 411–12); Michel de la Barberie married the daughter of Etienne Daurat, an *écuyer* without office, and Nicolas Basville de Lamoignon, a son of the first president, married Louise Bonnin, daughter of the governor of the Château of Nantes (Bluche, "L'Origine des magistrats," pp. 73–74, 236); Claude Foucault married into the established *épée* family of Bessencourt (BN, Cabinet des Titres, *dossiers bleus*, 101, 277), and so on.

40. BN, Cabinet des Titres, *pièces originales*, 206; *dossiers bleus*, 61, 672.

41. Ibid., *dossiers bleus*, 79; MSS. Fr. 32138, fol. 127.

42. Bluche, "L'Origine des magistrats," pp. 291–92; BN, MSS. Fr. 32785, fol. 353.

43. La Chesnaye Des Bois, *Dictionnaire*, X, 502–11.

44. Ibid., III, 656; BN, Cabinet des Titres, *dossiers bleus*, 115; MSS. Fr. 32353, fols. 169–70; AN, MM 818[1], fols. 342–43.

45. BN, Cabinet des Titres, *dossiers bleus*, 96; *nouveau d'Hozier*, 43.

46. BN, MSS. Fr. 32484, fol. 83; Bluche, "L'Origine des magistrats," pp. 116–17.

47. BN, Cabinet des Titres, *cabinet d'Hozier*, 169.

48. BN, MSS. Fr. 32354, fols. 979–80; 32356, fols. 160–61. In BN, Cabinet des Titres, *dossiers bleus*, 352, there is an interesting list of those persons who attended the wedding

ceremony of André-Pierre Habert (received at Parlement in 1659) and Françoise Le Gendre, daughter of a *maître des requêtes*, on April 20, 1682. They are almost exclusively members of Parlement and other Parisian sovereign courts, *maîtres des requêtes*, and councillors of state.

49. In his *Revolt of the Judges*, pp. 14–21, Moote notes how magistrates at every level could cooperate against encroachments by the royal administration. But in an earlier article, he emphasized that the *parlementaires* normally put their own vested interests before those of the other members of the judiciary, who themselves followed a similar pattern: "The greatest esprit de corps lay within each tribunal, with some cooperation among the Sovereign Courts of Paris, less between the Parlement of Paris and the provincial parlements, still less between the lesser courts and the sovereign tribunals." A. Lloyd Moote, "The Parlementary Fronde and Seventeenth-Century Robe Solidarity," *French Historical Studies*, II (1962), 341–42. Although Moote here refers specifically to magisterial attitudes in the midst of political and jurisdictional conflict with the crown, his words can also be applied to the *parlementaires'* views of their social status.

50. Bartet to Mazarin, July 31, AAE, 905, fol. 310; Abbé Thoreau to Mazarin, July 30, ibid., 906, fols. 184–86.

51. Maréchal L'Hôpital to Mazarin, July 27, AAE, 905, fols. 291–92.

52. Bishop of Anglure to Mazarin, July 31, AAE, 906, fols. 187–88.

53. See the letters of Abbé Thoreau, Archbishop Pierre de Marca of Toulouse, and various bishops to Mazarin in July and August in AAE, 906, fols. 192, 194, 198, 204, 206, 210, 213, 215–17, 242, 268. The remonstrances of the bishops and letters written by several bishops and Chancellor Séguier on this affair are in BN, Baluze MS. 114, fols. 3–20, 22–25v, 29–30v.

54. AAE, 274, fol. 368; 275, fols. 470–72v (Fréjus and Coutances); AN, X¹a 8391, fols. 198v–201 (message to Parlement, July 30, 1658).

55. Mazarin to the Bishop of Fréjus, August 21, 1658, AAE, 279, fols. 101–03. See the opinions of Séguier and Servien in letters addressed to Mazarin and Le Tellier in August, in ibid., 292, fols. 70–73; 905, fols. 388–90v, 405–07; BN, MSS. Fr. 6894, fols. 110–11.

56. AN, X¹a 8391, fol. 201. In August 1660, the king opted for Parlement when the judges became involved in precedence quarrels with other Parisian sovereign courts. Ibid., 8392, fols. 145v–64v. In February 1666, several bishops preceded the judges at the funeral ceremony of Anne of Austria. When the judges complained, Louis said that he was under no obligation to render account to Parlement for his decisions, but he agreed to receive remonstrances and make proper adjustments in the future. Ibid., 8394, fols. 76–77v of 1666 section.

57. Père d'Avrigny, *Mémoires pour servir à l'histoire universelle de l'Europe depuis 1600, jusqu'en 1716 avec des réflexions et remarques critiques* (Nîmes, 1733), II, 30.

58. "Recueil des écrits qui ont esté faits sur le différend entre messieurs les pairs de France et messieurs les présidens à mortier du Parlement de Paris, pour la manière d'opiner aux lits de justice (Paris, 1664)." AN, U 903, pp. 7–104 (paginated manuscript). Some of the memoirs in this volume bear no date, so it is possible that they were prepared not in 1662 as I have assumed, but in 1664 when the conflict between the peers and the presidents flared again. However, because the following paragraphs trace the controversy in both years, the problem of dating presents few difficulties for the historian interested in understanding the positions taken by both sides. Whether they were expressed in 1662 or in 1664, the opinions of both the peers and the presidents were clear and consistent, and the resolution of this affair remained the same.

59. Ibid., p. 7.

60. Ibid., pp. 9–20. Avrigny agrees in his *Mémoires*, II, 27–28.

61. AN, U 903, pp. 19–20. Since the mid-sixteenth century the *parlementaires* had asserted their supremacy over the Estates General as a way to elevate their own political and social importance. See Maugis, *Histoire du Parlement*, I, bk. III, chap. 5, and Shennan, *The Parlement of Paris*, pp. 216–18.

62. Second memoir of the peers. AN, U 903, pp. 27–87.

63. Second memoir of the *présidents à mortier*. Ibid., pp. 99–104.

64. Report to Parlement, April 4, 1662. AN, X¹a 8394, fols. 90v–92.

65. Memoir on the *lit de justice*, AAE, 917, fol. 6.

66. AN, X¹a 8394, fol. 37v. As early as January 1663, the judges had decided at a *mercuriale* to draw up additional memoirs and to delegate three persons to search Parlement's registers for evidence supporting their claims. BN, MSS. Fr. 10907, fols. 145–46.

67. Their memoir, dated January 25, 1664, is in AN, X¹a 8394, fols. 48v–58.

68. Ibid., fol. 49.

69. Ibid., fol. 52.

70. Ibid., fol. 55v.

71. *Journal*, II, 125–28.

72. The decree is published in ibid., p. 125, n. 1. Parlement registered it on April 29. AN, U 903, pp. 105–06.

73. See below, pp. 142, 145.

74. "Mémoire pour faire voir que Mrs. les Ducs et Pairs doibvent estre salués de Bonnet par M. le Premier Président du Parlement de Paris quand il demande leurs advis." AAE, 1594, fols. 387–94. On this affair in the eighteenth century, see Bluche, *Les Magistrats*, pp. 272–74; Ford, *Robe and Sword*, pp. 177–78; and Brancourt, *Le Duc de Saint-Simon*, pp. 219–20.

75. François Bertaut, sieur de Fréauville, *Les Prérogatives de la robe* (Paris, 1701).

76. Bertaut entered Parlement in 1666 after a brief tenure at the Parlement of Rouen. After serving in the *grand' chambre*, he received his letters of honor in 1697. He died in 1703. BN, Cabinet des Titres, *dossiers bleus*, 89; *pièces originales*, 309; MSS. Fr. 22728, fol. 606. The common seventeenth-century orthography is Bertrand de Fraville.

77. Bertaut, *Les Prérogatives*, p. 34.

78. Ibid., pp. 63, 360.

79. Ibid., pp. 141, 287.

80. Ibid., chap. 3, *passim*.

81. Ibid., chaps. 8–9, *passim*.

82. Ibid., pp. 221, 251. Further on (p. 378) he bluntly states that "il est nécessaire que les armes cèdent à la justice."

83. Ibid., pp. 243–45.

84. Ibid., pp. 241–42, 274–75.

85. Ibid., pp. 267–68, 284–85.

86. Ibid., pp. 141–42; chap. 4 is devoted to the subject of the venality of offices.

87. Ibid., p. 405.

88. Louis de Rouvroy, duc de Saint-Simon, *Mémoires*, ed. Arthur Michel de Boislisle (Paris, 1879–1930), XXV, 322. See the duke's "history" of Parlement on pp. 319–39, where he expresses similar opinions. See also Brancourt, *Le Duc de Saint-Simon*, pp. 211–32.

89. See the discussion of Charles Paul Hurault de l'Hôpital, seigneur de Belesbat, in Lionel Rothkrug, *Opposition to Louis XIV: The Political and Social Origins of the French Enlightenment* (Princeton, 1965), pp. 342–48.

90. Hay du Chastelet, *Traitté*, p. 49. Even a widely circulated book on etiquette published in 1671 pointed out that deference and respect were due the *parlementaires*, "sur lesquels rejalit quelque rayon de Sa Majesté, de la loy, dont ils sont dépositaires au nom du Prince."

Antoine de Courtin, *Nouveau Traité de la civilité qui se pratique en France, parmi les honnestes gens* (Paris, 1671), p. 56.

91. Hay du Chastelet, *Traitté*, pp. 62–63.

CHAPTER 3. ROYAL POLICY AND THE SOURCES OF PARLEMENTAIRE WEALTH

1. Moote, *Revolt of the Judges*, chaps. 2–5, *passim*, makes this point clear.

2. As defined by Bluche, *Les Magistrats*, pt. II, *passim*.

3. "Si on néglige la relative primauté des rentes, la répartition des fortunes parlementaires apparaît donc diverse, variable à l'extrême." Ibid., p. 155. See also Mousnier, *La Vénalité*, bk. III, chap. 2.

4. These figures are taken from a sample of the account books for the years 1653, 1657, 1661, 1665, and 1673. B. Maz., MSS. 3008, 3010, 3013, 3017, 3021. These registers, one for each year between 1645 and 1688, record both current salary payments and those for past increments in salary that a councillor or his predecessor *en charge* had accumulated.

5. Mousnier, *La Vénalité*, p. 426. On the relation between salaries and the prices of offices, see also Ford, *Robe and Sword*, p. 154.

6. The registers of the Parisian Chambre des Comptes include several volumes that illustrate the mathematics of augmentation procedures. See AN, P 3241, 3254, 3351.

7. On the relation between augmentations and office prices, see above, pp. 15–16. Parlement's account books (see above, n.4) reveal that most judges were entitled to salaries three or four times greater than the amounts listed on p. 63.

8. See above, n.4.

9. AN, P 3241, 3254, 3351.

10. AN, 144AP, 65, dossier 3.

11. Colbert, II, 367–68 (letter to intendants, December 18, 1674); AAE, 938, fols. 360–63 (edict of December 1674).

12. AN, U 2117, fol. 287v.

13. See Fouquet's marginal comments on a rough draft of an edict of December 1659 as well as his letter to Mazarin of April 9, 1660, in AAE, 908, fol. 387; 910, fols. 170–71. Colbert's remarks are in a financial memorandum to the king dated 1663 in Colbert, II, 43.

14. AN, E 349^A, fol. 113. Supporting decrees are in ibid., fol. 426; 349^B, fols. 1, 322; 349^C, fols. 286–87.

15. AN, X^1a 8393, fol. 130v (August 4, 1662). Protests at the Cour des Aides about reduced *augmentation des gages* payments began as early as December 1660. BS, MS. 904, fols. 673–75; AN, Z^1a 164, fol. 279.

16. Dreyss, I, supplement to Pellisson's memoir of 1661.

17. For example, see the letter of *Président à Mortier* Novion to Colbert, dated April or May 1662, in BN, Mélanges Colbert MS. 108, fols. 5–6. This collection of correspondence contains several letters on this subject. See also Clément's comments in Colbert, II, cix.

18. AN, X^1a 8392, fols. 344v–45v; E 349^C, fol. 221.

19. See above, n.4.

20. B. Maz., MS. 3013, *passim*. The figures cited were compiled from all the entries in this volume that applied to each *parlementaire*.

21. Indeed, the crown was much more rigorous with lesser royal officials. In December 1661 Louis ordered that *all* hereditary *gages* be paid only in return for a tax. Members of the sovereign courts, however, were exempted from this forced loan. See AN, X^1a 8658, fols. 90–92; a conciliar decree of January 1664 in AN, E 1722, fol. 23, explains this affair.

22. Mousnier, *La Vénalité*, pp. 432–33.

23. Ford, *Robe and Sword*, p. 155.

24. Isambert, XIX, 86–88.

25. Chéruel, *De L'Administration de Louis XIV*, p. 118. Hurt, "The Parlement of Brittany and the Crown," pp. 413–14, 433, exaggerates the importance of Louis's threats of 1673. Although he concedes that the edict was not enforced, he nevertheless portrays it as an attack on magisterial wealth.

26. They received as much as 693 *livres*, 5 *sous* per trip. AN, X^{1}b 9440, *passim*.

27. The impact of the procedural codes on Parlement is discussed in greater detail below in chapter 6.

28. BN, MSS. Fr. 16532, fols. 481–82, 485–86.

29. AN, X^{1}a 8660, fols. 525–28. The crown issued a similar decree in March 1671. BN, MSS. Fr. 16532, fols. 306–07v.

30. On this issue, see AN, X^{1}a 8394, fols. 84–86v, 89v–92; 8665, fols. 122v–24; 8667, fols. 362–76v; and BN, MSS. Fr. 16532, fols. 124–29v.

31. BN, MSS. Fr. 16532, fols. 130–38.

32. Marc Venard, *Bourgeois et paysans au XVIIe siècle: Recherche sur le rôle des bourgeois parisiens dans la vie agricole au sud de Paris au XVIIe siècle* (Paris, 1957), p. 34.

33. Bluche, *Les Magistrats*, pt. II, chap. 4.

34. Even in the sixteenth century, Parlement's right to register alienation of royal demesne was considered "positive and certain" (Maugis, *Histoire du Parlement*, I, 676), and series X^{1}a of Parlement's registers in the seventeenth century is full of royal decrees of alienation. On the judges' purchase of royal demesne after the Fronde, see the notations next to the councillors' names on a list of Parlement's members drawn up for Colbert in the early 1660s in Georges Depping, ed., *Correspondance administrative sous le règne de Louis XIV* (Paris, 1850–1855), I, 33–70.

35. Full documentation of this point would require several pages. Only an examination of notorial records for individual judges would yield a precise assessment, but the time-consuming nature of this work limited my investigation to documents that dealt with *parlementaires* as a group. For examples of grants of justice, see the cases of Gilbert des Voisins (1653), Maupeou (1654), Maugis (1654), Le Roy (1655), Miron (1659), Pinon (1659–60), Bailleul (1661), Lamoignon (1662), and Genou (1663) in BN, n.a.f. 8377, fols. 45v–58v, and Maupeou (1662) and Miron (1659) in AN, X^{1}a 8663, fol. 59v; 8661, fol. 197v.

36. As with justice privileges, complete documentation would require several pages. Research in AN, series E, U, and X^{1}a has uncovered three grants of *châtellenie* to *parlementaires* between 1653 and 1665, three grants of *foire* between 1653 and 1672, 13 grants of *chauffage* between 1653 and 1673, and one grant of *péage* in 1658.

37. AN, U 2109, fol. 157; 2111, fol. 156v; 2112, fol. 492; 2113, fol. 344v; 2114, fol. 397v; 2116, fols. 186v, 190, 197, 206, 297, 311v, 327; X^{1}a 8391, fol. 70v.

38. Compiled from AN, X^{1}a 8659, fols. 273v, 277; 8664, fol. 370; U 2116, fol. 259; BN, n.a.f. 8386, fols. 64, 65v.

39. Compiled from AN, X^{1}a 8658, fol. 56; 8659, fol. 511v; 8660, fol. 465.

40. Compiled from ibid., 8389, fol. 185v; 8393, fol. 165v; 8661, fols. 219–33; 8662, fol. 77v; 8670, fol. 332v; U 2107, fol. 444v; 2116, fols. 252–55.

41. Salary list of officials in the royal household, dated January 1, 1657. AAE, 903, fols. 36–78.

42. Colbert, V, 590, n.1 (Périgny); BN, n.a.f. 2771, fol. 146 (Longueil); Mélanges Colbert MS. 138, fols. 362–63 (Fouquet).

43. AN, X^{1}a 8392, fols. 52v–53v.

44. AN, P 2854, fol. 121 (Regnault); Jean Loret, *La Muse historique*, ed. J. Ravenel and E.

V. de La Pelouze (Paris, 1857–1878), II, 280 (Novion); BN, n.a.f. 1643, fol. 163 (Sevin); Mélanges Colbert MS. 118, fol. 239 (Bailleul).

45. Jean de Boislisle, ed., *Mémoriaux du conseil de 1661* (Paris, 1905–1907), I, 131.

46. Depping, ed., *Correspondance administrative*, I, 48, 53–54 (Feydeau and Longueil); AAE, 902, fol. 156 (Prévost); BN, Baluze MS. 176, fol. 11 (Champlâtreux); MSS. Fr. 6893, fol. 108 (Bazoches).

47. AAE, 903, fols. 36–78, *passim.*

48. In a letter dated December 2, 1667, Lamoignon had asked Secretary of State for Foreign Affairs Lionne to intercede in Parlement's behalf before the pope on this issue. AAE, 291, fols. 289–90. On December 14, 1668, and February 14, 1669, Parlement officially thanked the king and the ambassador to Rome, the Duc de Chaulnes, for their successful negotiations. AN, X¹a 8396, no fol. The council's decree enforcing the pope's grant of *indult* is mentioned in AAE, 926, fols. 183–84 (June 1668).

49. The first president received an annual pension of 10,000 *livres*, the *gens du roi*, 6,000. The members of the Parlement of Pontoise received a hereditary pension of 6,000 *livres* a year. See the account books cited above in n.4.

50. AN, P 3430, fols. 10–99v. Several other *parlementaires* are listed in this volume.

51. Ibid., 3434, fols. 11, 17v.

52. AN, K 899, dossier 1, no. 31.

53. Fouquet to Mazarin, August 4, 1656. AAE, 900, fol. 254.

54. President Périgny to Fouquet, BN, Baluze MS. 149, fols. 187–88; Mazarin to Abbé Fouquet about loans made by presidents Le Coigneux, Mesmes, and Novion, AAE, 269, fol. 157; payment on a loan of President Maupeou, AN, P 3277, fols. 75v–76; Novion to Colbert, May 1667, BN, Mélanges Colbert MS. 144, fol. 3.

55. AAE, 274, fol. 260. In a letter dated May 5, 1657, Mazarin informed Fouquet and Servien that he had instructed a Monsieur Coiffer to distribute "secret gifts" to certain magistrates in the sovereign courts. Ibid., fol. 222. In his memoirs, the financier Gourville reported giving 500 *écus* to those *parlementaires* who seemed to exert an influence on their colleagues. He is cited in Chéruel, *Histoire de France*, II, 266.

56. Mazarin to Fouquet, October 28, 1659. AAE, 281, fols. 289–92.

57. Colbert, II, 81–82.

58. Bernard Schnapper, *Les Rentes au XVIe siècle, histoire d'un instrument de crédit* (Paris, 1957), pp. 153–63.

59. On the crown's partial reliance on *rentes* for income in the seventeenth century and the procedures of issuance and payment, see Dent, *Crisis in Finance*, pp. 46–54.

60. For the participation of sixteenth-century *parlementaires* in *rentes*, see the table in Schnapper, *Les Rentes*, p. 172. For the judges' interest in the bonds after the Fronde, see the entries in Depping, ed., *Correspondance administrative*, I, 33–70; the receipts of payments in the genealogical collections in BN, Cabinet des Titres, particularly the volumes in *pièces originales* under the family name; and litigation records in AN, E and P (e.g., E 1770, fol. 139; P 3285, fols. 79, 81). Bluche testifies to the large amount of *rentes* in *parlementaire* fortunes in the eighteenth century in his *Les Magistrats*, pp. 212–16.

61. On Parlement's opposition to royal *rente* policy during the reigns of Henry IV and Louis XIII, see Schnapper, *Les Rentes*, pp. 266–69, 276–78; Moote, *Revolt of the Judges*, pp. 39–40; David Buisseret, *Sully and the Growth of Centralized Government in France, 1598–1610* (London, 1968), p. 89.

62. Cubells, "Le Parlement de Paris pendant la Fronde," pp. 179–84.

63. Moote, *Revolt of the Judges*, pp. 81, 164, 231, 239, 243, 246–49, etc. See also Normand, *La Bourgeoisie*, pp. 266, 279–87; Joubleau, *Etudes sur Colbert*, I, 47–49.

64. Dent, *Crisis in Finance*, pp. 51–52. For Parlement's decrees on *rentes* during the Fronde, see BN, MSS. Fr. 16533, fols. 491–94, 517–21, 538–46.

65. AN, X¹a 8389, fol. 33; K 695, no. 32. Royal orders to stop the assemblies are in AMG, A¹ 139, fols. 42–44v.

66. The report is anonymous. AAE, 892, fol. 179. On the Parisian disturbances, see also Le Tillier to Mazarin, June 21, ibid., fols. 137–40, and on Parlement's sessions, see AN, X¹a 8389, fol. 35 ff.

67. BN, MSS. Fr. 16533, fols. 486–88v.

68. AN, K 695, no. 32. July 10, 1653.

69. AN, E 1701, fol. 9.

70. See the contemporary manuscript journal which discusses these events in BN, MSS. Fr. 5844, fols. 205–06v, 208v–09, 212. For a list of the judges who attended *rentier* assemblies, see ibid., 16533, fols. 478–79v.

71. Ibid., 17355, fols. 212–14; AN, X¹a 8389, fols. 242v–44.

72. BN, n.a.f. 1506, fol. 27. The conciliar registers date the decree April 11. AN, E 1701, fol. 57.

73. As is evident from an extract of a conciliar decree of March in BN, MSS. Fr. 17335, fol. 225, and the manuscript journal, ibid., 5844, fol. 262v.

74. See the manuscript journal, BN, MSS. Fr. 5844, fols. 265, 268; AN, X¹a 8389, fol. 264 ff.; and a memorandum dated May 8, 1654, in AAE, 893 *bis*, fol. 37.

75. Servien to Mazarin, June 19, AAE, 893 *bis*, fol. 77; Mazarin to Abbé Fouquet, June 8, BN, MSS. Fr. 23202, fol. 124.

76. AAE, 893 *bis*, fol. 173. July 26, 1654.

77. See their correspondence of July and August 1654 in translated code in ibid., fols. 181, 189–90, 191–93.

78. Servien and Fouquet to Mazarin, August 1, ibid., fols. 189–90. A memorandum on this issue prepared for Mazarin by the *prévôt des marchands* on August 5 is in ibid., fol. 214.

79. See the lengthy letters sent to Mazarin by Servien, Fouquet, and Maréchal L'Hôpital in early August in ibid., fols. 189–90, 191–93, 196–97.

80. Servien and Fouquet to Mazarin, August 1, ibid., fols. 191–93.

81. Ibid., fols. 202–04.

82. Anonymous to Mazarin, August 6, ibid., fols. 215–18. The cardinal was clearly distressed at this time. See the segments of a letter he wrote to Colbert on August 25 in Gabriel-Jules de Cosnac, *Mazarin et Colbert* (Paris, 1892), I, 441.

83. AAE, 893 *ter*, fols. 244–46v.

84. AN, X¹a 8389, fols. 393v–94v; BN, MSS. Fr. 17335, fol. 237; undated memorandum prepared for the cardinal by the *prévôt des marchands*, AAE, 893 *bis*, fols. 259–61. In a letter to Mazarin dated August 27, Servien reminded the cardinal that the royal council was divided on how to resolve this issue. The final decision, he emphasized, would rest with the cardinal alone. AAE, 893 *bis*, fols. 287–88v.

85. Abbé Fouquet to Mazarin, August 20, AAE, 893 *ter*, fols. 272–76. First President Bellièvre had hoped for the same outcome in a letter to the cardinal dated August 22 in BI, Godefroy MS. 274, fol. 315.

86. Mazarin to Abbé Fouquet, August 23, 1654. BN, MSS. Fr. 23202, fols. 143–45.

87. Parlementary letter to the king, dated September 5, 1654. AN., X¹a 8389, fols. 393v–94v.

88. A point Moote makes throughout his *Revolt of the Judges*.

89. On Fouquet's policies of expediency in the context of the monarchy's financial difficulties, see Dent, *Crisis in Finance*, pt. I, chaps. 1–2, and the same author's "An Aspect of the Crisis of the Seventeenth Century: The Collapse of the Financial Administration of the French Monarchy (1653–1661)," *Economic History Review*, ser. 2, XX (1967), 241–56.

90. Mazarin to Colbert, September 10, 1656. AAE, 274, fol. 53.

91. Fouquet to Mazarin, May 20, 1657. Ibid., 902, fol. 85. As early as April 1656, the

Hôtel de Ville reported to Parlement about the scarcity of funds to meet interest payments on *rentes*. AN, X¹a 8390, fols. 322–23v.

92. BN, n.a.f. 1506, fols. 34, 35; 1509, fols. 30, 35v–39; Martin and Besançon, *L'Histoire du crédit*, pp. 54–55.

93. Bishop of Tulle to Mazarin, July 9, 1659. AAE, 907, fols. 119–20.

94. See the letters exchanged between Le Camus and Mazarin, September and October 1657, AAE, 275, fol. 69; 902, fols. 226–27; Fouquet to Mazarin, January 6, 1660, ibid., 910, fols. 1–4.

95. See the letter of the *prévôt des marchands*, Alexandre de Sève, to Mazarin, November 1658, AAE, 905, fol. 485, and the requests for overdue *rente* payments filed by several *rentiers*, including *parlementaires*, dated March 5, 1659, in AN, K 695, no. 38.

96. BN, MSS. Fr. 4215, fols. 9–15.

97. Fouquet to Mazarin, July 12, and Mazarin to Le Tellier, July 16, AAE, 907, fols. 195–97; 279, fols. 386–95.

98. In order to follow Fouquet's tactics, the reader is referred to the brief sketch of this affair in Jules-Auguste Lair, *Nicolas Foucquet, procureur général, surintendant des finances, ministre d'état de Louis XIV* (Paris, 1890), I, 501–05, and the *surintendant*'s letters to Mazarin in March and April 1660 in AAE, 900, fols. 103–04v; 910, fols. 134–41v, 170–71, 177–79. Even the interest paid on the more recent *rentes* was reduced by only one-third instead of the originally planned one-half. Although disgruntled, the *rentiers* accepted this solution in September 1660, expecting that the partial suppression of interest paid on recent *rentes* would ensure prompt payment on existing *rentes* in the future. See their remonstrance to the king dated September 23, 1660, in BN, MSS, Fr. 16533, fols. 522–25. On Parlement's interest in the *anciennes rentes*, see Joubleau, *Etudes sur Colbert*, I, 37.

99. Fouquet to Mazarin, March 1660, AAE, 284, fols. 261–71. For examples of how individual *parlementaires* received special consideration on *rentes* after 1660, see letters throughout the correspondence of Le Tellier (e.g., AMG, A¹ 168, fol. 337; 169, fol. 36), Colbert (e.g., BN, Mélanges Colbert MSS. 105, fols. 9–10, 61; 113, fol. 390; 117 *bis*, fol. 643; 121 *bis*, fol. 1081) and Mazarin (e.g., AAE, 284, fols. 313v–14; 910, fols. 91–97, 134–41v).

100. See the letters exchanged between Mazarin, Fouquet, and *Prévôt des Marchands* Sève in April 1660 in AAE, 284, fol. 334; 910, fols. 177–79, 190–91. Mazarin clearly threatened Sève into cooperating with Pinon.

101. AAE, 910, fol. 197.

102. Mazarin to Fouquet, May 16, 1660. AAE, 284, fols. 359–60v. The cardinal expressed his hope that Fouquet would one day sit down and calmly explain in detail how he had engineered such a perfect coup. Such letters testify to the great influence Fouquet enjoyed in formulating royal financial policy.

103. AN, X¹a 8392, fol. 433.

104. On the activities of the *Chambre de Justice*, see below, pp. 120–21.

105. Berrier (perhaps an agent of Colbert) to Colbert, May 10, 1662, in François Ravaisson-Mollien, ed., *Archives de la Bastille* (Paris, 1886–1904), I, 37–38; Sève to Colbert, May 12 and 13, 1662, BN, Mélanges Colbert MS. 108, fols. 555–56, 571–72.

106. Reported in Le Tellier to Achille II de Harlay (who replaced Fouquet as *procureur général* of Parlement in 1661), July 10, 1662. AMG, A¹ 174, fol. 63.

107. Ravaisson, II, 89–90.

108. Colbert, II, 39 ff.

109. Pierre Clément, *Histoire de Colbert et de son administration* (Paris, 1874), I, 154–56; Chéruel, *Histoire de l'administration*, II, 179–85; BN, MSS. Fr. 16533, fols. 507–08; n.a.f. 1506, fol. 47v.

110. Clément, *Histoire de Colbert*, I, 156. Most of Louis's advisers were less ambitious than

Colbert, suggesting in the Conseil d'Etat that only eight million *livres* of *rentes* be liquidated. It was Colbert who desired to repurchase all *rentes*. Ormesson, *Journal*, II, 154–56.

111. AN, E 1725, fol. 138 (June 11, 1664); Colbert to Séguier, June 3, 1664, Colbert, VII, 226.

112. "Remonstrances au roy sur le projet du remboursement des rentes de l'Hostel de Ville." BA, MS. 672, fols. 520–28v.

113. *Journal*, II, 149–56. On the disturbances in Paris, see the letters written to Colbert, Séguier, and the Doge of Venice in April and June 1664 in Ravaisson, III, 457–60, 462, and Séguier to Colbert, June 9, in BN, Mélanges Colbert MS. 121, fol. 323.

114. Le Tellier to Séguier, June 8, 1664. AMG, A¹ 185, fols. 307–08.

115. Ibid., fols. 306v, 312–13.

116. Foucault to Colbert, July 14, 1664. Colbert, VII, 402.

117. BN, Clairambault MS. 444, fols. 457–63.

118. Ravaisson, II, 360. Clément notes that the king even reimbursed some *parlementaires* for losses they had suffered in the *rente* operations. See his *Histoire de la vie et de l'administration de Colbert, contrôleur général des finances . . . précédée d'une étude historique sur Nicolas Fouquet* (Paris, 1846), pp. 61–62.

119. BN, n.a.f. 1506, fol. 51v.

120. Ibid., fol. 71v.

121. On the ordinance of 1672, see Robert M. Jennings and Andrew P. Trout, "Internal Control: Public Finance in Seventeenth-Century France," *Journal of European Economic History* I (1972), 651–56.

122. Isambert, XVIII, 69–71; AN, X¹a 8664, fols. 436–37v. The promise to pay 5.5 percent interest on many *rentes* issued before 1665 is mentioned in a conciliar decree of March 18, 1669, in BN, MSS. Fr. 16533, fol. 506, and in a royal declaration of April 7, 1672, in AN, X¹a 8669, fols. 280–81v.

123. Isambert, XIX, 5; Colbert, II, 248–49, and nn.1–3; BN, n.a.f. 1506, fol. 78v. In 1672, Colbert had preferred to raise taxes rather than create new *rentes*, but First President Lamoignon was of the opposite opinion and Louis accepted his advice. Colbert, visibly angered, reportedly told the first president, "Vous triomphez . . . [but] après les emprunts [rentes] il faudra les impôts pour les payer." Anonymous, *Vie de M. le premier président de Lamoignon*, pp. xxxviii–xxxix; A.-C. Chévrier, *Eloge de Guillaume de Lamoignon, premier président au Parlement de Paris* (Paris, 1856), p. 34.

124. BN, MSS. Fr. 16524, fols. 179–86v; 21016, fols. 817–32v; Isambert, XIX, 151–52, 202 and n.1.

125. Bluche, *Les Magistrats*, p. 214, estimates that at least two-thirds of the *parlementaires* in the eighteenth century had a large stake in *rentes*. J.-P. Poisson's study of notorial records in the late seventeenth century shows how *rentes* on the Hôtel de Ville continued to dominate private credit transactions. "Introduction à l'étude du rôle socio-économique du notariat à la fin du XVIIe siècle: 3 offices parisiens en 1698," *XVIIe Siècle*, no. 100 (1973), pp. 3–17.

126. As does Clément, *Histoire de Colbert*, I, 163 ff., although he qualifies the minister's success.

CHAPTER 4. PARLEMENT IN OPPOSITION, 1653–1660

1. For the early parts of this section, I am indebted to Ernest-Désiré Glasson, *Le Parlement de Paris, son rôle politique depuis le règne de Charles VII jusqu'à la Révolution*, 2 vols. (Paris, 1901), and the works on Parlement by Maugis, Moote, and Shennan cited in previous notes.

2. For example, in a declaration of February 21, 1641, Louis XIII had limited to two the

number of remonstrances the court could issue on financial decrees. But even he allowed that the court could have cognizance of public affairs with the king's consent. Normand, *La Bourgeoisie*, pp. 269–71.

3. Thus, the successive royal attacks on the privileges of the *trésoriers de France*, whom the court had doggedly defended before the Fronde, met with little resistance in the 1650s. Jean-Paul Charmeil, *Les Trésoriers de France à l'époque de la Fronde* (Paris, 1964), pp. 397–408.

4. Roland Mousnier, "Le Conseil du roi de la mort de Henri IV au gouvernement personnel de Louis XIV," *Etudes d'Histoire Moderne et Contemporaine*, I (1947), 29–67; Georges Pagès, "Le Conseil du roi sous Louis XIII," *Revue d'Histoire Moderne*, XII (1937), 293–324.

5. Moote, *Revolt of the Judges*, pp. 158–67.

6. The edicts are listed in AN, P 2602, fols. 415v–19.

7. Bluet to Mazarin, January 1, 1653. AAE, 892, fol. 30.

8. Moote, *Revolt of the Judges*, pp. 357–58.

9. Fouquet to Mazarin, August 5, 1654. AAE, 893 *bis*, fols. 209–10v.

10. Anonymous to Mazarin, August 6, 1654. Ibid., fols. 215–18. See also the letters of Séguier and Servien to the cardinal on August 9 and 12 on fols. 221–23, 229–39v.

11. BN, Baluze MS. 113, fols. 56–57.

12. See above, p. 75.

13. BA, MS. 6352, fols. 25–83 (account of the *lit de justice*).

14. BN, MSS. Fr. 17871, fol. 340 ff.

15. AN, X^{1}a 8390, fol. 79v ff.

16. Ibid., fols. 94–95v; U 2107, fols. 64–65v.

17. Colbert, I, 234.

18. See the anonymous report of the incident in AAE, 894, fol. 103. In a letter to Mazarin dated May 14, Le Tellier reported that Turenne ordered Bellièvre to spread the rumor. Ibid., fol. 106.

19. AN, X^{1}a 8390, fol. 121v.

20. Moote, *Revolt of the Judges*, p. 360; Chéruel, *Histoire de France*, II, 262 ff.

21. AAE, 894, fol. 116; Lair, *Foucquet*, I, 357–60.

22. BI, Godefroy MS. 528, fols. 297–98. See also an anonymous letter of protest about the proposed changes to Bellièvre, dated 1656, on fols. 266–77. The government of Holland did indeed plan to devalue French currency. See another letter to the first president on fol. 295.

23. Ibid., fol. 308. The entire memoir is on fols. 301–32v.

24. Parlement's activity may be followed in AN, X^{1}a 8390, fol. 230 ff.; 8299 *bis* (third chamber of *enquêtes*), fols. 39v–41; BN, MSS. Fr. 10907 (*mercuriales*), fols. 141–43.

25. AN, X^{1}a 8390, fol. 243 ff.; AMG, A^1 146, fols. 265, 278, 488.

26. Letter dated May 5, 1656, AAE, 898, fols. 76–79. Le Tellier spoke to deputies of Parlement on May 1 making similar charges, but to no avail. BN, Cinq Cents Colbert MS. 213, fols. 442–46v.

27. Speech to Parlement, February 6, 1656. AAE, 898, fols. 19–22v.

28. Colbert, I, 239–40 (February 19, 1656).

29. See Louis's letter cited in n. 26 and the registers of the Parisian Cour des Aides, BS, MS. 904, fols. 555–57 (April 1656).

30. Roquemarre to Mazarin, May 1656. AAE, 900, fol. 47.

31. Fouquet to Mazarin, June 20, 1656. Ibid., fols. 87–92.

32. See his letter of June 26 in ibid., fols. 105–07. The king sent Séguier a similar letter on June 22. Ibid., 898, fol. 121.

33. Lair, *Foucquet*, I, 373–75.

34. Parlement registered the decree on June 30. AN, X^{1}a 8659, fols. 467–68. See also Fouquet to Mazarin, June 30, AAE, 900, fols. 109–12.

35. René Pillorget, "Les Problèmes monétaires français de 1602 à 1689," *XVIIe Siècle*, nos. 70–71 (1966), p. 127.

36. August 10, 1656. AAE, 901, fol. 237. In a letter to Le Tellier dated August 29, 1656, Séguier spoke of the "advantages" Parlement won in the *affaire des monnaies*. BN, MSS. Fr. 6893, fol. 302.

37. On the continued resistance by Parlement and the public to the monetary edicts, see Germain Martin, *La Surintendance de Fouquet et les opérations de crédit public* (Paris, 1914), p. 26, and the following letters dated August 1656: Mazarin to the Duchesse de Chevreuse, AAE, 901, fol. 274; Séguier to Le Tellier, BM, Harleian MS. 4489, fol. 48; Séguier to Le Tellier, BN, MSS. Fr. 6893, fols. 287–88v.

38. Lair, *Foucquet*, I, 437–38; Fouquet to Mazarin and Mazarin to Le Tellier, May 23 and 29, 1658, AAE, 905, fols. 111–12; 906, fol. 140. In November 1659, Parlement reiterated its cognizance of monetary affairs. AN, X^{1}a 8392, fol. 4.

39. On the feuds of the *gens du roi* with each other and the crown, see Louis André, ed., *Deux Mémoires historiques de Claude Le Pelletier* (Paris, 1906), pp. 78, n.1, 82, n.3; Lair, *Foucquet*, I, 295; Colbert to Mazarin, June 4 and September 10, 1656, in Colbert, I, 241–42, 259–61.

40. AAE, 901, fols. 73–74v.

41. Moote, *Revolt of the Judges*, p. 357; Chéruel, *Histoire de l'administration*, II, 28 ff.

42. BN, MSS. Fr. 18592, fols. 154–56v.

43. See the letters written to Séguier, Le Tellier, and Mazarin on this matter in November and December 1659 in BM, Harleian MS. 4491, fols. 270–71, 374, 378–79; BN, MSS. Fr. 6897, fols. 91–92, 135v; AAE, 908, fols. 372–73, 396–97. For Parlement's action, see AN, X^{1}a 8392, fols. 153v–54v; K 695, no. 39. The affair is discussed briefly in Lair, *Foucquet*, I, 555–56.

44. Letter of a "resident of Holland" to Ambassador De Thou in October 1659. Ravaisson, I, 249.

45. BN, MSS. Fr. 6898, fols. 162–63v (April 19, 1660).

46. Ibid., fols. 177–80, 225–28; AAE, 910, fols. 222–25.

47. AAE, 900, fols. 103–04v (March 13, 1660).

48. AAE, 910, fols. 192–96v (April 22, 1660). On May 8 (fols. 207–08v) Fouquet expressed similar sentiments to the cardinal.

49. Mazarin to Fouquet, March 18, 1660. AAE, 284, fols. 261–71.

50. Lair, *Foucquet*, I, 556.

51. Ibid. See also Le Tellier to Talon, May 17, 1660. BN, MSS. Fr. 6898, fol. 210.

52. Ravaisson, I, 257, n.1. Indeed, Parlement's activity against the monopoly continued through December 1660. See the letters exchanged between Fouquet and Mazarin in AAE, 281, fols. 516–18v, 557–58v; 908, fols. 389–91v, and AN, X^{1}a 8392, fol. 206v.

53. AN, X^{1}a 8390, fols. 561–63, 568–69, 572–73; BN, MSS. Fr. 17288, fols. 420–22v.

54. AN, X^{1}a 8390, fols. 690, 713 ff.; 8299 *bis*, fols. 14v–15; AAE, 902, fol. 225; Séguier to Le Tellier, July 5, 1657, BN, MSS. Fr. 6894, fol. 34; BN, n.a.f. 8372, fols. 139v–40.

55. See the letters of Fouquet to Mazarin in March 1660 in AAE, 900, fols. 103–04v; 910, fols. 91–97. See also Séguier's note to Le Tellier of February 1660 in BN, MSS. Fr. 6898, fol. 86.

56. AN, U 2109, fols. 10, 164–67v, 176–79, 180–81, 211v–19, 221, 371.

57. AN, X^{1}a 8392, fols. 58v–59, 224v, 229–30.

58. Fouquet to Mazarin, March 11, 1660. AAE, 910, fols. 91–97.

59. BN, MSS. Fr. 6898, fols. 13–15 (January 23, 1660). See also AN, X^{1}a 8392, fols. 25v–26, and Fouquet to Mazarin, January 31, AAE, 910, fols. 31–36. Several provincial parlements followed suit with similar decrees. Ravaisson, I, 218–19.

60. AN, X¹a 8392, fols. 29v–30. The records of Huby's interrogation by several councillors of state in January 1660 are in BN, MSS. Fr. 6898, fol. 18 ff.

61. Fouquet to Mazarin, February 5, 1660. AAE, 910, fols. 39–45.

62. BN, MSS. Fr. 6898, fols. 37–39 (January 30, 1660). See his other letters to Mazarin and Le Tellier on February 3 in ibid., fols. 45–46 and AAE, 910, fols. 37–38. Some of this correspondence has been published in an appendix in René Kerviler, *Le Chancelier Pierre Séguier* (Paris, 1874).

63. BN, MSS. Fr. 6898, fols. 78–80v.

64. As reported in a letter of Le Tellier to Séguier, February 13, 1660. BM, Harleian MS. 4491, fols. 29–30.

65. AAE, 910, fols. 39–45.

66. AAE, 284, fols. 147–48v (February 12, 1660).

67. BN, MSS. Fr. 6898, fols. 88–90 (conciliar decree dated February 24); AN, U 2109, fols. 86v–87v.

68. Kerviler, *Séguier*, pp. 622–23 (March 3, 1660).

69. Letter of March 6, 1660. Ravaisson, I, 226.

70. AAE, 910, fol. 74 (February 22).

71. For the early part of this section, I am indebted to the articles by Mousnier and Pagès cited in n. 4 and the excellent studies by Arthur Michel de Boislisle, *Les Conseils du roi sous Louis XIV* (Paris, 1884), especially chaps. 1–4, and Antoine, *Le Conseil du roi*, pp. 293–96, 446–47, 521–36.

72. Moote, *Revolt of the Judges*, pp. 57–58, 85–86, 120–23, 160 ff.; Normand, *La Bourgeoisie*, p. 265; BN, MSS. Fr. 18467, fols. 157–60v (memorandum against conciliar evocations dated 1645).

73. This affair is treated briefly in Glasson, *Le Parlement de Paris*, I, 402–04. See also Fouquet to Mazarin, July 1, 1656. AAE, 900, fol. 120.

74. Benoise to Bellièvre, May 5, 1656. BI, Godefroy MS. 274, fol. 366.

75. See the anonymous letters to Mazarin from agents in Paris and Bordeaux, dated May 1656, in AAE, 900, fols. 39–40, 47, and the registers of the Paris Cour des Aides, BS, MS. 904, fol. 584 ff.

76. AN, X¹a 9326 (*mercuriales*); 8390, fol. 418; Séguier to Le Tellier, August 15, 1656, BM, Harleian MS. 4489, fols. 36–37.

77. BN, MSS. Fr. 17315, fols. 104–07, 139–52v; 17288, fols. 523–37v; n.a.f. 7982, fol. 334^A–H. There is some duplication in these memoranda. The records of the councils in AN, E and V⁶ (see bibliography for volumes consulted) contain other evocations not included in the memoranda. These too warrant consideration because Parlement might have prepared more than the four memoranda I uncovered.

78. A copy of one such pamphlet is in BN, Morel de Thoisy MS. 394, fols. 45–49v. Another issued in 1658 when the judges again clashed with the councils over evocations is in BN, Joly de Fleury MS. 1051, fols. 19–23v. The *parlementaires* were particularly interested in an article in the ordinance of Blois that stated: "Déclarons que nous n'entendons doresnavant bailler aucunes lettres d'évocation de nostre propre mouvement...."

79. See his memorandum on Parlement's decree of August 18 in Colbert, I, 252–58.

80. AAE, 900, fol. 344. See also the letters of Séguier and *Maître des Requêtes* Poncet to Le Tellier in August 1656 in BN, MSS. Fr. 6893, fols. 287–88v, 302, 308, 321–22.

81. Colbert, I, 252–58.

82. AAE, 900, fols. 324–26v.

83. See the chancellor's letters to Le Tellier in late August 1656 in BN, MSS. Fr. 6893, fols. 285, 299, 302. In Séguier's papers there is an interesting memorandum (though not in

his hand) that substantiates his claims against Parlement. See the "Discours sur l'authorité des parlements et du conseil privé du roi" in ibid., 17315, fols. 96–103v. See also his memoirs on the evocation controversy in BM, Harleian MS. 4489, fols. 42–43v, and AAE, 900, fols. 311–14v.

84. Letter of August 28, 1656, cited in AAE, 900, fols. 337–39.

85. Letter of September 7, 1656. Colbert, I, 258–59.

86. See the letters of Balthazar and other *maîtres des requêtes* to Séguier in late August 1656 in BM, Harleian MS. 4489, fols. 164–65, 166; Séguier to Le Tellier, August 29, BN, MSS. Fr. 6893, fol. 297; and Bellièvre to Mazarin, September 4, AAE, 900, fol. 347. Parlement's orders are in AN, X¹a 8390, fol. 434v ff.

87. Langlois to Bellièvre, August 30, BI, Godefroy MS. 274, fols. 386–87; AN, X¹a 8390, fols. 441–42v (Parlement's orders for remonstrances). The remonstrances of the *maîtres des requêtes* are in BN, MSS. Fr. 17288, fols. 243–53v; BM, Harleian MS. 1680, fols. 103–05; BI, Godefroy MS. 182, fols. 123–24.

88. Letter to Mazarin, September 5, 1656. AAE, 291, fols. 260–63v.

89. BN, Morel de Thoisy MS. 394, fols. 52v–54.

90. Ibid., fols. 20–43v.

91. AN, X¹a 8660, fols. 15–17. Another list of cases returned to Parlement is in BN, MSS. Fr. 18467, fols. 1–4.

92. AN, X¹a 8660, fols. 7–8.

93. For the Parisian Cour des Aides, see BS, MS. 904, fol. 589 ff., and BN, Morel de Thoisy MS. 394, fols. 68–71v. For the Parlement of Toulouse, see BM, Harleian MS. 4490, fols. 38, 40.

94. See Mousnier, "Le Conseil du roi," p. 61, and Louis's response to Parlement's remonstrances of August 1656, cited in Glasson, *Le Parlement de Paris*, I, 402, and a pamphlet in BN, Joly de Fleury MS. 1051, fols. 27–30v.

95. BN, MSS. Fr. 17315, fols. 167–73v.

96. AN, X¹a 8391, fol. 100v ff.; Colbert to Mazarin, July 7, 1658, AAE, 905, fol. 240.

97. AN, X¹a 8391, fols. 207v–17v. A pamphlet published by Parlement a century later (1752) referred to Talon's speech of 1658 as an "excellent discourse." BN, n.a.f. 7981, fol. 70v.

98. AN, X¹a 8391, fols. 235v–36.

99. AAE, 905, fols. 399–402v.

100. Letter of August 21, 1658. Ibid., fols. 405–07v; cf. with Servien's advice on the same date on fols. 408–09.

101. See Mazarin's letters to Fouquet, Servien, and Séguier on August 25 in AAE, 279, fols. 129–30v, 132v–33; Mazarin, *Lettres*, IX, 36–37.

102. See Mazarin's harsh letter to Nesmond dated August 26, 1658, in AAE, 279, fol. 140.

103. See the letters exchanged between Mazarin and Fouquet in August 1658 on this subject in ibid., fols. 138v–39v; 905, fols. 349–52v, 395–96.

104. On Lamoignon's service to the king in the provinces, see the letters of Séguier, Le Tellier, and the king dated September 1657, in AMG, A¹ 150, fol. 186; BN, MSS. Fr. 6894, fols. 44–45v; AAE, 291, fols. 395–96. On his selection by Mazarin and his reception at the court, see Le Tellier to Séguier, September 1, 1658, BM, Harleian MS. 4491, fol. 170, and Mazarin to Lamoignon, December 3, 1658, AAE, 279, fol. 215.

105. AN, X¹a 8391, fols. 309v–11 (Talon's report to the court).

106. Colbert to Mazarin, January 3, 1659. AAE, 907, fol. 1.

107. On Parlement's conflicts with the councils on evocations in 1659 and 1660, see AN,

X^{1}a 8391, fols. 60v, 378, 383, 407v; 8392, fol. 169; K 695, no. 37; BS, MS. 904, fols. 635–38 (Cour des Aides). A list of cases evoked from Parlement in 1660 is in BN, n.a.f. 8386, fol. 311.

108. BN, Morel de Thoisy MS. 50, fols. 240v–41v (extract of conciliar registers).

109. Letter to Mazarin dated December 17, 1658. AAE, 905, fols. 532–34.

110. Mazarin to Fouquet, December 9, 1658. AAE, 279, fols. 224–25.

111. AAE, 906, fol. 66; Ravaisson, I, 82 and n.1.

112. Parlement protested the "violation of law [and] the oppression given to justice by these irregular procedures." AN, X^{1}a 8391, fols. 467–69v. Louis's motives are described by Le Tellier in a letter to Mazarin on July 16, 1659, in BN, MSS. Fr. 4215, fols. 23v–28.

113. AAE, 907, fols. 151–52 (July 5, 1659).

114. BN, MSS. Fr. 4213, fols. 9v–15 (July 8, 1659).

115. Le Tellier to Mazarin, July 16, 1659. AAE, 907, fols. 207–10v.

116. The marquis was subsequently exonerated. Ravaisson, I, 88–89.

117. See n.115 as well as Séguier to Le Tellier, August 28, 1658, Ravaisson, I, 87; Fouquet to Mazarin, August 27, AAE, 907, fols. 347–48; AN, X^{1}a 8390, fol. 474.

118. AAE, 908, fol. 20.

119. See Séguier's memorandum on evocations dated March 20, 1659, in BN, MSS. Fr. 17288, fol. 445.

120. Mousnier, "Le Conseil du roi," p. 66.

121. AAE, 908, fol. 70.

122. Ormesson, *Journal*, II, 677.

123. Letter of September 23, 1653. BN, n.a.f. 6210, fol. 55.

124. AN, U 2105, fols. 457–59; 2106, fol. 438v; Séguier to Mazarin, October 6, 1653, AAE, 891, fol. 216v.

125. AAE, 891, fols. 229–31 (records of Bertaut's trial); Ormesson, *Journal*, II, xl–xli.

126. AN, U 2105, fols. 431–32; E 1699, fols. 33–36v.

127. AN, X^{1}a 8389, fol. 59v ff.

128. Letters dated May 5, 1653, and August 24, 1654. AAE, 892, fols. 254–55v; 893 *ter*, fols. 249–52v.

129. Glasson, *Le Parlement de Paris*, I, 384–85.

130. Lair, *Foucquet*, I, 280. Courtin to Séguier, April 1654, BI, Godefroy MS. 274, fol. 289 states that Croissy-Fouquet actually spent some time in Anjou "putting his affairs in order" before leaving France!

131. AN, X^{1}a 8390, fol. 475v; U 2106, fols. 317–18.

132. BN, MSS. Fr. 17013, fols. 355–62v (index to Vallée's trial records).

133. AAE, 902, fol. 371.

134. Lair, *Foucquet*, I, 395–401; Chéruel, *Histoire de France*, III, 47–48; La Cour Grulart to Achille II de Harlay, April 9, 1657, BI, Godefroy MS. 274, fols. 402–03.

135. Even a partial listing of works that deal with Jansenism as a theological doctrine and as a system of ethics would expand a footnote into a volume. The reader may consult the excellent bibliographies in Jean Delumeau, *Le Catholicisme entre Luther et Voltaire* (Paris, 1971); L. Willaert, *Bibliotheca janseniana belgica*, 3 vols. (Paris, 1949–1951); and Jean Orcibal, *Jean Duvergier de Hauranne, abbé de Saint-Cyran et son temps* (Paris, 1948).

136. The most detailed exposition of this thesis appears in two studies by Lucien Goldmann: *Le Dieu caché: Etude sur la vision tragique dans les 'Pensées' de Pascal et dans le théâtre de Racine* (Paris, 1955), pt. II, chaps. 5–6; and "Remarques sur le jansénisme: La Vision tragique du monde et de la noblesse de robe," *XVIIe Siècle*, no. 19 (1953), pp. 177–95. For scholars who expressed similar ideas before Goldmann published, or who were influ-

enced by his thesis, consult the bibliography for works by Xavier Azéma, Paul Bénichou, Franz Borkenau, Augustin Gazier, Henri Lefèbvre, Gérard Namer, and Eberhard Weis.

137. Critics have pointed out that not all the judges were attracted to Jansenism, that Jansenism had equal appeal among the clergy and the high nobility, and that the relations between Jansenism and the robe might be reduced simply to a matter of literacy, the robe being a large portion of that thin slice of French society that could read and respond to novel intellectual currents. Others note that many judges were avid supporters of the Jesuits, that Jansenist magistrates were often wealthy, and that the Marxists have little justification in defining the robe as a "class." See René Taveneaux, *Jansénisme et politique* (Paris, 1965), p. 21; Delumeau, *Le Catholicisme*, pp. 179–80; Bruno Neveu, "Un Parlementaire parisien érudit et janséniste: Jean Le Nain (1609–1698)," *Paris et Ile-de-France: Mémoires*, XVI–XVII (1965–1966), 200; and the objections of Roland Mousnier that Goldmann faithfully includes in *Le Dieu caché*, p. 115, n.1.

138. For this view, see Louis Cognet, *Le Jansénisme* (Paris, 1961), p. 48; Antoine Adam, *Du Mysticisme à la révolte: Les Jansénistes du XVIIe siècle* (Paris, 1968), p. 191.

139. For fuller analysis of relations between the *parlementaires* and the Jansenists from 1653 to the Peace of the Church in 1668, with special attention to the historiography of the subject, see Hamscher, "The Parlement of Paris and the Social Interpretation of Early French Jansenism," *Catholic Historical Review*, in press.

140. On the varieties of Gallicanism, see A. Latreille, E. Delaruelle, and J.-R. Palanque, *Histoire du catholicisme en France* (Paris, 1956–1962), II, 355–71; H. G. Judge, "Church and State Under Louis XIV," *History*, XLV (1960), 219–20; Victor Martin, *Le Gallicanisme politique et le clergé de France* (Paris, 1928), chaps. 1–3.

141. Robert Génestal, *Les Origines de l'appel comme d'abus* (Paris, 1951), pp. 1–5; Moïse Cagnac, *De L'Appel comme d'abus dans l'ancien droit français* (Paris, 1906), pp. 23–27, 37–41, 92–99. Although the purpose of the General Assembly of the Clergy, which met every five years for six months, was to expedite administrative and financial matters, the deputies often dealt with religious controversy, including Jansenism. See Pierre Blet, *Le Clergé de France et la monarchie: Etude sur les assemblées générales du clergé de 1615 à 1666*, 2 vols. (Rome, 1959).

142. Paule Jansen, *Le Cardinal Mazarin et le mouvement janséniste français, 1653–1659* (Paris, 1967).

143. On the formulation and reception of the bull as well as the events that followed, see Adam, *Du Mysticisme à la révolte*, pt. III, chap. 2; Blet, *Le Clergé*, II, 180–83; René Rapin, *Mémoires de la Compagnie de Jésus sur l'église et la société, la cour, la ville et le jansénisme, 1644–1669*, ed. Léon Aubineau (Paris, 1865), II, 164–70.

144. BN, MSS. Fr. 477, fols. 13v–19v. Contemporary documents and memoirs that deal with Jansenism rarely mention Jansenists in Parlement by name, relying instead on vague phrases like the Jansenist "party" or "faction." Yet Marca's assertion that only two or three Jansenists sat in the court might have been correct. Modern scholars (see nn. 136–38) have uncovered only a few *parlementaire* families with Jansenist sympathies: the Le Nains, Roberts, Briquets, Bignons, and certain among the Harlays, Fouquets, and Portails.

145. Supporters of the Jansenists submitted several memoranda to Parlement that attempted to arouse the judges against the bull by defending the court's right and obligation to intervene in religious affairs when Gallican liberties were at stake. See: BN, n.a.f. 1525, fols. 197–205v, 207–12v, and Godefroi Hermant, *Mémoires sur l'histoire ecclésiastique du XVIIe siècle (1630–1663)*, ed. Augustin Gazier (Paris, 1905–1910), III, 384–85, 395–97.

146. Adam, *Du Mysticisme à la révolte*, pp. 212–15; Edmond Préclin and Eugène Jarry, *Les Luttes politiques et doctrinales aux XVIIe et XVIIIe siècles* (Paris, 1955), chap. 9, *passim*.

147. See the letters exchanged between Mazarin and Fouquet on May 12 and 17, 1657, in AAE, 274, fol. 242; 902, fols. 75–76.

148. BN, Baluze MS. 176, fols. 277–78 (May 16, 1657).

149. Ibid., 113, fols. 344–45v (May 22, 1657). On Parlement's fear that the bull would initiate an inquisition, see also Hermant, *Mémoires*, III, 399–403, 414–15, 459–60, and Rapin, *Mémoires*, II, 485.

150. BN, MSS. Fr. 477, fols. 19v–29 (1657).

151. Ibid., fols. 29–44v (Marca's account of the *lit de justice* and the negotiations with the nuncio).

152. Ibid.; François Gaquère, *Pierre de Marca (1594–1662)* (Paris, 1932), pp. 270–71. In his *Mémoires* (III, 581–91), the Jansenist Hermant noted that Parlement's reception of the bull distressed the sect: "Although the disciples of Saint Augustine had given Parlement a great many writings on this important occasion, . . . the councillors of the chambers of *enquêtes*, who previously had appeared so zealous in their opposition to the bull, soon became reconciled [to the crown]. . . . Most of them remained satisfied with the declaration in its modified form."

153. Hermant, *Mémoires*, IV, 24–25; Rapin, *Mémoires*, II, 497–503.

154. See Marca's memoranda to Mazarin in 1657 in AAE, 904, fols. 179–91v; 906, fol. 27; BN, MSS. Fr. 477, fols. 313–18.

155. Louis XIV to Séguier, September 11, 1659. BN, MSS. Fr. 6896, fol. 68.

156. BN, Baluze MS. 114, fols. 103–04v (August 11, 1659). How the council's activity could generate support for the Jansenists is evident from a letter Fouquet wrote Mazarin on November 30, 1655. At that time, anti-Jansenists at the Sorbonne censured Antoine Arnauld's *La Fréquente Communion*. Fouquet explained that Jansenists on the faculty had filed an *appel comme d'abus* at Parlement and that several of Mazarin's advisers had urged the cardinal to have the council evoke the case. Fouquet hoped for another solution to this dilemma, however, because "it is certain that this contest over jurisdiction has thrown Parlement to the side of the Jansenists." AAE, 894, fols. 408–10v.

157. Mazarin to Lamoignon and to Abbé Roquespine, a permanent delegate to the General Assembly of the Clergy, August 28, 1659. AAE, 280, fols. 238–39, 242–43.

158. Le Tellier to Mazarin, September 6, 1659, AAE, 907, fols. 36–38v; Le Tellier to Séguier, October 5, BM, Harleian MS. 4491, fol. 212; Mazarin to Le Tellier, September 15, BN, MSS. Fr. 6896, fol. 87.

159. The discussion between the king, Fouquet, Le Tellier, and Marca in April 1661 is the subject of an anonymous memoir in BN, MSS. Fr. 476, fols. 117v–23.

160. Ibid.; AAE, 910, fols. 288–91 (conciliar decree dated April 13, 1661).

161. The change in Parlement's position toward Jansenism after 1661 is investigated in Hamscher, "The Parlement of Paris."

162. Louis's deteriorating relations with Rome in the 1660s and the impact this had on his relations with Parlement are examined at greater length below in chapter 5.

Chapter 5. Parlement in Submission, 1661–1673

1. Isambert, XVIII, 13–15. The idea of establishing such a commission was not new. At least four others met in the first half of the seventeenth century. For a list of the *chambres de justice* that had convened since 1527 as well as an examination of their organization and function, see John F. Bosher, "'Chambres de Justice' in the French Monarchy," in Bosher, ed., *French Government and Society, 1500–1850: Essays in Memory of Alfred Cobban* (London, 1973), pp. 19–40.

2. For a list of members, see Georges Mongrédien, *L'Affaire Foucquet* (Paris, 1956), pp. 94–95.

3. BS, MS. 848, fols. 501–02v.

4. BN, Morel de Thoisy MS. 403, fols. 1–6 (Lamoignon), 6v–21 (Talon).

5. The published decrees and decisions of the chamber fill over five hundred folios in BN, Clairambault MS. 766. The fines the tribunal levied, in alphabetical order, are on fols. 499–576.

6. In 1661 tax farmers contributed 37 million *livres* to the royal treasury; by 1671 this figure had increased to 60 million although the number of farms remained relatively stable. Pierre Goubert, *Louis XIV and Twenty Million Frenchmen*, trans. Anne Carter (New York, 1970), p. 123.

7. Isambert, XVIII, 9–12. On the reorganized Conseil des Finances, see Boislisle, *Les Conseils du roi*, chap. 4, and James E. King, *Science and Rationalism in the Government of Louis XIV, 1661–1683* (Baltimore, 1949), pp. 159–62.

8. Much of the information in this paragraph is taken from Goubert's fine synthesis of Colbert's financial reform in *Louis XIV*, pp. 114–27.

9. BN, n.a.f. 1506, fol. 45.

10. BN, Clairambault MS. 766, fols. 149–51.

11. See the king's comments on financial reform in Dreyss, II, 524–31, 545–52. The *Gazette* is cited in Boislisle, ed., *Mémoriaux*, I, lxxxvii.

12. Dreyss, II, 379 (introduction to 1661).

13. Pellisson, *Histoire de Louis XIV*, I, 2.

14. Nicolò Barozzi, ed., *Relazioni degli stati europei lette al senato degli ambasciatori Veneti nel secolo decimosettimo*, ser. 2, III (Venice, 1863), p. 102 (report of Alvise Grimoni).

15. By far the best treatment of the trial is the second volume of Lair's *Foucquet*, which is based on a careful examination of the thousands of documents presented during the trial. Good summary accounts are also in the works of Adolphe Chéruel, Pierre Clément, Louis Matte, and Georges Mongrédien, which are listed in the bibliography. The second volume of Ormesson's *Journal* is largely devoted to the trial because he was a member of the Chamber of Justice, and many documents from the trial are preserved in his family's papers in AN, 144AP. The second volume of Ravaisson's collection of sources is also rich in documentary material on the Fouquet affair.

16. Colbert had expressed his dissatisfaction with Fouquet's policies as early as 1659 in his memorandum to Mazarin on financial affairs. See above, pp. 10–11.

17. On this affair, see Lair, *Foucquet*, II, 34–35, 163–65. On the various requests by Parlement, Fouquet, his wife, and mother for the transfer of the case and the response of the royal administration, see AN, X¹ª 8389, fols. 127v–28; 8393, fols. 124–30 (July and August 1662); 144AP, 74, dossier 8; Ravaisson, II, 12–15, 57–61; BN, Joly de Fleury MS. 2502, fols. 182–206 (La Reynie's papers on the Chamber of Justice).

18. On the conduct of Talon and Lamoignon, see Lair, *Foucquet*, II, 95 ff.; Ormesson, *Journal*, II, lxxxi–lxxxv, 25, 46; Ravaisson, II, 83–84, 144, n.1; Colbert to Séguier, December 12, 1662, BN, MSS. Fr. 17401, fol. 331; Colbert to Louis XIV, August 27, 1663, Colbert, II, 14–15.

19. Ormesson, *Journal*, II, 27; Ravaisson, II, 162 and n.1.

20. AN, 144AP, 71, dossier 5.

21. Lair, *Foucquet*, II, 95 ff.; Mongrédien, *L'Affaire Foucquet*, pp. 105–06; Anonymous, *Vie de M. le premier président de Lamoignon*, pp. xxiii–xxix. In memoranda of 1662 and 1663 to the king about affairs at the Chamber of Justice, Colbert also saw these conflicts as the motives for the first president's procrastination. Colbert, II, 54–59; VII, 213–18.

22. For example, as early as October 16, 1661, an informant named Lafosse had written to Chancellor Séguier about Fouquet's implicating document and its mention of Lamoignon "cum maximo elogio." Ravaisson, I, 383–84.

23. On the "Conseil des Trois," see Boislisle, ed., *Mémoriaux*, I, introduction.

24. Lair, *Foucquet*, I, 556.

25. For a brief biographical sketch, see Moréri, *Le Grand Dictionnaire historique*, V, 526–27.

26. "Je permis à mon procureur général de résigner à son fils cette charge, qui n'avait pas coutume de passer ainsi de père en fils." Dreyss, II, 227.

27. On the close ties between Colbert and Harlay, see a sample of their correspondence for the year 1675 in BN, MSS. Fr. 17414, fols. 8, 9, 11, 12, 15, 18, 53–55, 65, and so on. Some of the letters they exchanged have been published in Depping, ed., *Correspondance administrative*, II, *passim*. For Harlay's opinions on age dispensations, see above, p. 26.

28. "Recueil sur le Parlement par Harlay, procureur général," B. Maz., MS. 2902. See especially chap. 2, fols. 1–7.

29. Saint-Simon, *Mémoires*, II, 54–55.

30. See above, pp. 20–21, 23–24, 125–26.

31. Lamoignon's role in judicial reform is discussed at length in chapter 6.

32. For example, see Lamoignon's conduct in the reception of the edict that stabilized office prices, above, pp. 20–21, and his reaction to Parlement's acceptance of the 1667 code on civil procedure, below, pp. 143–44.

33. Colbert, II, 55.

34. Ibid., I, 258–59.

35. Ibid., p. 259 (Mazarin's reply of September 9).

36. Ibid., pp. 259–60 (Colbert's reply of September 10).

37. Isambert, XVII, 403–05. For an analysis of the decree, see Antoine, *Le Conseil du roi*, pp. 553–54 and Boislisle, ed., *Mémoriaux*, I, 373–76. Séguier wrote the rough draft. BN, MSS. Fr. 17871, fols. 371–73. Of this decree, Louis recalled in his memoirs that, "in effect, all the parlements, which had until then [1661] caused difficulty by refusing to defer to the decrees of my council, received... the decree by which I forbade them to continue this abuse, permitting them only to complain to me about that which they believed that my council would have ordered against equity and against form." Dreyss, II, 400 and n.1.

38. BM, Harleian MS. 4442, fols. 431–33 (July 16, 1661).

39. AN, X¹a 8392, fols. 390–91.

40. The entire discourse, from which excerpts are given below, is in ibid., fols. 399–406v.

41. Ibid., fol. 431. The judges had already decided on the day of Talon's speech (August 5) to meet at the home of the first president "and examine there the subjects that give rise to contradictions between the decrees of the councils and those of our court," and to draw up memoranda for the king. BN, MSS. Fr. 10907, fol. 144.

42. For example, see Shennan, *The Parlement of Paris*, pp. 277–78; Glasson, *Le Parlement de Paris*, I, 406; and Edouard Laferrière, *Rivalité des parlements avec les intendants et le conseil du roi* (Paris, 1866), p. 26 ff.

43. Dreyss, II, 378. Antoine notes that "anarchy" in the Privy Council resulted in special regulations for the activities of that body in 1673. *Le Conseil du roi*, pp. 63–67.

44. Boislisle, ed., *Mémoriaux*, II, 233 (session of the council, July 25, 1661).

45. AMG, A¹ 258, fols. 112–13 (June 12, 1671).

46. BN, MSS. Fr. 17414, fol. 159 (May 6, 1678).

47. Antoine, *Le Conseil du roi*, pp. 63–67.

48. This discussion is based upon an examination of the following cartons and volumes of conciliar records in series E (*Conseil du Roi*) and V⁶ (*Conseil Privé*) at the Archives Nationales, all of which fall between the years 1661 and 1673: E 1712, 1714, 1716, 1717, 1719, 1720, 1723, 1726–28, 1730–32, 1735, 1739, 1741, 1742, 1745, 1747, 1748, 1750, 1753, 1758, 1760, 1766, 1769; V⁶ 419, 420, 423, 425, 428, 433, 439, 449, 466, 470, 484, 502, 510, 531, 534, 536, 555, 563, 592. Also useful were Parlement's registers, BN, Joly de Fleury MS. 1051, and Boislisle, ed., *Mémoriaux*.

49. For example, on August 2, 1664, the council returned to Parlement the case of a Monsieur Olivier, which had generated conflict between the two bodies in the 1650s. AN, X¹a 8394, fols. 192–94v; 8664, fol. 133. On June 18, 1671, the council also rescinded two evocations to the great satisfaction of the judges (ibid., 8396, no fol.), and on January 11, 1672, the council returned to Parlement the criminal case of a Monsieur Perrier, complete with an apology (AN, E 1766, fols. 15–17). These are only a few of the cases that could be cited.

50. For example, see the case of several merchants who had refused to pay a royal tax in BN, Joly de Fleury MS. 1051, fols. 210–12. In November 1668, Parlement had established a tax to support abandoned children in Paris; the council nullified, but Le Tellier reestablished the tax. AAE, 927, fol. 544. In August 1669, the council also returned to Parlement a *régale* case, which it had evoked, when the judges substantiated their jurisdictional claim. AN, E 1753, fols. 347–49v. Many additional examples could be cited.

51. And this was not always the case in the 1650s. For an example of the quantity of *règlements de juges* in Parlement's favor, see AN, V⁶ 466 and 563, *passim*.

52. See, for example, several cases in ibid., 502.

53. For a concise review of Parlement's authority in Paris, see Shennan, *The Parlement of Paris*, chap. 3.

54. Isambert, XVIII, 100–03.

55. According to Clément, *Histoire de Colbert*, II, 338–39.

56. Colbert, VI, 403.

57. AN, U 2116, fol. 248. For other examples of La Reynie's cooperation with the *parlementaires*, see Jacques Saint-Germain, *La Reynie et la police au grand siècle d'après de nombreux documents inédits* (Paris, 1962), pp. 265, 267–68, 271, 280, 311–12, and Pierre Clément, *La Police sous Louis XIV* (Paris, 1866), chap. 10.

58. Georges Pagès, *Les Institutions monarchiques sous Louis XIII et Louis XIV* (Paris, 1961), p. 109.

59. The reader is referred to the lists of decrees on Parisian police matters that Parlement both registered and issued between 1653 and 1673, and 1628 and 1676, in BN, n.a.f. 8494, fols. 258–63; MSS. Fr. 8092. On the issue of guilds for the single year 1671, the magnitude of Parlement's labors can be seen in AN, X¹a 8668, *passim*. Interesting regulations dated September 7, 1660, on the Hôpital Général and the treatment of the poor and vagabonds in the city are in AN, X¹a 8392, fols. 181–85v. All these records show Parlement's extensive participation in the administration of Paris both before and after 1667.

60. The fascinating reports of Chrétien and Parlement's decrees are in AN, X¹a 8395, fols. 278–318.

61. Minutes of some ten sessions held between October 28 and December 24, 1666, with copies of the legislation that resulted are in BN, MSS. Fr. 16847, fols. 9–149v. Louis mentions the group in Dreyss, II, 222.

62. Saint-Germain, *La Reynie*, p. 16, asserts that Lamoignon and Harlay did sit on the commission, but the minutes do not mention them.

63. BN, MSS. Fr. 16847, fols. 31–41v.

64. Ibid., fols. 53–61.

65. See the comments of Colbert and his uncle, Councillor of State Henri Pussort, in ibid., fols. 17–20, 23–29v.

66. Parlement's decree of 1663 is in ibid., fols. 136–43v. The royal edict of December 1666 is in Isambert, XVIII, 93–94. In 1658, Parlement had already issued an important decree on street lighting. Shennan, *The Parlement of Paris*, p. 90.

67. On the early intendants, see Gabriel Hanotaux, *Origines de l'institution des intendants des provinces* (Paris, 1884), and several articles by Edmond Esmonin published in a volume of his work entitled *Etudes sur la France des XVIIe et XVIIIe siècles* (Paris, 1964). Esmonin corrects

many of the errors in Hanotaux's pioneer work. See also: David Buisseret, "A Stage in the Development of the French *Intendants:* The Reign of Henri IV," *Historical Journal,* IX (1966), 27–38; M. Bordes, "Les Intendants de province aux XVIIe et XVIIIe siècles," *L'Information Historique,* XXX (1968), 107–20; and Pagès, "Essai sur l'évolution des institutions administratives en France," pp. 8–57, *passim.*

68. On the evolution of the intendants and the opposition they generated in the venal bureaucracy during the ministries of Richelieu and Mazarin, see two articles by Roland Mousnier: "Etat et commissaire: Recherches sur la création des intendants des provinces (1634–1648)," in *Forschungen zu Staat und Verfassung: Festgabe für Fritz Hartung* (Berlin, 1958), and "L'Evolution des institutions monarchiques en France et ses relations avec l'état social," *XVIIe Siècle,* nos. 58–59 (1963), pp. 57–72.

69. For local studies on the intendants, consult the bibliography for the works by Pierre Dubuc, Louis Duval, Henri Fréville, Georges Livet, and J. Néraud. Edmond Esmonin, *La Taille en Normandie au temps de Colbert* (Paris, 1913), also has much useful information.

70. In his *Revolt of the Judges,* Moote has some excellent sections that place the intendants in the context of Richelieu's and Mazarin's "governmental revolution." See especially chap. 2. The struggle of the intendants with all levels of the judiciary before the Fronde can be followed in two editions of Chancellor Séguier's correspondence with these officials prepared by A. D. Lublinskaya and Roland Mousnier, listed in the bibliography.

71. Ibid., pp. 160–61.

72. See above, p. 87.

73. On the reestablishment of the intendants after the Fronde, see three articles on this subject by Edmond Esmonin listed in the bibliography. On the royal attacks on the *trésoriers de France* and the *élus,* see Roland Mousnier, "Recherches sur les syndicats d'officiers pendant la Fronde: Trésoriers généraux de France et élus dans la révolution," *XVIIe Siècle,* nos. 42–43 (1959), pp. 76–117.

74. The thesis that follows can only be substantiated or discounted by research on the provincial intendants under Louis XIV. Renewed scholarly interest in the intendants during the king's personal rule is necessary because the standard work on the subject, Charles Godard, *Les Pouvoirs des intendants sous Louis XIV, particulièrement dans les pays d'élections de 1661 à 1715* (Paris, 1901), needs the verification of more extensive and local archival research.

75. On the intendants as investigators, see King, *Science and Rationalism,* chap. 6.

76. On Colbert and the intendants, see Georges Pagès, "Le Gouvernement et l'administration monarchique en France à la fin du règne de Louis XIV," *Revue des Cours et Conférences,* ser. 1 (1936), pp. 1–9; ser. 1 (1937), pp. 289–98, 610–19, 703–12; and Mousnier, "L'Evolution des institutions monarchiques," *passim.*

77. Pagès, "Le Gouvernement et l'administration monarchique," p. 613. Godard also found little intrusion by the intendants into the judicial business before the regular courts. *Les Pouvoirs des intendants,* pp. 47–50, 67, 69, 72.

78. Colbert, II, 209–10.

79. This statement is based on an examination of the conciliar records cited above in n. 48.

80. Dreyss, I, 250–51.

81. Ibid., II, 443–44.

82. For example, in October 1663 Parlement ordered a *maître des deniers* to show his accounts to the court. The council suspended this order. AN, E 367^A, fol. 221. On May 28, 1661, the council ordered Parlement to obey a tariff edict of 1651. Ibid., 1714, fol. 78. In April 1662, Parlement ordered the arrest of a collector of the *taille* and the council also nullified this order. AN, V^6 439, no. 86. In May 1661, the council ordered several merchants who had protested a tax at the court to pay despite their appeal. Ibid., 425, no. 23 (similar cases in 428, nos. 2, 21, 44). For evocations of cases involving Protestants, see AN, E 1719,

fol. 68; 1720, fol. 167; 1723, fol. 77; 1758, fol. 226. The councils' orders to Parlement about the codes of civil and criminal procedure are discussed in chapter 6. The historian of Parlement's *arrêts de règlement* notes that the political content in these regulations declined drastically after 1661. Geneviève Deteix, *Les Arrêts de règlement du Parlement de Paris* (Paris, 1930), p. 120.

83. AN, E 1723, fol. 55.

84. Isambert, XVIII, 105–06. Concise analyses of this title are in Charles-Bon-François Boscheron Des Portes, *Histoire du Parlement de Bordeaux, depuis sa création jusqu'à sa suppression (1451–1790)* (Bordeaux, 1877), II, 195–97, and Marc-Antoine Rodier, *Questions sur l'ordonnance de Louis XIV, du mois d'avril 1667* (Toulouse, 1777), pp. 2–11.

85. This point is emphasized in Jacques-Antoine Sallé, *L'Esprit des ordonnances de Louis XIV, ouvrage où l'on a réuni la théorie et la pratique des ordonnances* (Paris, 1755–1758), I, 2.

86. Colbert, VI, 5–12. Also, see above, p. 11.

87. On the early work of the Council of Justice and the exclusion of the sovereign courts from its deliberations, see Ernest-Désiré Glasson, *Histoire du droit et des institutions de la France* (Paris, 1887–1903), VIII, 181–85; Glasson, *Le Parlement de Paris*, I, 418–26; Adhémar Esmein, *Histoire de la procédure criminelle en France* (Paris, 1882), pp. 177–80; Francis Monnier, *Guillaume de Lamoignon et Colbert, essai sur la législation française au XVIIe siècle* (Paris, 1862), p. 48 ff.; Pierre Clément, "La Réforme des codes sous Louis XIV, d'après les documents inédits," *Revue des Questions Historiques*, VII (1869), 115–44. The labors of this council on the problems of civil and criminal procedure are discussed at length in chapter 6.

88. Minutes of the proceedings of the Council of Justice survive only for the period from September 25 to October 25, 1665. They are published in Colbert, VI, 369–91, on which the following discussion is based.

89. Glasson, *Le Parlement de Paris*, I, 413–14.

90. These sessions are analyzed in Clément, "La Réforme des codes," *passim*, and in Monnier, *Lamoignon et Colbert*, p. 71 ff. The minutes of the conferences in 1667 as well as those held in 1670 to consider the ordinance on criminal procedure have been published under the title: *Procès-Verbal des conférences tenues par ordre du roi pour l'examen des articles de l'ordonnance civile du mois d'avril 1667 et de l'ordonnance criminelle du mois d'aoust 1670* (Paris, 1757).

91. *Procès-Verbal*, pp. 475–79.

92. See the first president's elaboration of these points in a debate with Pussort in ibid., pp. 475–504.

93. See above, p. 68.

94. AN, X¹a 8395, fols. 96v, 98, 102v, 110–11.

95. Isambert, XIX, 70–73.

96. AN, X¹a 8397, no fol. (entry under April 5, 1672).

97. Ormesson, *Journal*, II, 631.

98. Shennan, *The Parlement of Paris*, p. 278. Monnier, *Lamoignon et Colbert*, p. 108, agrees and gives credit for the letters to Louvois without, however, documenting his assertion.

99. Published lists of the edicts of February and March are in AAE, 938, fols. 90–91v. Fifteen edicts registered by Parlement on March 23 are listed in AN, X¹a 8397, no fol.

100. As noted above, the Council of Justice discussed this issue in one of its early sessions. See also Glasson, *Le Parlement de Paris*, I, 409, and Ormesson, *Journal*, II, 404.

101. AN, X¹a 8395, fol. 226. See also Le Tellier to Séguier, January 25, 1668, AMG, A¹ 212, fol. 359.

102. See an unsigned account of Lamoignon's report to Parlement in late January 1668 in AAE, 296, fol. 313v.

103. AN, X¹a 8393, fol. 111.

104. For Lamoignon in action, see ibid., fols. 62–63v, 69, 74, 202–04, 224v–26. The tax on *greffiers* was the only financial issue of any consequence that generated conflict between crown and Parlement in the 1660s. The king eventually compromised on his original proposal and reduced the tax by two-thirds for the clerks at Parlement. See ibid., and BN, n.a.f. 8449, fols. 17–26, 115, 120–22v; AN, P 4985; Ravaisson, II, 29–32, 35, 50, 55, 101–02, 104–06, 117–18.

105. Colbert, VI, 16.

106. For similar interpretations, see Shennan, *The Parlement of Paris*, p. 278, and Judge, "Church and State Under Louis XIV," p. 220.

107. For the historical literature on Louis XIV's relations with Rome after 1661, see the bibliography in Paul Sonnino, *Louis XIV's View of the Papacy (1661–1667)*, University of California Publications in History, 79 (Berkeley, 1966), and the footnotes in Judge, "Church and State Under Louis XIV."

108. AN, X¹a 8393, fols. 233v–52v. The records of the sessions Parlement held with the faculty between January and May 1663 are in BN, MSS. Fr. 17647, fols. 1–118. On the issue of the theses, see also Louis André, *Michel Le Tellier et Louvois* (Paris, 1943), pp. 115–32.

109. Charles Jourdain, *Histoire de l'Université de Paris, au XVIIe et au XVIIIe siècles* (Paris 1888), I, 418–19, and BN, MSS. Fr. 17647, fols. 81–83v.

110. See Blet, *Le Clergé de France*, II, 315–16, and Martin, *Le Gallicanisme*, chap. 8 for analyses of the text of the Six Articles.

111. Alfred Cauchie, *Le Gallicanisme en Sorbonne, d'après la correspondance de Bargellini, nonce de France (1668–1671)* (Louvain, 1903), pp. 11–14.

112. Paul Viollet, *Le Roi et ses ministres pendant les trois derniers siècles de la monarchie* (Paris, 1912), p. 116.

113. Blet, *Le Clergé de France*, II, 318–19; Sonnino, *Louis XIV's View of the Papacy*, p. 68.

114. Blet, *Le Clergé de France*, II, 318–20.

115. See the account of the *lit de justice* in 1664 in BA, MS. 5414, and the comments of Ormesson on Parlement's action in 1665 in his *Journal*, II, 350.

116. Jacques Boileau, ed., *Recueil des diverses pièces concernant les censures de la faculté de théologie de Paris sur la hiérarchie de l'Eglise et sur la morale chrétienne* (Münster, 1666), pp. 59–62 (brief), 92–96 (bull).

117. Ibid., pp. 170–93; Jourdain, *Histoire de l'Université de Paris*, I, 424.

118. Boileau, ed., *Recueil*, pp. 63–91. See also the memorandum of Harlay, Talon, and Bignon to the king in BN, MSS. Fr. 6899, fols. 118–49.

119. Blet, *Le Clergé de France*, II, 324.

120. The phrase is Blet's. Ibid., p. 325.

121. Judge, "Church and State Under Louis XIV," p. 221.

122. On this and the following issue, see Blet, *Le Clergé de France*, II, 326–31. Talon's speech is in AN, X¹a 8394, fols. 10v–27v.

123. The records of the tribunal are in AN, X¹b 9699–9703. The regulations for "ecclesiastical and regular communities" and the protest of the Bishop of Amiens about them are in the manuscript journal of the tribunal's clerk, Nicolas Dongois, in AN, U 750, fols. 112v–38, 141, 187–88v. The royal administration was well aware of the judges' activities. In December, Talon and Le Tellier still hoped to find precedents for legitimizing the tribunal's regulations. See Le Tellier's letters to Talon dated December 4, 18, and 25, 1665, in AMG, A¹ 196, fols. 294–95, 439–40, 545.

124. Blet, *Le Clergé de France*, II, 334–35; Le Tellier to Nesmond, December 4, 1665, AMG, A¹ 196, fol. 296; Esprit Fléchier, *Mémoires sur les Grands Jours d'Auvergne en 1665*, ed., A. Chéruel (Paris, 1862), pp. 391–93. In *La Réforme ecclésiastique du diocèse de Clermont au XVIIe*

siècle (Paris, 1956), pp. 194–95, Louise Welter notes that the legislation of the *Grands Jours* on monastic discipline remained in force.

125. Latreille *et al.*, *Histoire du catholicisme*, II, 374–94; Cynthia Dent, "The Council of State and the Clergy During the Reign of Louis XIV: An Aspect of the Growth of French Absolutism," *Journal of Ecclesiastical History*, XXIV (1973), 256–58.

126. Blet, *Le Clergé de France*, II, 336. For Louis's comments on the Talon affair, see Dreyss, I, 33; II, 76–79.

127. Adam, *Du Mysticisme à la révolte*, p. 255 ff.; Rapin, *Mémoires*, III, 421–71; Sonnino, *Louis XIV's View of the Papacy*, pp. 80–81.

128. Blet, *Le Clergé de France*, II, 340.

129. The declaration of February 10, 1673, is in Isambert, XIX, 67–69. For Parlement's support of the king, see AN, X^{1}a 8397, *passim*. Parlement's alliance with the king is reportedly a theme of Pierre Blet, *Les Assemblées du clergé et Louis XIV de 1670 à 1693* (Rome, 1972), but I have not examined this book myself.

130. See Harlay's correspondence with Colbert and Seignelay in 1681 in BN, MSS. Fr. 17416, *passim*. See also the letters the *procureur général* sent to Colbert on January 18, March 21, and April 15, 1673, in BN, Mélanges Colbert MS. 163, fols. 115, 457–58, 560–61, and Le Tellier's letters to Harlay on March 24 and 30, 1680, in BN, MSS. Fr. 17415, fols. 141, 143.

131. Shennan, *The Parlement of Paris*, pp. 278–79.

132. See, for example, Hurt, "The Parlement of Brittany and the Crown," *passim*, and Eugene Asher, *Resistance to the Maritime Classes: The Survival of Feudalism in the France of Colbert*, University of California Publications in History, 66 (Berkeley, 1960), chap. 5. The second volume of Depping, ed., *Correspondance administrative* contains many letters that indicate resistance by provincial parlements to Louis XIV.

133. Moreover, not all provincial parlements opposed the crown during the personal rule of Louis XIV. The historians of the parlements of Bordeaux and Dijon report relative calm after 1667. See Boscheron Des Portes, *Histoire du Parlement de Bordeaux*, II, 195, and Elisabeth-François de Lacuisine, *Le Parlement de Bourgogne depuis son origine jusqu'à sa chute* (Dijon, 1864), III, 137.

134. In his book, *Revolt of the Judges*, and an article, "Law and Justice Under Louis XIV," in Rule, ed., *Louis XIV and the Craft of Kingship*, A. Lloyd Moote notes the limits of Louis's control of Parlement and the rest of the judiciary. As regards the *parlementaires*, he emphasizes that the judges continued to rely upon "secondary" and "tertiary" means of resistance to oppose some policies throughout the reign. He notes that "the counting of remonstrances is not an accurate way to measure officials' opposition to Louis's personal reign, since it overlooks their highly effective tactic of retreating to secondary and even tertiary defense and their equally successful substitution of slowing down implementation of royal decisions in place of openly remonstrating against them" (*Revolt of the Judges*, p. 363). Applying these ideas to the entire judiciary, Moote notes in the article that "as the personal reign of Louis XIV continued, the role of the robe became more modest, to be sure. But beneath the relatively calm surface, the judiciary was as active as ever, changing its direction and preparing for a chance to reassert itself" (p. 230). Moote is certainly correct in pointing out some of the limits of Louis XIV's control of the court, such as the survival of Parlement's administrative authority, the overlap of public and private law, and the availability of other weapons than remonstrances to the judges. Such a view is certainly a welcome relief from the many unsubstantiated and exaggerated assertions about Parlement's decline that litter so many histories of Louis XIV. Nevertheless, Moote does not show, for the Parlement of Paris at any rate, that such "secondary" and "tertiary" means of resistance (which he does not clearly define) posed any appreciable threat to Louis's control of the court while he lived. The

difficulty in Moote's interpretation seems to reside in equating the robe in general with the Parlement of Paris in particular, and in inferring the opposition of the Parisian courts because it existed in the provinces.

CHAPTER 6. PARLEMENT AND LOUIS XIV'S "REFORMATION OF JUSTICE"

1. This chapter considers only those aspects of Louis XIV's "reformation of justice" that had a potential impact on the Parlement of Paris. No space, for example, is devoted to regulations that dealt specifically with judicial procedures in the royal councils, the chambres des comptes, or the Châtelet. Nevertheless, most of the major legislation of the 1660s and 1670s applied to the entire Parisian and provincial judiciary as well as to the Parlement of Paris. Future historians thus may find Parlement's experience instructive for assessing the impact of the "reformation of justice" on other courts.

2. Several works discuss Louis XIV's judicial reforms, but none deal adequately with the impact of this legislation on the magistracy. See, for example, Clément, "La Réforme des codes," *passim;* Monnier, *Lamoignon et Colbert, passim;* Glasson, *Histoire du droit,* VIII, 177–95; Esmein, *Histoire de la procédure criminelle,* pp. 177–259, 327–46; Arthur Engelmann *et al., A History of Continental Civil Procedure,* trans. R. W. Millar, Continental Legal History Series, 7 (Boston, 1927), pp. 708–47; Carl Ludwig von Bar *et al., A History of Continental Criminal Law,* trans. T. S. Bell, Continental Legal History Series, 6 (Boston, 1916), p. 259 ff. Other, earlier works are cited in the notes below.

3. Colbert, VII, 164–83 (memorandum to Mazarin, October 1, 1659).

4. Ibid., VI, 361–67.

5. Ibid., p. 368 (letter of September 6, 1661).

6. The memorandum of May 15 is in ibid., pp. 5–12, and is analyzed in Pierre Clément, "Projet de réforme dans l'administration de la justice, par Colbert," *Revue Rétrospective,* ser. 2, vol. IV (1835), 247–63. The memoirs to Colbert on the subject of judicial abuse are discussed below.

7. See above, pp. 141–44.

8. The minutes of the sessions of 1667 and 1670 are published in *Procès-Verbal.*

9. Colbert, VII, 164–83. Sandras de Courtilz wrote of the minister: "Colbert's only interest in reforming procedure was to provide the people with more funds to devote to commerce." *Vie de Colbert,* p. 194.

10. For example, in a memorandum to the king dated October 22, 1664, Colbert condemned both the great number of judicial officials in the kingdom, which extended the length and cost of litigation, and age dispensations for candidates for the judiciary, which permitted youthful and uneducated individuals to assume judicial office. Colbert, VI, 3–5.

11. Esmein, *Histoire de la procédure criminelle,* pp. 180–92. The memoirs of the councillors of state fill several hundred folios in BN, Clairambault MS. 613.

12. Most of these reports are in BN, Mélanges Colbert MS. 33. Others are in ibid., 123 *bis,* fols. 639–40; 129 *bis,* fols. 597–98; MSS. Fr. 5069; 16484, fols. 388–90; BI, Godefroy MS. 106, fols. 36–39, 86–93v; AN, U 945^B, fol. 2. Because Esmein has analysed the memoirs submitted by the councillors of state (see the previous note), the citations in the following notes concentrate on these other reports that are less familiar to historians.

13. Colbert, VI, 369–71 (session of September 25, 1665). See also Colbert's memoir of May 15 in ibid., pp. 5–12, and his letter to Le Tellier, April 27, 1664, AMG, A^1 184, fols. 524–25. A list of *maîtres des requêtes* who supposedly visited the provinces to prepare reports on judicial abuse is in BN, Clairambault MS. 613, fol. 871.

14. On this point, see Esmein, *Histoire de la procédure criminelle,* pp. 192–93. Fortunately,

enough of the other memoirs have survived to compensate for the lack of detailed provincial reports.

15. On this point, see, for example, an untitled memoir, in BN, Mélanges Colbert MS. 33, fols. 218–26; "Mémoire pour la réformation de la justice," ibid., fols. 302–26; "Mémoire sur le règlement et réformation de la justice," ibid., fols. 344–53; "Mémoire au roy sur la réformation de la justice et des études de droit," AN, U 945ᴮ, fol. 2; Esmein, *Histoire de la procédure criminelle*, p. 181. Most of the other memoirs also encouraged "universal" reform.

16. See, for example, Pussort's comments in BN, Clairambault MS. 613, pp. 401–05 (paginated manuscript) and Harlay's views in BN, Mélanges Colbert MS. 33, fols. 68–71.

17. Most of the memoirs touched upon these problems. For example, see "Mémoire pour la réformation de la justice—19 Juin 1665," BN, Mélanges Colbert MS. 33, fols. 113–41; "Plainct de la justice au roy," a 22-page manuscript, BN, MSS. Fr. 5069. See also Esmein, *Histoire de la procédure criminelle*, pp. 181–85.

18. Cited in Esmein, *Histoire de la procédure criminelle*, p. 182.

19. In BN, Clairambault MS. 613, see the memoirs of councillors of state Aligre (p. 5), Barillon de Morangis (p. 33), La Mauguerie (p. 277), and Pussort (p. 409 ff.). Most of the memoirs condemned the proliferation of judges, especially in lesser jurisdictions. For example, see the anonymous memoir in BN, Mélanges Colbert MS. 123 *bis*, fols. 639–40. On the call for a reduction or abolition of *épices*, see the following reports: "Mémoire pour servir au dessein que le roy a de corriger les abus de la justice et d'abréger les procès," ibid., 33, fols. 157–63; "Pour abolir la chiquane pour jamais," ibid., fols. 192–99; "Mémoire pour le faict de la justice et abbréviation des procès," ibid., fols. 216–17.

20. In BN, Mélanges Colbert MS. 33, see the memoir on fols. 113–41 and Harlay's comments on fols. 68–71. See also Godefroy's report in BI, Godefroy MS. 106, fols. 86–93v.

21. Esmein, *Histoire de la procédure criminelle*, pp. 181–85. See also Harlay's memoir in BN, Mélanges Colbert MS. 33, fols. 68, 71–72v, other memoirs on fols. 1–4, 5, and 7–13v, and the anonymous memoir in AN, U 945ᴮ, fol. 2.

22. "Mémoire des abus qui se commettent au Parlement en l'administration de la justice tout contre les ordonnances et règlements qu'autrement," BN, MSS. Fr. 16484, fols. 388–90. For similar views, see Harlay's memoir in BN, Mélanges Colbert MS. 33, fol. 76v, and Esmein, *Histoire de la procédure criminelle*, pp. 188–92.

23. See Orgeval's memoir in BN, Mélanges Colbert MS. 33, fols. 364–73, and the memoir on fols. 157–63.

24. "Réflexions politiques sur une proposition faicte au roy pour la réformation de la justice en France," ibid., fols. 56–62v.

25. Almost all the memoirs were hostile to seigneurial and *prévôts des maréchaux* courts, which were notorious for their lack of precision in judging litigation and for the assessment of heavy court costs. See Harlay's memoir in ibid., fols. 93–94, an anonymous report dated 1664 in BI, Godefroy MS. 106, no fol., and Esmein, *Histoire de la procédure criminelle*, pp. 184–85.

26. See Esmein's discussion of this point in *Histoire de la procédure criminelle*, pp. 185–86.

27. The memoirs in BN, Mélanges Colbert MS. 33 are more specific on abuses in civil procedure than those submitted by the councillors of state. For example, see professor of law Doujat's report, "Plan général de la réformation de justice" (fols. 30–37v) as well as the memoirs on fols. 157–63, 218–26, 302–26v, 344–53.

28. Very little scholarship exists on French civil procedure in the seventeenth century. Even the many fine studies on French law in the *ancien régime* by Joseph Declareuil, Alfred Gautier, Ernest-Désiré Glasson, Paul Viollet, and François Olivier-Martin deal more with the content and evolution of public and private law than with procedural issues. As a result, the comments here on civil procedure are based on contemporary sources—the memoirs to

Colbert (cited in the previous notes), the royal ordinance of 1667 (in Isambert, XVIII, 103–80)—and on several eighteenth-century commentaries on this legislation that often relate particular provisions of the ordinance to previous judicial practices: Philippe Bornier, *Conférences des ordonnances de Louis XIV* (Paris, 1755), I, *passim;* Daniel Jousse, *Nouveau Commentaire sur l'ordonnance civile du mois d'avril 1667* (Paris, 1753); Rodier, *Questions;* and Sallé, *L'Esprit des ordonnances*, I, *passim.* There is also some useful information in the literature cited above in n. 2.

29. See the memoirs in BN, Mélanges Colbert MS. 33, fols. 157–63, 192–99, 216–17, 328–34v.

30. On malpractice by *procureurs*, see the memoir in ibid., fols. 113–41. For complaints about the conduct of *greffiers* and advocates, see the reports filed by Harlay and Orgeval in ibid., fols. 79, 364–67v, and the memoir in BN, MSS. Fr. 16484, fols. 388–90.

31. See BN, Mélanges Colbert MS. 33, fols. 113–41, 157–63.

32. For example, see "Advis pour l'abbréviation des procès dans les cours de Parlement," and Gomont's report in ibid., fols. 174–83, 422–25. The authors conveniently forgot that poor parties often could not afford such sums for deposit.

33. Fortunately, a fine study exists on French criminal procedure in the *ancien régime:* Esmein's *Histoire de la procédure criminelle.* See also the memoirs to Colbert (cited in previous notes), the criminal ordinance of 1670 (in Isambert, XVIII, 371–423), and the commentaries on this legislation: Bornier, *Conférences des ordonnances*, II, *passim;* Daniel Jousse, *Nouveau Commentaire sur l'ordonnance criminelle du mois d'août 1670* (Paris, 1763); and Sallé, *L'Esprit des ordonnances*, II, *passim.*

34. Esmein, *Histoire de la procédure criminelle*, pp. 188–92.

35. For example, see the memoir in BN, Mélanges Colbert MS. 33, fols. 113–41.

36. See "Traicté de la réformation de justice et de l'abbréviation des procès," ibid., fols. 200–14, and the memoirs on fols. 174–83, 422–25; MSS. Fr. 16484, fols. 388–90.

37. This suggestion was not intended as an attack on privilege, but solely as a solution to the purely logistical problem of reducing the flow of cases into the court to a manageable level. See BN, Mélanges Colbert MS. 33, fols. 113–41 and Harlay's comments on fols. 84v–85.

38. See Harlay's memoir and "Articles sur l'abbréviation des procès" in ibid., fols. 84, 228–34v, and two short memoirs in AAE, 909, fols. 393–99v, 400.

39. BN, Clairambault MS. 613, pp. 417–19.

40. Colbert, VI, 18–22.

41. This paragraph compares Pussort's memoir in BN, Clairambault MS. 613 with Colbert's memoir of May 15, 1665, in Colbert, VI, 5–12.

42. Esmein, *Histoire de la procédure criminelle*, pp. 186–88.

43. In 1654 the magistrates decided to hold a *mercuriale* every three months (BN, n.a.f. 8339, fol. 146), but the court's registers do not indicate that this was ever enforced with regularity. Nevertheless, even if the judges assembled for a *mercuriale* only once a year, they could still accomplish a great deal because their sessions often extended over a number of weeks and even months.

44. Jean Dufresne, ed., *Journal des principales audiences de Parlement avec les arrests qui y ont été rendus* (Paris, 1733), pp. 716–18. Various single sessions and preliminary reports leading to this decree are described or mentioned in BN, MSS. Fr. 16520, fols. 103v–15v; n.a.f. 7981, fol. 226; AN, U 437 (December 12, 1657).

45. In December 1659, Parlement fined several *procureurs* for violating this decree and issued additional regulations that "carried the revocation of useless procedures used by *procureurs*." BN, n.a.f. 8449, fols. 147–50.

46. The court also reiterated an earlier decree of April 29, 1657, that set the fees *greffiers* could charge. Similar regulations were issued for *huissiers* in 1658. Ibid., fols. 243–55.

47. See this date in AN, U 437 and X¹a 9326.

48. See this date in ibid. as well as U 2108, fols. 335v–42v. In general, these regulations were intended "to diminish the length and cost of litigation, [and to ensure that judicial officials] did not require parties to pay greater sums they they should."

49. BN, n.a.f. 8449, fols. 175–76. See also the comments of an anonymous *parlementaire* at the *mercuriale* of 1658 in BI, Godefroy MS. 216, fols. 111–17.

50. AN, U 2167, fols. 143v–58.

51. This was especially true concerning the provisions dealing with *épices*. Daniel Jousse, *Nouveau Commentaire sur les ordonnances des mois d'août 1669 et mars 1673* (Paris, 1756), pp. 176, 184–91, 198, 204.

52. This despite the attempt of bailliage officials to have the Grand Conseil issue an injunction against the decree. See AN, U 2114, fols. 99v–100v, 141–42v, 166v–67v, and Lamoignon's comments on this affair at the sessions the *parlementaires* held with deputies of the Council of Justice, in *Procès-Verbal*, pp. 100–03.

53. Several decrees Parlement issued in January 1661 on the conduct of *greffiers* and *procureurs*, registration of *épices*, and the observance of delay periods are in AN, U 2110, fols. 71v–73; 2112, fols. 470v–73v; X¹a 8392, fols. 237v–38. In April 1664, the court again ordered lesser judges to hear cases even if court costs and *épices* were not forthcoming, "so that grave and atrocious crimes might not go unpunished." AN, X¹a 8394, fols. 110v–11. In the same year, the judges issued regulations on the signing of judicial documents as well as a decree intended to reduce the length and cost of litigation involving the seizure of property. Ibid., fol. 122; U 2167, fols. 96–101. On January 2, 1665, Parlement reiterated previous regulations on the conduct of *huissiers*, sergeants, and archers. BN, n.a.f. 8395, fol. 173v. Finally, on July 16, 1665, the *grand' chambre* issued a significant decree that facilitated the swift judgment of appellate cases. Appeals were to be placed on special dockets and judged within three months of their reception, and *épices* were limited to the appellate request alone and not all the pieces that might be attached. AN, U 1086, fols. 227v–30. Many decrees on these and other judicial topics are scattered throughout Parlement's records for the period 1661–1665.

54. Sallé, *L'Esprit des ordonnances*, I, 434–98. The minute of the decree, signed by Lamoignon, is in AN, X¹b 8865.

55. See Sallé's comments on title 31, article 14 of the ordinance of 1667 in *L'Esprit des ordonnances*, I, 434. See also Jousse, *L'Ordonnance civile*, p. 476.

56. The records are in BN, n.a.f. 2475, fols. 3–52. The conferences resumed in May 1696.

57. See a sample of several sessions held between 1661 and 1664 in ibid., fols. 10v–12v, 17v–21, 24–25v, 41–43.

58. The only serious study of the *Grands Jours* in general is G. Trotry, *Les Grands Jours des parlements* (Paris, 1908), but unfortunately this work contains little specific information on the tribunal of 1665. More extensive accounts exist in Eugène Bonnemère, *La France sous Louis XIV (1643–1715)* (Paris, 1874), I, 346 ff., and in Pierre Clément's essay on Nicolas Potier de Novion in *Portraits historiques* (Paris, 1855), pp. 109–45, but both of these authors relied heavily on Fléchier's *Mémoires* of the tribunal's activities to the exclusion of archival sources. Many documents on the *Grands Jours* of Auvergne exist in several archives and libraries, and I elaborate on these in my article, "Les Réformes judiciaires des Grands Jours d'Auvergne, 1665–1666," *Cahiers d'Histoire*, in press. The following notes are not comprehensive, but they provide an idea of the sources that are available.

59. See the comments of Clément in Colbert, VI, xxx–xxxii.

60. Dated August 31, 1665. AN, X¹a 8394, fols. 214–15. See also Novion's comments on the authority of his court in a letter to Colbert dated November 24, 1665, in Depping, ed., *Correspondance administrative*, II, 166.

61. See the entries in a manuscript journal kept by the tribunal's *greffier*, Nicolas Dongois, in AN, U 750.

62. See above, p. 150.

63. BN, Mélanges Colbert MS. 132, fols. 29–31.

64. Ibid., 133, fols. 20–29.

65. AN, U 750, fols. 143, 186v–87; X¹b 9700 (reports on litigation), entry for December 30, 1665; letters of Novion and Fortia to Colbert in Depping, ed., *Correspondance administrative*, II, 162, 169–70; A. de Boislisle, "Les Grands Jours de Languedoc (1666–1667)," *Comité des Travaux Historiques et Scientifiques. Bulletin Philologique et Historique*, nos. 1–2 (1886), 75.

66. AN, U 750, fols. 167–71v.

67. About these regulations, Fléchier concluded that "it is enough to know that they are all intended to regulate the order, security, and use of documents in the *greffier*'s office, and to prevent the seigneurs and subordinate judges from disposing of them as they please and abusing their judicial authority." *Mémoires*, pp. 214–15.

68. AN, U 750, fol. 228.

69. "Nous avons projetté un règlement très utile pour toute la justice selon la nécessité que nous y avons recognue dans les provinces." BN, MSS. Fr. 17881, fol. 213v.

70. AN, U 750, fol. 228v.

71. Ibid., fols. 228v–39.

72. Colbert, VI, 396–401. See the analysis of the letter in Esmein, *Histoire de la procédure criminelle*, pp. 202–06.

73. On Lamoignon's plans, see Monnier, *Lamoignon et Colbert*, pp. 4–7, and the two studies by Glasson, *Le Parlement de Paris*, I, 425, and *Histoire du droit*, VIII, 185–86.

74. For this study, I examined the editions of 1703 (Paris) and 1768 (Nancy).

75. BN, n.a.f. 2431, fols. 92–102v.

76. Cited in the anonymous *Vie de M. le premier président de Lamoignon*, p. xxxiii.

77. As noted previously, minutes for only three of the Council of Justice's sessions in 1665 have survived. On the council's work from October 1665 to January 1667, see Auzanet's letter in Colbert, VI, 396–401.

78. AN, X¹a 8395, fols. 29v–30v.

79. Esmein, *Histoire de la procédure criminelle*, pp. 202–06; Glasson, *Histoire du droit*, VIII, 186; Monnier, *Lamoignon et Colbert*, p. 59 ff. Why Louis consented to these sessions remains unclear. He said he hoped the meetings would bring additional "perfection" to the code. Perhaps he agreed as a favor to the first president. At any rate, Colbert was not pleased with the king's decision.

80. Isambert, XVIII, 103–80.

81. For example, all types of exceptions (when a party challenged a court's jurisdiction) were combined into single procedural steps and documentation. The same was done for both oral and written proof. See title 9, article 1; title 20, article 6; Jousse, *L'Ordonnance civile*, pp. xviii–xix, 275. In a similar vein, title 8, articles 1, 6, and 13 combined *demandes* and *garants* for judgment at the same time and reduced their cost. Ibid., pp. 80, 82, 91.

82. On *greffiers*, see title 10, article 2; title 14, article 1; title 11, articles 8, 17, 26, and 33; Jousse, *L'Ordonnance civile*, pp. 113, 133, 142–47; and Sallé, *L'Esprit des ordonnances*, I, 117, 137–38. On *procureurs*, see title 6, article 5, and Jousse, *L'Ordonnance civile*, p. 75.

83. Title 9, article 5, and title 13 abolished the practice of defendants requesting excessive documentation for inheritance contests or research on cases before they came before a judge. Rodier, *Questions*, pp. 120–23, 225–27. Title 11, article 11 reduced the categories of written

procedure from five to three. Ibid., p. 156. Title 21 limited the instances when judges and court-appointed experts could visit a locality to collect evidence and reduced their fees. Sallé, *L'Esprit des ordonnances*, I, 244. The code also repealed article 48 of the ordinance of Moulins that permitted the arrest and detention of defendants in a civil suit and limited this practice to a few specific instances. See title 34, article 1, and Jousse, *L'Ordonnance civile*, pp. 545–54.

84. For example, see titles 3, 7, 22 (articles 1–3); Jousse, *L'Ordonnance civile*, pp. 32–34; Rodier, *Questions*, p. 386; Sallé, *L'Esprit des ordonnances*, I, 256–81.

85. For example, judges were denied *épices* on the procedures whereby plaintiffs demanded judgment of a case because the defendant had failed to appear or to present sufficient documents, when litigants filed an appeal during litigation on a specific legal point, or when parties challenged the competence of a particular judge to hear a case. See title 11, articles 5 and 24, title 24, article 27, and the comments of Jousse, *L'Ordonnance civile*, pp. 111, 381–82. Title 19 detailed procedures for cases involving sequestered property, ensuring that the officials involved did not overcharge for their services. Rodier, *Questions*, p. 314.

86. Jousse also noted that a principle of the code was that "tout ce qui peut être jugé à l'audience doit y être jugé." *L'Ordonnance civile*, pp. 172, 204. See also Sallé, *L'Esprit des ordonnances*, I, 185, and Engelmann *et al.*, *Continental Civil Procedure*, pp. 714–18.

87. According to a contemporary document that compares practices before and after the code. BN, n.a.f. 8449, fols. 224–25.

88. Title 35, article 39.

89. See Rodier's comments on title 17 in *Questions*, pp. 289–90, and title 6, article 2 in Jousse, *L'Ordonnance civile*, p. 62.

90. For a list of these articles, see Jousse, *L'Ordonnance civile*, p. 395.

91. In his *Histoire du droit* (VIII, 187), Glasson praised the code because "not a useful rule was omitted [and] . . . not a useless resolution had been inserted." We will have occasion to qualify Glasson's estimation of the code, but his words suffice to point out the great merit of this legislation which should not go unrecognized.

92. The debates are in *Procès-Verbal*. The classic study of these sessions is Monnier, *Lamoignon et Colbert*. See also two articles on Pussort: the sketch by R. Pillorget in Mousnier *et al.*, *Le Conseil du roi*, and E. Paringault, "Le Conseiller d'état Henri Pussort, réhabilitation historique," *L'Investigateur. Journal de l'Institut Historique de France*, ser. 4, vol. X (1870), pp. 143–57, 167–75.

93. *Procès-Verbal*, p. 7.

94. Ibid., pp. 71–72.

95. Ibid., pp. 112–13.

96. Ibid., pp. 38–40.

97. Ibid.

98. Ibid., p. 236.

99. This quotation is taken from two discourses in ibid., pp. 38–40, 40–48. Lamoignon expressed similar sentiments at a later session. Ibid., pp. 475–79.

100. Ibid., pp. 75–76, 475–79.

101. Ibid., pp. 40–48.

102. Ibid., pp. 475–79.

103. Ibid., pp. 101–03. President Novion, who had presided over the reforms of the *Grands Jours*, remarked in an earlier session "that justice is rendered better in the Parlement of Paris than in any other court of the realm, and [the potential prosecution of judges] would weaken the law as well as diminish the esteem of the magistrates." Ibid., pp. 40–48.

104. Ibid., pp. 49–50.

105. Ibid., p. 382.

106. Ibid., p. 237.

107. Ibid., pp. 488–89.

108. Ibid., pp. 480–96, *passim.*

109. Ibid., pp. 496–504.

110. Monnier, *Lamoignon et Colbert*, pp. 88–89.

111. See, for example, *Procès-Verbal*, pp. 453–56.

112. August 13, 1669. Isambert, XVIII, 341–61. In this year, the crown also issued legislation for *eaux et forêts* and regulations on the procedures used by the chambres des comptes. Ibid., 219–311, 311–19.

113. Three royal decrees appeared in August 1669 at the same time the king issued the judicial edict just cited. One repeated the articles of the code that reduced the number of written procedures. Ibid., 340–41. Another established special *greffiers des affirmations* in all royal courts to handle documents dealing with court costs levied by judges who visited a particular locality to collect and verify evidence. Ibid., 339–40. A third decree reviewed the procedures whereby appellants deposited a sum of money at their court of appeal, which they forfeited if they lost their contest. Again, the intent here was to reduce the number of appeals in the judiciary. Ibid., 336–39, reprinted in full in Colbert, VI, 395–96, and discussed in Sandras de Courtilz, *Vie de Colbert*, pp. 191–92. Another edict of the same year concentrated on the procedures of documentation for the code's second title, and in April 1671 another decree extended these provisions to many other documents used in civil cases. AN, X¹a 8667, fols. 250–52v; 8668, fols. 403v–07.

114. AN, X¹a 8667, fols. 42–46v.

115. Ibid., fols. 246v–49v.

116. On the interim chamber established in 1667, see Isambert, XVIII, 190, and the letters of Séguier to Harlay, February 4, 1668 (BN, MSS. Fr. 16485, fol. 197), and Le Tellier to Harlay, November 28, 1668 (AAE, 927, fol. 546). The chamber was continued in 1670 and 1671 and became a permanent feature of the court until at least 1691. AN, X¹a 8668, fols. 259v–60; U 2116, fol. 320.

117. AN, X¹a 8867, fols. 244v–46; Sandras de Courtilz, *Vie de Colbert*, pp. 181–82.

118. An extract of the decree is in Isambert, XIX, 86–88, and it is reprinted in full in Jousse, *Nouveau Commentaire sur les ordonnances des mois d'août 1669 et mars 1673*. In this year, the crown also issued the famous commerical code (Isambert, XIX, 91–107) as well as regulations on the procedures used by the Conseil d'Etat (AN, E 1770, fols. 3–21v).

119. Published versions of the decrees are in BN, MSS. Fr. 16582, fols. 5–12 (March 24) and AAE, 938, fols. 36–39 (July 10).

120. AN, E 1744, fols. 274–76.

121. August 27, 1668. Ibid., 1748, fol. 32. For a similar case involving the *chambre de l'édit* of the Parlement of Rouen and an appeal to the Parlement of Paris, see September 23, 1668, in ibid., fol. 75. In a similar case, the council ordered "défenses à tous ceux qui auront esté partis dans les arrests . . . de contrevenir à [the ordinance of 1667 in appellate matters]." Ibid., fol. 76.

122. Ibid., 1768, fol. 45.

123. *Journal*, II, 561. Councillors of state Voisin and Pussort researched the case of these judges and prepared reports for the king. AN, E 1748, fol. 100.

124. AN, E 1748, fol. 79.

125. April 1, 1669. Ibid., 1749, fols. 109–11.

126. Bornier, *Conférences des ordonnances*, I, appendix of several hundred pages.

127. AN, E 1756, fol. 477. Similar decisions are in ibid., 1749, fols. 295–97, and Bornier, *Conférences des ordonnances*, I, ccxxviii–ccxxxviii.

128. BN, MSS. Fr. 17413, fol. 140.

129. See portions of their correspondence in ibid., 5267, fol. 19 (1678); 17415, fols. 23, 40, 42, 44, 172, 215 (1679–1680); 21118, fols. 495–96, 598–600 (1682–1683).

130. Ibid., 17414, fol. 66.

131. For example, the articles which prohibited *greffiers* from issuing documents in duplicate and triplicate and those which forbade litigants to issue rejoinders and surrejoinders in the course of litigation were not enforced. See title 14, articles 2 and 3, and Engelmann *et al.*, *Continental Civil Procedure*, pp. 714–18. Similarly neglected was title 17, article 16, which prohibited judges from applying other than summary procedures for certain types of cases. Sallé, *L'Esprit des ordonnances*, I, 192.

132. The decree is in Bornier, *Conférences des ordonnances*, I, 9–10.

133. Englemann *et al.*, *Continental Civil Procedure*, pp. 720–22.

134. Ibid.

135. See above, p. 99. On the edict of 1669, see Jousse, *Nouveau Commentaire sur les ordonnances des mois d'août 1669 et mars 1673*, pp. 1–2. At one of the sessions of 1667, Lamoignon even proposed to increase the categories of parental ties that would justify evocations. *Procès-Verbal*, p. 335.

136. And these figures pertain to the interim chamber that sat from 1667 to 1669, which possessed *less* authority than the permanent *tournelle civile*. See the unsigned note in AAE, 296, fol. 301v.

137. BN, MSS. Fr. 16581, fols. 115–18 (printed).

138. See the preface of a declaration of March 24, 1673, that created special dockets for appellate cases in ibid., 16582, fols. 5–12 (printed).

139. Dufresne, ed., *Journal des principales audiences;* Claude Le Prestre, ed., *Questions notables de droit, décidées par plusieurs arrests de la cour de Parlement* (Paris, 1679). The decrees in these works were rendered by Parlement on appellate cases that local customs could not decide, usually on questions such as the succession to property, the transfer of fiefs, the condition of minors, and so on. J. Huet, ed., *Notables Arrêts des audiences du Parlement de Paris depuis 1657 jusques en 1664* (Paris, 1664) contains similar judgments for an earlier period, and a comparison of it with the above volumes reveals that Parlement's role in interpreting law had not declined as a result of the code.

140. In September 1667, Parlement ordered all courts in its jurisdiction to obey the code. BN, n.a.f. 1506, fol. 58. In May 1669, the court revised its regulations on the conduct and fees of *procureurs* and *huissiers* to conform to the code. Ibid., 8349, fols. 161v, 174. A decree of December 1668 established procedures for lesser courts for the subrogation of appeals. BS, MS. 1081, fol. 439. On February 15, 1670, the court defined the duties and fees of *greffiers des présentations* (who registered documentary evidence presented to the court) following the guidelines of the code and the edict of 1669. AN, X¹a 8396, no fol. In June 1671, Parlement established similar regulations for officials involved in the seizure and auctioning of property, and in January and March 1672, the *parlementaires* set forth procedures for officials at the Châtelet. BN, MSS. Fr. 16532, fol. 29; AN, X¹a 8397, no fol. These are only a few of the decrees Parlement issued on procedural matters after the issuance of the code.

141. BN, n.a.f. 8350, fol. 95v.

142. AN, X¹a 8396, no fol.

143. BS, MS. 849, pp. 165–75 (results of the *mercuriale*).

144. See above pp. 166–67.

145. Engelmann *et al.*, *Continental Civil Procedure*, pp. 730–33. Similarly, title 21, article 12, did not apply in areas where the custom of Paris was in force, and articles 9–11 were taken from this custom. Moreover, title 27, article 8, was always practiced in Parlement, and article 6 applied specifically to provincial sovereign courts. Sallé, *L'Esprit des ordonnances*, I, 245, 247–48, 334, 336.

146. Hamscher, "Les Réformes judiciaires des Grands Jours d'Auvergne."

147. See titles 11 and 17 of the code and Shennan, *The Parlement of Paris*, p. 66.

148. For additional comments on *épices*, see above, p. 66.

149. The conciliar records in AN, E and V[6] consulted for this study have been cited in previous chapters. The reader is also referred to the manuscript bibliography.

150. The code is published in Isambert, XVIII, 371–423.

151. Title 14, article 1.

152. Title 14, article 2.

153. See titles 12 and 13 as well as Sallé, *L'Esprit des ordonnances*, II, 136 ff.

154. On *greffiers*, see title 6, articles 9, 12, 15–19, and title 7, article 7. On the handling of documents, see title 23 and Esmein, *Histoire de la procédure criminelle*, pp. 330–33.

155. A list of the appropriate articles is in Jousse, *L'Ordonnance civile*, p. 395.

156. Esmein, *Histoire de la procédure criminelle*, pp. 228–37.

157. See titles 24, 25, 28, and Bernard Schnapper, "Les Peines arbitraires du XIIIe siècle au XVIIIe siècle (doctrines savantes et usages français)," *Tijdschrift Voor Rechtsgeschiedenis*, XLII (1974), 94–100.

158. Esmein, *Histoire de la procédure criminelle*, pp. 228–37. See also Bar *et al.*, *Continental Criminal Law*, pp. 259–63, 278; Alfred Gautier, *Précis de l'histoire du droit français* (Paris, 1882), II, 377–79.

159. Esmein, *Histoire de la procédure criminelle*, pp. 214–15; Schnapper, "Les Peines arbitraires," pp. 93–94, 99–100.

160. Sallé, *L'Esprit des ordonnances*, II, 9–11.

161. March 23, 1676. BN, MSS. Fr. 17414, fol. 74.

162. See the letters patent dated July 2, 1659, in AN, U 2108, fols. 386v–88.

163. Ibid., 2114, fol. 251; X[1]a 8393, fols. 194, 206v–07; 8395, fols. 14v–17v, 38, 41–42, 44v–45.

164. Esmein, *Histoire de la procédure criminelle*, pp. 224–28; Hamscher, "Les Réformes judiciaires des Grands Jours d'Auvergne."

165. The sessions extended from June 6 to July 8, 1670. The minutes are in *Procès-Verbal* under separate pagination.

166. For more details on these issues, see ibid., pp. 13–19, 153–64; Esmein, *Histoire de la procédure criminelle*, pp. 206–11; and Paringault, "Le Conseiller d'état Henri Pussort," pp. 170–71.

167. *Procès-Verbal*, pp. 13–19.

168. Ibid., pp. 79–81, 108–10, 139.

169. See title 6, article 13, and ibid., p. 108.

170. Esmein, *Histoire de la procédure criminelle*, pp. 338–41.

171. Ibid., p. 339. In 1696 Sandras de Courtilz wrote that many criminals escaped prosecution "lorsqu'il n'y a point de partie civile pour fournir aux frais." *Vie de Colbert*, pp. 182–86.

172. Esmein, *Histoire de la procédure criminelle*, pp. 341–46.

173. Ibid., pp. 340–41.

174. Ibid., p. 338.

175. See above, pp. 10–13.

176. See above, pp. 20–25.

177. See above, pp. 25–27.

178. AN, MM 263, fols. 159–68; Jourdain, *Histoire de l'Université de Paris*, I, 474–81.

179. On Louis's motives for these two innovations, see Jourdain, *Histoire de l'Université de Paris*, I, 434–38; Alfred de Curzon, *L'Enseignement du droit français dans les universités de France aux XVIIe et XVIIIe siècles* (Paris, 1920), chap. 2; G. Péries, *La Faculté de droit dans l'ancienne Université de Paris (1160–1793)* (Paris, 1890), pp. 319–24.

180. AN, MM 263, fols. 169–79.

181. Ibid., fols. 183–91.

182. Péries, *La Faculté de droit*, pp. 241–46; Marie-Antoinette Lemasne-Desjobert, *La Faculté de droit de Paris aux XVIIe et XVIIIe siècles* (Paris, 1966), p. 34.

183. Péries, *La Faculté de droit*, p. 298. On the *parlementaires'* desire to encourage practical legal education, see Lemasne-Desjobert, *La Faculté de droit*, pp. 109–16.

184. Memoir signed by Fouquet in BN, Joly de Fleury MS. 1706, fol. 68. Parlement reiterated these decrees on September 7, 1661. AN, U 2110, fols. 403–05v.

185. Jourdain, *Histoire de l'Université de Paris*, I, 434–38.

186. On the failure of certain aspects of Louis's reforms, see Péries, *La Faculté de droit*, pp. 256–57, 337–40, and Lemasne-Desjobert, *La Faculté de droit*, pp. 100–01.

187. Curzon, *L'Enseignement*, chap. 5, *passim;* Lemasne-Desjobert, *La Faculté de droit*, pp. 115–16.

188. Including members of the Le Pelletier, Maupeou, Verthamon, and Gilbert des Voisins families. Péries, *La Faculté de droit*, pp. 283–88.

189. Ibid., p. 288.

190. Larrey, *Histoire*, III, 535.

191. Sandras de Courtilz, *Vie de Colbert*, p. 158. He elaborates on pp. 158–66.

192. BN, Morel de Thoisy MS. 264, fols. 250–79v.

193. Cited in the anonymous *Vie de M. le premier président de Lamoignon*, p. xxxi.

Bibliography

I. Primary Sources: Manuscripts

It became evident in the early stages of research for this study that only an extensive examination of unpublished documents could define the relations between the Parlement of Paris and the crown after the Fronde. The publication of source material for most periods of French history has lagged considerably behind that of books and articles on specialized topics owing to the large quantity of documents available for analysis. This is especially true for the reign of Louis XIV, when the growth of the royal bureaucracy produced a corresponding increase in the volume of official records. Furthermore, no single collection of documents, published or in manuscript, is in itself adequate for tracing the activities and development of Parlement. The many facets of the *parlementaires'* authority, duties, and vested interests ensured that they dealt continually not only with the king and his ministers and advisers, but also with other Parisian and provincial officials and a broad spectrum of issues. The historian of Parlement must be eclectic in his research, shuffling through a wide variety of materials in many archives. An examination of Parlement's own registers inevitably leads to the records of other institutions, public and private correspondence, and documents related to particular subjects scattered throughout many collections. This book is based substantially on manuscript sources in nine libraries and archives located in Paris and London. This section of the bibliography describes these sources, with particular attention to the usefulness of various collections at each repository.

A. Archives des Affaires Etrangères (AAE)

1. Mémoires et Documents: France

This series contains the largest single collection of Cardinal Mazarin's correspondence as first minister between 1643 and 1661. This study drew heavily on volumes 269–277, 279–285, 291, and 292, which contain copies of many letters that he sent during the years 1653–1661. Volumes 890–910 contain most of the extant letters and memoranda that he received between 1652 and 1661. Together, these two groups of the cardinal's papers constitute an important source for tracing the activities of the central government in the mid-seventeenth century. They reveal the daily formulation of policy in the highest circles of the royal administration and provide evidence about Mazarin's methods of soliciting advice, delegating responsibility, and supervising the implementation of his decisions. Parlement and the issues that concerned it appear frequently in the letters he exchanged with Le Tellier, Séguier, Fouquet, Servien, Colbert, and a network of informants in Paris and the provinces.

Also useful in this series are volumes 29 and 201, which contain documents pertaining to the activities of the king's councils between 1533 and 1681, and 1547 and 1674 respectively. Volumes 169 and 170 are devoted to accounts of *lits de justice* at Parlement between   *247*

1561 and 1714, and volume 203 has some interesting documents on the Parisian sovereign courts, 1360–1679. Volumes 89 and 364 contain letters of various public figures (including Mazarin) from 1643 to 1655 and 1477 to 1658, and volume 233 has several excerpts from the memoirs of Saint-Simon on Parlement's quarrel with the dukes and peers in 1664. Other volumes in this series include miscellaneous papers of various secretaries of state during the personal rule of Louis XIV. Occasionally, these contain notes, reports, and correspondence relating to Parlement's activities after 1661. Of these, the most useful volumes and their dates are 916 (1663), 917 (1664), 919 (1665), 921 (1667), 926 (1668), 927 (1668), 934 (1671–1672), and 938 (1673–1674). Volumes 1593 and 1594 contain similar papers that pertain exclusively to the Ile-de-France region between 1651 and 1696. Among them are copies of speeches that *parlementaires* delivered to their colleagues, reports on sessions of Parlement's *mercuriales*, several memoranda on the court's conflicts with the dukes and peers, and some letters addressed to Mazarin.

2. Personnel

Volume 49 has an anonymous eighteenth-century memoir on Mazarin's career as first minister.

B. *Archives du Ministère de la Guerre (AMG), série* A[1]

The minutes of the correspondence that Michel Le Tellier dispatched in his capacity as secretary of state for war between 1643 and 1677 form several hundred volumes in this series. The volumes consulted for this study, which fall between the years 1653 and 1673, were 139, 146, 149, 150, 153, 156, 157, 164, 168–170, 174, 184, 185, 193, 195, 196, 199–204, 206, 212, 213, 235, and 256. Reading the script of these hastily written minutes requires considerable time and patience, but Le Tellier's prominent role in the formulation of royal policy, which extended far beyond the conduct of military affairs, makes the effort worthwhile. His instructions to officials at all levels of the judicial, financial, and military administrations, sprinkled with rough drafts of edicts and conciliar decrees, provide information about the genesis and execution of royal programs and the growth of the monarchy's bureaucratic apparatus. His letters to Mazarin and Séguier frequently mention Parlement's conflicts with the crown.

C. *Archives Nationales (AN)*

1. Salle des inventaires

In the mid–nineteenth century, an archivist by the name of Alphonse Grün culled Parlement's registers and prepared a list of all the officials received by the court between 1669 and 1790. He also carefully noted those magistrates who had received age dispensations. Grün's list remains in manuscript form and is located in the reference room under the title, "Table des lettres de provision, de dispenses et de vétérans, et des réceptions ... au Parlement de Paris de Septembre 1669–1790."

2. Série AP (Archives Privées)

Collection 144AP contains many papers of the Ormesson family over several centuries on microfilm. Many documents that were assembled for use in the *Chambre de Justice* between 1661 and 1665 concern financial administration under Mazarin and Fouquet, while other papers, private in nature, show a magisterial family's interest in the purchase and price of offices, the *droit annuel*, and the acquisition and management of estates.

3. Série E (Conseil du Roi)

The decrees of the king's council constitute an indispensable source for investigating the crown's relations with its judicial institutions. The council advised the king, issued and enforced royal policies, coordinated the other branches of the royal administration, and rendered judicial and administrative decisions on every conceivable type of national and regional issue. Series E contains the minutes of the decrees issued by the following sections of the king's council: the Conseil d'En haut (or d'Etat), the Conseil d'Etat et des Finances, the Conseil royal des Finances (after 1661), and the Conseil des Dépêches. (The archives of the Conseil Privé are catalogued separately; see below, *série* V⁶).

For the purposes of this study, conciliar records not only helped to define the policies of Mazarin and Louis XIV, but also provided a reliable way to trace the conflicts between the councils and Parlement that dominated their relations after the Fronde, particularly on matters concerning evocations and royal taxation. Because the archives of the various councils are so voluminous, the historian not searching for a particular decree must be content with examining a sample of relevant volumes. Those consulted for this study, which contain decrees from the period 1653–1673, were 304^A, 327^B, 339^C, 349^{A-B-C}, 357^B, 367^A, 383^B, 450^{A-B-C}, 462^B, 1683 (all of which include decrees primarily from the Conseil d'Etat et des Finances and the Conseil royal des Finances), and 1685, 1689, 1699, 1701, 1705, 1706, 1708–1712, 1714, 1716, 1717, 1719, 1720, 1722, 1723, 1725–1728, 1730–1732, 1735, 1739, 1741, 1742, 1744, 1745, 1748–1750, 1753, 1755, 1756, 1758, 1760, 1766, and 1768–1770 (all of which contain decrees primarily from the Conseil des Dépêches and the Conseil d'En haut).

4. Série K ("Monuments" Historiques)
The documents in this series are a mixed lot, ranging from institutional records and official correspondence to private papers, memoirs, and treatises. The most useful cartons for the period 1653–1673 are 695, which contains reports on the activity of the Parlement of Paris and other royal courts in the seventeenth century; 701, which has accounts of several of Parlement's plenary sessions; and 899, which includes some original notes, letters, and working papers of Colbert.

5. Série M (Ordres Militaires et Hospitaliers, Universités, Collèges, Titres Nobiliaires)
Volume 271 has information on the professional and social backgrounds of seventeenth- and eighteenth-century magistrates. It proved useful in drawing up the genealogies of the councillors who entered Parlement after the Fronde.

6. Série MM (Ordres Militaires et Hospitaliers, Universités, Collèges, Titres Nobiliaires)
Like M 271, volumes 404, 700^B, 703, and 818^1 in this series have genealogical information on seventeenth- and eighteenth-century magistrates. Volume 263 contains documents dealing with Parlement's relations with the faculty of law at the University of Paris and the reformation of legal education in 1679, 1680, and 1682.

7. Série O¹ (Maison du Roi)
This series, which contains the papers of the secretary of state for the king's household, is relatively complete only for the eighteenth century. The volumes for the mid-seventeenth century contain only copies of letters which illustrate the format of royal documents. Occasionally, however, one of the letters refers to a *parlementaire* of the period under consideration in this study. Volumes 2, 3, 10–12, 17, and 19 were of limited value.

8. Série P (Chambre des Comptes de Paris)
The records of the Parisian Chambre des Comptes are very incomplete. They consist primarily of copies of some of the original registers that were destroyed by fire in 1737. What remains, however, can be used profitably. For example, volumes 2602 and 2603 contain information on the issues discussed by the officials of this court in their plenary sessions in the period 1654–1673, often with speeches of the *gens du roi* and occasional

reference to activity at Parlement. Other volumes have valuable information on the transfer of offices (*quittances*), pensions, accounts of magisterial salaries and the augmentations associated with them, and financial litigation that involved *parlementaires*. The volumes consulted for this study were 2854, 3231–3235, 3239, 3241, 3242, 3246, 3252–3254, 3258, 3259, 3270, 3271, 3273–3285, 3287, 3351, 3430–3435, 4981, and 4985.

9. Série U (Extraits et Copies de Pièces Judiciaires)
This is a series of documents that relates to judicial administration in its broadest sense, covering a wide variety of courts over several centuries. For this study, the most important volumes were 2105–2117 and 2167, which cover the years 1653–1673 in the Le Nain Collection. This collection, which was prepared in the late seventeenth and early eighteenth century under the supervision of Jean V Le Nain, councillor at Parlement, includes excerpts from Parlement's registers of *Conseil Secret* in series X¹a (see below). Le Nain and his aides selected what they considered to be the most important entries in these registers from 1636 through the reign of Louis XIV. Historians may disagree with their selections and will want to consult the original registers, but the collection allows the researcher to use the *Conseil Secret* portion of the court's records in an abbreviated format.

Other volumes in series U have valuable information on specific issues. Volume 437 has the minutes for many of Parlement's *mercuriales*, 1607–1694; 750 is Nicolas Dongois's manuscript journal of the activities of the *Grands Jours* of Auvergne, 1665–1666; 903 contains copies of many of the memoranda written by the *présidents à mortier* and the dukes and peers during their contest over precedence in 1662 and 1664; and 939 has an interesting memorandum on the *droit annuel* in the seventeenth century. A report to Colbert on the abuses in judicial administration is in 945[B]; excerpts from the registers of the king's councils, some of which deal with their conflict with Parlement over evocations, are in 947; 1086 and 1087 contain several decrees issued by Parlement between 1659 and 1665 that the court's clerks failed to copy in the official registers.

10. Série V⁶ (Conseil Privé ou des Parties)
The Privy Council was the judicial section of the king's council. It had jurisdiction in several categories of litigation in first instance and on appeal, issued decrees of evocation and *cassation*, and settled jurisdictional disputes between royal courts. Like the conciliar records in series E, the decrees in this series provide another method for tracing Parlement's conflicts with the king's council after the Fronde, particularly on the subject of evocations. These documents are difficult to use in a comprehensive fashion, however, because each carton for the mid–seventeenth century contains at least a hundred decrees, and there was normally a carton for each month. In preparing this study, only a random sample of cartons for the years 1653–1673 was consulted: 317, 319, 327, 391, 394, 395, 398–400, 403, 418–420, 423, 425, 428, 433, 439, 449, 455, 466, 470, 48ᴬ, 488, 493, 502, 510, 522, 531, 534, 536, 555, 563, and 592.

11. Série X¹a (Parlement de Paris, Civil: Registres)
The many thousands of registers and cartons that comprise Parlement's records are catalogued in several subseries arranged chronologically, each indicating whether the documents are civil or criminal in content and whether they are registers or the minutes from which the registers were copied. Series X¹a comprises the registers of civil litigation and X¹b is its counterpart in minutes; criminal registers form series X²a, and X²b contains criminal minutes, and so on. A group of registers in series X¹a known as *Conseil Secret*, which date from 1636, contain the most useful documents for historians interested in Parlement's relations with the central government. Unlike most of the court's records, which pertain strictly to litigation, the registers of *Conseil Secret* deal with affairs that were of general concern to the judges, usually those discussed in the *grand' chambre* and in

plenary sessions. The entries note the request of magistrates for plenary sessions and *mercuriales*, and they describe the issues that the judges raised in these meetings. They also record decisions to protest a royal decree by written remonstrance or a visit to the king, often with a copy of the contested legislation. The registers of *Conseil Secret* also contain the speeches of the first president and the *gens du roi*, copies of some of the decrees registered by the magistrates, most of the regulations and instructions Parlement issued to lesser tribunals, and notations on the reception of new councillors.

Although these registers are of decisive importance for a study of Parlement, the brevity of most of the entries limits their value. For example, the registers do not contain the views of individual judges (except the first president and the *gens du roi*) nor do they provide details on how each magistrate voted to pursue a particular course of action. Full texts of remonstrances and elaborate reports of discussions are lacking. Entries rarely note the outcome of negotiations with the crown, and they offer no information about discussions within the individual chambers of *enquêtes* and *requêtes*. For the historian as detective, therefore, the registers of *Conseil Secret* provide both valuable clues about the issues that concerned the judges and a broad account of their relations with the central government. But the researcher must consult other published and manuscript sources to discover the resolution of conflicts and the opinions of the judges and the leading figures in the royal administration. This study made extensive use of volumes 8389–8398, which are the registers of *Conseil Secret* for the years 1653–1673.

Another group of registers in series X¹a comprises all the edicts, declarations, ordinances, letters patent, and conciliar decrees that Parlement registered as well as the regulations and instructions that the judges dispatched to lesser courts. These records are instructive in several respects. First, many royal statutes and most of Parlement's decrees have not survived in published form. Second, the *parlementaires* often used their regulatory powers over lesser tribunals to oppose the execution of royal policies. Third, a comparison of the original royal legislation sent to Parlement and recorded in the registers of *Conseil Secret* with the finished products registered by the court exemplifies the element of compromise that was such an integral part of the judges' relations with the crown. Volumes 8658–8670 comprise these registers for the years 1653–1673.

Two additional volumes in series X¹a proved quite useful. The fragments of the registers of the third chamber of *enquêtes* in 8299 *bis* reveal in microcosm the issues raised by the judges in the *grand' chambre* and in plenary sessions. Volume 9326 contains many of the regulations that the magistrates issued from their *mercuriales* between 1607 and 1698.

12. Série X¹b (Parlement de Paris, Civil: Minutes)

The companion series in minutes to X¹a is important because Parlement's clerks often failed to copy into the registers some of the issues discussed by the judges and much of the legislation that they examined and promulgated. For example, carton 8865 contains a significant decree on judicial procedures which Parlement issued in 1665 but which was not copied into the register for that year; occasionally a rough draft or a fragment of a remonstrance has survived in the minutes. In order to compensate for omissions in the registers, I consulted the minutes of *Conseil Secret* for the years 1653–1673 as well. They are in cartons 8858–8870.

Several cartons that lack counterparts in the registers of X¹a also proved useful: 9440 includes the official reports of judges who visited the provinces to collect evidence on litigation between 1635 and 1681, often with information on their *épices*; 9699–9703 contain the records of the *Grands Jours* of Auvergne, complete with reports that councillors filed on litigation and inspection tours, minutes of judicial proceedings, and copies of decrees that the tribunal issued to regional courts.

13. Série Y (Châtelet de Paris)

The records of the Châtelet, the criminal court for the *prévôté* of Paris, had only limited value for this study. Because this court was under Parlement's jurisdiction, however, its registers occasionally contain decrees that the *parlementaires* issued to regulate its conduct and procedures. Two such decrees issued in 1663 and 1664 are catalogued as numbers 16753 and 16762.

14. Série Z¹a (Cour des Aides de Paris)

Like the records of the Chambre des Comptes and the Châtelet, the registers of the Parisian Cour des Aides are neither as complete nor as detailed as those of Parlement. Nevertheless, volumes 164 and 165, which are similar in format to Parlement's registers of *Conseil Secret*, contain a partial account of this financial court's plenary sessions in the seventeenth century. Entries occasionally mention events at Parlement, and they provide a rare glimpse into how the Cour des Aides responded to royal policies after the Fronde.

D. *Bibliothèque de l'Arsenal (BA)*

A few manuscripts at this library have information on Parlement after the Fronde. Volume 672 contains many memoranda on the *droit annuel*, age dispensations, and *rentes* on the Hôtel de Ville. Volume 2483 has extracts from the registers of the chambers of *requêtes* between 1632 and 1728 that complement Parlement's registers of *Conseil Secret* in series X¹a at the Archives Nationales. Discourses of *parlementaires*, particularly the first president and the *gens du roi*, as well as accounts of several *lits de justice* are among the documents in volumes 2856, 5414, and 6352. Volume 5860 contains several anonymous memôirs dating to the second half of the seventeenth century that discuss Parlement's right to participate in affairs of state. Supporting documents for these essays are in volume 3482.

E. *Bibliothèque de l'Institut de France (BI), collection Godefroy*

The several hundred volumes that comprise this collection contain both public and private papers assembled by the eminent historiographer of Louis XIV, Denis Godefroy. Many of the documents are invaluable for the historian of Parlement after the Fronde. Volume 274, for example, is full of the correspondence of Mazarin, Fouquet, Séguier, Bellièvre, and several *maîtres des requêtes* in the 1650s. Many letters discuss Parlement's opposition to royal financial and religious policies as well as the judges' conflicts with the king's councils and the *maîtres des requêtes* over evocations. Volume 106 includes several memoranda addressed to Colbert on the subject of abuses in judicial administration, and volume 216 has a report on one of Parlement's *mercuriales* in 1658. Memoranda and correspondence dealing with Parlement's opposition to royal coinage policy in 1656 are located in volume 528. Volume 182, which is partially devoted to the Parlement of Paris in the seventeenth century, has several interesting letters and reports of royal ministers and advisers on the court's activities after the civil wars, particularly its clashes with the crown over conciliar evocations.

F. *Bibliothèque du Sénat (BS)*

This library has only a few manuscripts dating from the *ancien régime*. Volume 848 contains copies of some of Parlement's remonstrances between 1649 and 1661. Their usefulness is limited, however, because most of them are not dated. Volume 849 has the results of some of Parlement's *mercuriales* in the seventeenth century. Volume 904 has extracts from the plenary sessions of the Parisian Cour des Aides from 1610 to 1686. Volume 1081 contains partial records of Parlement's second chamber of *requêtes* for the years 1580–1718.

G. *Bibliothèque Mazarine (B. Maz.)*
This library holds the account registers that list the payment of salaries to the magistrates at the Parlement of Paris. Twenty-six registers, volumes 3004–3029, cover the years 1645–1688. I consulted volumes 3008, 3010, 3013, 3017, and 3021 for this study. Volume 2902 is Achille III de Harlay's essay on the organization and authority of Parlement.

H. *Bibliothèque Nationale (BN)*
  1. Cabinet des Titres
Except for notarial records, the six manuscript collections that comprise the Cabinet des Titres form the major source for genealogical research on the *ancien régime*. Each collection is arranged alphabetically by family name. In all, several thousand families are represented, but rarely do all six collections include each individual family. The researcher may find anything from a single-sentence notation on a family's geographical origin or a drawing of a coat of arms to a relatively complete genealogy with birth, death, and marriage certificates, *rente* receipts, litigation records, and other assorted memorabilia of a family. Because genealogical records and charts frequently contain inaccuracies and omissions, one should corroborate any data taken from one collection in this series with material from the other collections as well as additional published and manuscript sources. Below is a list of the six collections with the volumes that had significant information on the professional and social backgrounds of the 208 councillors who entered Parlement between 1653 and 1673.
  a. Cabinet d'Hozier. 29, 31, 42, 67, 68, 103, 138, 146, 158, 162, 169, 222, 248, 252, 266, 316, 318, 337.
  b. Carrés d'Hozier. 64, 96, 135, 137, 268, 491.
  c. Chérin. 16, 24, 38, 68, 84, 155, 183.
  d. Dossiers bleus. 17, 58, 61, 66, 69, 79, 89, 96, 101, 113, 115, 124, 131, 136, 137, 139, 142, 148, 161, 169, 183, 188, 199, 203, 207, 227, 230, 235, 242, 248, 255, 264, 265, 277, 280, 299, 304, 310, 314, 317, 320, 327, 331, 336, 339, 345, 348, 352, 356, 364, 368, 417, 419, 432, 447, 450, 473, 478, 496, 518, 536, 550, 555, 560, 564, 568, 580, 590, 593, 597, 602, 609, 613, 625, 626, 631, 649, 661, 673, 677.
  e. Nouveau d'Hozier. 27, 29, 39, 43, 69, 132, 147, 310.
  f. Pièces originales. 54, 205, 206, 227, 271, 309, 357, 425, 453, 520, 540, 570, 828, 1054, 1270, 1326, 1357, 1376, 1469, 1551, 1552, 1655, 1819, 1820, 2025, 2083, 2084, 2092, 2247, 2320, 2523, 2616, 2752, 2760, 2796, 3018.

  2. Collection Baluze
Assembled by one of Colbert's librarians, Etienne Baluze, this collection is rich in documents relating to all aspects of royal administration during the reign of Louis XIV. Volumes 113 and 114 contain many papers assembled by Archbishop Pierre de Marca of Toulouse that deal primarily with ecclesiastical affairs in the 1650s. Marca's many letters and memoranda to Mazarin, supplemented with the correspondence of other leading figures in the central government, are especially valuable for tracing Parlement's response to Jansenism. Volumes 175 and 176 contain many letters addressed to Mazarin between 1643 and 1660, especially by Colbert. Correspondence of Nicolas Fouquet seized by royal agents on his arrest in 1661 comprises volumes 149 and 150. These contain letters that he both dispatched and received between 1656 and 1661. Volume 325 has correspondence of various public figures between 1639 and 1662, some of which was addressed to Mazarin. Volume 177, which contains papers relating to the monarchy's quarrel with Rome over the *régale*, has letters and memoranda by Colbert and the *gens du roi* of Parlement on this subject. They provide insight into Parlement's involvement in ecclesiastical affairs during the personal rule of Louis XIV.

3. Collection Cinq Cents Colbert

Most of the volumes in this collection contain papers that Colbert collected on various aspects of royal administration in the seventeenth century. Particularly valuable for this study were volumes 212, which provides information on Parlement's conflicts with the dukes and peers over precedence and with the king's councils over evocations, and 259 and 260, which contain lists of the estimated market values of judicial and financial offices throughout France in 1665. Volume 155 has documents pertaining to Parlement's involvement in the infallibility controversy in the early 1660s; volume 251 includes many decrees issued by Parlement and the royal councils between 1661 and 1667; and volume 213 has a discourse that Le Tellier delivered to deputies from Parlement in 1656.

4. Collection Clairambault

This collection was prepared in the second half of the seventeenth century under the supervision of Pierre de Clairambault, genealogist of the order of Saint-Esprit. Like the Baluze and Cinq Cents Colbert collections, it contains documents on all aspects of royal administration during the personal rule of Louis XIV. Three volumes in particular were crucial for this study. Volume 613 has the reports that councillors of state submitted to Colbert in preparation for the "reformation of justice." Volume 756 contains a wealth of information on the *droit annuel* and office prices at Parlement as well as miscellaneous accounts of the court, records of office transfers, letters the king sent to Lamoignon, and so on. Volume 444 contains documents on these subjects as well as several items on Parlement's involvement in ecclesiastical affairs in the 1660s, the judges' conflicts with the dukes and peers in 1664, and Colbert's reform of *rentes*. Other volumes that proved useful are 766, which contains the published decrees of the *Chambre de Justice*, and 443, which has some general information on Parlement's activities during the years 1660–1662.

5. Collection Joly de Fleury

Although this collection was assembled by an eminent *parlementaire* in the eighteenth century, several volumes are of interest to the historian of Parlement during the reign of Louis XIV. Because many of the issues that occupied the magistrates of Parlement in the eighteenth century had precedents in the past, the topically arranged volumes in this collection often contain memoranda that analyse the activities of the central government in the previous century and original documents that date to the post-Fronde era. For example, volume 1051, which is devoted to the subject of conciliar evocations, has memoranda and decrees concerning Parlement's jurisdictional conflicts with the king's councils in the 1650s. Similarly, volume 2129, which deals with offices at Parlement, has several references to the venality of offices and the *droit annuel* in the seventeenth century. Information on Parlement's relations with the Parisian faculty of law during the reign of Louis XIV and on the judges' interest in reforming legal education can be found in volume 1706. Volume 2502 contains original papers of La Reynie on the trial of Fouquet.

6. Collection Mélanges Colbert

This collection includes over eighty volumes of the correspondence that Colbert received between 1661 and 1674. They complement Clément's published edition of the letters and memoranda that the minister addressed to others. For this study I consulted volumes 102, 103, 105–109, 113, 114, 117 *bis*, 119, 121–123 *bis*, 126–127 *bis*, 129 *bis*–134 *bis*, 137 *bis*, 138, 140, 141, 144, 147, 155, 157 *bis*, 158, 162, 163, and 176 *bis*. Other volumes in this collection contain documents on specific subjects. Volume 7, which deals with the sovereign courts of Paris between 1597 and 1707, has letters and memoranda concerning Parlement's activities in ecclesiastical affairs in the 1650s and 1660s. Volume 33, like Clairambault 613, has several hundred folios of reports submitted to Colbert in 1664 and 1665 on the subject of abuses in judicial administration.

7. Collection Morel de Thoisy

This collection is composed primarily of published works on public and civil law, but a few volumes of manuscripts are included. Volume 50 has several documents on Parlement between 1648 and 1660, the most interesting being several discourses of the *gens du roi* and memoranda on Parlement's conflicts with the crown written by *Avocat Général* Denis Talon. His report that discusses abuses in judicial administration is in volume 264. Discourses by Talon and Lamoignon before the *Chambre de Justice* are in volume 403. Volume 394 contains a memorandum by Talon on Parlement's opposition to conciliar evocations as well as extracts from the registers of Parlement and the councils on this subject.

8. Manuscrits Français (MSS. Fr.)

Among the most useful documents in this collection are the letters and memoranda of leading figures in the royal administration. Volumes 6892–6900 contain much of the correspondence that Le Tellier received between 1653 and 1678, and volumes 4211–4215 contain letters that he exchanged with Mazarin in 1653 and in 1659. Because both series are rich in letters received by Le Tellier, they complement the Archives du Ministère de la Guerre's collection of the letters and instructions he dispatched. Copies of letters sent by Le Tellier as chancellor of France between 1677 and 1685 are located in volumes 5267, 10985, and 21118. Each of these registers, however, contains almost identical material.

Volumes 17395–17412 contain much of the correspondence that Chancellor Séguier received between 1658 and 1669. Séguier's influence in the highest circles of the central government declined drastically after the death of Mazarin, and in consequence his correspondence after 1661 has little value to the historian of institutions. But during the 1650s Séguier still exercised considerable authority, especially in matters regarding the judiciary, and he actively participated in the formulation of royal policies. The letters and memoranda he received between 1656 and 1661 both in this collection and at the British Museum (see below) contain valuable information on the problems confronted by the royal administration after the Fronde as well as on Parlement's opposition to royal programs. Volume 17871 has some of the chancellor's working papers in his own hand, and volume 17881 contains some correspondence addressed to him, notably reports from the *parlementaires* at the *Grands Jours* of Auvergne.

The correspondence received by Achille III de Harlay as *procureur général* is not voluminous, but volume 17413, which covers the years 1665–1674, has many letters addressed to him by Le Tellier and Colbert. Several volumes of his correspondence for later years, especially 17414 (1675–1678) and 17415 (1679–1680), were also useful for this study.

Letters and memoranda of Guillaume de Lamoignon, Pomponne II de Bellièvre, and Jérôme I and II Bignon are rare; yet some papers of Bellièvre have survived in volumes 16519 and 16575, and materials collected for the lives of Lamoignon and Jérôme I Bignon—including letters, reports, discourses, and career information—are located in volumes 23985 and 5926 respectively. Some speeches of Lamoignon, Talon, and other *gens du roi* in the 1650s and 1660s are scattered throughout volumes 15226, 16522, and 21148.

Like Baluze MSS. 113 and 114, volumes 476 and 477 in *manuscrits français* contain important material for understanding religious issues in the 1650s, particularly Jansenism. Assembled by Archbishop Marca, they include some of the letters and memoranda he addressed to Mazarin on this subject as well as accounts of proceedings at Parlement, the king's council, and the General Assemblies of the Clergy. Volume 23202 has much of the extant correspondence that Mazarin exchanged with his confidant, the Abbé Basile Fouquet, between 1651 and 1660.

Several volumes in *manuscrits français* include partial records of Parlement's *mercuriales:* 10907 for the period July 1613 to July 1739; 16520 for the years 1607–1658; 16580 for the years 1496–1663. An anonymous journal, volume 5844, was helpful for tracing events in Paris between 1652 and 1655, and volumes 10276 and 10277 are unpublished portions of Jean Vallier's journal for the years 1654–1657, which also mention events in the capital city. The records for the trial of Claude Vallée are located in volume 18465, and an index to them is in volume 17013. Several volumes concern Parlement's authority in the city of Paris. Volume 8092 has many decrees issued by the court concerning Paris between 1628 and 1676. Regulations issued by both Parlement and the royal councils on the same subject between 1663 and 1666 can be found in volume 16847. This volume also contains the minutes of the meetings that councillors of state and *maîtres des requêtes* held in late 1666 to prepare for the "reformation of police" in Paris.

Volumes that were indispensable for drawing up the genealogies of the councillors who entered Parlement after the Fronde include 14018, 22728, 32138, 32139, 32353, 32354, 32464, 32484, 32785, 32786, 32933, and 32987. Together, they contain a wealth of information on the professional and social backgrounds of *parlementaires, maîtres des requêtes,* and leading Parisian families in the *ancien régime.*

Often the most valuable documents for investigating specific issues are not in a compact set of memoranda, registers, or correspondence. Rather, they lie hidden in volumes classified as *mélanges,* or miscellany, which typically include material on diverse topics with broad chronological limits. Often such volumes were part of a collection compiled for a public figure such as Chancellor Séguier and *Procureur Général* Harlay. Correspondence, reports, and extracts from the registers of Parlement and the king's councils that pertain to Parlement's opposition to conciliar evocations in the 1650s are located in volumes 15466, 16484, 16485, 17288, 17315, and 18467. Many documents dealing with Parlement's conflicts with the crown over *rentes* on the Hôtel de Ville are located in volumes 15533, 16484, 16532, 16533, 17335, 21016, and 21758. Documents concerning Parlement's opposition to other aspects of royal financial policy can be found in volumes 15533, 16532, 17288, and 18508. Still other volumes contain numerous letters, memoranda, and extracts from the registers of Parlement and the king's councils concerning the *droit annuel,* Parlement's hostility to tax farmers, and the *parlementaires'* offices, official income, pensions, and age dispensations. Among the volumes that figured prominently in this study are 7654, 10791, 11058, 11110, 14029, 15533, 16524, 16530, 16532, 16581, 16582, 18230, 18495, 18508, and 21016. Information on Parlement's role in judicial administration, the crown's plans for a "reformation of justice," and the formulation of procedural legislation is located in volumes 5069, 15533, 16484, 16485, 16532, 16580–16582, 17288, 17349, and 21600. Volumes 4252 and 17647 have material on Parlement's relations with the faculty of theology at the Sorbonne during the infallibility controversy of 1663. Other volumes that have useful miscellaneous information are 18469 and 18592, which were part of Séguier's collection. Alphabetical and subject indexes to the Le Nain Collection are in volumes 21309–21323, 21333–21360.

9. Manuscrits Nouvelles Acquisitions Françaises (n.a.f.)

Volume 1525 contains many letters and memoranda that reveal the response of Parlement, the central government, and the papacy to Jansenism in the decades after the Fronde. Many documents in volume 7982 deal with Parlement's conflict with the king's councils over evocations in the 1650s. Some correspondence addressed to Séguier in the mid–seventeenth century is in volume 6210, and volumes 2770 and 2771 contain letters of several *parlementaires* arranged in alphabetical order. Memoranda and discourses of magistrates at Parlement, especially First President Lamoignon, are located in volumes 2429–2431. Volume 9734 provides a brief history of Le Tellier's career written by Claude Le

Pelletier, and volume 9807 includes an informative memorandum on the *droit annuel* in the seventeenth century. Minutes of the conferences sponsored by Parlement between August 1661 and May 1665 for the advocates attached to the court fill most of volume 2475. Volume 1506 provides a lengthy list of royal decrees issued between 1643 and 1700, and documents on various *lits de justice* at Parlement between 1620 and 1761 are located in volume 8451. Decrees issued by Parlement on the conduct of *greffiers* and *huissiers* attached to the court are among the items in volumes 8449 and 8450, and some ordinances on Parisian police matters that Parlement registered between 1412 and 1689 are included in volume 8494. Volumes 7981 and 7982 are full of contemporary essays and memoranda on the organization and authority of Parlement in the seventeenth century, the judges' claim to nobility, the court's participation in affairs of state, and its relations with the king's councils. Alphabetical and subject indexes to the Le Nain Collection are in volumes 2229–2307, 2309–2323, and 8234–8424 (the last being the most detailed).

I. The British Museum (BM)

1. Harleian Manuscripts

Under circumstances that remain unclear, many volumes of material that Chancellor Pierre Séguier collected in his lifetime have found their way into this collection. Six volumes in particular, 4442 and 4489–4493, were valuable for this study because they contain letters and memoranda addressed to the chancellor by royal ministers and secretaries of state, leading ecclesiastical personages, and financial and judicial officials in the provinces during the years 1656–1662. Some of this correspondence relates to Parlement's conflicts with the crown, especially over royal financial, judicial, and religious policies. Volume 4468 contains letters that link Croissy-Fouquet to Condé, and volume 1680 has a remonstrance that the *maîtres des requêtes* sent to the king about their quarrel with Parlement over evocations.

2. Egerton Manuscripts

Volume 1674 has information on Lamoignon's career before he became first president of Parlement.

II. Primary Sources: Published Correspondence, Memoirs, Journals, Genealogies, and Contemporary Histories

André, Louis, ed. *Deux Mémoires historiques de Claude Le Pelletier.* Paris, 1906.

Anon. *Vie de M. le premier président de Lamoignon.* Paris, 1781.

Anon., ed. "Lettres écrites au chancelier Séguier à l'occasion du procès Fouquet." *Le Cabinet Historique,* XI (1885), 13–24, 39–54.

Aubert de La Chesnaye Des Bois, François-Alexandre. *Dictionnaire de la noblesse.* 19 vols. Paris, 1863–1876.

Auzanet, Barthélemy, ed. *Arrestez de M. le p. p. de L[amoignon]. Arrestez ou lois projettées dans des conférences de M. le p. p. de L. pour les pays coutumiers de France et pour les provinces qui s'y régissent par le droit écrit.* Paris, 1703.

Avrigny, Père d'. *Mémoires pour servir à l'histoire universelle de l'Europe depuis 1600, jusqu'en 1716 avec des réflexions et remarques critiques.* 2 vols. Nîmes, 1733.

Bacquet, Jean. *Oeuvres.* 2 vols. Lyon, 1744.

Barozzi, Nicolò, ed. *Relazioni degli stati europei lette al senato degli ambasciatori Veneti nel secolo decimosettimo.* Serie 2, *Francia.* 3 vols. Venice, 1857–1863.

Barthélemy, Edouard de, ed. *Correspondance inédite de Turenne avec Michel Le Tellier et avec Louvois.* Paris, n.d.

Bertaut, François, sieur de Fréauville. *Les Prérogatives de la robe.* Paris, 1701.

Bluche, François. "L'Origine des magistrats du Parlement de Paris au XVIIIe siècle." *Paris et Ile-de-France: Mémoires*, V–VI (1953–1954), entire issue.

Boileau, Jacques, ed. *Recueil des diverses pièces concernant les censures de la faculté de théologie de Paris sur la hiérarchie de l'Eglise et sur la morale chrétienne.* Münster, 1666.

Boislisle, Jean de, ed. *Mémoriaux du conseil de 1661.* 3 vols. Paris, 1905–1907.

Castel de Saint-Pierre, Abbé Charles-Irénée. *Annales politiques, 1658–1740.* Ed. J. Drouet. Paris, 1912.

Chérin, Louis Nicolas Henri, ed. *Abrégé chronologique d'édits, déclarations . . . et lettres patentes des rois de France de la troisième race concernant le fait de noblesse.* Paris, 1788.

Colbert, Jean-Baptiste. *Lettres, instructions et mémoires.* Ed. Pierre Clément. 7 vols. Paris, 1861–1882.

Courtin, Antoine de. *Nouveau Traité de la civilité qui se pratique en France, parmi les honnestes gens.* Paris, 1671.

Depping, Georges, ed. *Correspondance administrative sous le règne de Louis XIV.* 4 vols. Paris, 1850–1855.

Desmaisons, François-C., ed. *Nouveau Recueil d'arrêts et règlements du Parlement de Paris.* Paris, 1667.

Dreyss, Charles, ed. *Mémoires de Louis XIV pour l'instruction du Dauphin.* 2 vols. Paris, 1860.

Dufresne, Jean, ed. *Journal des principales audiences de Parlement avec les arrests qui y ont été rendus.* Paris, 1733.

Fléchier, Esprit. *Mémoires sur les Grands Jours d'Auvergne en 1665.* Ed. Adolphe Chéruel. Paris, 1862.

Foucault, Nicolas-Joseph. *Mémoires.* Ed. J. Baudry. Paris, 1862.

Hay du Chastelet, Paul. *Traitté de la politique de France.* Cologne, 1669.

Hérault de Gourville, Jean. *Mémoires.* Ed. Léon Lecestre. 2 vols. Paris, 1894–1895.

Hermant, Godefroi. *Mémoires sur l'histoire ecclésiastique du XVIIe siècle (1630–1663).* Ed. Augustin Gazier. 6 vols. Paris, 1905–1910.

Hozier, Louis Pierre d'. *Armorial général de la France.* 10 vols. Paris, 1738–1768.

Huet, J., ed. *Notables Arrêts des audiences du Parlement de Paris depuis 1657 jusques en 1664.* Paris, 1664.

Isambert, François-André, *et al.*, eds. *Recueil général des anciennes lois françaises depuis l'an 400 jusqu'à la révolution de 1789.* 29 vols. Paris, 1822–1833.

Jovet, Laurent, ed. *La Bibliothèque des arrests de tous les parlemens de France.* Paris, 1669.

La Chesnaye Des Bois. *See* Aubert de La Chesnaye Des Bois, François-Alexandre.

La Rocque de La Lontière, Gilles-André. *Traité de la noblesse, de ses différentes espèces.* Rouen, 1710.

Larrey, Isaac de. *Histoire de France sous le règne de Louis XIV.* 4 vols. Rotterdam, 1718.

Le Prestre, Claude, ed. *Questions notables de droit, décidées par plusieurs arrests de la cour de Parlement.* Paris, 1679.

Limiers, H.-P. de. *Histoire du règne de Louis XIV.* 7 vols. Amsterdam, 1717.

Loret, Jean. *La Muse historique.* Ed. J. Ravenel and E. V. de La Pelouze. 4 vols. Paris, 1857–1878.

Louis XIV. *Mémoires pour l'instruction du Dauphin. See* Dreyss, Charles, ed.

———. *Oeuvres.* Ed. Philippe-A. Grouvelle. 6 vols. Paris, 1806.

Loyseau, Charles. *Cinq Livres du droict des offices.* Paris, 1613.

———. *Traité des ordres et simples dignitez.* Paris, 1613.

Lublinskaya, A. D., ed. *Lettres et mémoires adressés au chancelier P. Séguier (1633–1649).* Leningrad, 1966.

Mazarin, Jules. *Lettres.* Ed. Adolphe Chéruel. 9 vols. Paris, 1872–1906.

Mousnier, Roland, ed. *Lettres et mémoires adressés au chancelier Séguier (1633–1649).* 2 vols. Paris, 1964.

Néron, Pierre, and Girard, Etienne, eds. *Recueil d'édits et d'ordonnances royaux.* 2 vols. Paris, 1720.

Ormesson, Olivier Lefèvre d'. *Journal.* Ed. Adolphe Chéruel. 2 vols. Paris, 1860–1861.

Pellisson, Paul. *Histoire de Louis XIV, depuis la mort du Cardinal Mazarin en 1661 jusqu'à la paix de Nimègue en 1678.* 3 vols. Paris, 1749.

Procès-Verbal des conférences tenues par ordre du roi pour l'examen des articles de l'ordonnance civile du mois d'avril 1667 et de l'ordonnance criminelle du mois d'aoust 1670. Paris, 1757.

Rapin, René. *Mémoires de la Compagnie de Jésus sur l'église et la société, la cour, la ville et le jansénisme, 1644–1669.* Ed. Léon Aubineau. 3 vols. Paris, 1865.

Ravaisson-Mollien, François, ed. *Archives de la Bastille.* 19 vols. Paris, 1866–1904.

Riencourt, Simon de. *Histoire de la monarchie françoise sous le règne de Louis le grand.* 2 vols. Paris, 1692.

Saint-Simon, Louis de Rouvroy, duc de. *Mémoires.* Ed. Arthur Michel de Boislisle. 51 vols. Paris, 1879–1930.

Sandras de Courtilz, Gatien. *Mémoires contenant divers événements remarquables arrivés sous le règne de Louis le grand.* Cologne, 1684.

_____. *La Vie de Jean-Baptiste Colbert, ministre d'état sous Louis XIV.* Cologne, 1696.

Soefve, Lucien, ed. *Nouveau Recueil de plusieurs questions notables, tant de droit que de coutumes.* 2 vols. Paris, 1682.

Vallier, Jean. *Journal.* Ed. Henri Courteault. 4 vols. Paris, 1902–1918.

III. Secondary Sources: Books and Dissertations

Abercrombie, Nigel. *The Origins of Jansenism.* Oxford, 1936.

Adam, Antoine. *Du Mysticisme à la révolte: Les Jansénistes du XVIIe siècle.* Paris, 1968.

Affre, Denis-Auguste. *De L'Appel comme d'abus, son origine, ses progrès et son état présent.* Paris, 1845.

André, Louis. *Michel Le Tellier et l'organisation de l'armée monarchique.* Paris, 1906.

_____. *Michel Le Tellier et Louvois.* Paris, 1943.

Antoine, Michel. *Le Conseil du roi sous le règne de Louis XV.* Genève, 1970.

Asher, Eugene. *Resistance to the Maritime Classes: The Survival of Feudalism in the France of Colbert.* University of California Publications in History, 66. Berkeley, 1960.

Aubert, Félix. *Histoire du Parlement de Paris, de l'origine à François Ier, 1250–1515.* 2 vols. Paris, 1894.

Azéma, Xavier. *Un Prélat janséniste: Louis Fouquet, Evêque et Comte d'Agde (1656–1702).* Paris, 1968.

Bar, Carl Ludwig von, *et al. A History of Continental Criminal Law.* Trans. T. S. Bell. Continental Legal History Series, 6. Boston, 1916.

Bataillard, Charles, and Nusse, Ernest. *Histoire des procureurs et des avoués, 1483–1816.* 2 vols. Paris, 1882.

Bénichou, Paul. *Morales du grand siècle.* Paris, 1948.

Bernard, Leon. *The Emerging City: Paris in the Age of Louis XIV.* Durham, 1970.

Billacois, François, *et. al. Crimes et criminalité en France sous l'ancien régime.* Paris, 1971.

Blet, Pierre. *Les Assemblées du clergé et Louis XIV de 1670 à 1693.* Rome, 1972.

_____. *Le Clergé de France et la monarchie: Etude sur les assemblées générales du clergé de 1615 à 1666.* 2 vols. Rome, 1959.

Bloch, Jean Richard. *L'Anoblissement en France au temps de François Ier.* Paris, 1934.

Bluche, François. *Les Magistrats du Parlement de Paris au XVIIIe siècle.* Paris, 1960.

Bluche, François, and Durye, Pierre. *L'Anoblissement par charges avant 1789.* 2 vols. Paris, 1962.

Boislisle, Arthur Michel de. *Les Conseils du roi sous Louis XIV.* Paris, 1884.

Bonnemère, Eugène. *La France sous Louis XIV (1643–1715)*. 2 vols. Paris, 1874.

Borkenau, Franz. *Der Übergang vom feudalen zum bürgerlichen Weltbild*. Paris, 1934.

Bornier, Philippe. *Conférences des ordonnances de Louis XIV*. 2 vols. Paris, 1755.

Boscheron Des Portes, Charles-Bon-François. *Histoire du Parlement de Bordeaux, depuis sa création jusqu'à sa suppression (1451–1790)*. 2 vols. Bordeaux, 1877.

Bosher, John F., ed. *French Government and Society, 1500–1850: Essays in Memory of Alfred Cobban*. London, 1973.

Brancourt, Jean-Pierre. *Le Duc de Saint-Simon et la monarchie*. Paris, 1971.

Buisseret, David. *Sully and the Growth of Centralized Government in France, 1598–1610*. London, 1968.

Cagnac, Moïse. *De L'Appel comme d'abus dans l'ancien droit français*. Paris, 1906.

Cans, Albert. *L'Organisation financière du clergé de France à l'époque de Louis XIV*. Paris, 1909.

Cauchie, Alfred. *Le Gallicanisme en Sorbonne, d'après la correspondance de Bargellini, nonce de France (1668–1671)*. Louvain, 1903.

Charmeil, Jean-Paul. *Les Trésoriers de France à l'époque de la Fronde*. Paris, 1964.

Chéruel, Adolphe. *De L'Administration de Louis XIV (1661–1672) d'après les mémoires inédits d'Olivier d'Ormesson*. Paris, 1850.

———. *Histoire de France sous le ministère de Mazarin (1651–1661)*. 3 vols. Paris, 1882.

———. *Histoire de l'administration monarchique en France depuis l'avènement de Philippe-Auguste jusqu'à la mort de Louis XIV*. 2 vols. Paris, 1855.

———. *Mémoires sur la vie publique et privée de Fouquet*. 2 vols. Paris, 1862.

Chévrier, A.-C. *Eloge de Guillaume de Lamoignon, premier président au Parlement de Paris*. Paris, 1856.

Clément, Pierre. *Histoire de Colbert et de son administration*. 2 vols. Paris, 1874.

———. *Histoire de la vie et de l'administration de Colbert, contrôleur général des finances . . . précédée d'une étude historique sur Nicolas Fouquet*. Paris, 1846.

———. *La Police sous Louis XIV*. Paris, 1866.

———. *Portraits historiques*. Paris, 1855.

Cognet, Louis. *Le Jansénisme*. Paris, 1961.

Cosnac, Gabriel-Jules de. *Mazarin et Colbert*. 2 vols. Paris, 1892.

Curzon, Alfred de. *L'Enseignement du droit français dans les universités de France aux XVIIe et XVIIIe siècles*. Paris, 1920.

Declareuil, Joseph. *Histoire générale du droit français des origines à 1789*. Paris, 1925.

Delumeau, Jean. *Le Catholicisme entre Luther et Voltaire*. Paris, 1971.

Dent, Julian. *Crisis in Finance: Crown, Financiers and Society in Seventeenth-Century France*. New York, 1973.

Desmaze, Charles. *Le Parlement de Paris, son organisation, ses premiers présidents et procureurs généraux*. Paris, 1859.

Deteix, Geneviève. *Les Arrêts de règlement du Parlement de Paris*. Paris, 1930.

Dictionnaire de biographie française. 12 vols. to date. Paris, 1933–1970.

Doolin, Paul. *The Fronde*. Cambridge, Mass., 1935.

Doucet, Roger. *Les Institutions de la France au XVe siècle*. 2 vols. Paris, 1948.

Dubuc, Pierre. *L'Intendance de Soissons sous Louis XIV, 1643–1715*. Paris, 1902.

Duval, Louis. *Etat de la généralité d'Alençon sous Louis XIV*. Alençon, 1890.

Engelmann, Arthur, *et al*. *A History of Continental Civil Procedure*. Trans. R. W. Millar. Continental Legal History Series, 7. Boston, 1927.

Esmein, Adhémar. *Histoire de la procédure criminelle en France*. Paris, 1882.

Esmonin, Edmond. *Etudes sur la France des XVIIe et XVIIIe siècles*. Paris, 1964.

———. *La Taille en Normandie au temps de Colbert*. Paris, 1913.

Ford, Franklin. *Robe and Sword: The Regrouping of the French Aristocracy After Louis XIV.* Cambridge, Mass., 1953.

Fréville, Henri. *L'Intendance de Bretagne (1689–1790).* 3 vols. Rennes, 1953.

Gaquère, François. *Pierre de Marca (1594–1662).* Paris, 1932.

Gaudry, Joachim-Antoine-Joseph. *Histoire du barreau de Paris depuis son origine jusqu'à 1830.* 2 vols. Paris, 1864.

Gautier, Alfred. *Précis de l'histoire du droit français.* 2 vols. Paris, 1882.

Gazier, Augustin. *Histoire générale du mouvement janséniste depuis ses origines jusqu'à nos jours.* 2 vols. Paris, 1922.

Génestal, Robert. *Les Origines de l'appel comme d'abus.* Paris, 1951.

Glasson, Ernest-Désiré. *Histoire du droit et des institutions de la France.* 8 vols. Paris, 1887–1903.

————. *Le Parlement de Paris, son rôle politique depuis le règne de Charles VII jusqu'à la Révolution.* 2 vols. Paris, 1901.

Godard, Charles. *Les Pouvoirs des intendants sous Louis XIV, particulièrement dans les pays d'élections de 1661 à 1715.* Paris, 1901.

Göhring, Martin. *Die Ämterkäuflichkeit im Ancien régime.* Berlin, 1938.

Goldmann, Lucien. *Le Dieu caché: Etude sur la vision tragique dans les 'Pensées' de Pascal et dans le théâtre de Racine.* Paris, 1955.

Goubert, Pierre. *Louis XIV and Twenty Million Frenchmen.* Trans. Anne Carter. New York, 1970.

Guiral, P.; Pillorget, R.; and Agulhon, M. *Guide de l'étudiant en histoire moderne et contemporaine.* Paris, 1971.

Hanotaux, Gabriel. *Origines de l'institution des intendants des provinces.* Paris, 1884.

Hanotaux, Gabriel, and La Force, Duc de. *Histoire du Cardinal de Richelieu.* 6 vols. Paris, 1933–1947.

Hardy, James D. *Judicial Politics in the Old Regime: The Parlement of Paris During the Regency.* Baton Rouge, 1967.

Jansen, Paule. *Le Cardinal Mazarin et le mouvement janséniste français, 1653–1659.* Paris, 1967.

Joubleau, Félix. *Etudes sur Colbert, ou exposition du système d'économie politique suivi en France de 1661 à 1683.* 2 vols. Paris, 1856.

Jourdain, Charles. *Histoire de l'Université de Paris, au XVIIe et au XVIIIe siècles.* 2 vols. Paris, 1888.

Jousse, Daniel. *Nouveau Commentaire sur les ordonnances des mois d'août 1669 et mars 1673.* Paris, 1756.

————. *Nouveau Commentaire sur l'ordonnance civile du mois d'avril 1667.* Paris, 1753.

————. *Nouveau Commentaire sur l'ordonnance criminelle du mois d'août 1670.* Paris, 1763.

Kerviler, René. *Le Chancelier Pierre Séguier.* Paris, 1874.

King, James Edward. *Science and Rationalism in the Government of Louis XIV, 1661–1683.* Baltimore, 1949.

Kossmann, Ernst. *La Fronde.* Leiden, 1954.

Lacuisine, Elisabeth-François de. *Le Parlement de Bourgogne depuis son origine jusqu'à sa chute.* 3 vols. Dijon, 1864.

Laferrière, Edouard. *Rivalité des parlements avec les intendants et le conseil du roi.* Paris, 1866.

Lair, Jules-Auguste. *Nicolas Foucquet, procureur général, surintendant des finances, ministre d'état de Louis XIV.* 2 vols. Paris, 1890.

Latreille, A.; Delaruelle, E.; and Palanque, J.-R. *Histoire du catholicisme en France.* 3 vols. Paris, 1956–1962.

Lefèbvre, Henri. *Pascal.* 2 vols. Paris, 1949–1954.

Lemasne-Desjobert, Marie-Antoinette. *La Faculté de droit de Paris aux XVIIe et XVIIIe siècles.* Paris, 1966.

Livet, Georges. *L'Intendance d'Alsace sous Louis XIV, 1648–1715.* Paris, 1956.

Lorris, Pierre-Georges. *La Fronde.* Paris, 1961.

Marion, Marcel. *Dictionnaire des institutions de la France aux XVIIe et XVIIIe siècles.* Paris, 1923.

Martin, Germain. *La Surintendance de Fouquet et les opérations de crédit public.* Paris, 1914.

Martin, Germain, and Besançon, Marcel. *L'Histoire du crédit en France sous le règne de Louis XIV.* Paris, 1913.

Martin, Victor. *Le Gallicanisme politique et le clergé de France.* Paris, 1928.

Matte, Louis. *Crimes et procès politiques sous Louis XIV.* Paris, 1910.

Maugis, Edouard. *Histoire du Parlement de Paris de l'avènement des rois Valois à la mort d'Henri IV.* 3 vols. Paris, 1913–1916.

Meyer, Jean. *La Noblesse bretonne au XVIIIe siècle.* 2 vols. Paris, 1966.

Mongrédien, Georges. *L'Affaire Foucquet.* Paris, 1956.

Mongrédien, Georges, ed. *Mazarin.* Paris, 1959.

Monnier, Francis. *Guillaume de Lamoignon et Colbert, essai sur la législation française au XVIIe siècle.* Paris, 1862.

Moote, A. Lloyd. *The Revolt of the Judges: The Parlement of Paris and the Fronde, 1643–1652.* Princeton, 1971.

Moréri, Louis. *Le Grand Dictionnaire historique.* 10 vols. Paris, 1759.

Mousnier, Roland. *Les Hiérarchies sociales de 1450 à nos jours.* Paris, 1969.

————. *La Vénalité des offices sous Henri IV et Louis XIII.* Rouen, 1945.

Mousnier, Roland, *et al. Le Conseil du roi, de Louis XII à la Révolution.* Paris, 1970.

Namer, Gérard. *L'Abbé Le Roy et ses amis, essai sur le jansénisme extrémiste intramondain.* Paris, 1964.

Néraud, J. *Les Intendants de la généralité de Berry.* Paris, 1922.

Neveu, Bruno. *Un Historien à l'école de Port-Royal: Sébastien Le Nain de Tillemont (1637–1698).* La Haye, 1966.

Normand, Charles. *La Bourgeoisie française au XVIIe siècle.* Paris, 1908.

Olivier-Martin, François. *Histoire du droit français des origines à la Révolution.* Paris, 1951.

Orcibal, Jean. *Jean Duvergier de Hauranne, abbé de Saint-Cyran et son temps.* Paris, 1948.

————. *Louis XIV contre Innocent XI.* Paris, 1949.

Pagès, Georges. *Les Institutions monarchiques sous Louis XIII et Louis XIV.* Paris, 1961.

————. *La Monarchie d'ancien régime en France (De Henri IV à Louis XIV).* Paris, 1928.

Péries, G. *La Faculté de droit dans l'ancienne Université de Paris (1160–1793).* Paris, 1890.

Préclin, Edmond, and Jarry, Eugène. *Les Luttes politiques et doctrinales aux XVIIe et XVIIIe siècles.* Paris, 1955.

Robin, Pierre. *La Compagnie des secrétaires du roi (1351–1791).* Paris, 1933.

Rodier, Marc-Antoine. *Questions sur l'ordonnance de Louis XIV, du mois d'avril 1667.* Toulouse, 1777.

Rothkrug, Lionel. *Opposition to Louis XIV: The Political and Social Origins of the French Enlightenment.* Princeton, 1965.

Rule, John C., ed. *Louis XIV and the Craft of Kingship.* Columbus, 1969.

Saint-Germain, Jacques. *La Reynie et la police au grand siècle d'après de nombreux documents inédits.* Paris, 1962.

Sallé, Jacques-Antoine. *L'Esprit des ordonnances de Louis XIV, ouvrage où l'on a réuni la théorie et la pratique des ordonnances.* 2 vols. Paris, 1755–1758.

Schnapper, Bernard. *Les Rentes au XVIe siècle, histoire d'un instrument de crédit.* Paris, 1957.

Shennan, J. H. *The Parlement of Paris.* Ithaca, 1968.

Sippel, Cornelius. "The *Noblesse de la Robe* in Early Seventeenth-Century France: A Study in Social Mobility." Ph.D. dissertation, University of Michigan, 1963.

Sonnino, Paul. *Louis XIV's View of the Papacy (1661–1667)*. University of California Publications in History, 79. Berkeley, 1966.

Stocker, Christopher. "Offices and Officers in the Parlement of Paris, 1483–1515." Ph.D. dissertation, Cornell University, 1965.

Swart, Koenraad Wolter. *The Sale of Offices in the Seventeenth Century*. The Hague, 1949.

Tapié, Victor-L. *La France de Louis XIII et de Richelieu*. Paris, 1967.

Taveneaux, René. *Jansénisme et politique*. Paris, 1965.

Trotry, G. *Les Grands Jours des parlements*. Paris, 1908.

Venard, Marc. *Bourgeois et paysans au XVIIe siècle: Recherche sur le rôle des bourgeois parisiens dans la vie agricole au sud de Paris au XVIIe siècle*. Paris, 1957.

Vian, Louis. *Les Lamoignons, une vieille famille de robe*. Paris, 1896.

Viollet, Paul. *Histoire du droit civil français*. Paris, 1893.

―――――. *Le Roi et ses ministres pendant les trois derniers siècles de la monarchie*. Paris, 1912.

Voltaire, [François Marie Arouet de]. *Siècle de Louis XIV*. Paris, 1903.

Welter, Louise. *La Réforme ecclésiastique du diocèse de Clermont au XVIIe siècle*. Paris, 1956.

Westrich, Sal. *The Ormée of Bordeaux: A Revolution During the Fronde*. The Johns Hopkins University Studies in Historical and Political Science, 89, no. 2. Baltimore, 1972.

Willaert, L. *Bibliotheca janseniana belgica*. 3 vols. Paris, 1949–1951.

Wolf, John. *Louis XIV*. New York, 1968.

Zeller, Gaston. *Les Institutions de la France au XVIe siècle*. Paris, 1948.

IV. SECONDARY SOURCES: ARTICLES

Blet, Pierre. "Le Clergé de France et ses assemblées (1615–1666)." *XVIIe Siècle*, no. 52 (1961), pp. 3–19.

Boislisle, A. de. "Les Grands Jours de Languedoc (1666–1667)." *Comité des Travaux Historiques et Scientifiques. Bulletin Philologique et Historique*, nos. 1–2 (1886), pp. 63–87.

Bordes, M. "Les Intendants de province aux XVIIe et XVIIIe siècles." *L'Information Historique*, XXX (1968), 107–20.

Buisseret, David. "A Stage in the Development of the French *Intendants:* The Reign of Henri IV." *Historical Journal*, IX (1966), 27–38.

Chauleur, André. "Le Rôle des traitants dans l'administration financière de la France de 1643 à 1653." *XVIIe Siècle*, no. 65 (1964), pp. 16–49.

Chaunu, Pierre. "Le XVIIe Siècle religieux: Réflexions préalables." *Annales: Economies, Sociétés, Civilisations* (mars-avril 1967), pp. 279–302.

―――――. "Jansénisme et frontière de catholicité (XVIIe et XVIIIe siècles), à propos du jansénisme lorrain." *Revue Historique*, CCXXVII (1962), 115–38.

Clément, Pierre. "Projet de réforme dans l'administration de la justice, par Colbert." *Revue Rétrospective*, ser. 2, vol. IV (1835), 247–63.

―――――. "La Réform des codes sous Louis XIV, d'après les documents inédits." *Revue des Questions Historiques*, VII (1869), 115–44.

Cubells, Mme. "Le Parlement de Paris pendant la Fronde." *XVIIe Siècle*, no. 35 (1957), pp. 171–201.

Dent, Cynthia. "The Council of State and the Clergy During the Reign of Louis XIV: An Aspect of the Growth of French Absolutism." *Journal of Ecclesiastical History*, XXIV (1973), 245–66.

Dent, Julian. "An Aspect of the Crisis of the Seventeenth Century: The Collapse of the

Financial Administration of the French Monarchy (1653–1661)." *Economic History Review*, ser. 2, XX (1967), 241–56.

Dessert, Daniel. "Finances et société au XVIIe siècle: A Propos de la Chambre de Justice de 1661." *Annales: Economies, Sociétés, Civilisations* (juillet-août 1974), pp. 847–82.

Deyon, Pierre. "A Propos des rapports entre la noblesse française et la monarchie absolue." *Revue Historique*, CCXXXI (1964), 341–56.

Dillay, M. "Les Registres secrets des chambres des enquêtes et des requêtes du Parlement de Paris." *Bibliothèque de l'Ecole des Chartes*, CVIII (1950), 75–123.

Dumont, F. "Royauté française et monarchie absolue au XVIIe siècle." *XVIIe Siècle*, nos. 58–59 (1963), pp. 3–18.

Esmonin, Edmond. "Les Arrêts du conseil dans l'ancien régime." *Bulletin de la Société d'Histoire Moderne* (1938), pp. 6–10.

————. "Un Episode du rétablissement des intendants après la Fronde: Les Maîtres des requêtes envoyés en chevauchées." *Revue d'Histoire Moderne et Contemporaine*, XII (1965), 217–28.

————. "Un Episode du rétablissement des intendants: La Mission de Morant en Guienne (1650)." *Revue d'Histoire Moderne et Contemporaine*, I (1954), 86–101.

————. "La Suppression des intendants pendant la Fronde et leur rétablissement." *Bulletin de la Société d'Histoire Moderne* (1935), pp. 114–19.

Goldmann, Lucien. "Remarques sur le jansénisme: La Vision tragique du monde et de la noblesse de robe." *XVIIe Siècle*, no. 19 (1953), pp. 177–95.

Goubert, Pierre. "Les Officiers royaux des présidiaux, bailliages et élections dans la société française au XVIIe siècle." *XVIIe Siècle*, nos. 42–43 (1959), pp. 54–75.

Hamscher, Albert. "The Parlement of Paris and the Social Interpretation of Early French Jansenism." *Catholic Historical Review*, in press.

————. "Les Réformes judiciaires des Grands Jours d'Auvergne, 1665–1666." *Cahiers d'Histoire*, in press.

Hartung, Fritz, and Mousnier, Roland. "Quelques Problèmes concernant la monarchie absolue." *Relazioni X Congresso Internazionale di Scienze Storiche* (Rome and Florence, 1955), IV, 3–55.

Hatton, Ragnhild M. "Louis XIV: Recent Gains in Historical Knowledge." *Journal of Modern History*, XLV (1973), 277–91.

Hurt, John J. "The Parlement of Brittany and the Crown, 1665–1675." *French Historical Studies*, IV (1966), 411–33.

Jennings, Robert M., and Trout, Andrew P. "Internal Control: Public Finance in Seventeenth-Century France." *Journal of European Economic History*, I (1972), 647–60.

Judge, H. G. "Church and State Under Louis XIV." *History*, XLV (1960), 217–33.

Major, J. Russell. "The Crown and the Aristocracy in Renaissance France." *American Historical Review*, LXIX (1964), 631–45.

Meuvret, Jean. "Comment les Français du XVIIe siècle voyaient l'impôt." *XVIIe Siècle*, nos. 26–27 (1955), pp. 59–82.

Moote, A. Lloyd. "The French Crown versus its Judicial and Financial Officials, 1615–1683." *Journal of Modern History*, XXXIV (1962), 146–60.

————. "The Parlementary Fronde and Seventeenth-Century Robe Solidarity." *French Historical Studies*, II (1962), 330–55.

Mousnier, Roland. "Le Conseil du roi de la mort de Henri IV au gouvernement personnel de Louis XIV." *Etudes d'Histoire Moderne et Contemporaine*, I (1947), 29–67.

————. "Etat et commissaire: Recherches sur la création des intendants des provinces (1634–1648)." In *Forschungen zu Staat und Verfassung: Festgabe für Fritz Hartung*. Berlin, 1958.

_____. "L'Evolution des institutions monarchiques en France et ses relations avec l'état social." *XVIIe Siècle*, nos. 58–59 (1963), pp. 57–72.

_____. "Quelques raisons de la Fronde: Les Causes des journées révolutionnaires parisiennes de 1648." *XVIIe Siècle*, nos. 2–3 (1949), pp. 33–78.

_____. "Recherches sur les syndicats d'officiers pendant la Fronde: Trésoriers généraux de France et élus dans la révolution." *XVIIe Siècle*, nos. 42–43 (1959), pp. 76–117.

Neveu, Bruno. "Un Parlementaire parisien érudit et janséniste: Jean Le Nain (1609–1698)." *Paris et Ile-de-France: Mémoires*, XVI–XVII (1965–1966), 191–230.

Pagès, Georges. "Le Conseil du roi sous Louis XIII." *Revue d'Histoire Moderne*, XII (1937), 293–324.

_____. "Essai sur l'évolution des institutions administratives en France du commencement du XVIe siècle à la fin du XVIIe." *Revue d'Histoire Moderne*, VII (1932), 8–57.

_____. "Le Gouvernement et l'administration monarchique en France à la fin du règne de Louis XIV." *Revue des Cours et Conférences*, ser. 1 (1936), pp. 1–9; ser. 1 (1937), pp. 289–98, 610–19, 703–12.

_____. "La Vénalité des offices dans l'ancienne France." *Revue Historique*, CLXIX (1932), 477–95.

Paringault, E. "Le Conseiller d'état Henri Pussort, réhabilitation historique." *L'Investigateur. Journal de l'Institut Historique de France*, ser. 4, vol. X (1870), pp. 143–57, 167–75.

Pillorget, René. "Les Problèmes monétaires français de 1602 à 1689." *XVIIe Siècle*, nos. 70–71 (1966), pp. 107–30.

Poisson, Jean-Paul. "Introduction à l'étude du rôle socio-économique du notariat à la fin du XVIIe siècle: 3 offices parisiens en 1698." *XVIIe Siècle*, no. 100 (1973), pp. 3–17.

Riley, Philip. "Louis XIV: Watchdog of Parisian Morality." *The Historian*, XXXVI (1973), 19–33.

Salmon, J. H. "Venal Office and Popular Sedition in Seventeenth-Century France." *Past and Present*, no. 37 (1967), pp. 21–43.

Schnapper, Bernard. "Les Peines arbitraires du XIIIe siècle au XVIIIe siècle (doctrines savantes et usages français)." *Tijdschrift Voor Rechtsgeschiedenis*, XLI (1973), 237–77; XLII (1974), 81–112.

Sorbier, M. "Biographie de Guillaume de Lamoignon, premier président du Parlement de Paris." *Mémoires de l'Académie Royale des Sciences, Arts et Belles-Lettres de Caen*, VI (1847), 319–59.

Stocker, Christopher. "Office as Maintenance in Renaissance France." *Canadian Journal of History*, VI (1971), 21–43.

_____. "The Politics of the Parlement of Paris in 1525." *French Historical Studies*, VIII (1973), 191–212.

Timbal, P. J. "L'Esprit du droit privé au XVIIe siècle." *XVIIe Siècle*, nos. 58–59 (1963), pp. 30–39.

Trévédy, J. "Sur le titre 'noble homme.'" *Revue Morbihannaise* (1902).

Vian, L. "Louis XIV au Parlement d'après les registres manuscrits du Parlement." *Revue des Questions Historiques*, XXXII (1882), 607–14.

Weis, Eberhard. "Jansenismus und Gesellschaft in Frankreich." *Historische Zeitschrift*, CCXIV (1972), 42–57.

Wolf, John B. "The Reign of Louis XIV: A Selected Bibliography of Writings Since the War of 1914–1918." *Journal of Modern History*, XXXVI (1964), 127–44.

Index